AFRICAN STAR OVER ASIA
The Black Presence in the East

AFRICAN STAR OVER ASIA
The Black Presence in the East

RUNOKO RASHIDI

WWW.BOOKSOFAFRICA.COM

AFRICAN STAR OVER ASIA
The Black Presence in the East

BY RUNOKO RASHIDI

Books of Africa Limited
16 Overhill Road
East Dulwich, London
SE22 0PH
United Kingdom

Web site: www.booksofafrica.com
Emails: admin@booksofafrica.com
sales@booksofafrica.com

Copyright Runoko Rashidi 2012

Reprinted in 2015, 2017, 2019, 2020, 2021, 2023, 2024

ISBN: 978-0-9566380-9-0

A CIP catalogue record for this book is available from the British Library.

Printed and bound in the United Kingdom by ImprintDigital.com

Contents

Part Two

AFRICAN STAR OVER ASIA: TRAVEL NOTES AND LETTERS

DEDICATED TO
PIONEER SCHOLARS
CHANCELLOR WILLIAMS,
JOHN G. JACKSON
AND IVAN VAN SERTIMA

Acknowledgements

Many people made invaluable contributions of many different kinds to the development and evolution of this text. For your scholarship, your technical, moral, spiritual and material support, your photographs, your logistical support, your encouragement, I am most grateful for all that you have done. These contributors include:

Dr. James E. Brunson, Wayne B. Chandler, Brenda Miller, Carol Strong, Hamara Holt, Paco D. Taylor, the First World Alliance, V.T. Rajshekar, Horen Tudu, Dr. Velu Annamalai, Charles S. Finch, MD, Njeri Khan, Dr. Charles B. Copher, Afrikan Echoes, Zawadi Sagna, Dr. Wesley Muhammad, Dr. Thabiti Asukile, Obadele Williams, Osunbunmi Gaida, John Halcomb, the Kerala Dalit Panthers, Pramod Kureel, Joy A. Nealy, M.D., Nias Harris, Nnamdi Kenneth King, Dr. Dieudonné Gnammankou, Emmanuel Mah, Nigel Watt, Zain Jacobs, and many, many more. I am most grateful.

Preface

African Star over Asia: The Black Presence in the East is about the African presence in Asia and the scholars who have contributed to our understanding of it. It is a product of more than thirty years in the making. It is the English-language companion volume to my French-language work *Histoire millénaire des Africains en Asie: Présence africaine en Asie de l'Antiquité à nos jours* (2005). It is the extension of the work of many people and the logical extension to *African Presence in Early Asia*, edited with Ivan Van Sertima. Indeed, since the last edition of that work in 1995 I have been regularly asked to compile a new volume on the subject. This work is the result.

My interest in the African presence in Asia began in the early 1970s. There were three primary catalysts. First, the stories of family and friends who had been in the US military and had served terms of duty in Vietnam. For the first time I heard accounts of indigenous Black people in Vietnam and Cambodia. It seemed so interesting. Second, as a young university student, after listening to an inspiring speech by political activist Kwame Ture about Pan-Africanism, African unity and African solidarity, I joined a local study group where the first book we dissected was Chancellor James Williams' *Destruction of Black Civilization*. And that was the third catalyst. These were life changing experiences for me. First, the knowledge that Black people lived all over the world, including Asia. Secondly, Dr. Ture's challenge to me to examine the African presence in far away places. And, thirdly, Dr. Williams' clear statement that African people had a long history before invasion, colonization and enslavement. This inspired me to want to find out what happened to those Africans who left Africa not only as a result of enslavement, but those Africans who left Africa in the far distant past.

The search to find out what happened to those Africans has been the core of my existence and it is my desire to tell that story that leads to this book today. It is also something that makes this a largely unique work, for we will not confine ourselves to the study of enslaved Africans in Asia, as so many scholars have done. We want to look at all of those Black people who have populated Asia from the beginning and in subsequent migrations. We want to look at

Black people, at African people, as the first people of Asia, as gods, goddesses and mythological figures, kings and queens, warriors and commanders, martyrs and saints, and, yes, as enslaved people and freed men and women. This book attempts to tell their story.

The foundation of *African Star over Asia* I have chosen to call the Ivan Van Sertima Papers. These are largely revisions and expansions of essays written for what Dr. Van Sertima called the *Journal of African Civilizations*. Orginally, they covered a thirteen year period from 1982 (thirty years ago) to 1995. I am just speaking of my essays on the African presence in Asia now. The entire volume of articles I composed for Dr. Van Sertima is much broader. The Asia essays were published in *Egypt Revisited* in 1982, *Nile Valley Civilizations* in 1984; *African Presence in Early Asia* in 1985 (Runoko Rashidi, Guest Editor) ; *African Presence in Early America* in 1986, Cheikh Anta Diop, *Volume 1: Great African Thinkers* in 1987; *African Presence in Early Asia* (2nd Edition, Runoko Rashidi Co-Editor) in 1988; Golden Age of the Moor in 1991, and, the major contribution—the *African Presence in Early Asia* (Runoko Rashidi, Editor and Ivan Van Sertima, Co-Editor) in 1995.

These contributions have been revised and expanded to keep them up to date and relevant, while also preserving their essence and the meticulous research that went into their composition. These essays cover much of the range of the African presence in ancient and, in the case of India and the Philippines, modern Asia. They look at African people as the Aboriginal people of Asia, as the spark and maintainers of civilization in Asia, and as enslaved and subjugated people in Asia. We are proud of these essays. If you have read the originals, we ask you to please read the revisions. There is much information contained therein, a great deal of it new information. We would only request that the reader forgive the inevitable overlap and repetition that comes with our attempts at synthesis.

But *African Star over Asia* is also a new work. The next section of the text, one of the newest sections, focuses on my recent travel experiences in Asia, and observations and reflections about the African presence there. Here, we look at the summation of my travels in India in South Asia; the mighty monuments of ancient Angkor, Thailand and Vietnam in Southeast Asia; a first hand account of the search for African people in China in East Asia; the highlights of my initial trip to Turkey in Southwest Asia; journeys to Jordan, Syria and

Lebanon on Asia's Mediterranean seaboard; the ancient temples of Central Java, Indonesia; and a look back at little known Myanmar (Burma), with its temple-fields at Bagan.

One can never discount the value of primary and onsite research. Many of these accounts are actually letters written during the course of my journeys to these lands, and one gets to experience with me and through me the goals and the fears, the hopes and expectations, the triumphs and disappointments encountered in search of the African presence in Asia. These accounts are largely unfiltered and unedited. Most of them are published here for the first time. They were not written just for scholars, but for consumption by all interested people. And they are passionately, unreservedly and unabashedly pro-African. I leave no doubts to the imagination as to my sentiments.

In has been our good fortune, in the course of our travels and researches to have visited many museums, and so the next section of *African Star over Asia* features a series of brief photo essays—the first on Southwest Asia—the next two on Southeast Asia, specifically ancient Iraq and Iran, and Vietnam and Thailand. Indeed, generally speaking and beyond the photo essays themselves, the photos in *African Star over Asia* are among its most one of its most outstanding features. Many of these photos are quite original and have never been published in any form or context.

One does not do this work alone. This is not an individual endeavor. And so we are pleased to introduce, reintroduce and bring to the front six other contributors to the search for the African presence in Asia. These contributors, brilliant one and all, are: Dr. Thabiti Asukile—the world's leading authority on the great historian Joel Augustus Rogers, who has contributed an insightful essay on J.A. Rogers and the African presence in Asia; V.T. Rajshekar—the veteran crusading journalist from South India who has contributed so much to our knowledge of the existence and plight of the Dalits: The Black Untouchables of India; Dr. Horen Tudu—a young and passionate South Asia Pan-Africanist whose roots are Santhali in Bangladesh; Paco D. Taylor an outstanding writer and historian based in Tucson, Arizona; Hamara Holt—a world traveler, a brilliant photographer and developing anthropologist; and Dr. Wesley Muhammad a remarkable scholar determined to uncover the historical relationships between Africa and Arabia, and the African Origins of Islam. Each of these contributors has buttressed my own researches on the African presence in Asia and brought exciting new dimensions to the study as well.

I have always enjoyed research and find bibliographic references absolutely vital. With that in mind we have included here more than thirty pages of such references to substantiate the current volume and help pave the way for volumes yet to come.

And there it is. We confess that *African Star over Asia* is not a complete work. Perhaps it is not possible, at least in one volume, to have a complete work on such a vast subject. No, it is not a complete work. But it is a substantial work. *African Star over Asia* leaves us with many questions. But it also answers a great many questions. Asia is an enormous area and yet we have tried here to touch on every major section of it. The African presence in Asia is a massive subject and yet we hope that we have contributed in a significant way to our understanding of it—an understanding that those Africans who left home so long ago so richly deserve.

Part One

AFRICAN STAR OVER ASIA: OVERVIEW AND ESSAYS – THE IVAN VAN SERTIMA PAPERS

"'What became of the Black people of Sumer?' the traveller asked the old man, for ancient records show that the people of Sumer were Black. 'What happened to them?' 'Ah,' the old man sighed. 'They lost their history, so they died'..."[1]

A Sumer Legend

1.1- OVERVIEW

This Sumer legend we think is a fitting way to begin this Introduction to the latest volume on the African presence in Asia, for it speaks to the consequences that face a people when they fail to document their history and refuse to tell their story. This Introduction and this book are part of the very much needed chronicle of the African presence in Asia. It is a story that must be told. Indeed, the story of the African presence in Asia is as fascinating as it is obscure. It is a story that begins perhaps 100,000 years ago. It does not begin with slavery

1.1.1- The African Presence in Asia: the first Diaspora

In truth we now know, based on DNA studies, that modern humanity originated in Africa, that African people are the world's original people, and that all modern humans can ultimately trace their ancestral roots back to Africa. Were it not for the primordial migrations of early African people, humanity would have remained physically Africoid, and the rest of the world outside of the African continent absent of human life. Since the first modern humans in Asia were of African birth, the African presence in Asia can therefore be demonstrated through the history of the Black populations that have inhabited the Asian land mass within the span of modern humanity.

Two recent DNA studies strongly substantiate this. According to the first report, "Chinese Roots lie in Africa":

> "Most of the population of modern China, one fifth of all the people living today, owes its genetic origins to Africa, an international scientific team said today in research that undercuts any theory that modern humans may have originated independently in China."[2]

Populations from East Asia always derived from a single lineage, indicating the single origins of those populations. It is now probably safe to conclude that modern humans originating in Africa constitute the majority of the current gene pool in East Asia.

Although few scholars today dispute the idea that the earliest ancestors of the human species evolved in Africa, there still is considerable debate over how modern humanity evolved from its more primitive ancestors.

Many anthropologists believe that humans may have migrated out of Africa in waves. More than a million years ago, humanity's primitive ancestors, known as Homo erectus, walked out of Africa to colonize Europe, the Middle East and Asia. On that everyone agrees.

Then several hundred thousand years later, some theorize, a second wave of more sophisticated tool-using humans migrated out of Africa and overwhelmed those earlier ancestors. According to that theory, "modern humans are descended solely from those especially sophisticated tool-users."[3]

An equally important report, "An Ancient Link to Africa Lives on in Bay of Bengal," focuses on the inhabitants of the Andaman Islands (a remote archipelago east of India), and states that they are the direct descendants of the first modern humans to have inhabited Asia. Writes Stanford University's Dr. Peter Underhill (a co-author of the report):

> "Their physical features—short stature, dark skin, peppercorn hair and large buttocks—are characteristic of African Pygmies. They look like they belong in Africa, but here they are sitting in this island chain in the middle of the Indian Ocean."[4]

Only four of the dozen or so tribal groups that once inhabited the island survive, with a total population of about five hundred people. This was before the December 2004 tsunami. These include the Jarawa (the largest group), who still live in the forest, the Onge, who have been settled by the Indian government, the Great Andamanese and the Sentinelese.

These studies of the Andamanese suggest that they are part of what is described as a "relict Paleolithic population, descended from the first modern humans to leave Africa."[5]

Dr. Underhill, an expert on the genetic history of the Y chromosome, said the Paleolithic population of Asia might well have looked as African as the Onge and Jarawa do now, and that "people with the appearance of present-day Asians might have emerged only later."[6]

1.1.2- The African presence in classical civilisations of Asia

But not only were African people the first inhabitants of Asia. There is abundant evidence to show that African people within documented historical periods created, nurtured or influenced some of ancient Asia's most important and enduring classical civilizations. Sumer, considered the first great civilization of Western Asia, is perhaps the most prominent example.

Flourishing during the third millennium B.C.E. between the mighty Tigris and Euphrates Rivers, Sumer set the guidelines and established the standards for the kingdoms and empires that followed her, including Babylon and Assyria. She has been acknowledged as an early center for advanced mathematics, astronomy and calendars, writing and literature, art and architecture, religion and highly organized urban centers, some of the more notable of which were Kish, Uruk, Ur, Nippur, Lagash, and Eridu.

While Sumer's many achievements are much celebrated, the important question of the ethnic composition of her population is frequently either glossed over or left out of the discussion altogether. As topical as Iraq is today and since the civilization of ancient Sumer has been claimed by other peoples, it is important to set the record straight and we believe that we can state without equivocation that Sumerian civilization was at least in some measure an extension of Nile Valley civilizations "of which Egypt was the noblest-born but not the only child."[7]

1.1.3- Racial classification and terminology

For well over a century, Western historians, ethnologists, anthropologists, archaeologists and other such specialists have generally and often arbitrarily used such terms as *Negroid, Proto-Negroid, Proto-Australoid, Negritic and Negrito* in labeling populations in Asia with Africoid phenotypes and African cultural traits and historical traditions. This has especially been the case with Black populations in South Asia, Southeast Asia and Far East Asia. In Southwest Asia, on the other hand, terms like *Hamites, Eurafricans, Mediterraneans and the Brown Race* have commonly been employed in denoting clearly discernible Black populations. In this work, we have chosen to reject such deliberately confusing nomenclature as obsolete and invalid, unscientific and racially motivated, and it is our intention to explore comprehensively the full impact and extent of the African presence in the human cultures and classical civilizations of early Asia.

Dr. Cheikh Anta Diop, whose work has in so many ways formed a model for much of our research efforts, expressed a keen understanding of the nature and ramifications of the phenomena. In a November 1985 interview with the *Journal of African Civilizations*, Charles S. Finch pointed out that, "There seems to be a growing consensus or idea in the literature of anthropology that there is no such thing as race."[8] Continuing, Dr. Finch noted that "One consequence of this thinking is the idea that Black people in India, Asia and the Pacific Islands who have almost the identical physical characteristics as Africans—that is, black skins, kinky hair, full lips, broad noses, etc.—are said to be totally unrelated to Africans."[9] In his response, Dr. Diop, speaking deliberately and uncompromisingly, pointed out that:

> "A racial classification is given to a group of individuals who share a certain number of anthropological traits, which is necessary so that they not be confused with others. There are two aspects which must be distinguished, the phenotypical and genotypical. I have frequently elaborated on these two aspects.
>
> If we speak only of the genotype, I can find a black who, at the level of his chromosomes, is closer to a Swede than Peter Botha is. But what counts in reality is the phenotype. It is the physical appearance which counts. This black, even if on the level of his cells he is closer than Peter Botha, when he is in South Africa he will live in Soweto. Throughout history, it has always been the phenotype which has been at issue; we mustn't lose sight of this fact. The phenotype is a reality, physical appearance is a reality. Now, every time these relationships are not favorable to the Western cultures, an effort is made to undermine the cultural consciousness of Africans by telling them, 'We don't even know what a race is.' It is the phenotype which has given us so much difficulty throughout history, so it is this which must be considered in these relations. It exists, is a reality and cannot be repudiated."[10]

1.1.4- What is to be done in respect to the African presence in Asia?

In this work we have tried to survey, at least to some extent, all of the major geographical regions in Asia and yet so very much, obviously, remain to be done.

There are so many parts of Asia that cry out for detailed study. For example, someone at a recent meeting asked me about the African presence in Sri Lanka. My response was, essentially:

"It all depends on what you mean by African. The majority Sinhalese population of Sri Lanka (formerly Ceylon) is itself generally very dark-complexioned. Then you have the Tamils from South India residing in Sri Lanka. They, also, are heavily melanated people. They are Dravidians, with some of them being quite black-complexioned. These are the Blacks who have fought the Sinhalese Sri Lanka government for independence, or at least a greater degree of autonomy. Then you have the group of Blacks arrived more recently from Africa in Sri Lanka called Kaffirs. They are very similar to the African populations in Iraq, Iran and Kuwait, and known in Pakistan as Sheedis and India as Siddis and Habshis. There seems to be only a few thousand of these Kaffirs in Sri Lanka but they represent the descendants of enslaved Africans brought to the island within the past several hundred years. These Blacks have distinct recollections of Africa. And certainly not to be left out of the discussion are the descendants of probably the original people of Sri Lanka, and these people are generally called Veddas or Veddoids and have a strong resemblance to some groups of Indigenous Australians. In respect to phenotype, all of these populations are Black."

Myanmar, Cambodia, and Vietnam should be special areas of research. On a 2002 visit to Myanmar my tour guide informed me that twenty miles south of the capitial Yangon resides a community of African pearl divers. Other guides in Southeast Asia have informed me of "unmixed" Black people in Cambodia. The Black presence in Vietnam today has scarcely been looked at, and very much the same could be said for Bangladesh. And what about the 13,000 islands of Indonesia, stretching from mainland Asia into the Pacific Ocean? What about Northeast Asia—Siberia? What about Korea? What of the African presence in Syria, Jordan, Lebanon and Palestine? What about African people in Uzbekistan and Kazakhstan and the high plateaus of Central Asia? So much of the work that must be done to have a "complete" picture of the African presence in Asia has scarcely even been outlined.

Perhaps it was expressed best by Dr. Chancellor Williams (to whom this work is in large measure dedicated) in his classic *Destruction of Black Civilization*. According to Dr. Williams, in respect to the African presence in Asia:

"I only made passing reference in the work to Blacks scattered outside of Africa over the world—not from the slave trade, but dispersions that began in prehistory. Fact alone indicates the great tasks of future scholarship on the real history of the race. We are actually just on the threshold, gathering up some important missing fragments. The biggest jobs are still ahead.

Ancient China and the Far East, for example must be a special area of African research. How do we explain such a large population of Blacks in Southern China—powerful enough to form a kingdom of their own? Or the Black people of... the Malay Peninsula, Indo-China, the Andamans and numerous other islands. The heavy concentration of Africans in India... open still another interesting field for investigation. Even the 'Negroid' finds in early Europe appear not to be as challenging as the Black population centers in Asia. Our concern is with great and dominant populations. These are the Blacks who have so puzzled Western scholars that some theorize that Asia or Europe may be the homeland of Africans after all. The African populations in Palestine, Arabia, and Mesopotamia are better known, although the centuries of Black rule over Palestine, South Arabia, and in Mesopotamia should be studied and elaborated in more detail. All of this will call for a new kind of scholarship, a scholarship without any mission other than the discovery of truth, and one that will not tremble with fear when that truth is contrary to what one prefers to believe."[11]

In summation, in brief, we contend that the history of the African presence in Asia, including the African presence in classical Asian civilizations, is one of the most significant, challenging and least written about aspects of the global African experience, and that even today, after an entire series of holocausts and calamities, the Black presence in Asia may exceed (especially if we include the Blacks of India) hundreds of millions of people. The works of pioneer historians and scholars like Rufus Lews Perry, James Marmaduke Boddy, Alphonso Orenzo Stafford, George Wells Parker, Drusilla Dunjee Houston, Joel Augustus Rogers, John Glover Jackson, Cheikh Anta Diop, Chancellor James Williams, Clyde-Ahmad Winters, James E. Brunson, Wayne B. Chandler, and numerous others, to varying degrees, have stressed this for a long time. We are attempting here to continue to carry this work forward energetically.

It is in this light and with this in mind that we present this volume. It is a summary of knowledge, a tying together of strings, a search for answers and an attempt to examine and survey several core areas. Among the most fundamental of these areas are:

1. The peopling and settlement of Asia from Africa, identifying African people as Asia's first modern human populations. That African people—Black people—are the aborigines of Asia, and that subsequent and periodic migrations and movements of African people into Asia occurred throughout antiquity.

2. The impact and extent of the African presence in the human cultures and classical civilizations of early Asia.

3. Discernible African elements and underpinnings of the major religions and philosophical movements in Asian antiquity.

4. Historical, anthropological, and linguistic relationships between Asia's Africoid, Mongoloid, Caucasoid, and Semitic populations.

5. The enslavement and subjugation of Black people in Asia.

6. Ancient and modern documentations and historiography of the African presence in Asia.

7. Major population centers and geographic locations of African populations in Asia, from antiquity to modern times.

8. Nomenclature and designations for African people in Asia.

9. The numbers and proportions of African people in Asia, from antiquity to modern times.

10. The status of African people in Asia today.

11. Are all of the Black people in Asia Africans?

And so with that, for now, we open the book to you and leave it to the reader to judge its merits. At the beginning of this Introduction we stated that the epic story of the African presence in Asia may have begun 100,000 years ago. In closing, we say that the story of the African presence in Asia has not ended yet. The story is not finished. It is not completed. The past is not dead and history is not done. Or, to state it more eloquently, and in the words of the great scholar and teacher Dr. Ivan Van Sertima (to whom this volume, along with John G. Jackson and Chancellor Williams, is dedicated):

"On that note we close. The Black role in Asia, as elsewhere in the world, has been submerged and distorted for centuries. But it has not been totally eclipsed and it rises now like a star which was hidden by a cloud but never faded into the oblivion of the night."[12]

Notes

1. Cited by Chancellor Williams, *The Destruction of Black Civilization*, rev. ed. (Chicago: Third World Press, 1974), 15.

2. Robert Lee Holts, "Chinese Roots Lie in Africa, Research Says," *Los Angeles Times*, September 29, 1998.

3. Holts. op. cit.

4. Nicholas Wade, "An Ancient Link to Africa Lives on in Bay of Bengal," *New York Times*, December 11, 2002.

5. Wade, op. cit.

6. Wade, ibidem

7. Ivan Van Sertima, *Egypt Revisited* (New Brunswick: Transaction Press, 1982), 8.

8. Charles S. Finch, *Great African Thinkers, vol. 1*: Cheikh Anta Diop, (New Brunswick: Transaction Press, 1986), 285.

9. Finch, op. cit.

10. Cheikh Anta Diop, *Great African Thinkers, vol. 1*: Cheikh Anta Diop, (New Brunswick: Transaction Press, 1986), 285.

11. Chancellor Williams, *The Destruction of Black Civilization, rev. ed.* (Chicago: Third World Press, 1974), 44.

12. Ivan Van Sertima, *African Presence in Early Asia* (New Brunswick: Transaction Press, 1995), 17.

1.2.- ESSAYS – THE IVAN VAN SERTIMA PAPERS –
Pioneer Contributions to the African Presence in Early Asia, 1883 to 1926: George Washington Williams to Drusilla Dunjee Houston

By Runoko Rashidi and James E. Brunson

1.2.1- Background and Intoduction

One of the most fascinating areas in the broad field of the African presence in Asian antiquity is its early documentation by African scholars. In this essay we have chosen to highlight the lives and works of seven pioneer African Diasporan scholars who published on the African presence in early Asia within the forty-three year time period from 1883 to 1926—an era in the United States beginning in the middle of the post-Reconstruction period and ending in the middle of the Harlem Renaissance.

Of course, the major scholars discussed here were not the only ones during this turbulent age whose works touched upon and embraced the African presence in early Asia. Nor were they the first. As early as July 18, 1827, for example, Samuel E. Cornish (ca. 1795-1859) and Jamaican-born John Brown Russwurm (1799-1851) in *Freedom's Journal* (the first African newspaper established in the United States) published an article entitled *"European Colonies in America"* in which was written that:

> "Ethiopia, a country of which the history is almost entirely shrouded in the night of ages and of which we know little or nothing, except that it must have been in its day a seat of high civilization and great power, probably the fountain of the improvement of Egypt and western Asia, was inhabited by Blacks. It then comprehended the country on both sides of the Red Sea, whence the Ethiopians are said by Homer to be divided into two parts. The great Assyrian empires of Babylon and Nineveh, hardly less illustrious than Egypt in arts and arms, were founded by Ethiopian colonies, and peopled by Blacks."[1]

Dr. Edward Wilmot Blyden (1832-1912) argued that "No people can interpret Africans but Africans."[2] In his essay entitled "The Negro in Ancient

History," which was the first article written by an African focusing on the Black presence in antiquity to be published in an American literary quarterly (appearing in the January 1869 issue of the *Methodist Quarterly Review*), Blyden referenced the work of Assyriologist Henry Creswicke Rawlinson (1810-1895), concluding "that the early inhabitants of South Babylonia were of a cognate race with the primitive colonists both of Arabia and of the African Ethiopia."[3]

In 1891 Edward Austin Johnson (1860-1944), a lawyer, educator and principal of Washington Public School in Raleigh, North Carolina, published *A School History of the Negro Race in America*. In a section of the work focusing on the "Origins of Race," Johnson pointed out that, "Three million Buddhists in Asia represent their chief deity, Buddha, with Negro features and hair."[4]

The writers who are the primary focus of this essay are a representative cross section of the most outstanding Africanist scholars of their era. Although we pay tribute to them here, it is fair to say that in spite of their work they are not especially well known today in African-centered circles. This is a pity, for they all led difficult, fascinating and highly remarkable lives. None of them, it must be said, seem to have made the study of the African presence in Asia the primary focus of their researches. Each of them, however, with varying degrees of significance, made qualitative contributions to the field. All of them were exceptionally brilliant and actively dedicated in their own way to the complete and total emancipation of African people

Reviewing their works today, in some cases more than a century after their initial publications, it is not hard to be critical. However, their work as historians and scholars must be weighed within the context of the times in which they lived, with all of the profound limitations and handicaps imposed upon them by severe economic disabilities and racial and gender discrimination.

And yet in spite of the innumerable difficulties and staggering obstacles placed in their paths, through their intellect, sacrifice, persistence, determination and the confidence that the work they were doing was a vital, almost sacred mission, they made immense contributions that have served as models, inspiration and guidance. These scholars, these courageous African men and women, were pioneers and trailblazers whose works, even today and in spite of obvious flaws, merit considerable praise and serious recognition.

1.2.2.- George Washington Williams (1849-1891)

Dr. George Washington Williams, a man generally credited as the first African-American to write a "scholarly general history" of Black people not only in America but antiquity, was born in Bedford Springs, Pennsylvania October 16, 1849. He graduated from Howard University in 1868 and studied at Newton Theological Seminary in Massachusetts, graduating in 1874. Williams traveled in Western Europe in 1884, to the Belgian Congo in 1890, and in January 1891 to Cairo, Egypt. Williams was an international traveler, the first Black member of the Ohio legislature, an orator, soldier, minister, journalist, jurist, writer, editor and an astute historian.

In 1883 G.P. Putnam's Sons published Dr. Williams' two volume work *History of the Negro Race in America from 1619 to 1880. Negroes as Slaves, as Soldiers, and as Citizens: Together with a Preliminary Consideration of the Unity of the Human Family, an Historical Sketch of Africa, and an Account of the Negro Governments of Sierra Leone and Liberia.* The work was reviewed in such mainstream publications as the Atlantic Monthly, the Nation, and the New York Times.

In the first volume, in a chapter entitled "The Negro in the Light of Philology, Ethnology, and Egyptology," while dwelling on the antiquity of Africans in Asia, Williams wrote that:

> "In Japan, and in many other parts of the East, there are to be found stupendous and magnificent temples that are hoary with age. It is almost impossible to determine the antiquity of some of them, in which the idols are exact representations of woolly-haired Negroes, although the inhabitants of those countries today have straight hair. Among the Japanese, black is considered a color of good omen. In the temples of Siam we find the idols fashioned like unto Negroes... Among the Hindus, Kali, the consort of Siva, one of their great Triad; Crishna, the eighth incarnation of Vishnu; and Vishnu also himself, the second of the Trimerti or Hindu Triad, are represented of a black color."[5]

> "Now, these substantial and indisputable traces of the march of the Negro races through Japan and Asia lead us to conclude that the Negro race antedates all profane history. And while the great body of the Negro races have been located geographically in Africa, they have been, in no small sense, a cosmopolitan people. Their wanderings may be traced from the rising to the setting sun."[6]

"Taking the whole southern portion of Asia westward to Arabia, this conjecture-which likewise was a conclusion drawn, after patient research, by the late Sir T. Stanford Raffles-accounts, more satisfactorily than any other, for the Oriental habits, ideas, traditions, and words which can be traced among several of the present African tribes and in the South-Sea Islands. Traces of this black race are still found along the Himalaya range from the Indus to Indo-China, and the Malay Peninsula, and in mixed form all through the southern states to Ceylon."[7]

Towards the end of his life Williams focused tremendous energy on the conditions of Africans in Africa under colonial rule, especially Central Africa. He traveled to the Belgian Congo in 1890 and wrote a scathing letter to King Leopold II of Belgium detailing the ruthless brutalities of European rule in Africa.

George Washington Williams died in Blackpool, England on August 2, 1891.

1.2.3- Rufus Lewis Perry (1843-1895)

Born into slavery in Smith County, Tennessee, Rufus Lewis Perry became a "Ph.D., Editor, Ethnologist, Essayist, Logician, Profound Student of Negro History, Scholar in the Greek, Latin and Hebrew Languages."[8] His parents, Lewis and Mary Perry, were owned by one Archibald Overton. Lewis Perry, an outstanding carpenter and mechanic, was empowered to work in Nashville where young Rufus attended a school for free Blacks (taught by Mrs. Sally Porter) until his father fled to Canada. In 1852 Perry was sold to a slave dealer who planned to take him to Mississippi. Perry had other plans, however, and, following his father's tradition, escaped to Canada, eventually becoming a prominent clergyman and graduating from Kalamazoo University in the class of 1861.

Perry entered the Kalamazoo Seminary in 1861 and was ordained as pastor of the Second Baptist Church in Ann Arbor, Michigan on August 9, 1861. Perry engaged in general missionary work and subsequently served as superintendent in a school for freed Africans. Like his father before him, "Perry was a Baptist minister. He was editor of the *Sunbeam* (Brooklyn) and the *People's Journal* (Columbus, Ohio), coordinate editor of the *American Baptist* (later the *Baptist Weekly*, New

York), and editor and publisher of the National Monitor (Brooklyn). For ten years, Perry served as corresponding secretary of the consolidated American Baptist Missionary Convention and, later, corresponding secretary of the American Educational Association and of the American Baptist Free Mission Society."[9] In 1887 the State University at Louisville conferred upon Perry, George Washington Williams and James Poindexter, the honorary degree of Doctor of Philosophy.

A dominant theme in Perry's work (and in the work of numerous other scholars as well) was the identification of both an ancient African and Asian land known to the Greeks as Ethiopia, and in the Biblical table of nations as Cush.

In 1887 the *Literary Union* published a paper read by Perry before the *Brooklyn Literary Union* entitled *The Cushite: or, The Children of Ham, (The Negro Race) As Seen by the Ancient Historians and Poets.* In the Introduction to *The Cushite*, Thomas McCants Stewart (1854-1923), the Union's president, wrote that: "THE CUSHITE", so ably and learnedly presented in the following pages by a Negro scholar, who has given years to the study of the subject, will prove invaluable to those who desire to know, 'what is truth?' And more; it will aid in the development of a nobler manhood, because of the information which it imparts, and because of the enthusiasm which it will arouse."[10]

In *The Cushite*, heavily referencing the Biblical table of nations, Dr. Perry wrote that: "The enemies of the Negro maintain that the distinguished Ethiopians and the Egyptians of such frequent and favorable mention, in both sacred and profane history, were not black men. They ingeniously explained the black men away and cunningly substituted some other race."[11] "The four sons of Ham were Cush, Mizraim, Phut and Canaan. These and their immediate descendants were the founders of great Negro or Cushite nations, traces of whose names and extraordinary deeds exist even unto this day. The term 'Cushite' comes directly from Cush whose sons were Nimrod, Seba, Havilah, Sabtah, and Raamah, who begat Sheba, Dedan, and Sabtecha.

Nimrod founded the city of Babylon and the Babylonian empire. Cush and his son Seba are the ancestral heads of the Cushites of southwestern Arabia, Abyssinia and of Nubia, which was originally called Seba by the Hebrews, (Isa. xliii. 3,) and Meroe by the Greeks and Romans."[12] "Canaan, the fourth son of Ham, begat the original inhabitants of Palestine called Canaanites, and was the progenitor of the Sidonians, afterwards called Phoenicians."[13]

In 1893, a far more comprehensive work of Dr. Perry's entitled *The Cushite, Or the Descendants of Ham as Found in the Sacred Scriptures and in the Writings of Ancient Historians and Poets from Noah to the Christian Era* was published in *Springfield*, Massachusetts. In this work there are separate chapters devoted to the semi-legendary Queen of Sheba (whose domain is believed to have embraced parts of both Africa and Asia), Nimrod (the Biblical son of Kush and founder of Mesopotamian civilization), and Memnon (the mythical African warrior-king from southwestern Asia and the most celebrated of the non-Hellenic heroes of antiquity).

By tradition, Memnon was slain by Achilles while defending Priam's Trojans when they were besieged by the fabulous coalition of Greek city-states immortalized in Homer's Iliad: "To Troy no hero came of nobler line, Or if nobler, Memnon, it was thine."[14] Of Memnon, Dr. Perry pronounced: "The distinguished Cushite whom Homer calls Memnon came and went like a meteor in the galaxy of illustrious Ethiopian monarchs. But the poet in classic song and the historian in legendary tradition have preserved enough of his brightness to indicate his rank and power among the contemporary potentates of the earth. He was king of the Ethiopians. He fought against the Greeks in the Trojan War; and after he had slain Antilochus, son of Nestor, was killed by Achilles."[15]

Dr. Perry expressively concluded that "Though slain by Achilles, Memnon is so embalmed in verse and prose by Homer, Hesiod, Virgil and others, that his name will last as long as the writings of these imperishable authors."[16]

Rufus Lewis Perry was a remarkable man. In his epic work Men of Mark Williams J. Simmons summed him up when he stated that, "Without doubt, Rufus L. Perry is one of the ablest men in the United States. He is a splendid type of the Negro genius."[17]

Rev. Perry died in his home at 1016 St. Mark's Avenue in Brooklyn, New York in June 1895, leaving behind a wife and seven children.

1.2.4- Pauline Elisabeth Hopkins (1859-1930)

Pauline Elizabeth Hopkins has been called "One of the most neglected early Black women writers."[18] Born in Portland, Maine, she was an editor, journalist, essayist, novelist, poet, publisher, public lecturer, actress, musician, and stenographer for the Bureau of Statistics on the Massachusetts Census of 1895 for four years. From the age of fifteen, after winning a literary contest sponsored by the African-American playwright, novelist, essayist, historian and abolitionist William Wells Brown (1814-1884), Hopkins went on to write prolifically.

At the age of twenty she completed her first play—*Slaves' Escape; or The Underground Railroad*, and soon became a founder and literary editor of The *Colored American Magazine*, "the first significant Afro-American journal to emerge in the twentieth century."[19]

During this period, she began to lecture on African history in churches and schools.

As an historian, the pinnacle of her writing career came in 1905. From February to July 1905 Hopkins wrote one of the earliest discourses on the global African presence in the form of a four-part series on "The Dark Races of the Twentieth Century," published in *The Voice of the Negro*. In the same year Hopkins authored and published a thirty-one page booklet entitled *A Primer of Facts Pertaining to the Early Greatness of the African Race and the Possibility of Restoration by its Descendants*—With Epilogue.

In *A Primer of Facts* Hopkins wrote that:

> "Nimrod first arose to national greatness as a monarch so that until this day his name is great among the princes of the earth. He was the founder of the great Assyrian Empire."[20]

In "The Dark Races of the Twentieth Century, Pt. 2: The Malay Peninsula, Borneo, Java, Sumatra and the Philippines" Hopkins' ideas about the Black presence in the Philippines and other parts of Southeast Asia and Australasia were emphasized as follows:

> "At the time of Magellan's discovery of these islands lying washed by the Pacific Ocean and the China Sea, the country was peopled by the tribes of Negritos, or descendants of African tribes. Wars and intermarriage have very nearly obliterated the traces of the original stock, and the remaining numbers live in the mountains and cultivate the land. Many interesting theories are offered as to the origin of Negroes in this archipelago. Some scientists say that he was driven from Africa, and others that he came from New Guinea."[21]
>
> "The presence of man in all sections is easily explained by migration, and there is nothing to show several distinct nuclei. Man started out from one point

alone, and by the power of adaptation he has finally covered the entire habitable globe. Therefore we must conclude that the Negritos of the Philippines and the other dark races of Australasia are of the family of Ham."[22]

Finally, she concludes:

"Then why not allow that the theory of Ethiopia as the mother of science, art, and literature is true? Surely we the descendants of Ham cannot be condemned and ridiculed for claiming that the ancient glory of Ethiopia was the beacon light of all intellectual advancement now enjoyed by mankind. History and the fragments founds in buried cities, though meager, give us a strong claim upon the attention of the world."[23]

At the completion of the series *The Voice of the Negro* pronounced that "Many people have written us and spoken to us about Miss Hopkins articles. Evidently they have awakened great interest in the history of the colored people of the world."[24]

Beginning as early as 1904, Pauline Elizabeth Hopkins began to suffer from poor health and for most of the rest of her life she labored in obscurity. She died in the Cambridge Relief Hospital on August 13, 1930 after she was horribly burned the previous day when her dress caught fire. She was buried on August 17 (Marcus Garvey's birthday) in the Hopkins family plot on Lilac Path, in the Garden Cemetery, Chelsea, Massachusetts. She had spent a full lifetime of making the well-being of her people her highest priority.

1.2.5- James Marmaduke Boddy (1866-1935)

Of the writers outlined here, Reverend James Marmaduke Boddy is probably the least known. He was born in Wrightsvlle, Pennsylvania in September in either 1866 or 1867, the son of James and Cassandra Boddy. His father was born in Pennsylvania; his mother in Maryland. He attended Roberts Vaux Grammar School in Philadelphia, graduated from Lincoln University in 1890 and the Princeton Theological Seminary in 1895. He also attended Albany Medical College. He was ordained as a Presbyterian minister in 1895 and pastored churches in Little Rock, Arkansas and St. Paul, Minnesota. Rev. Boddy also pastored at the Liberty Street Presbyterian Church of Troy, New York. Rev. Henry Highland Garnet, who made famous the expression "Let your motto be resistance", was pastor of the same church from 1839 to 1846. In 1906 Rev. Boddy married Elizabeth G. Davis of Troy, New York.

Boddy is described in the preamble to the March 1905 issue of the Colored American Magazine as "one of the most noted divines in the Presbyterian Church, a graduate of Lincoln and Princeton, ripe scholar, great preacher."[25] He was also one of the earliest African-American writers to tackle the issue of the Black presence in ancient East—specifically China and Japan.

In 1905 Boddy had at least three essays published in *The Colored American Magazine*. They were "The Ethnic Unity of the Negro and the Anglo-Saxon Race" in March, "Brain Weight and Intellectual Development: Physical Variations of the Nego and the Anglo-Saxon Races" in July, and "The Ethnology of the Japanese Race" in October of that year.

In the October 1905 issue of *The Colored American Magazine*, Boddy published a nine page essay entitled "The Ethnology of the Japanese Race," which attempted to document a prominent and indelible African strain running through early Japanese history and show that the Japanese are at least in part "Asian Negroes."

Referencing the work of ethnologist and anthropologist James Cowles Prichard (1786-1848), Boddy wrote that:

> "As to the color of the invaders who gave to the Japanese race their crisp hair and dark complexion we have the testimony of Prichard, who quotes from ancient Japanese state records of the empire, which speaks of the early invaders as 'Black Savages, who were very formidable.' They are also described as having 'peculiar features,' 'Crisp hair' and 'dark complexion.' Besides their Negro features, which are very observable, the early Japanese historians themselves have described for us the 'Black Barbarians of the South; the Black savages of the west,' who, in an age which antedates authentic history, 'came from the south in ships and settled in Japan.' (See Prichard's Researches Into the *Physical History of Mankind, Vol. IV.*, p. 492)."[26]

> "It is to be noted that the word savage, when used in the context of Prichard and Boddy, denoted strangers. Rev. Boddy concluded by saying that 'These immigrants mingled and amalgamated one with another and with the natives, and in time became a homogeneous race, whose predominating physical characteristics bespeak the unmistakable presence of a large Negro element.'[27] In ancient records, wrote Boddy, these Blacks were called, among other things,

'black cinnamon,' 'black barbarians,' and 'dark pygmies,' according to the whims or dictation of the various authors."[28]

Reverend James Marmaduke Boddy died on November 17, 1935 in Hennepin, Minnesota—more than thirty years after the publication of his Colored American essays. And researchers defied attempts to find what became of him in those last thirty years. In spite of those missing three decades, however, his legacy is golden.

1.2.6- Alphonso Orenzo Stafford (1871-1941)

In contrast to Boddy, the major details of the life of educator and historian Alphonso Orenzo Stafford are fairly well known. Stafford was born in Alexandria, Virginia on May 5, 1871. At an early age he came to the District of Columbia where he was educated in the public schools. Stafford completed the teacher training course at the Miner Normal School in Virginia and became an elementary school teacher in the District of Columbia. While teaching he studied law at Howard University, but never practiced. He later took courses at the University of Pennsylvania and Columbia University.

Around the beginning of the twentieth century Stafford began teaching in the public schools in Baltimore. This was during the era when African-American teachers were beginning to take over the responsibilities for the instruction of African-American youth from White teachers. Stafford eventually taught in Washington, D.C., ultimately serving as Principal of the Lincoln School, the Harrison School, and Burville and Phillips.

Stafford eventually served on the staff of Chaney Training College for Teachers (which later became Chaney State College in Chaney, Pennsylvania), and assisted Booker Taliaferro Washington (1856-1915) and his staff in the study of Africa. Commenting on Stafford, Carter G. Woodson (1875-1950) noted that, "His coworkers and superiors give him a high rating as an educator. He had the bearing of a gentleman of the highest culture; and teachers, children, and parents profited by contact with him."[29]

Professor Stafford was also an important early contributor to *Journal of Negro History*, published by the Association for the Study of Negro Life and

History and edited by Harvard trained Dr. Woodson. His first contribution to the *Journal of Negro History*, "The Mind of the African Negro as Reflected in His Proverbs," was published in its inaugural issue in January 1916. Stafford's next article, "Antar, the Arabian Negro Warrior, Poet and Hero," appeared in the second issue of the *Journal of Negro History* in April 1916. Antar has been referred to as the "national hero of the Arabs." Regarding Antar, Stafford wrote that:

Regarding the heroic figure Antar, Stafford wrote that:

> "His fame as a literary character transcends that of the modern authors of black blood, such as Pushkin in Russia, and the elder Dumas in France. After his death the fame of Antar's deeds spread across the Arabian Peninsula and throughout the Mohammedan world. In time these deeds, like Homeric legends, were recorded in a literary form and therein is found that Antar,... has become the Achilles of the Arabian Iliad, a work known to this day after being a source of wonder and admiration for hundreds of years to millions of Mohammedans as the 'Romance of Antar.' The book, therefore, ranks among the great national classics like the 'Shah-nameh' of Persia, and the 'Nibelungen-Lied' of Germany. Antar was the father of knighthood. He was the champion of the weak and oppressed, the protector of women, the impassioned lover-poet, the irresistible and magnanimous knight. 'Antar' in its present form probably preceded the romances of chivalry so common in the twelfth century in Italy and France."[30]

In November 1940 the *Negro History Bulletin*, which, like the *Journal of Negro History*, was founded and edited by Carter Woodson, devoted a special issue to the African presence in Asia to which Stafford contributed three brief essays: "Antar," "Africa and Asia," and "Why Study Asia with Respect to Africa."

After a full lifetime of working for the uplift of African people A.O. Stafford passed away in March 1941. According to Dr. Woodson, "The Association for the Study of Negro Life and History in particular and the Negro race in general suffered a great loss in the passing of Alphonso Orenzo Stafford on March 22, 1941. He was helpful to the Association from its very beginning, and through it he made various contributions to the intellectual progress of the country."[31] And, in perhaps his finest tribute to Stafford, Dr. Woodson stated that "When the Association for the Study of Negro Life and History was organized in 1915 Stafford was the first to invite its attention to the importance of penetrating the African background."[32]

1.2.7.- Georges Wells Parker (1882-1931)

George Wells Parker, historian and activist, was born September 18, 1882, the son of Abraham W. Parker of Petersburg, Virginia and Augusta Bing of Charleston, South Carolina. After moving to Nebraska he attended Creighton University in Omaha until his junior year in 1909-10. Robert A. Hill described Parker as "a medical student in Omaha and scion of one of that city's oldest black families."[33] Later in life Parker became an enthusiastic supporter of Marcus Garvey and performed a dynamic function in aiding African people relocating to Omaha in 1916 and 1917.

On April 1, 1917 Parker delivered a speech before the Omaha Philosophical Society entitled "The African Origin of the Grecian Civilization." Still referenced today, "The African Origin of the Grecian Civilization" was published in the *Journal of Negro History* in July 1917.[34]

George Wells Parker was an exceptional scholar, perhaps even ahead of his time, who wrote with a pronounced degree of confidence, clarity and sharpness. Parker believed that, "That No race can lay claim to such glory as can the African race, and when the truth is known, as it must be known some day, all other races will bow to it, not because they wish, but because truth is a tyrant that admits of no falsity."[35]

Along with John Edward Bruce (1856-1924) and the Rev. John Albert Williams (1866-1933), George Wells Parker founded the Hamitic League of the World, of which the extraordinary bibliophile Arthur Alfonso Schomburg (1874-1938) became a member.[36]

The term Hamitic was a popular and progressive expression used at the time to denote African people. It was a term particularly applied to the great and ancient African builders of grand civilizations. The declared aims of the Hamitic League of the World were:

> "To inspire the Negro with new hopes; to make him openly proud of his race and of its great contributions to the religious development and civilization of mankind and to place in the hands of every race man and woman and child the facts which support the League's claim that the Negro Race is the greatest race the world has ever known."[37]

In 1918 the Hamitic League of the World published a twenty-nine page pamphlet by Parker entitled *The Children of the Sun* which contained an enlightening section highlighting the African presence in classical African, Asian and European civilizations. *The Children of the Sun* which contained a fascinating section highlighting the ethnic composition of classical Asian civilizations. Of Southwest Asia, Parker wrote that:

> "In the great Mesopotamian valley, where flourished Chaldea, Babylon and Assyria, evidences of the rule of African peoples have become so persistent that the most famous scholars simply attribute the glory of these mighty empires to African blood and let it go at that. True, that the ancient writers knew there were black empires and said so, but modern man has always had the habit of believing that the ancients never knew what they were talking about.[38]

After an incisive examination of ancient languages and religions, Persia and Phoenicia, India and Arabia, Parker concludes his comments on Asia as follows:

> "And this ends the survey of Asia. Fifty years ago one would not have dreamed that science would defend the fact that Asia was the home of the black races as well as Africa, yet it has done just that thing. Now when we gaze on the ruins of Assyria's palaces or stand in wrapt wonder before the fallen winged beasts which guarded her gates; when we stand silently upon the spot that once was Babylon and ponder upon the mighty walls built by this grand and wondrous mistress of the Euphratean plain or reverently uncover before the tumbled pillars of sanctuaries built in the long ago to forgotten gods; when we marvel at the depth of love and the majesty of grief that built the Taj Mahal or scan the perfumed literatures of India and Persia and Arabia, let us not forget that the secret, like the secret of all things wonderfully and aesthetically beautiful, lies with Africa, the mother of civilization and of nations."[39]

1.2.8.- Drusilla Dunjee Houston (1876-1941)

Race woman, teacher, journalist and historian, Drusilla Dunjee Houston has earned a high-ranking place in the struggle to redeem Africa's role in world history. She was born in Winchester, Virginia in 1876, the daughter of John William and Lydia Taylor Dunjee, and spent most of her life in the United States Southwest, principally Oklahoma and Arizona.

Drusilla's father, John William Dunjee, was an educator, church building missionary and fund raiser for the American Baptist Home Mission Society. He is principally credited with instilling in young Drusilla a strong sense of ethnic identity and "race pride." Visits to the Houston home by her father's close colleagues included such luminaries as Frederick Douglass and Blanch K. Bruce. As a young woman she lived with her family in Minneapolis, Minnesota before settling down in Oklahoma.

At the age of twenty-two Drusilla married Price Houston—a storekeeper eleven years her senior. Together they bore a daughter. In McAlester, Oklahoma she opened the McAlester Seminary—an educational institution which she maintained for a dozen years. In Oklahoma City Houston worked with her brother Roscoe Dunjee (1883-1965), the editor of *The Black Dispatch*—an Oklahoma City weekly newspaper.

As a journalist, Houston aggressively covered numerous cases of white atrocities against the Black citizens of Oklahoma. But it is as a bold and uncompromising historian that Houston comes to our attention here. *Reading The Negro* by Dr. W.E.B. DuBois (published in 1915) inspired her to research African people and their contributions to the world's civilizations.

Houston's crowning achievement was the publication of the *Wonderful Ethiopians of the Ancient Cushite Empire, Book I: Nations of the Cushite Empire. Marvelous Facts from Authentic Records*. *Wonderful Ethiopians* was originally published in 1926 in Oklahoma City by the Universal Publishing Company, and was intended as the first volume of a three volume set. *Wonderful Ethiopians* is a pioneering work that not only contains comprehensive chapters devoted to ancient African civilizations along the Nile, but continues the ethnographic survey into Asia where it examines and illuminates the strong African influences on classical Asian civilizations. Houston looks extensively at the African background to European civilizations and even ponders the role of Africans in ancient America.

According to Ms. Houston:

> "Out of anthropology, ethnology, geology, paleontology, archaeology, as well as history, I have dug up an irrefutable arsenal of facts that Harvard or Yale or cowardly scholarship in our race dare not refute. How can a leadership point the forward way that is utterly ignorant of the past?"[40]

Wonderful Ethiopians was favorably reviewed in a number of newspapers by Arthur Alfonso Schomburg, in the *Amsterdam News* by Joel Augustus Rogers, and in the *Pittsburgh Courier* by Robert L. Vann. Schomburg (1874-1938), the brilliant bibliophile, noted that:

> "I can assure everyone that the author must have used considerable oil in her lamp represented by her exhaustive research, the indefatigable labor that resulted in the astonishing compilation before me… We are indebted to Drusilla D. Houston for this illuminating and comprehensive book."[41]

Joel Augustus Rogers (1883-1966), himself a tremendous historian, journalist and scholar, recommended that *"The Wonderful Ethiopians* be placed in every Negro home and school in the land."[42] Robert L. Vann emphasized that "We know of no book published in the last 25 years which offers such reputable inspiration to the Black people of the earth."[43] A. Philip Randolph's newspaper, *The Messenger*, commented that:

> "Mrs. Houston has done what few other Negro authors have had the necessary patience and perseverance to do… She has delved deep into the… past to show that the literature, art, music, religion and customs of the Greeks and the early torch bearers of civilization were all permeated and influenced by the Ethiopians."[44]

Ten of the seventeen chapters in *Wonderful Ethiopians* focus on the African presence in early Asia. After thoroughly exploring Africa's Nile Valley civilization Ms. Houston proceeds to examine the African presence in early Arabia, before going on to the Tigris-Euphrates, then Pakistan and India, before finishing up with Persia and Media. And this was in 1926!

Regarding Arabia she says:

> "Arabia was once a portion of the ancient Cushite Empire. Some authorities claim that it was the original seat of Ethiopian culture."[45]
>
> "Arabia was originally settled by two distinct races, an earlier Cushite Ethiopian race and a later Semitic Arabian. The Cushites were the original Arabians and dwelt there before Abraham came to Canaan. Ancient literature assigns their first settlement to the extreme southwestern point of the peninsula. From thence they spread northward and eastward over Yemen, Hadhramaut and Oman. A proof that they were Hamites lay in the name Himyar or dusky, given to the ruling race. The Himyaritic language, now lost, but some of which is preserved, is African in origin and character. Its grammar is identified with the Abyssinian."[46]

Regarding Southwestern Asia, she says succinctly:

"We know that Nimrod was the son of Cush. Babylon had two elements in her population in the beginning. The northern Accadians and the southern Sumerians were both Cushites. The finds of recent explorations in the Mesopotamian valley reveal that these ancient inhabitants were black, with the cranial formation of Ethiopians."[47]

Of India, she notes that:

"The Dravidians in ethnic type are Ethiopian and are the race of India from which her civilization originated. Megasthenes said that the natives of India and Ethiopia were not much different in complexion or feature. Dravidians are short like the race of the Mediterranean called Iberians and the Chaldeans. Their complexions are black or very dark."[48]

Houston was also the author of a syndicated column entitled the "Wondrous History of the Negro" and for years she was a feature writer for the Associated Negro Press. On April 11, 1937 in the historic St. Paul African Methodist Episcopal church in St. Louis, Missouri, before a packed audience, she gave an address entitled "The Negro Woman in a Changing Social Order." Her presentation was described as "one of the most profound and illuminating addresses ever heard in St. Louis."[49]

After a remarkable life, on February 2, 1941, in Phoenix, Arizona Drusilla Dunjee Houston succumbed to tuberculosis. At the time of her death she was working on another book on African history. The last years of her life were spent in relative seclusion, and until recently *Wonderful Ethiopians* itself seemed destined for obscurity. Fortunately, however, in 1985 William Paul Coates of Black Classic Press in Baltimore, Maryland reprinted *Wonderful Ethiopians* in its entirety, supplemented with excellent Introduction, Afterword and Commentary by W. Paul Coates, Asa G. Hilliard III, and James G. Spady, respectively.

1.2.9.- Conclusion

Although the story of the African presence in early Asia has been described as somewhat obscure, its documentation is by no means new, as the admirable and relevant works of the scholars discussed in this essay, Dr. George Washington Williams, Dr. Rufus Lewis Perry, Pauline Elizabeth Hopkins,

Rev. James Marmaduke Boddy, Alphonso Orenzo Stafford, George Wells Parker, and Drusilla Dunjee Houston, along with a host of others, effectively demonstrate. Indeed, their collective works can be credited with having developed and sustained a foundation from which the present generation of scholars can move confidently forward.

Notes

1. Samuel E. Cornish and John B. Russwurm, "*European Colonies in America,*" Freedom's Journal, July 18, 1827, 1.
2. Edward Wilmot Blyden, quoted in George Shepperson, "Notes on Negro American Influences on the Emergence of African Nationalism," in Melvin Drimmer, ed., *Black History* (Garden City: Doubleday, 1969), 494.
3. Edward Wilmot Blyden, "*The Negro in Ancient History,*" The Methodist Quarterly Review (January 1869), 78.
4. Edward A. Johnson, *The Negro Race in America* (Raleigh: Edwards & Broughton, 1891), 12.
5. George Washington Williams, *History of the Negro Race in America*, vol. 1 (New York: G.P. Putnam's 1883), 17.
6. Williams, 18.
7. Williams, 19.
8. William J. Simmons, *Men of Mark, Eminent, Progressive and Rising* (1887; rpt. Chicago: Johnson, 1970), 425.
9. Sylvia M. Jacobs, *The African Nexus* (Westport: Greenwood Press, 1981), 70. "Perry was almost adamant in his belief that the `duty' of Afro-Americans to help in the `development' of Africa. He maintained that, under the guise of philanthropy, the European rivals were plotting to gain a foothold on the continent. But Perry had no doubt that God had reserved Africa for the Africans and that in the end Africa would be a black man's continent." Jacobs, 71.
10. Thomas McCants Stewart, *Introduction to The Cushite*, by Rufus Lewis Perry (Brooklyn: The Literary Union, 1887), vi. Thomas McCants Stewart was a lawyer, pastor, author, editor and educator. He was born of free parents in 1854 in Charleston, South Carolina. In 1898, after attending Howard University and graduating from the University of South Carolina, Stewart moved to Honolulu. From 1915 to 1921 he lived in England, and died in St. Thomas, Virgin Islands January 7, 1923.
11. Simmons, 427.
12. Rufus Lewis Perry, *The Cushite* (Brooklyn: The Literary Union, 1887), 9-10.
13. Perry, 10.
14. Homer, *The Iliad.*

15. Rufus Lewis Perry, *The Cushite, Or the Descendants of Ham as Found in the Sacred Scriptures and in the Writings of Ancient Historians and Poets from Noah to the Christian Era* (Springfield, MA: Willey & Co., 1893), 119.

16. Perry, 121.

17. Simmons, 429.

18. Ann Allen Shockley, "*Pauline Elizabeth Hopkins: A Biographical Excursion in Obscurity*," Phylon 33 (Spring 1972), 22.

19. Abby Arthur Johnson, and Ronald M. Johnson, "*Away from Accommodation: Radical Editors and Protest Journalism, 1900-1910,*" *Journal of Negro History* (July 1977), 325. *The Colored American Magazine* began publication in May 1900. On the magazine's cover it describes itself as, "A Monthly Illustrated Magazine Devoted to the Interests of the Colored Race." *The Colored American Magazine* was published by the Moore Publishing and Printing Company in New York City and sold for ten cents a month or $1.00 a year.

20. Pauline Elizabeth Hopkins, *A Primer of Facts Pertaining to the Early Greatness of the African Race and the Possibility of Restoration by its Descendants-With Epilogue Compiled and Arranged from the Works of the Best Known Ethnologists and Historians* (Cambridge: P.E. Hopkins & Co., 1905), 10.

21. Pauline Elizabeth Hopkins, "The Dark Races of the Twentieth Century, Pt. 2: The Malay Peninsula, Borneo, Java, Sumatra and the Philippines," *The Voice of the Negro* (March 1905), 190.

22. Hopkins, 191.

23. Hopkins.

24. Editorial Page, *The Voice of the Negro* (June 1905).

25. Editorial Page, *The Colored American Magazine* (March 1905).

26. James Marmaduke Boddy, "The Ethnology of the Japanese Race," *The Colored American Magazine* (October 1905), 582.

27. Boddy, 582.

28. Boddy, 583.

29. Carter G. Woodson, "Alphonso Orenzo Stafford," *Journal of Negro History* (January 1941), 278.

30 Alphonso Orenzo Stafford, "Antar, The Arabian Negro Warrior, Poet and Hero," *Journal of Negro History 1, No. 2* (1916), 155. Stafford's third article for the *Journal of Negro History*, "The Tarik E' Soudan," was published in April 1917. It was essentially a review of the brilliant West African scholar Abderrahman es-Sadi's classic history of the Sudan. In this article Stafford wrote that:

"The sixteenth century was the golden age of science and literature in Timbuctoo. Her scholars with the University of Sankore as a center had so generously contributed to the world's thought that they had brought to that country no less fame than its statesmen and warriors by their constructive work and daring deeds. The country, however, was finally invaded by the Moors and the scattering of the talented class resulting thereby led to the inevitable decline of culture." A.O. Stafford, "The Tarik E' Soudan," *Journal of Negro History* (April 1917), 139.

31. Woodson, 277.

32. Woodson, 278.

33. Robert A. Hill, ed., *The Marcus Garvey and Universal Negro Improvement Association Papers, vol. 1* (Berkeley: University of California Press, 1983), 522.

34. "This short article in the *Journal of Negro History* is important for its age, 1917! It anticipates George G.M. James' *Stolen Legacy* and Martin Bernal's *Black Athena* using substantially the same approach." Asa G. Hilliard III, *Free Your Mind: Return to the Source African Origins and Master Keys, rev. ed.* (East Point: Waset Educational Productions, 1991), 86.

35. Born in San Juan, Puerto Rico, Schomburg once explained that "The Negro must remake his past in order to make his future. Though it is orthodox to think of America as the one country where it is unnecessary to have a past, what is a luxury of the nation as a whole becomes a prime social necessity for the Negro. For him, a group tradition must supply its compensation for persecution, and race pride is the simple antidote for prejudice." Arthur A. Schomburg, "The Negro Digs Up His Past." In the *New Negro, ed.*, Alain Locke (New York: Arno Press and the New York Times, 1968), 231.

36. Quoted by Robert A. Hill, *Introduction to The Crusader* (New York: Garland, 1987), xx.37. Hill, xxi.

38. George Wells Parker, *The Children of the Sun* (Omaha: The Hamitic League of the World, 1918), 12-13.

39. Parker, 22.

40. Drusilla Dunjee Houston, Quoted on the Back Cover, *Wonderful Ethiopians of the Ancient Cushite Empire* (Baltimore: Black Press, 1985).

41. Quoted by W. Paul Coates, *Introduction to Wonderful Ethiopians of the Ancient Cushite Empire, ii.*

42. Coates.

43. Quoted by Coates, ii.

44. Quoted on the Back Cover, *Wonderful Ethiopians.*

45. Houston, 110.

46. 113.

47. 162.

48. 223.

49. "St. Louis Hears Drusilla Dunjee Houston in Talk," *Black Dispatch* (April 17, 1937).

1. Runoko Rashidi and Ivan Van Sertima at Compton College in 1982

2. George Washington Williams

3. Rev. Rufus Lewis Perry

4. Pauline Elizabeth Hopkins

5. Rev. James Marmaduke Boddy

6. George Wells Parker

7. Drusilla Dunjee Houston

8. John Glover Jackson. Photo by James E. Brunson

9. Chancellor James Williams

10. Cheikh Anta Diop

1.3.- The African Presence in Early Southwest and Southern Asia through the Eyes of Nineteenth Century European Scholars

The critical elements in the bold and adventurous Phoenician city-states; ancient Sumer, the seminal high-culture of Southwestern Asia; Elam, with its capital of Susa—the home of Memnon and the tomb of the Biblical prophet Daniel; and the mighty Indus Valley civilization can each in their own way be ultimately traced back to Africa's Nile Valley.

The claim of so many scholars that these were "Semitic" civilizations or civilizations of "mysterious" origin is one of the great frauds of recent times. This has not, however, always been the case, and this is particularly true of the nineteenth century. Ironically, it was in this period, the zenith of European imperialism, with most of the world's surface conquered in the name of white supremacy and manifest destiny, that history, archaeology and related sciences, as we currently know them, made giant strides.

European and American scholars at this time had an almost unhindered access to the treasures of the world's past, in many ways largely hidden up to then. Some of the most interesting postulations in respect to the place of Black people in the formation of early civilizations, in fact, were made during this transitional period, before the modem standardizations of history's major themes.

Godfrey Higgins (1772-1833), comes under this category. Through the publication of *The Celtic Druids: Or, An Attempt to Show, That the Druids were the Priests of Oriental Colonies who Emigrated from India*, and Were the Introducers of the First or Cadmean System of Letters, and the Builders of Stonehenge, or Carnac, and of Other Cyclopean Works, in Asia and Europe in 1829, and a much more massive work, *Anacalypsis: An Attempt to Draw Aside the Veil of the Saitic Isis* or an *Inquiry into the Origin of Languages, Nations and Religions*, published posthumously in 1836, Higgins was able to show an initial and all pervasive Black presence and influence upon early Asia's major civilizations. His numerous references to the Black Buddhas of India, the Black god Krishna and the Black Memnon of Trojan War fame, along with many others, establish Higgins as basic reading material for students searching out the story of the Black presence in Asian antiquity.

Higgins was convinced, along with many others, that mankind itself, of which the Black race was the first representative, owed its origins to Asia, and specifically India, rather than Africa. The ugly face of racism can also, unfortunately, be found in Higgins' work, for while he vociferously argued that the Black man was the original man, he was equally emphatic in his insistence that while first, he had subsequently become obsolete and utterly incapable of competing with newer and more evolved races. Cited below are Higgins' exact words:

> "Now I suppose, that man was originally a Negro, and that he improved as years advanced and he travelled Westwards, gradually changing from the jet black of India, through all the intermediate shades of Syria, Italy, France, to the fair white and red of the maid of Holland and Britain. On the burning sands and under the scorching sun of Africa, he would probably stand still, if he did not retrograde. But the latter is most likely to have happened; and, accordingly, we find him an unimproved Negro, mean in understanding, black in colour."[1]

What could be more explicit?

Born in Paris on January 17, 1837, Francois Lenormant was a French archaeologist and member of the Academy of Inscriptions and Belles-Lettres. Brilliant even as a youth, Lenormant at the young age of fourteen published a major paper on Greek inscriptions at Memphis, Egypt. In the 1869 publication of volume one of *Ancient History of the East*, Lenormant asserted an influential Cushite presence in early Western Asia:

> "Of these two great nations who constituted the mass of the population of Chaldea, one was of the race of Ham and of the Cushite branch. The presence of Cushites in Chaldea and Babylonia is attested by the Bible, by Berosus, and by the universal testimony of antiquity.[2]
>
> In this state, the first regularly organised government in the world, the preponderance and dominion among the various tribes belonged at first to the Hamites of the Cushite race."[3]

In volume two of *Ancient History of the East*, which appeared in 1871, Lenormant continued his established theme with the early Canaanites and their kith and kin—the Phoenicians, and in another section, the Southern Arabians. The following statements are typical of Lenormant:

"The Phoenicians, as we read in the tenth chapter of Genesis, as they themselves asserted, and as their descendants informed Saint Augustine, belonged to the race of Canaan, who were, according to the biblical tradition, of the posterity of Ham. They were but a branch however, not the whole of the race, a branch among the most celebrated and the most permanent. In this book we shall speak specially of the Phoenicians, because they alone of their race played an important part in history; but first of all, by way of introduction, we must say a few words on the Canaanites in general, on their origin and their migrations, up to the time when the Sidonians or Phoenicians separated themselves from the other nations sprung from the same source, and organized themselves into distinct communities.

The Canaanites at first lived near the Cushites, their brethren in race, on the banks of the Erythraean Sea, or Persian Gulf."[4]

Of the Southern Arabians:

"We may perceive the remembrance of a powerful empire founded by the Cushites in very early ages, apparently including the whole of Arabia Felix, and not only Yemen proper.

Circumcision established in Yemen from remotest antiquity, and several other pagan usages, still practiced in our days, appear to be of Cushite origin. Lokman, the mythical representative of Adite wisdom, resembles Aesop, whose name… seems to indicate an Ethiopian origin. In India, also, the whole literature of tales and apologues apparently come from the Sudras. Perhaps this style of fiction… may represent a style peculiar to the Cushites."[5]

Francois Lenormant died in Paris on December 9, 1883.

John D. Baldwin, an American antiquarian, was the next writer to make significant additions to our knowledge of an ancient and overwhelmingly preeminent Ethiopian impact on the development of Asian high cultures. The year 1872 saw the publication of Baldwin's most relevant work, that being *Pre-Historic Nations; or, Inquiries Concerning Some of the Great Peoples and Civilizations of Antiquity, And their Probable Relations to a Still Older Civilization of the Ethiopians or Cushites of Arabia.*

Pre-Historic Nations, still interesting reading today, contains chapters on early Arabia, the Phoenician city-states, Mesopotamia, India, Egypt and North Africa, and Western Europe. According to Baldwin, "The Cushite race appeared first in the work of civilization." And in further detail: "The Hebrews saw nothing geographical more ancient than this land of Cush… The people described in the Hebrew Scriptures as Cushites were the original civilizers of Southwestern Asia; and that, in the deepest antiquity, their influence was established in nearly all the coast regions, from the extreme east to the extreme west of the Old World."[6]

Although written at a time when archaeology and related sciences were still in their infancy, *Pre-Historic Nations*, like Anacalypsis before it, is a tremendous repository of eye-witness accounts, both ancient and modern, of Black history in early Asia. *Pre-Historic Nations* does contain, however, major drawbacks which are obvious and cannot be overlooked. Baldwin, like Higgins, had major problems with geography, as the text's lengthy subtitle suggests. The following statement neatly sums up Baldwin's position: "The original Ethiopia was not in Africa, and the ancient home of the Cushites or Ethiopians, the starting point of their great colonizing and civilizing, movements, was Arabia."[7] "At that time Arabia was the exalted and wonderful Ethiopia of old tradition—the centre and light of what, in Western Asia, was known as the civilized world."[8]

Pre-Historic Nations, following tradition is also marred by racist thinking, through which Baldwin, when pressed, transforms as if by magic history's great Ethiopians into dark Caucasoids:

> "In modern times, it has commonly been assumed, without proper inquiry, that the Ethiopians were of course Africans. This grave mistake has been the source of much misunderstanding and confusion… Careful students of antiquity now point out that 'the people of Ethiopia seem to have been of the Caucasian race,' meaning white men."[9]

The English antiquarian Gerald Massey (1828-1907) grew up in an atmosphere of intense intellectual activity, and it is interesting to note that among his London contemporaries were Karl Marx and Charles Darwin. Much to Massey's credit, his works are also refreshingly free of the blatantly racist commentaries so often included in antiquarian works. Massey was consistent in his geography and dedicated to truth irrespective of the consequences. Indeed, his statement, "Africa the birthplace and Egypt the mouthpiece," succinctly summarizes his philosophy and is just as profound today as when it was originally penned.[10]

Massey's largest emphasis on the African foundations of Asian history and religions is contained in volume two of *A Book of the Beginnings: Containing an*

Attempt to Recover and Reconstitute the Lost Origines of the Myths and Mysteries, Types and Symbols, Religion and Language, with Egypt for the Mouthpiece and Africa as the Birthplace. Volume 1, Egyptian Origines in the British Isles, was published in 1881. Over two thirds of the text is devoted solely to Hebrew origines in Egypt. Moving east, *Book of Beginnings* includes a comprehensive comparative vocabulary of Akkadian/Assyrian and Egyptian words, followed by a telling chapter entitled "Egyptian Origines in Assyria."[11]

Born in Toulouse, August 3, 1844, Marcel-Auguste Dieulafoy, was a French archaeologist who from 1884 to 1886 conducted major excavations at the ancient site of Susa, in what is now Iran. It is said that Dieulafoy thoroughly represented a generation of learned Frenchmen of the nineteenth century who were without university education and specialized training. But their familiarity with classical civilization combined with technical education led them to take an interest in wide-ranging aspects of history and archeology.

The results of the excavations at Susa were published successively from 1890 to 1892 under the title *L'Acropole de Suse: d'après les fouilles exécutées en 1884, 1885, 1886, sous les auspices du Musée du Louvre* (French Edition). In the first section, on Susa's history and geography, Dieulafoy devoted considerable space to the region's early ethnic compositon of at least some of Susa's residents.

Dieulafoy's legacy is significant in that he focused on only one area; concluding that the African element in the city of Sua in ancient Iran was highly prominent and may have survived even into modem times. The text is accompanied by a set of extremely rare and quite distinct photographs of Susians with clearly distinct Africoid features—meaning full lips, broad noses, and tightly curled hair.

Reflecting upon the excavations as Susa, Dieulafoy stated that:

> "On removing a tomb placed across a raw-brick wall which was part of the fortifications of the Elamite gate, the workers uncovered a funeral urn. The urn was encased in a masonry covering composed of enameled bricks. These came from a panel depicting a personage superbly dressed in a green robe with yellow, blue, and white embroidery. He wore a tiger skin and carried a cane or a golden spear. Most surprising of all, the personage whose lower jaw, beard, neck, and hand I found was black. His lips were thin, the beard thick; the embroidery, of archaic style, seemed to be the work of Babylonian artisans.

In other Sassanid walls built of earlier materials, were found glazed bricks revealing two feet shod in gold, a very well-shaped hand, a wrist covered with bracelets; the fingers held one of those long canes that became the emblem of the sovereign power under the Achaemenides. A piece of the robe bore the coat-of-arms of Susa, partly hidden under a tiger skin. Finally, a flowered fringe on a brown background. His head and feet were black. It was even evident that the whole decoration had been designed to blend with the dark complexion of the face. Only powerful personages had the right to carry long canes and wear bracelets. Only the governor of fortified post could have his image embroidered on his tunic. Yet, the owner of the cane, the master of the citadel was black. It is therefore highly probably that Elam was ruled by a black dynasty and, judging by the features of the face already described, an Ethiopian dynasty…"[12]

L'Acropole de Susa was unfortunately printed in limited quantities which are now extremely scarce. There has never been an English translation that we are aware of. Dieulafoy died after a short illness in February 1920.

The last of the major nineteenth century writers we examine here whose works prominently address the Black presence in early Asia are Henry Creswicke Rawlinson (1810-1895) and Canon George Rawlinson (1812-1902). The former is perhaps best known for his work from 1835 to 1844 in deciphering Mesopotamia's cuneiform scripts. Through his linguistic background Rawlinson was able to identify effectively the Cushite roots in West Asian scripts. The following passage was taken from his commentary to the 1858 publication of the *The History of Herodotus. A new English Version, Edited with Copious Notes and Appendices… Embodying the Chief Results, Historical and Ethnographical, Which have been Obtained in the Progress of Cuneiform and Hieroglyphical Discovery* is representative of Rawlinson's views:

> "Recent linguistic discovery tends to show that a Cushite or Ethiopian race did in the earliest times extend itself along the shores of the Southern Ocean from Abyssinia to India. The whole peninsula of India was peopled by a race of this character before the influx of Arians; it extended from the Indus along the seacoast through the modern Beloochistan and Kerman, which was the proper country of Asiatic Ethiopians; the cities on the northern shores of the Persian Gulf are shown by the brick inscriptions found among their ruins to have belonged to this race; it was dominant in Susiana and Babylonia, until overpowered in the one country by Arian, in the other by Semitic intrusion; it can be traced, both by dialect and tradition, throughout the whole south coast

of the Arabian peninsula, and it still exists in Abyssinia, where the language of the principal tribe (the Galla) furnishes, it is thought, a clue to the cuneiform inscriptions of Susiana and Elymais, which date from a period probably a thousand years before our era."[13]

George Rawlinson, Camden Professor of Ancient History at the University of Oxford from 1861 to 1889, echoed his brother's assessment on these Asiatic Ethiopians. Utilizing Biblical references as the primary evidence, in one of his finest works, *The Origin of Nations: In Two Parts on Early Civilizations, On Ethnic Affinities, etc.*, published posthumously in 1912, Rawlinson traces the geneaologies of the races of man, with special emphasis on the Blacks or Hamites. His conclusions: "The author of Genesis unites together as members of the same ethnic family the Egyptians, the Ethiopians, the Southern Arabians, and the primitive inhabitants of Babylon."[14]

Notes

1. Godfrey Higgins, *Anacalypsis, vol. 1* (London: Longman, 1836), 284.
2. Francois Lenormant, *Ancient History of the East, vol. 1* (London: Asher & Co., 1869), 342.
3. Lenormant, 348.
4. Lenormant, vol. 2, 144.
5. Lenormant, 296, 318.
6. John D. Baldwin, *Pre-Historic Nations* (New York: Harper &Brothers, 1872), 17-18.
7. Baldwin, 21.
8. Baldwin, 47.
9. Baldwin, 48.
10. Gerald Massey, *Ancient Egypt, vol. 1* (New York: Samuel Weiser, 1970).
11. Gerald Massey, *Book of Beginnings*, vol. 2 (Secaucus: University Books, 1881, rpt. 1974).
12. Marcel A. Dieulafoy, *L'Acropole de Susa* (Paris: Hachette, 1892), 44
13. George and Henry Rawlinson, *History of Herodotus*, vol. 1 (London: John Murray, 1858), 650.
14. George Rawlinson, *Origin of Nations* (New York: Charles Scribners' Sons, 1912), 214.

1.4.- The African Presence in Asia in the Works of James Cowles Prichard

James Cowles Prichard, M.D. (1786-1848) was an influential British ethnologist described as one of the founders of the science of anthropology. Prichard was the author of the massive text, *Researches into the Physical History of Man*, originally published in London in 1813. George W. Stocking, editor of a revised reissue of the work, pointed out that, "To Prichard, the continued existence of tribes of 'wooly-haired blacks' from the Andaman Islands east to the South Pacific suggested the early diffusion of a black race over a much wider area."[1]

Reverend James Marmaduke Boddy referenced Prichard in his 1905 article on the "Ethnology of the Japanese Race," which sought to demonstrate an identiable African presence in early Japan.[2] Although Prichard was distinctly biased in his views about race and ethnicity, an examination of his work indicates that many of the European scholars of his era were well aware of the position, stature and prominence of Black people in antiquity. In a notable section of his work "On the Physical Characters of the Ancient Indians," Prichard acknowledged that for a long time, both physically and culturally, the dominant people in ancient India were Black. In support of this he cites, for example, the observations of a number of well-known classical Greek and Roman authors. He points first to Herodotus (ca. 450 B.C.E.), and notes that "It is remarkable that Herodotus, in his enumeration of the forces of Xerxes, mentions a tribe of Ethiopians from the eastern parts of Asia, who were drawn out in the same division of the army with the Indians."[3]

Another notable source was the Greek historian Arrian (ca. 150 B.C.E.). In his work *the Indica*, Arrian said of the people of India that, "Those farther to the south are somewhat more like the Ethiopians, and they are black in their complexion, and their hair is black, but they are not likewise flat nosed, nor is their hair woolly; but those who live farther northward most resemble the Egyptians in their persons."[4]

In more recent times Prichard cites one of his contemporaries, Francis Wilford, an officer in the Indian Army, whose writings appeared in the monumental, twenty-volume *Asiatic Researches*, first published in Calcutta from

1788 to 1839. The initial twelve volumes of *Asiatic Researches* were reprinted in London from 1806 to 1812. A widely recognized scholar during his day, Wilford ultimately concluded that "**it cannot reasonably be doubted, that a race of Negroes formerly had pre-eminence in India.**"[5]

And then, after examining the art of early India, Prichard himself concluded that, "There can be no doubt that the prototypes from which they were designed, were either Negroes properly so called, or that they were possessed of physical characteristics similar to those of the natives of Africa."[6]

Notes

1. George W. Stocking, Jr., "From Chronology to Ethnology: James Cowles Prichard and British Anthropology 1800-1850." *In Researches into the Physical History of Man*, by James Cowles Prichard, rev. ed. (Chicago: University of Chicago Press, 1973), liv.
2. James Marmaduke Boddy, "The Ethnology of the Japanese Race," *The Colored American Magazine* (October 1905), 582.
3. James Cowles Prichard, *Researches into the Physical History of Man* (Chicago: University of Chicago Press, 1973), 389.
4. Prichard, 390.
5. Prichard, 391.
6. Prichard, 395.

1.5.- Sitting at the Feet of a Forerunner: an April 1987 Meeting and Interview with John G. Jackson

1.5.1.- Overview by Runoko Rashidi

John Glover Jackson, one of our greatest cultural historians, was born on April 1, 1907, in Aiken, South Carolina. Never short of cutting remarks, Jackson would sometimes say that "I was born on April Fool's Day, and I've been a fool ever since!" Obviously, this was not the case.

At the age of fifteen Jackson moved from South Carolina to Harlem, New York, where he entered Stuyvesant High School. During his student days he began to do historical research and was soon writing short essays about African-American history and culture. These essays were impressive enough that in 1925, while still a high school student, he was invited to write articles for Marcus Garvey's newspaper, the *Negro World*.

In addition to these growing activities as a writer in 1930 Jackson became a lecturer at both the Ingersoll Forum and the Harlem Unitarian Church. Among his teachers and associates during this formative phase of his life were Hubert Henry Harrison (whom Jackson would later refer to as the "Black Socrates"), Arthur Alfonso Schomburg (the great bibliophile and founder of the Schomburg Library), Joel Augustus Rogers (a journalist and master historian who probably did more to popularize African history than any scholar of the twentieth century), and Dr. Willis Nathaniel Huggins (a chief mentor to both John G. Jackson and John Henrik Clarke).

Willis Nathaniel Huggins, a little known figure today, but without whom *Introduction to African Civilizations* might have never been written, was born February 7, 1886, in Selma, Alabama. Huggins comes boldly to us as one of the most active African-American scholars and supporters of Ethiopia after its invasion and occupation by Italian fascists from 1935 to 1941. Indeed, beginning in 1935, Dr. Huggins was named executive director of the International Council of the Friends of Ethiopia and was commissioned to deliver an appeal on behalf of Ethiopia to the League of Nations in Geneva, Switzerland.

This is a critical and insufficiently documented phase in the saga of African people and Jackson was always anxious to point it out and discuss it. In 1932 Jackson became the Associate Director of the Blyden Society. Named after Edward Wilmot Blyden, one of the outstanding African-American leaders of the nineteenth century, the Blyden Society acted most gallantly as an Ethiopian support group. Among the very early and most talented students to come out of the Blyden Society was Dr. John Henrik Clarke. Professor Jackson had a remarkable memory, possessed a keen sense of humor, and enjoyed sharing his life story with those he thought could appreciate it. One mid-1980 afternoon in Chicago he told me that:

> "Rogers introduced me to Dr. Willis Nathaniel Huggins who had a B.A. from the University of Chicago, an M.A. from Columbia University, a Ph.D. from Fordham University, and he did historical research at Oxford University in England. Around 1932, Dr. Huggins established a little group to study African history at the Harlem YMCA. He called the group the Blyden Society. After Rogers introduced me, he asked me to join it. He was Director. He made me Associate Director. Among our students were Bayard Rustin and John Henrik Clarke. Rustin decided to pull out and join the communists. Clarke was writing poetry. He told me that I changed his life. He said that he was wasting his time writing poetry, which only a damn fool would write. Huggins and I told him that he should be a historian. He says that we put him on the right track."

In 1934, along with Dr. Huggins, Jackson wrote *A Guide to the Study of African History: Directive Lists for Schools and Clubs*. In 1937, the same team wrote *An Introduction to African Civilizations* with *Main Currents in Ethiopian History*. The latter work, a direct precursor of *Introduction to African Civilizations*, was actually published by the Blyden Society. According to Jackson's biographer Larry Crowe, "Huggins would also open what some think to be the first Black book store in Harlem, The Blyden Book Store on 7th Avenue."

John Jackson lived in New York for five decades. Although these were exceptionally arduous years for him, with race-prejudice, poverty and illness his familiar companions, he continued to produce well-researched, informative and provocative texts. In 1939 he authored *Ethiopia and the Origin of Civilization, and Pagan Origins of the Christ Myth in 1941*. His discerning literary contributions to The Truthseeker Magazine were published regularly from 1930 until 1955. In addition to *Introduction to African Civilizations* and his works with

Dr. Huggins, Jackson authored several major books, including *Man, God, and Civilization, Christianity Before Christ*, and *Ages of Gold and Silver*.

I first read *Introduction to African Civilizations* in 1978 during a trip to Mexico. I was young and enthusiastic, and this was my first big international trip. Although the trip itself was poorly planned, I managed to salvage it because I brought along Jackson's book. Soon, I became enraptured by it. With Dr. Chancellor James Williams' *Destruction of Black Civilization* and *Malcolm X Speaks*, it became a critical text in my career as a historian. John G. Jackson showed that African people were a global people, and that the history of the African did not begin as a servant and slave. Psychologically, at least, Jackson's work helped liberate me as a human being.

John G. Jackson taught and lectured at colleges and universities throughout the United States, including City College of New York and Northeastern University. I met Professor Jackson for the first time in 1982 while working at Compton College. I remember him as a large, elderly, light-complexioned Black man who spoke with a deep booming voice. It was my job at the college to develop cultural awareness programs and bring in guest speakers. Getting Professor Jackson was one of my first big triumphs, and I believe that it was one of his only lectures given in California. His lecture was memorable, but what I most vividly recall were our private conversations, sometimes during meals, other times hunting in used book stores, and still other times just strolling around campus.

After our initial encounter, we spent many hours in person and on the phone dissecting history, scholarship, politics, and much more. John Glover Jackson died in Chicago, Illinois in October 1993. The twilight years of his life were spent in a nursing home in southside Chicago.

He remains one of my great heroes.

1.5.2.- Interview by Runoko Rashidi and James E. Brunson

R/B: Some older writers tried to make the early Sumerians, or the black-headed people, into Turanians. What are your views on this?

Jackson: The Sumerians were the people who lived in the valley of the Tigris and Euphrates. They formed the original civilization in that area and it was pre-Semitic. The Semites got their culture from them. That's one trouble that we have with these people who call themselves Semites, because they claim that they were the world's first civilized people. Similarly, if you read the average book on the history of Egypt you will be told that the Egyptians were the first civilized people in Africa, and that the y then went down and civilized Ethiopia. But we know better now, because two archaeologists from the Oriental Institute of the University of Chicago discovered an Ethiopian civilization that predated that of Egypt, so there's no argument there.

R/B: We wanted to ask you about some of the diffusionists. Could you give us some ideas on the works of Albert Churchward?

Jackson: Well Churchward was a disciple of Gerald Massey. So he left us some outstanding books like *The Origin and Evolution of the Human Race, The Signs and Symbols of Primordial Man, The Origin and Evolution of Religion. The Origin of Freemasonry*, and so on. They are all very scholarly works.

R/B: What type of climate was Churchward writing these books in, and what kind of reaction did he receive?

Jackson: He got a very negative reaction. Because here was a man that in 1921, in *The Origin and Evolution of the Human Race*, said that the human race started in Africa at least two-million years ago. His fellow anthropologists laughed at him. This was in 1921. About three or four years later a fossil was uncovered in Africa that was about two-million years old. I think Churchward died in 1929, so he had a chance to laugh at his critics before he died.

R/B: How did you first hear about the works of Albert Churchward?

Jackson: I heard about them through Dr. Hubert Harrison, who was Staff Lecturer for the Board of Education in New York. He had read *Signs and Symbols of Primordial Man* and reviewed *The Origin and Evolution of Religion for Amsterdam News*, and lectured about them. After Harrison died I went to the library to do research. I looked up Churchward's works and then saw where he mentioned his 'dear friend Gerald Massey.' And then I looked up Massey and found out that Massey was the master and Churchward was the disciple. That was in 1930.

R/B: What do you know about the lives and works of the Rawlinson Brothers?

Jackson: There were two of them. The oldest was Sir Henry Rawlinson. He made the major breakthrough in deciphering some of the important ancient languages of the Near East including Sumerian, Akkadian, Babylonian, and so on. He said that there was a common connection between these languages and Egyptian as well, and that the Ethiopian language was the foundation of all of them. His brother, George Rawlinson, was professor of ancient history at Oxford University. He was also a high official in the Church of England and the Canon of Canterbury. So they called him Canon Rawlinson of Canterbury. They were both first-class scholars. Sir Henry Rawlinson was the great Orientalist. His brother was the great ancient historian.

R/B: What do think of the current linguists who have the opinion that there was a distinct difference between the early Sumerian and Ethiopian languages, and that there was no connection between them?

Jackson: I think that they're trying to cover up something. A lot of them have taken the position that the African is the low man on the totem pole and everybody had to be ahead of him. Some of these people are just plain lying because they have to have capital in order to operate. James Henry Breasted is a fine example. He published a high school textbook in 1916 called Ancient Times. It had two very fine chapters on Egypt and he plainly states in there that the ancient Egyptians were not white folks, but 'a brown-skinned race.' And then he needed money to establish the Oriental Institute and to do research in Egypt. John D. Rockefeller, Jr. gave him 1.5 million dollars, and then Breasted got out a new edition of his book and the Egyptians became 'members of the great white race.' In other words, in order to get Rockefeller's money he had to switch over the Egyptians to 'the great white race.'

R/B: Could you give us a little background on W.J. Perry and Grafton Elliot Smith?

Jackson: Perry was an Englishman and a disciple of Grafton Elliot Smith. Smith was a physical anthropologist, specializing mainly in anatomy, who traced most of the world's early civilizations to Egypt. He made a scholarly study of mummies in Egypt and other parts of the world. Probably his most outstanding work was a book called Human History. He said that the Egyptian civilization was the first, and that all the others came out of it. Smith did a credible job, but Perry was a much better man in all respects. Smith was a British imperialist.

R/B: You've referred to a scholar named Forlong in your works. Exactly, who was Forlong?

Jackson: Major General J.G.R. Forlong was a Scottish scholar. In my book Man, God and Civilization I put him down as an Englishman, but I found out later that he was born in Scotland. He went to India while in the British army as an engineer to help build railroads. His great contribution was a two volume work called Rivers of Life.

R/B: In one of his books Cheikh Anta Diop mentions that the worship of Buddha, or the work attributed to Buddha, was probably brought to India by Egyptian priests fleeing from the persecutions of the Persian invaders of Egypt.

Jackson: It could have happened that way. We do know that Diodorus Siculus, the Greek historian of the first century B.C. said that all of the astronomical knowledge of the Babylonians was brought in by a colony of Egyptian priests.

R/B: Could you talk a little bit about your relationship and interactions with J.A. Rogers?

Jackson: Yes, that's easy. I came to New York in 1922. Rogers had been traveling through the South and he was coming back to New York. Rogers did a lecture for Dr. Hubert H. Harrison, who was my teacher and Rogers' friend. It was Harrison's forum but he let Rogers do the talking. I attended the lecture. Rogers and I became acquainted and became friends. Later on, Rogers introduced me to Dr. Willis N. Huggins who had a B.A. from the University of Chicago, an M.A. from Columbia University, a Ph.D. from Fordham University, and he did historical research at Oxford University in England. Around 1932 Dr. Huggins established a little group to study African history at the Harlem Y.M.C.A. He called the group the Blyden Society. After Rogers introduced me, he asked me to join it. He was the Director. He made me the Associate Director. Among our students were Bayard Rustin and John Henrik Clarke. Rustin decided to pull out and join the Communists. Clarke was writing poetry. He told me that I changed his life. He said that he was wasting his time writing poetry which only a damn fool would write. Huggins and I told him that he should be a historian. He says that we put him on the right track.

R/B: Rogers makes a reference in one of his books to a General Ganges of India. Are you acquainted with this reference?

Jackson: I saw that reference, but it's probably mythology. There's a Ganges River in India, but I don't think that there was really any such person. So that's probably mythology.

R/B: Where did these early Black scholars like Rogers get the funds for their travels and research?

Jackson: Well I can tell you about Rogers. He came from Jamaica in the West Indies. He settled in Chicago. He eventually took a job as a Pullman porter so he could visit different cities and libraries and do research. I got an interesting story about that. The story was that in a lot of large cities a lot of libraries were for whites only. Black people weren't permitted to go into them. So Rogers had to pay the Pullman conductor to go to the libraries and take out books from them. The conductor said 'Rogers, I believe you're a damn fool. But if you want to throw away your money that way, I'm willing to cooperate.' Rogers was a field anthropologist. He traveled to sixty different nations and did a lot of research and observing. He had been told when he was a child in Sunday School that God had cursed the Black Man and made him inferior. Rogers wanted to prove that the Black Man was not inferior.

1.6.- Cheikh Anta Diop on Asia: Highlights and Insights

Dr. Cheikh Anta Diop has been justly called the pharaoh of Nile Valley studies, and we are well aware that the *African origin of Ancient Egyptian civilization* was the major focus of his more than forty years of research. It is impossible, however, as Diop made clear; to isolate the populations and civilizations of early Africa from the rest of the world. Asia must also be taken into consideration in this respect, if only to be examined as an extension of the African cradle land. Diop, as usual, has done this remarkably well. Indeed, his work on Asia has blazed as brilliant a trail as his more comprehensive work on continental Africa. If he is not the pharaoh of Afro-Asian studies as well, he is the author, at least, of some of the most profound explorations of the subject.

Diop's concern is not only with Africa as the cradle of civilization but as the cradle of humanity as well. For a long time the cradle of humanity was actually placed in Asia. This was done for three reasons: (1) the ancient presence in Asia of all three major ethnic groups or races: Black, White, and Yellow; (2) the discovery of Homo erectus in Java at a time when Africa had not become a target for archaeological and palaeontological excavation; and (3) the Biblical tradition which puts the cradle of humanity in Western Asia with the creation of Adam and Eve. With new discoveries, however, the cradle of humanity has become ever firmly entrenched in Africa and seems more and more destined to remain there.

In addition to Homo erectus, who was the first hominid to journey into Asia (the arrival of hominids in Europe is a much later development), the Great Lakes region of East-Central Africa also produced the first modern human populations (Homo sapiens sapiens) yet identified, which, as a result of migrations, came to populate Asia.

Both Homo erectus and Homo sapiens sapiens, born originally in Africa, were undeniably Black:

> "The man born in Africa was necessarily dark-skinned due to the considerable force of ultraviolet radiation to the equatorial belt. As he moved toward the

more temperate climes, this man gradually lost his pigmentation by a process of selection and adaptation."[1]

There were different routes with varying degrees of difficulty that the Africans could have taken as they left the Great Lakes region. These routes included the Nile Valley, the Suez Isthmus, Palestine and from there to far Asia, Oceania and Europe. "It is in the light of this route that the human presence in Palestine can be traced. No one was born there. They came from elsewhere."[2] Another migration route would have led out of Africa's Horn easterly along the coasts of South Asia.

1.6.1.- The Origin and Evolution of the "Yellow Race"

As a working hypothesis Diop postulates that the "Yellow race" is probably the result of extensive co-mingling between Whites and Blacks at an extremely early age in human history. He argues that the melanin content of "Yellow peoples," as well as physical characteristics, such as prognathism, lips and nose, are those of "mixed breeds." Of course, these characteristics would become further distinguished by centuries and millennia of forced adaptation to environmental factors, among the most critical of which were wind currents.[3]

Certainly, traces of Blacks have been found in both the prehistoric and historic periods throughout the latitudes of Northeastern Asia.[4] Japan, for example, occupying the extreme eastern extensionsof Asia, is assumed by many to have been historically composed of an essentially homogeneous population and culture, the accumulated evidence (much of which has been quietly ignored) places the matter in a vastly different light, and though far more study needs to be done on the subject, it seems indisputable that Black people in Japan played an important role from the most remote phases of antiquity through at least the eighth century.[5]

Importantly, Diop calls our attention to a Japanese proverb: "**For a samurai to be brave he must have a bit of black blood**."[6] We also have the report, regarding Japan, of Sakanouye Tamuramaro (ca. 800 C.E.) the Black general who led the Japanese armies into battle against the Ainu, who were the neolithic inhabitants of Japan, and who se name harkens back to the ancient Anu of Nile

Valley fame. Tamuraro's successful generalship ultimately won him the Japanese shogunate.[7]

A scientific study, summarized in the Los Angeles Times newspaper in September 1998, noted that "Most of the population of modern China—one fifth of all people living today—owes it genetic origins to Africa."[8] An Africoid presence is visible throughout China's early periods.[9] The recent work of art historian James Brunson is critical here, because it substantially adds to Diop's own work in the area. Brunson, in fact, has gone considerably farther than anyone else in exploring China's early Black presence. He shows that China's historic period was alive with an active Black participation. The Shang, for example, China's first dynasties, apparently had a Black background, so much so that the conquering Chou described them as having "black and oily skin."[10]

The initial kingdoms of Southeast Asia emerged by the third century; the region first attracting attention as a rich source of coral, forest and mineral products, all of which were extremely valuable. The first kingdom of Southeast Asia is called Funan, and located in what is now southern Cambodia (Cambodia) and Vietnam. Much of our knowledge of early Southeast Asia is derived from Chinese and Indian sources. Chinese historical documents speak of the Funanese (the builders of the earliest kingdom in Southeast Asia) as "ugly and black. Their hair is curly."[11] The Khmer men, essentially the same as the Funanese, were described by the Chinese as "small and black."[12] In 1923 Harvard University anthropologist Roland Burrage Dixon (1874-1935) noted that the ancient Khmers were physically "marked by distinctly short stature, dark skin, curly or even frizzly hair, broad noses and thick negroid lips."[13]

Funan began to decline in stature in the sixth century due to loss of the vital trade routes coupled with major agricultural reverses. Her last king, Rudravarman, 514-539 C.E., was a devotee of Vishnu and sent several diplomatic missions to China whose influence in the region was then expanding.

Chen-La was the successor kingdom to Funan, and emerged as the result of a political marriage between the grandson of Rudravarman and a Chen-La princess, following which the center of regional power was shifted north, where stone was abundant and utilized as the major building material for the first time. The history of Chen-La is much the same as that of Funan. At some point late in the eighth century trade with India was disrupted, resulting in an administrative break down while Chen-La collapsed into a feuding group of small and insignificant states, and for a short time the regional power shifted to Indonesia where the Shailendra dynasty was ruling with vigor.

The most significant and long-lived of the South Asian states was centered at Angkor, Cambodia, and was much more empire than kingdom. The roots of Angkor can be traced back to Funan, Chen-La, and the Shailendras of Indonesia, Indianized states all. The people of Angkor were the Khmers. Angkor was designed to be completely self sufficient, and was filled with great stone temples and a large and thriving population. The key factor was a magnificent irrigation project, the basis of which was a series of huge artificial reservoirs fed by the local rivers and linked to each other by a rectangular grid system of canals. The reservoirs, called barays, were placed at the highest point in the river system, and were utilized to supply an immense chain of irrigation channels spreading out over the low lands.

During the more than 640 years of Angkor's life, great rulers emerged one after the other, leaving their marks upon the world in the form of stupendous temple islands, the vast artificial lake known as the Indratataka, and the temple mountains of Angkor Wat and Angkor Thom and Bayon, among the most conspicuous.

Even during her greatness Angkor was afflicted with ongoing battles with the Champa Kingdom in Vietnam. Champa, in Central Vietnam, shared many elements of Angkor's material culture, but was somewhat weaker and less fortunate in location and natural resources.

The ultimate fate of the Black kingdoms of Southeast Asia can be effectively linked to the rising influx of Mongoloid racial types from the north. The story of the Black kingdoms of Southeast Asia is, in essence, the story of African people in early Asian history; builders of the earliest kingdoms, only to be overwhelmed in the end. The early and intermittent African influence in Asia, however, is permanent and everlasting, and the Asian nations of today, whether conscious of it or not, have merely raised themselves under tutelage of Blacks.

1.6.2.- Could Egyptian Civilzation have been of Asian Origin?

Mesopotamia

Diop argues that it is important to distinguish between what can be deduced from a strict examination of historical documents and what is claimed beyond those documents. To assign Pharaonic Egyptian civilization an Asian origin, or, for that matter, any foreign origin, it is necessary to be able to show a prior cradle of civilization outside of Africa. Diop establishes that there is no tangible evidence of this, and points out that the world's oldest recorded date, 4236 B.C.E., is from Africa, when the calendar was already in use in Kmt. If there was a contemporary or simultaneous high-culture in Western Asia, Diop argues, the material basis for it is vague and uncertain, suggesting that the most ancient civilization of West Asia (Sumer) has been artificially embellished and given an unsubstantiated precedence over the Nile Valley. He points out that:

> "Egypt's pyramids, temples, and obelisks, its abundance of columns at Luxor and Karnak, its avenues of Sphinxes, the colossi of Memnon, its rock carvings, its underground temples with proto-Doric columns (Deir el-Bahri) at Thebes, are an architectural reality still palpable today, historical evidence that no dogma can blow into thin air. In contrast, what did Iran and Mesopotamia produce prior to the eighth century (epoch of the Assyrians)? Only shapeless clay mounds."[14]

Even conservative Sumerologists date the beginnings of Sumer's initial dynastic period at not earlier than 2750 B.C.E., whereas Kmt's dynastic history was in motion, at the latest, by 3100 B.C.E., and thus it is small wonder that Diop regards the synchronization of Egyptian and Mesopotamian history as a political necessity "resulting from ideology, not from fact." The goal behind this strategy is to attempt to successfully explain Egypt through Mesopotamia, that is Western Asia, thus denying Egypt its African roots. "If we remain within the realm of authentic facts, we are," he says, "forced to view Mesopotamia as a belatedly born daughter of Egypt."[15]

Diop does not end his discussion of Mesopotamia at this point but seeks to examine, though briefly, the ethnicity of the Sumerians themselves, whose thousand-year existence is essentially one of city-states and only seldom that of large kingdoms and empires. Who were these Sumerians of Mesopotamia, Diop asks, who occupy such a prestigious, if disputed, position in world history?

1.6.3.- The status of Mesopotamia and the Blackheads of Sumer

> "Since the civilizations of ancient Sumer and Elam, like those of Egypt, have been claimed by other peoples, it is important to set the record straight. Like Egypt, they are partial extensions from the old Ethiopian center and show the extraordinary vitality and unsuspected range of the civilization of which Egypt was the noblest-born but not the only child."[16]

Ancient Sumer, the Biblical land of Shinar, was the formative civilizing influence of early West Asia. Flourishing during the third millennium B.C.E., Sumer set the tone and established the guidelines for the kingdoms and empires which succeeded her. Frequently designated as, or linked with, Chaldea and Babylonia, Sumer embraced the Tigris/Euphrates river valley from the base of the Persian Gulf north to Akkad, a distance of about 300 miles.

While Sumer's many cultural achievements are much celebrated, the important question of her ethnic composition is frequently glossed over or left out of the discussion altogether. While it would be foolish to assert that Sumer's inhabitants were homogeneous or exclusive to any particular racial type, it seems rather obvious that the bright light of Sumerian civilization can only be attributed to the arrival of Black migrants from Africa's Nile Valley.

On the relationship between the Nile Valley and Sumer, Diop draws attention to several points of corroborative evidence, which are listed below:

1. The Hebraic traditions support the idea that the Sumerians were Black migrants from the Nile Valley. Genesis states that "Cush (Ethiopia) begat Nimrod: he began to be a mighty one in the earth… And the beginning of his kingdom was Babel… in the land of Shinar (Sumer)."[17]

2. The evidence of The Epic of Gilgamesh, a passage from which Diop cites: "Father Enlil, Lord of the countries, Father Enlil, Lord of the True Word, Father Enlil, Pastor of the Blacks…"[18]

3. The stature of Anu, "the primitive god, father of Ishtar, has the same Negro name as Osiris the Onian."[19] Anu was the great father of the gods, including Ishtar and Enlil, in Sumerian religious mythology. Anu was also a name frequently associated with the early Blacks of the Nile Valley and related areas. The Anu Seti, for example, lived on the banks of the Upper Nile, in the Sudan. The Anu-Tehennu were the early Black inhabitants of Libya. The ancient people of Arabia Petraea were called the Anu. According to Diop, "These Blacks [the

Anu] were probably the first to practice agriculture, to irrigate the valley of the Nile, build dams, invent sciences, arts, writing, the calendar. They created the cosmogony contained in The Book of the Dead, texts which leave no doubt about the Negroness of the race that conceived the ideas."[20]

4. (A) The Egyptian traditions, as reported by the Roman historian Diodorus Siculus, ca. 40 B.C.E., on the origins of the Chaldeans, who were the descendants of the Sumerians. The Egyptians considered the Chaldeans a transported colony of Egyptian astronomer-priests.[21] (B) The close resemblance of the ancient ziggurats in Mesopotamia and Iran to the step-pyramids of Africa. Diop notes, for example, that the Tower of Babel, also known as "Birs-Nimroud" and the "Temple of Baal," was probably the astronomical observatory of the Chaldeans. He then raises the question, "What, then, would be more normal than the existence of step pyramids in Saqqara, in Babylon (Kushite city of Bel), in the Ivory Coast (in the form of bronze weights), and in Mexico where Negro emigration across the Atlantic is attested by Mexican authors and archeologists themselves?"[22]

Of the most outstanding of the Blackheads Diop singles out Gudea, ca. 2300 B.C.E., the Africoid ruler of the kingdom of Lagash. Interestingly enough, Gudea, in spite of the general scarcity of stone in Mesopotamia, which Diop makes abundantly clear, had numerous, almost life-size statues of himself carved from hard black diorite, as though he could have actually anticipated the historical dilemma his African descendants would find themselves in, and they us left his personal calling cards in the medium of stone that would shout to the world his African roots.

1.6.4.- From Sumer to Elam

The Awan Dynasty was the first dynasty of Elam (Ancient Iran), founded by king Peli at the dawn of Iranian history in the twenty-seventh century B.C.E. Awan was an area of Elam whose location is not given, but is often believed to be north of the city of Susa. A royal list found in Elam gives twelve names of the kings of the Awan dynasty. The Elamites themselves were contemporaries and sometimes rivals of the Blackheads of neighboring Sumer (Ancient Iraq). It is also known that the Awan kings carried out incursions in Iraq, where they ran up against the most powerful city-states of this period—Kish and Lagash.

Elam was a contemporary of Sumer, and like Sumer itself the African presence seems to have been exceptionally prominent. Elam was the first great civilization of ancient Iran and Diop does not let it go without comment. The politically significant and far-famed city of Susa was a boundary phenomenon in the histories of both Elam and Sumer, and at least for the present the history of Elam is largely the history of Susa and its environs.

Susa was generally thought by the ancients of the Greco-Roman world to be the residence of the legendary Black warrior-king Memnon—identified as one of the most heroic figures of the Trojan War. Indeed, the father of Memnon—Tithonus—in Greek mythology was the founder of Susa. The story of Memnon was one of the most widely circulated of the non-Hellenic heroes of antiquity. His father was Tithonus and his mother was Eos, the Greek goddess of the dawn. Memnon is mentioned in the works of the writers as Hesiod, Virgil, Ovid, Pindar, Diodorus Siculus, Aeschylus, Pausanias, Strabo and Apollonius of Tyana, among others. Arctinus of Miletus composed an epic poem entitled Ethiopia in which Memnon was the leading figure.

By tradition, Memnon was slain by Achilles while defending Priam's Trojans when they were besieged by the fabulous coalition of Greek city-states immortalized in Homer's Iliad: "To Troy no hero came of nobler line, Or if nobler, Memnon, it was thine."[23] Robert Graves, in volume two of Greek Myths, refers to Memnon as "black as ebony but the handsomest man alive."[24] But Memnon is also firmly associated with King Nebmare Amenhotep III of Kmt, circa 1360 B.C.E. As a result, "Memnon thus unites the Eastern with the Western Ethiopians; and the less we regard him as an historical personage, the more must we view him as personifying the ethnic identity of the two races."[25]

Nor was Diop the first African scholar in modern times to take note of Memnon. Of Memnon, Dr. Rufus Lewis Perry, a great African-American scholar working in the late nineteenth century, pronounced: "The distinguished Cushite whom Homer calls Memnon came and went like a meteor in the galaxy of illustrious Ethiopian monarchs."[26]

Perry concluded that, "Though slain by Achilles, Memnon is so embalmed in verse and prose by Homer, Hesiod, Virgil and others, that his name will last as long as the writings of these imperishable authors."[27]

After Perry, William Leo Hansberry was the next African scholar to make prominent mention of Memnon. Hansberry noted that:

"The early Greek traditions record the father of Memnon (King of the Ethiopians) was holding sway in Persia, or Susa, and that it was from this point that Memnon, with a consolidated army of Ethiopians and soldiers from India, marched to the successor of his kinsmen at Troy. What, then, if the old Ethiopian stock had succeeded in holding its own in part at least of the Persian area down to the time of the Trojan War, and what if the royal houses of Ethiopia, Susa, and Troy VI were related through intermarriage in a manner similar to what seems to have been the case in Ethiopia and Egypt."[28]

And, finally, in this regard, we cite the work of Frank Snowden. Snowden wrote, in his scholarly work *Blacks in Antiquity: Ethiopians in the Greco-Roman Experience*, that:

"A legendary character of divine descent that came to be regarded as Ethiopian and black during the transmission of a myth is Memnon, son of Tithonus and Eos. Though associated with the east and Asia in certain, particularly early, accounts, Memnon was eventually localized unmistakably in Egypt and Ethiopia also. King of the Ethiopians as early as Hesiod but perhaps even before, in the Aethiopis of Arctinus, Memnon went to the aid of Priam at Troy, where he distinguished himself by his nobility and his bravery, killed Antillochus but spared his father, and finally met his death at the hands of Achilles.

As to an eastern origin it was Susa with which Memnon was frequently associated. In the course of time Memnon acquired both an Asian and an African provenence. Diodorus, for example, was acquainted with Asian and African versions. For in one instance Memnon, the son of Tithonus, according to Diodorus, was sent by Teutamus, the king of Assyria to Priam with a force of twenty thousand troops, one half Ethiopian and the other half from Susa. In this version Memnon had built a palace in the upper city of Susa called Memnonium in his honor. This attribution, however, was disputed, Diodorus reminds us, by the Ethiopians bordering upon Egypt, who maintained that Memnon was a native of their country and, in support of their claim, pointed to a place which bore his name. Strabo also knew two traditions—Susa was founded by Tithonus, the father of Memnon, and its acropolis was Memnonium, but he also mentions Memnon in Abydos and Thebes."[29]

In addition to references to Memnon Diop points to the historical Black presence in early Iran from the time of Elam into the Persian period. In this regard, he focused especially on the work of Marcel Dieulafoy from his late nineteenth century excavations at Susa.[30]

Diop also cites supporting statements on the physical characteristics of the people, as noted by Georges Contenau fifty years later.[31] Contenau described the Susian as "a probable product of some mixture of Kushite and Negro with his relatively flat nose, dilated nostrils, prominent cheekbones, and thick lips, is a racial type well observed and well depicted."[32]

1.6.5.- The twilight of Elam B.C.E.

Kutik-Inshushinak (also known as Puzur-Inshushinak) was a king of Elam, in what is now Iran, from about 2240 to 2220 B.C.E., and the last ruler from the Awan dynasty. Kutik-Inshushinak's first position was as governor of the historic and splendid city of Susa, which he may have held from a young age. About 2250 B.C.E., his father died, and he became crown prince in his stead. He built extensively on the splendid citadel at Susa, and encouraged the use of the Linear Elamite script to write the Elamite language. After his death Susa was overrun by the Third Sumerian Dynasty of Ur.

The beginning of the seventh century B.C.E. ushered in the twilight of Elam B.C.E. This was the epoch marked by the wars with the Assyrians, whose imperial ambitions cast a giant shadow over all of western Asia and northern Africa. In all the annals of human history, it is difficult to find any people with an appetite for bloodshed and carnage to rival that of the Assyrians. The civility they did possess was borrowed from the Sumerian Blackheads. Their chief contribution to the modern world was their ability to preserve the religious and secular texts of their predecessors.

The Assyrian state with its capital of Nineveh was a vast military machine. The Assyrians introduced the first large armies with iron weapons, and unlike many nations of antiquity, placed no dependence on foreign mercenaries whose loyalties might shift at any time. The bulk of the Assyrian armies consisted of archers and heavily armed spearmen and shield bearers, horsemen and heavy chariots. These armies were well trained, absolutely ferocious, and utterly merciless, and employed battering rams and formidable siege machines.

The Assyrians elevated warfare to an exact science. They were not content to merely conquer peoples; they must completely destroy them. Around the smoking ruins that had been cities would stretch lines of tall stakes, on which were impaled the bodies of the defeated community leaders, flayed alive. Scattered about were huge mounds of the viciously mutilated bodies of the dead and dying. Those who survived the holocaust were deported to other regions of Assyrian control.

Under the reign of Ashurbanipal, 669-626 B.C.E., the Assyrians reached their destructive zenith. In 667 B.C.E. Kmt was invaded. In 663 B.C.E. she was again invaded; this time with Ashurbanipal himself at the head of what must have seemed like the legions of Hell. The African countryside was wasted; its splendid cities plundered. The many magnificent temples of Waset, living repositories of the greatness that was Kmt, were looted and set ablaze. On his return to Nineveh, Ashurbanipal besieged the great Phoenician city of Tyre. In a panic Tyre's ruler sent to Nineveh his own family heavily laden with rich tribute and his own daughter for Ashurbanipal's harem.

After the Kamite and Phoenician conquests, and the defeat of a host of lesser states, the Assyrians directed their attention towards Elam. Elam, a highly formidable state in her own right, who had often struck terror in the regions of the near east, had long contested the territorial ambitions of the Assyrians and, seizing the initiative, took the war to Nineveh's doorstep. So much of Assyria's energies were directed to the Elamitic wars that Kmt, in 655 B.C.E., was able to regain her independence. At any other time Ashurbanipal would have led an army to stamp out the revolt. The Elamite war effort however had grown so intense and exhausting that the Assyrians had to give up Kmt to maintain Asia.

In 639 B.C.E., after a prolonged resistance, Susa was overwhelmed. Her ziggurat was destroyed. The royal family was sent to its fate in Nineveh. The Assyrians made an example out of Susa. For twenty-five days their armies marched over Susa's remains, scattering salt over the ruins. "Wild beasts," declared Ashurbanipal, "would now be her occupants."[33] To a people conscious of a proud past there could be no greater humiliation.

When after many years of hard and intense fighting the Assyrians finally took Susa, they savaged it with a ferocity rarely equaled in human history. Ashurbanipal's own texts recall in horribly triumphant detail the looting and razing of temples, the destruction of sacred groves, the desecration of royal tombs, the seizure of the statues of Elamite deities, the removal of royal memorials, the sowing of ruined ground with salt, and the deportation of people, livestock, and even rubble from the devastated city. The style of the report suggests that the destruction of Susa was a sweepingly calculated effort designed to shock the entire world and proclaim Susa's total earthly eradication.

Although in a severely diminished capacity, after the devastation of Susa, the Blacks of Elam remained an important regional factor. Herodotus finds them represented as Persian auxiliaries in the Greco-Persian wars.[34] During this same period southern Baluchistan, extreme eastern Iran and western Pakistan, was known as Gedrosia, "the country of the dark folk." The Persian ruler Cyrus erected his winter capital at a rebuilt Susa, and it was in this now Persian city that the Biblical prophet Daniel resided. Even today, the very same site is thought to house the tomb of Daniel. According to George Rawlinson, writing in the late nineteenth century, "Even now the ancient Susiana is known as Khuzistan, the land of Khuz, or of the Cushite."[35]

1.6.6.- The Phoenicians

Next in importance for Diop, after the early Asian civilizations of Mesopotamia (Southern Iraq) and Iran, is Phoenicia. This was the name given by Greeks in the first millennium B.C.E. to the coastal provinces of modern Lebanon and northern Palestine, although occasionally the term seems to have been applied to the entire eastern Mediterranean seaboard from Syria to Palestine.

Phoenicia was not considered a nation, in the strict sense of the word, but rather as a chain of coastal cities of which the most important were Sidon, Byblos, Tyre and Ras Shamra. To the Greeks, the term Phoenician, from the root "phoenix," had connotations of "red," with the assumption that the name was derived from the physical appearance of the people themselves.

The Phoenicians were a coastal branch of the Canaanites who, according to Biblical tradition, were the brothers of Cush (Ethiopia) and Mizraim (Egypt), members of the Hamite, or Kamite, ethnic family. The Bible says that the Canaanites, Ethiopians and Egyptians were all Black and of Nile Valley origin.[36]

Diop claims that:

> "Phoenician history is therefore incomprehensible only if we ignore the Biblical
> data according to which the Phoenicians, in other words, the Canaanites, were

originally Negroes, already civilized, with whom nomadic, uncultured white tribes [as represented by Abraham] later mixed."[37]

From this period, towards the middle of the second millennium B.C.E., the term Leuco (White) Syrians came to be applied to the newly arrived populations. Ultimately, Diop believed, the people of Abraham and the already settled Canaanites fused to become the historical Hebrews.

While acknowledging the Biblical data, Diop cautions that the economic relations shared by Kmt and the Phoenicians should not be minimized in explaining the strong sense of solidarity which generally existed between them. There was frequently a Kamite presence: military, diplomatic, religious and/or commercial, both in the Canaanite hinterland and the Phoenician city-states themselves, and Diop goes on to state that, "Even throughout the most troubled periods of great misfortune, Egypt could count on the Phoenicians as one can count more or less on a brother."[38]

Looking at Phoenician religious mythology, Diop finds himself almost peering into a mirror of Kmt. He highlights, for example, the importance of Taaut, who was none other than the Thoth (thought), or Tehuti, of the Kamites. In both cultures he was the inventor of sciences and letters. This information may be found in the fragments of Sanchroniatho and, in the texts of Ras Shamra, we find that the original home of the national heroes of Phoenicia is placed in the south, near the borders of Kmt.

Spurred on by increasing population pressures, the Phoenicians, who were becoming increasingly mixed racially, had by the middle of the second millennium B.C.E. developed a prowess on the seas, and were in the process of establishing a network of colonies and trading posts that not only brought them fame and prosperity but introduced in some cases, and reinforced in others, vital elements of the cultural attributes of the Southern world. Indeed, Diop says, "It seems impossible to exaggerate the essential role played by Negroes and Negroids at a time when the European races were still uncivilized."[39]

Of course the most famous colony of the Phoenicians was Khart-Haddas (new town) later known as Carthage. Khart-Haddas was established in 814 B.C.E. on the North African coast, in what is now Tunisia. The colony was supposedly founded by Dido, who was a queen of the Phoenician city of Tyre, although the name itself may have actually been a title indicating female royalty, as opposed to a proper name.

1.6.7.- Arabia

The Arabian Peninsula, first inhabited more than 8,000 years ago, was early populated by Blacks. Once dominant over the entire peninsula, the African presence in early Arabia is most clearly trace able through the Sabeans. The Sabeans were the first Arabians to step firmly within the realm of civilization. The southwestern corner of the peninsula was their early home. This area, which was known to the Romans as Arabia Felix, is today called Yemen. In antiquity this region gave rise to a high degree of civilization because of the fertility of the soil, the growth of frankincense and myrrh, and the close proximity to the sea and consequently its importance in the trade routes.

We hear of the Sabeans in the tenth century B.C.E. through the fabled exploits of its semi-legendary queen. This woman had all the qualities of an exceptional monarch and appears to have ruled over a wealthy domain embracing parts of both Africa and Arabia. She is known as Bilqis in the Koran, Makeda in the Kebra Negast, and the Queen of Sheba in the Bible. The three of these documents provide a relatively clear picture of a highly developed state distinguished by the pronounced overall status of women.

Bilqis/Makeda was not an isolated phenomenon. Several times, in fact, do we hear of prominent women in Arabian history; the documents they are mentioned in providing no commentary on husbands, consorts, or male relatives. Either their deeds or inheritance, perhaps both, enabled them to stand out quite singularly. The Sabeans apparently possessed a dedicated matrifocal culture and society.

Around the beginning of the first millennium B.C.E., the period in which Bilqis/Makeda is thought to have lived, we find the emergence of a number of large urban centers characterized by elaborate irrigation systems. With the domestication of the camel, the Southern Arabians could effectively exploit the region's greatest natural resources—frankincense and myrrh—which from the earliest historical periods were much prized and sought after. The purest and most abundant sources of frankincense and myrrh were in Southern Arabia and Somalia (Punt?), across the Red Sea in Africa

In Diop's view, Arabia was once an exclusively Kushite domain with a high civilization in the south, upon which was imposed nomadic white ethnic elements from the north and east. In elaborating this theme, Diop relies significantly upon the research of nineteenth century French Assyriologist and archaeologist Francois Lenormant (1837-1883), whose works constituted for him a rich source of information on the Black presence in early Western Asia.

Of the Southern Arabians Lenormant noted that:

> "We may perceive the remembrance of a powerful empire founded by the Cushites in very early ages, apparently including the whole of Arabia Felix, and not only Yemen proper. Circumcision established in Yemen from remotest antiquity, and several other pagan usages, still practiced in our days, appear to be of Cushite origin. Lokman, the mythical representative of Adite wisdom, resembles Aesop, whose name... seems to indicate an Ethiopian origin. In India, also, the whole literature of tales and apologues apparently come from the Sudras. Perhaps this style of fiction... may represent a style peculiar to the Cushites."[40]

Two of the outstanding men of African heritage in early Arabia that Diop shines light upon are Lokman—thought to be the architect of the Marib Dam and a great sage of the east on whose life Aesop's is thought to have been modeled—and Antarah—the fabulous hero of pre-Islamic Arabia. According to the great Jamaican born scholar Joel A. Rogers (1883-1966):

> "Lokman is the most celebrated sage of the East. So great is his fame there that there is still a saying, 'To teach wisdom to Lokman,' which is the equivalent of 'Carrying coals to Newcastle.' In Islam his fame equals that of Solomon in the Christian-Jewish world. Mohammed quoted him as an authority and named the thirty first chapter of the Koran after him.
>
> Much that is said about him is legendary. The Arabs say that he lived about 1100 B.C.E., was a coal-black Ethiopian with woolly hair, and was the son of Baura, who was a son or a grandson of a sister of Job. Lokman is often confused with Aesop, who was also a Negro, and who, it appears, adapted some of Lokman's fables to his own use."[41]

Antar was a dashing knight, poet, champion of the weak and oppressed and protector and lover of women, highly esteemed by the sons of the desert, whose deeds of valor became a part of the literary heritage of the Arabic-speaking world." Of Antar, African-American scholar A.O. Stafford pointed out that:

"His fame as a literary character transcends that of the modem authors of black blood, such as Pushkin in Russia, and the elder Dumas in France. After his death the fame of Antar's deeds spread across the Arabian Peninsula and throughout the Mohammedan world. In time these deeds, like Homeric legends, were recorded in a literary form and therein is found that Antar has become the Achilles of the Arabian Iliad, a work known to this day after being a source of wonder and admiration for hundreds of years to millions of Mohammedans as the 'Romance of Antar.' The book, therefore, ranks among the great national classics like the 'Shah-nameh' of Persia, and the 'Nibelungen-Lied' of Germany. Antar was the father of knighthood. He was the champion of the weak and oppressed, the protector of women, the impassioned lover-poet, the irresistible and magnanimous knight. 'Antar' in its present form probably preceded the romances of chivalry so common in the twelfth century in Italy and France."[42]

By the beginning of the seventh century the seeds of Islam were already ripe and Africa was instrumental in its growth. According to tradition, the first Muslim killed in battle was Mihdja—a Black man. Another Black man, Bilal, was such a pivotal figure in the development of Islam that he has been referred to as "a third of the faith." Bilal was Islam's first muezzin. Today Bilal has a large tomb and mosque in Damascus, Syria.

Five years after the proclamation of Islam (615), a number of Muslims sought refuge in neighboring Ethiopia in order to escape the persecutions of the Kurayshites in Mecca Their sojourn in Ethiopia greatly impressed these early Muslim migrants and influenced the future development of their new faith. Muslim biographical sources (tabakat) enumerate not a few Ethiopian converts to Islam who migrated to Medina and ranked amongst the Prophet's companions. They were referred to as the 'Ethiopian monks' (ruhban al-habasha).[43] It was this relationship which caused Muhammad to declare that, "Who brings an Ethiopian man or an Ethiopian woman into his house, brings the blessing of God there."[44]

Another prominent Black man in Arabia, Ata ibn Abi Rabah (ca. 700), became a mufti at Makkah. He was born in southern Arabia of Nubian parents. Eventually he moved to Makkah and became a famous teacher and jurisconsult there. In his later years his reputation spread far and wide. According to some accounts, including that of the brilliant Black writer and historian Uthman Amr ibn-Bahr al-Jahiz, the prophet Muhammad himself was partly of African lineage.

According to al-Jahiz, the guardian of the sacred Kaaba—Abd al-Muttalib, "fathered ten Lords, Black as the night and magnificent." One of these men was Abdallah, the father of Muhammad.[45]

1.6.8.- Pakistan and India

Exceptionally valuable writings expressing intimate connections between early India, ancient Egypt and Ethiopia have existed for more than two thousand years. In the first century B.C.E., for example, the famous Greek historian Diodorus Siculus penned that, "From Ethiopia he (Osiris) passed through Arabia, bordering upon the Red Sea as far as to India... he built many cities in India, one of which he called Nysa, willing to have remembrance of that (Nysa) in Egypt where he was brought up."[46]

Apollonius of Tyana, who is said to have visited India near the close of the first century C.E., was convinced that, "The Ethiopians are colonists sent from India, who follow their forefathers in matters of wisdom."[47]

The Christian writer Eusebius, born in Palestine in 264 C.E. and appointed Bishop of Nicaea in 325 C.E., has been called the "Father of Church History." The basis for this reputation is his Historia Ecclesiastica. Eusebius' work is particularly important to us because of its preservation of the tradition that, "*In the reign of Amenophis III, a body of Ethiopians migrated from the country about the Indus, and settled in the valley of the Nile.*"[48]

Also important is The Itinerarium Alexandri, a Latin work written about 345 C.E. for the Roman emperor Constantius. The Itinerarium Alexandri, 110 says that, "India, taken as a whole, beginning from the north and embracing what of it is subject to Persia, is a continuation of Egypt and the Ethiopians."[49]

1.6.9.- The Indu Valley Civilization

The riverine civilization of the Indus Valley (in the area now known as Pakistan) is included by Diop in the Zone of Confluence. It marks its eastern limits. The Indus Valley Civilization, also known as the Harappan civilization—named after one of its largest and most studied sites—Harappa, flourished from about 2200 B.C.E. to 1700 B.C.E. The complex actually had extensions reaching from the river Oxus in Afghanistan in the north to the Gulf of Gambay in India in the south.

At its height, the Harappans engaged in regular commercial relations with Iraq and Iran. This much we know with certainty. We are equally certain that the founders of the Harappan civilization were Black. This is verifiable through the available physical evidence-skeletal remains, the eye-witness accounts preserved in the Rig Veda, artistic and sculptural remains, the regional survival of Dravidian languages (including Brahui, Kurukh and Malto) and the essential role of these languages, which are now being used in the decipherment of the Harappan script. We should also take into account the prominence accorded the mother goddess in the Harappan cities and the sedentary nature of the Harappan people themselves. Walter Fairservis claims that the Harappans cultivated cotton and may have domesticated the chicken.[50]

The decline and fall of the Indus cities has been linked to several factors. The most important of these are: the reduction of agricultural productivity due to over cultivation; an escalation in local flooding, as a result of tectonic fluctuations in the area of the Lower Indus; a proliferation of human and cattle populations; and the increasingly frequent incursions of Indo-Aryan patriarchal, nomadic clans from Central Asia and later Iran. The name Iran, in fact, means the "land of the Aryan."

1.6.10.- Two cradles and the zone of confidence

Western Asia, some of whose civilizations we have briefly surveyed, and Byzantium as well, are placed by Diop in the Zone of Confluence, which for him is the middle ground between the Southern or Black Cradle and the Northern or White Cradle. In addition to each cradle's racial distinctions, there were cultural patterns peculiar to each.

For Diop, and this is critical in his view of the evolution of the world, the Zone of Confluence, or overlap, as a cradle in itself, out of which emerged the Semitic world. He states that, "Anthropologically and culturally speaking, the Semitic world was born during protohistoric times from the mixture of white-skinned and black-skinned people in Western Asia."[51] At this juncture, Diop asserts, we go beyond the point of working hypothesis into the realm of provable fact, which is where we want to go and where we must go for a serious understanding of the ethnic composition and evolution of a geographical region encompassing probably the most complex and confusing collection of physical types in the world.

The Southern Cradle, confined to Africa, was characterized by the matriarchal family and the emancipation of women in domestic life; the creation of the territorial state; an attraction to things foreign, whether manners, styles or peoples; an international or worldly, as opposed to a local or provincial, outlook; and a "sort of social collectivism having as corollary a tranquility going as far as unconcern for tomorrow and a material solidarity of right for each individual." In the moral sphere, the Southern Cradle reflects ideals of peace, justice and goodness, with an optimistic view devoid of a concept of guilt or original sin.[52]

Regarding matriarchy, Diop notes that it is a well-balanced and harmonious dualism, defended and protected by both sexes, where irrespective of sexual distinctions "each and everyone could fully develop by following the activity best suited to his physiological nature."[53]

The Northern Cradle, on the other hand, was characterized by the patriarchal family; the city-state, "outside of which a man was an outlaw"; a fear and hostility towards things foreign; individualism, moral and material solitude; and what could only be called a pessimistic view of existence itself. The Northern Cradle introduced cremation, while the Southern Cradle utilized burial as a method of disposing of the dead.[54]

1.6.11.- The dispersal of the Nomads

"Behold, he shall come up as clouds, and his chariots shall be as a whirlwind: his horses are swifter than eagles. Woe unto us! for we are spoiled."[55]

Who were these people of the Northern Cradle, these nomads, and how did they come to wreak such havoc and destruction upon the civilized world, especially the long established agricultural settlements of the Blacks? This was, first of all, not an isolated phenomenon and the movements of the Aryan tribes into Iran, Pakistan and India reflect a major turning point in the history of mankind and the overall ascendancy of the Indo-European speakers in the world at large. The Kassite rulers of Babylon, for example, in power for roughly five hundred years beginning about 1600 B.C.E. had Indo-Aryan names. So did the rulers of the kingdom of Mitanni (1500 B.C.E. to 1370 B.C.E.) on the Upper Euphrates. There were Indo-European elements amongst the Hyksos invaders of Egypt, ca. 1720 B.C.E. Such elements could also be found within the Hittite aristocracy of Turkey and northern Syria of the same period.

A western branch of Indo-European speakers, the Achaeans, who were cousins of the Aryans, violently attacked the settled populations of early Greece, besieged and sacked Troy, and conquered the centuries-old civilization of Minoan Crete around 1450 B.C.E. Two centuries later appeared the Dorians, also Indo-Europeans, even more violent than their Achaean predecessors. The Dorians rapidly proceeded to assault the surviving cities of Crete, and either exterminated, reduced to vassalage, or chased away many of the former inhabitants of Greece itself. We see some of the results of the Dorian conquests in the brief rise of the Sea Peoples, who, fleeing from the encroachments of other nomads even more aggressive than themselves, shattered the Hittites, conquered the Libyan populations, and invaded Kmt three times in the reigns of Merenptah (19th dynasty) and Ramses III (20th dynasty).

Since the late nineteenth century the Indo-European homeland has been placed somewhere in the vast Eurasian steppes between the frontiers of China on the east and the plains of Central Europe on the west. This veritable sea of grass was the true breeding ground of nomads. By the fifth millennium B.C.E. these steppes were peopled by scattered tribes united by common cultural traditions and a proto-Indo-European language which separated ultimately into local dialects with a common root.

The Eurasian steppes was also the home of the wild ancestors of the horse, which was rapidly domesticated, and with the development and evolution of increasingly sophisticated and elaborate harnesses, saddles, stirrups and related gear, effectively exploited by the region's nomadic populations. Whether this occurred first among the Indo-Europeans themselves or the Mongoloids further to the east is not known, but there is no question that the Indo-Europeans made the first significant impact in their application of this development. The same can be said for the spoked-wheel chariot which the Indo-Europeans may or may not have invented, but certainly perfected.

Whether in the hunt or in war, the steppe dwellers made use of the powerful compound bow, strengthened with bone and sinew in a manner designed to increase its resilience. The compound bow and the light, spoked-wheel chariot constituted the ultimate military weaponry of their era, making those that possessed and effectively utilized them highly formidable, if not absolutely irresistible, on the battlefield. Metallurgy was exposed to the Indo-European tribes north of the Caucasus no later than 2500 B.C.E., which enabled them to acquire a wide range of copper and bronze weapons and tools.

Now armed with military technologies second to none, by the end of the third millennium B.C.E. the Indo-European tribes, including the Aryans, were in full motion, carrying their families and all worldly possessions on their backs and in their wagons. Whether motivated by drought, excess populations, or forces and factors that have not been fully explained, these northern nomads were heading like a great human juggernaut towards new and unknown lands, uprooting who le peoples in their path. The Southern world, ill prepared to de fend itself against the onslaught, was rocked to its foundations.

What sort of people were these Indo-European intruders from the steppes? What kind of mentality did they have and how did they see themselves and the world? Diop is so brilliant on these issues that it is necessary to quote him at length:

> "The ferocity of nature in the Eurasian steppes, the barrenness of those regions, the overall circumstances of material conditions, were to create instincts necessary for survival in such an environment. Here, Nature left no illusion of kindliness: it was implacable and permitted no negligence; man must obtain his bread by the sweat of his brow. Above all, in the course of a long, painful existence, he must learn to rely on himself alone, on his own possibilities. He could not indulge in the luxury of believing in a beneficent God who would shower down abundant means of gaining a livelihood; instead, he would conjure up deities maleficent and cruel, jealous and spiteful: Zeus, Yahweh, among others.
>
> "In the unrewarding activity that the physical environment imposed on man, there was already implied materialism, anthropomorphism (which is but one of its aspects), and the secular spirit. This is how the environment gradually molded these instincts in the men of that region, the Indo-Europeans in parti-

cular. All the peoples of the area, whether white or yellow, were instinctively to love conquest, because of a desire to escape from those surroundings. The milieu chased them away; they had to leave it or succumb, try to conquer a place in the sun in a more clement nature. Invasions would not cease, once an initial contact with the Black world to the south had taught them the existence of a land where the living was easy, riches abundant, technique flourishing.

"Man in those regions long remained a nomad. He was cruel. The cold climate would engender the worship of fire, to remain burning from the fire of Mithras (in Persian mythology, Mithras was the god of the light and truth, later of the sun) to the flame on the tomb of the Unknown Soldier under the Arch of Triumph and the torches of the ancient and modern Olympics. Nomadism was responsible for cremation: thus the ashes of ancestors could be transported in small urns. This custom was perpetuated by the Greeks; the Aryans introduced it to India after 1450 B.C., and that explains the cremation of Caesar, and of Gandhi in our own epoch.

"Obviously, man was the pillar of that kind of life. Woman's economic role was much less significant than in Black agricultural societies. Consequently, the nomadic patriarchal family was the only embryo of social organization. The patriarchal principle would rule the whole life of the Indo-Europeans."[56]

If we have quoted the author at length here, it is because we regard these passages as representative of Cheikh Anta Diop at his finest: incisive, succinct, uncompromising, almost brutally direct.

The Aryan tribes may have begun to make their presence felt in the Harappan complex as early as the end of the third millennium B.C.E., and their increasingly bold and frequent raids added, with the progression of time, the finishing touches to a civilization already well into its late period. The invaders seemed to have been well aware of their impact on the Blacks and were quite conscious of the destruction around them:

"The people to whom these ruined sites, lacking posts, formerly belonged, these many settlements widely distributed, they, O' Vaisvanara, having been expelled by thee, have migrated to another land."[57]

"Through fear of you (Agni) the dark people went away, not giving battle, leaving behind their possessions, when, O' Vaisvanara, burning brightly for Puru, and destroying the cities, you did shine."[58]

The Aryans may have deliberately shattered the dams and reservoirs of the Blacks, and their warrior god Indra is said to have freed the waters by rolling stones like wagon wheels. As Purandara, the "fort-destroyer," Indra gave the Aryans victory over the Blacks in their strongholds, walled towns and newly fortified cities.

Raiding now gave way to settlement. By 800 B.C.E. the Aryans had extended their conquests from Pakistan to the entire Gangetic plain of India east to the river Jamuna. Their new dominions they called Aryavarta (the Aryan Land). This era, which is called the Vedic Period by historians, reflects the consolidation of Aryan power and institutions in North India, and the extermination of many of the conquered Blacks, the subordination of many others, and untold numbers of other Blacks who simply left the region, to establish, for example, the Dravidian kingdoms of South India.

Two of the most interesting institutions we find in Aryavarta, and later in South India with the spread of Aryan ideas, are the suttee and jati. Diop has effectively pointed to the patriarchal character and the practice of cremation among the descendants of the Northern Cradle, and nowhere is this seen more vividly than in the suttee, one of India's most awesome and awful rituals. The suttee was the self-immolation of the devout Hindu widow on the funeral pyre of the deceased husband. The suttee rite accomplished two goals: the wife could continue to serve her husband-in the next life, and would save both souls for thirty-five million years! If she cannot burn herself, she must at least remain chaste. If not, she will go to hell. If the deceased died on a distant battlefield, the widow might take an article of his clothing, and with this in her possession successfully burn herself. If the widow were pregnant or had an infant child, she might be honorably spared the suttee.[59]

Jati pertains to what is in the West called caste, which is actually a Portuguese term and concept based on what they saw in India. Caste however, Diop argues, is actually an indigenous African institution, which was also in existence in the Black dominated civilizations of Western Asia, and Pakistan and India. When the Aryans entered these regions they found this system, which was based on labor, already intact and functionally operational. Diop says that, "the caste system of social organization assures a greater permanence and equilibrium to a society than does the system of classes created by the Aryans in Rome and Greece," and the "criteria of color has a low priority indeed without any ethnic connotations."[60] On this latter issue however, Diop is in sharp disagreement with a number of African-centric researchers, including myself. The Aryan aristocracy did adopt certain elements of the prevailing social system. One has to recall that the Aryans were essentially nomads, and after hundreds of years of interaction with the Blacks and an adjustment to settled life, this seems only natural. But the caste system was modified with a cold blooded racist logic, with the Whites on top, the mixed races in the middle and the mass of the conquered Blacks at the bottom. This is not to deny that there were Black priests and tribal or provincial leaders who managed to gain prominence in the essentially Aryan but still evolving social structure. The masses however, the vast multitude of the Blacks, were placed at the bottom and were called the Sudras.

As early as the Rig Veda, believed to have been composed between 1500 B.C.E. to 1000 B.C.E., we find in Aryavarta the notion that the Sudras sprang from the feet of Brahma (God) and were destined to serve the upper castes in any capacity required, most often as landless agricultural laborers. In religious mythology the Sudras were regarded as untruth itself, and were always identified with the color Black. Caste in early India was inseparable from race. Indeed, the term jati was closely connected with varna, a Sanskrit word which literally means color or complexion.[61]

This was the rigid and ugly reality for the Black masses in conquered India. Servitude became the basis of their lives for generation after generation after generation. Their reward for perfect service: a higher birth in the next life. This chain of subordination was not broken until the reign of Mahapadma Nanda in the fourth century B.C.E., known as "the exterminator of the Kshatriya race."

In the Mauryan dynasty, which was again of Sudra origin, social gains were also made by the Sudra caste, but this is a much later period of Indian history. By this era, 300 B.C.E., a physical amalgamation of sorts had taken place, but it had not been a total synthesis, and the original racial distinctions had only been blurred, not completely forgotten. They still have not been forgotten today, although the original four castes have now proliferated into thousands of sub-castes and outcastes, or "untouchables."

The social structure of Iran (the land of the Aryan) seems to have paralleled that of the Indian Aryavarta in its racial element. The Iranian upper caste was composed of the Aryamen, who were divided into priests, chariot driving nobles, herdsmen and artisans. Apparently the lower caste was recognized as distinct in race for the name of this caste was pishtra, literally color.[62]

When Buddhism finally emerges in the sixth century B.C.E. it comes in the form of a protest against Hinduism. The significance of caste is relatively minor in Buddhism, and it therefore comes as no surprise that it developed such a large and rapid following in the sectors of India where the Blacks existed in large numbers. Diop points out that "it would seem that Buddha was an Egyptian priest, chased from Memphis by the persecutions of Cambyses. This tradition would justify the portrayal of Buddha with wooly hair. Historical documents do not invalidate this tradition... There is general agreement today on placing in the sixth century not only Buddha but the whole religious and philosophical movement in Asia with Confucius in China, Zoroaster in Iran. This would confirm the hypothesis of a dispersion of Egyptian priests at that time spreading their doctrine in Asia."[63]

1.6.12.- Dravidians

It is safe to say that when we speak of the Dravidians as a people we are speaking of the living descendants of the Harappan people of the ancient Indus Valley who were pushed into South India as the result of the Aryan invasions. This is certainly consistent with Dravidian traditions which recall flourishing cities that were either lost or destroyed in antiquity. The term "Dravidian," however, encompasses both an ethnic group and a linguistic group. The ethnic group is characterized by straight to wavy hair textures, combined with Africoid physical features.

Dravidian, in addition to its ethnic component, however, is an important family of languages spoken by more than a hundred million people, primarily in South India. These languages include Tamil (the largest element), Kannada, Malayalam (from which the name of the Asian country Malaya is derived), Telegu and Tulu. The term "Dravidian" itself is apparently an Aryan corruption of Tamil.

The Dravidians were an unusually advanced seafaring people, with the Cholas, in particular, distinguishing themselves amongst the dominant maritime powers of their era. Through its ports, the great kings of Chola traded with

Ethiopia and Somalia, Iran and Arabia, Cambodia and China, Sumatra and Sri Lanka, exporting spices and camphor, ebony and ivory, quality textiles and precious jewels.

The Dravidian kingdoms and the Dravidian people were quite well known internationally. When Augustus became head of the Roman world, for example, the Dravidian kingdoms sent him a congratulatory embassy. Dravidian poets describe Roman ships, which carried bodyguards of archers to ward off pirates, while the Dravidian kings employed bodyguards of Roman soldiers.

Notes

1. Cheikh Anta Diop, "Africa: Cradle of Humanity," *Nile Valley Civilizations*, ed. Ivan Van Sertima (New Brunswick: Transaction Press, 1984), 27.
2. Diop, 26.
3. Diop, *African Origin of Civilization*, trans. Mercer Cook (New York: Lawrence Hill & Company, 1974), 280-81.
4. "African-Like Stone Age Hut is Unearthed in Japan," Associated Press, February 15, 1986.
5. Diop, 281.
6. Beatrice L. Fleming and Marion L. Pryde, *Distinguished Negroes Abroad* (Washington, D.C: Associated Publishers, 1946), 3-9. Of the Black people of early Japan, the most picturesque single figure was Sakanouye no Tamuramaro
7. Tamuramaro was not only the first man to bear the title of Sei-i-tai-Shogun, he was also the first of the warrior statesmen of Japan. In later ages he was revered by military men as a model commander and as the first recipient of the title shogun-the highest rank to which a warrior could aspire. George Sansom, *A History of Japan to 1334* (Stanford: Stanford University Press, 1958), 105. Lois M. Jones, "Sakanouye Tamura Maro," *Negro History Bulletin 4, No. 2* (1940), 31. Beatrice J. Fleming and Marion J. Pryde, *Distinguished Negroes Abroad* (Washington, D.C.: Associated Publishers, 1946), 3-9. W.E.B. DuBois, *The World and Africa: An Inquiry Into the Part that Africa Has Played in World History* (1946; rpt. New York: International Publishers, 1965), xi.
8. *Los Angeles Times*, September 29, 1998.
9. "It is clear that the majority of archaeological finds of the early Recent period in South China indicate a culture continued to the southwestern part of the area, characterized by chipped stone implements of the archaic chopper-chopping tool traditions of the palaeolithic, by the hunting of small game animals, and mollusks. The single population with the Negroid elements of the rest of Southeast Asia, widely substantiated for this stage, and apart from the contemporary Mongoloid inhabitants to the north." Kwan-chih Chang, *The Archaeology of Ancient China*, rev. ed. (New Haven: Yale University Press, 1968), 76-77.

10. James E. Brunson, *Black Jade: African Presence in the Ancient East* (DeKalb: Kara, 1985).

11. Quoted in Lawrence Palmer Briggs, *The Ancient Khmer Empire* (Philadelphia: American Philosophical Society, 1951), 16.

12. Quoted in Briggs, 50.

13. Roland B. Dixon, *The Racial History of Man* (New York: Scribner's, 1923), 226. Dixon had the distinction at Harvard of being anthropologist Franz Boas' first doctoral student.

14. Diop, *African Origin of Civilization*, 101.

15. Diop, 106.

16. Ivan Van Sertima, *Egypt Revisited* (New Brunswick: Transaction Press, 1982), 8.

17. Genesis 10: 8-10.

18. Diop, 105.

19. Diop, 105.

20. Diop, 77.

21. Diop, 101.

22. Diop, 102.

23. Homer, *The Iliad*, cited by Hansberry, 82.

24. Robert Graves, *The Greek Myths, vol. 2* (Harmondswork: Penguin Books, 1960), 315.

25. George Rawlinson, *Ancient Monarchies, Vol. 1* (New York: Dodd, Mead & Co., 1881), 48.

26. Rufus Lewis Perry, *The Cushite, Or the Descendants of Ham as Found in the Sacred Scriptures and in the Writings of Ancient Historians and Poets from Noah to the Christian Era* (Springfield, MA: Willey & Co., 1893), 119.

27. Perry, 121.

28. Hansberry, 53-54.

29. Frank Snowden, *Blacks in Antiquity* (Cambridge: Belknap Press, 1970), 151.

30. Franck Op. cit.

31. Diop, 104. Georges Contenau (April 9, 1877—March 22, 1964) was a French archaeologist, orientalist and religious historian and an expert in the field of culture and religion of the civilizations of the Near and Middle East. He was professor at the University of Brussels from 1932 to 1947, chief curator of Oriental antiquities at the Musée du Louvre from 1937 to 1946, and led several archaeological expeditions to Susa, Sidon and Nahavand. From 1946 to 1957 he was director general of the French Archaeological Mission in Iran.

32. Contenau, cited by Diop, 104.

33. D.D. Luckenbill, *Ancient Records of Assyria and Babylonia, vol. 2* (Chicago: University of Chicago Press, 1927), 309-312.

34. Herodotus, *The Histories*, trans. Aubrey de Selincourt (New York: Penguin Books, 1972), 468.

35. George Rawlinson, *Ancient Monarchies, Vol. 1* (New York: Dodd, Mead & Co., 1881), 50.

36. Genesis 9.

37. Diop, *African Origin of Civilization*, 107-108.

38. Diop, 108.

39. Diop, 119.

40. Francois Lenormant, *Ancient History of the East, vol. 2* (London: Asher & Co., 1869), 296, 318. Born in Paris on January 17, 1837, Francois Lenormant was a French archaeologist and member of the Academy of Inscriptions and Belles-Lettres. At the age of fourteen he published a major paper on Greek inscriptions at Memphis, Egypt. Francois Lenormant died in Paris on December 9, 1883.

41. J.A. Rogers, *World's Great Men of Color, vol. 1* (New York: Collier, 1972), 67.

42. A.O. Stafford, *"Antar, The Arabian Negro Warrior, Poet and Hero," Journal of Negro History 1, No. 2* (1916), 155.

43. Y. Talib, *"The African Diapora in Asia,"* in UNESCO General History of Africa. Vol. 3, *Africa from the Seventh to the Eleventh Century, ed. M. El Fasi* (Berkeley: University of California Press, 1988), 710-11.

44. E. Cerulli *"Ethiopia's Relations with the Muslim World,"* in UNESCO *General History of Africa. Vol. 3, Africa from the Seventh to the Eleventh Century*, ed. M. El Fasi (Berkeley: University of California Press, 1988), 576.

45. 'Uthman' Amr ibn-Bahr al-Jahiz, *The Book of the Glory of the Black Race*, trans. *Vincent J. Cornell* (Los Angeles: Preston, 1981), 50.

46. Diodorus Siculus. Bk 1: 11, 12.

47. Flavius Philostratus, *The Life of Apollonius of Tyana, Book VI.*

48. Eusebius. Quoted by George Rawlinson in Ancient Monarchies, V. 1, p. 49.

49. The Itinerarium Alexandri, 110.

50. Walter A. Fairservis, *"The Script of the Indus Valley Civilization," African Presence in Early Asia, eds.* Ivan Van Sertima and Runoko Rashidi (New Brunswick: Transaction Press, 1985), 64-79.

51. Diop, *African Origin of Civilization*, XV.

52. Diop, *Cultural Unity of Black Africa* (Chicago: Third World Press, 1978), 195.

53. Diop, 120.

54. Diop, 195.

55. Jeremiah 5:13.

56. Diop, *African Origin of Civilization*, 112-13.

57. *Hymns of the Rig Veda*, quoted by T. Burrow, *"The Aryan Invasion of India," The Encyclopedia of Ancient Civilizations, ed. Arthur Cotterell* (New York: Mayflower Books, 1980), 184.

58. *Hymns of the Rig Veda.*

59. "It must not be imagined that the Brahmans have legally possessed the means of dragging the devoted victim to the pile, by any other chains than those of superstition… The main crime of the Brahmans then has been the fabrication, from these flimsy

materials, of the soul-enfeebling chain of superstition, and decking it with flowers of heavenly promise. There is, besides these, another powerful motive which operates in conjunction with them. Among the Hindus a woman, after the decease of her husband, loses entirely her consequence in his family, and is degraded to a situation little above that of a menial. She is told that if she become a Suttee, she will not only escape from that life of assured debasement and contempt, but will ascend to a state as preeminently exalted; and will thus (whatever the crimes of the parties may have been) save both her own soul, and the souls of her husband and her husband's family from purgatory and future transmigration. I now turn me to a different picture... which various other authorities before, as well as my own local inquiries, oblige me to say is not infrequent... 'Bancha-ramu, a native of Mujil-poora, a place about a day's journey from Calcutta, dying, his wife went to be burnt with the body. All the previous ceremonies were performed: she was fastened on the pile, and the tire was kindled; but the night was dark and rainy. When the tire began to scorch this poor woman, she contrived to disentangle herself from the dead body, and creeping from under the pile hid herself among some brushwood. In a little time it was discovered that there was only one body on the pile. The relations immediately took the alarm and searched for the poor wretch. The son soon dragged her forth, and insisted that she should throw herself on the pile again, or hang or drown herself. She pleaded her life at the hands of her own son, and declared that she could not embrace so horrid a death: but she pleaded in vain. The son urged that he should lose his caste, and that, therefore he would die or she should. Unable to persuade her, the son and others present then tied her hands and feet, and threw her on the funeral pile, when she quickly perished." Charles Coleman, *The Mythology of the Hindus* (London: Parbury, Allen & Co., 1832), 166-73.
60. Diop, *Precolonial Black Africa* (Westport: Lawrence Hill, 1987), 16, 12.
61. One of the very best discussions of this subject is Vulindlela Wobogo's "Diop's *Two Cradle Theory* and the *Origin of White Racism*," Black Books Bulletin, ed. Haki R. Madhubuti (Chicago: Institute of Positive Education, 1976) vol. 4, Winter, 21-29.
62. A.T. Olmstead, *History of the Persian Empire* (Chicago: University of Chicago Press, 1948), 22.
63. Diop, *African Origin of Civilization*, 287.

1.7.- From the Center to the Fringe: the Persistence of Racial Myths in Physical Anthropological Theory

The Hamitic Hypothesis and the anthropological concepts of Brown and Mediterranean races are grounded in the racist thinking of the late eighteenth, nineteenth, and early twentieth centuries—the heyday of European imperialism and manifest destiny. During this period, it is well known, Black populations in Africa, Asia, Australia, the South Pacific, and the Western Hemisphere were essentially divided, dispossessed, colonized, and thoroughly dominated by competing White nations. These concepts have effectively provided the basis for the removal of Black people from the center of world civilizations to the fringe. The Sumerians—the illustrious Blackheaded people of ancient Iraq—are a prime example.

Of the physical anthropologists that have examined actual Sumerian remains and published the results, the works of L.H.D. Buxton, Mario Cappieri, Henry Field, Arthur Keith, and T.K. Penniman stand out. The reader should be aware, however, that none of these scientists was honest enough to call a Black a Black; resorting instead to the use of ridiculous ethnic euphemisms, and for Sumerian physical types presented us with "Hamites, Mediterraneans, and members of the Brown race." In reference to a skull found during the course of excavations at Kish, for instance, Buxton wrote that:

> "It undoubtedly belongs to the same type as that which Grafton Elliot Smith has called the Brown race and which Sergi has termed Mediterranean. This type is widely spread throughout the whole region and extends from the Mediterranean to India. It formed the main bulk of the ancient inhabitants of Egypt and has been called the Proto-Egyptian type."[1]

1.7.1.- The Hamitic hypothesis

"Ham was the middle child of Noah's three sons, Shem, Ham, and Japheth. The name 'Ham' means 'hot,' 'heat,' and by application, 'black'... The name 'Ham' is patronymic of his descendants."[2] The four sons of Ham were: Ethiopia, Kmt, Libya, and Canaan. The lines of Ham's descendents, as described in Genesis, represent a kind of mythologized ethnology. Until the late eighteenth century, it was generally accepted that Hamites were Black people. The extraordinary results of Napoleon Bonaparte's occupation of Egypt starting in 1798, however, became the historical impetus for Europeans to transform the Hamites into white people.

Briefly stated, according to Edith Sanders, "The Hamitic hypothesis states that everything of value ever found in Africa was brought there by the Hamites, allegedly a branch of the Caucasian race."[3] Charles G. Seligman (1873-1940) explained the civilizing role of the Hamites in Africa in the following manner: "The civilizations of Africa are the civilizations of the Hamites, its history the record of these peoples... The incoming Hamites were pastoral 'Europeans'—arriving wave after wave—better armed as well as quicker witted than the dark agricultural Negroes."[4] As recently as 1987, St. Clair Drake noted that, "The term 'Hamitic' is still used by Africanists whose attempts to purge it of racist implications have not yet been entirely successful."[5]

1.7.2.- The Brown race

In 1966, Wyatt MacGaffey wrote that:

> "Recently the term Hamite for the Caucasoid ideal has fallen into disfavor, but certain authors speak of the Brown Race. This concept is without scientific value, and must be regarded as a myth with specific ideological functions related to the colonial situation."[6]

The Brown race has a dual ancestry. Although originally created by Giuseppe Sergi, the notion of the Brown race was substantially modified by G. Elliot Smith[7]. Australian born Grafton Elliot Smith (1871-1937), who was eventually knighted, was a prominent anatomist and a hyper diffusionist who believed that most, if not all, of the world's early monumental high-cultures, from Sumer to China to the Western Hemisphere, were rooted in the Nile Valley. Included within Smith's Brown race were the ancient Kamites, Sumerians, Elamites, and Dravidians. Smith was an outspoken racist who believed that "The Negro and the Australian are more primitive than any other living peoples."[8]

1.7.3.- The Mediterranean race

The term Mediterranean Race may have been coined by Giuseppe Sergi (1841-1936), Professor of Anthropology in the University of Rome. In 1901, Sergi's book *The Mediterranean Race: A Study of the Origin of European Peoples* was published by Walter Scott of London. Sergi's views were at least as racist as those of Smith. According to Sergi:

> "The most degraded of existing races, such as the Australians, Tasmanians, Papuans, Veddahs, Negroes, Hottentots, and Bosjemen, as well as the aboriginal forest tribes of India, are typically dolichocephalic."[9]

Anthropologist Carleton S. Coon, the author of numerous works on physical anthropology and a fierce and ardent champion of the concept of the Mediterranean Race, was extremely influential in shaping the views of physical anthropologists in the twentieth century. With Coon's researches, writings and viewpoints, however, Dr. Cheikh Anta Diop was not impressed and commented thus: "Coon's work contributes nothing new. If all the specimens of races and sub-races described by him lived in New York today, they would reside in Harlem."[10]

Dr. Diop, in his most eloquent and scholarly manner, adequately summarizes the matter for us:

> "Anthropologists have invented the ingenious, convenient, fictional notion of the 'true Negro,' which allows them to consider, if need be, all the real Negroes on earth as fake Negroes, more or less approaching a kind of Platonic archetype, without ever attaining it. Thus, African history is full of 'Negroids,' Hamites, semi-Hamites, Nilo-Hamites, Ethiopoids, Sabaeans, even Caucasoids! Yet, if one stuck strictly to scientific data and archaeological facts, the prototype of the White race would be sought in vain throughout the earliest years of present-day humanity. The Negro has been there from the beginning; for millennia he was the only one in existence. Nevertheless, on the threshold of the historical epoch, the 'scholar' turns his back on him, raises questions about his genesis, and even speculates 'objectively' about his tardy appearance.[11]

If the African anthropologist made a point of examining European races 'under the magnifying glass,' he would be able to multiply them ad infinitum by grouping physiognomies into races and sub-races as artificially as his European counterpart does with regard to Africa. He would, in turn, succeed in dissolving collective European reality into a fog of insignificant facts."[12]

Notes

1. L.H.D. Buxton, cited by Stephen Langdon, *Excavations at Kish, vol. 1* (Paris: Paul Geuthner, 1924), 58-59.
2. Walter Arthur McCray, *The Black Presence in the Bible, vol. 1* (Chicago: Black Light Fellowship, 1990), 54.
3. Edith R. Sanders, "*The Hamitic Hypothesis; Its Origin and Functions in Time Perspective,*" *Journal of African History 10, No. 4* (1969), 532.
4. Charles G. Seligman, *The Races of Africa* (New York: Henry Holt, 1930), 96.
5. St. Clair Drake, *Black Folk Here and There, vol. 1* (Los Angeles: Center for Afro-American Studies, UCLA, 1987), 129.
6. Wyatt MacGaffey, "*Concepts of Race in the Historiography of Northeast Africa,*" *Journal of African History 7, No. 1* (1966), 16.
7. MacGaffey, 3.
8. Grafton Elliot Smith, *Human History* (New York: Norton, 1929), 123.
9. Giuseppe Sergi, *The Mediterranean Race: A Study of the Origin of European Peoples* (London: Walter Scott, 1901), 22.
10. Cheikh Anta Diop, *African Origin of Civilization: Myth or Reality*, trans. and ed. Mercer Cook (Westport: Lawrence Hill, 1974), 238.
11. Diop, 274.
12. Diop, 275.

1.8.- The African Presence in Ancient Iraq: the Blackheads of Sumer

A very important part of Southwest Asia is the country that we now call Iraq. In truth, Iraq has had an African presence for thousands and thousands of years. Indeed, the first civilization of Southwest Asia, known as Sumer and located in Southern Iraq (formerly Mesopotamia "the land between the two rivers") was dominated by Black people.

Flourishing during the third millennium B.C.E. between the mighty Tigris and Euphrates Rivers, Sumer set the guidelines and established the standards for the kingdoms and empires that followed her including Babylon and Assyria. Sumer, as is well known, has been acknowledged as an early center for advanced mathematics, astronomy and calendars, writing and literature, art and architecture, religion and highly organized urban centers, some of the more notable of which include Kish, Uruk, Ur, Nippur, Lagash and Eridu.

While Sumer's many achievements are much celebrated, the important question of the ethnic composition of her population is frequently either glossed over or left out of the discussion altogether. As topical as Iraq is today and since the civilization of ancient Sumer has been claimed by other peoples, it is important to set the record straight and we believe that we can state without equivocation that Sumerian civilization was but an extension of Nile Valley civilizations "of which Egypt was the noblest-born but not the only child."

To buttress our claims about Sumer's African origins we first point out that the ancient Sumerians referred to themselves as the "Black headed people." And there is no doubt that the oldest and most exalted deity of the Sumerians was Anu, a name that loudly recalls thriving Black populations at the dawn of history including Africa itself, the Arabian Peninsula, India and even Europe. Equally important is the skeletal evidence exhumed from ancient Sumerian cemeteries, Biblical references in which Nimrod (the Old Testament founder of Sumer) is described as a son of Kush (Ethiopia), architectural similarities, eye witness accounts and oral traditions. All of this data points to and supports an early African origin for the Sumerians of ancient Iraq.

1.8.1.- Lord Enki

Enki, whose name means Lord of the Earth, was one of the most important and most interesting figures in the Sumerian pantheon. Enki began his career as the local deity of the city of Eridu, and like Oannes, to whom he is very similar, became the personification of the watery element in general.

Because the Persian Gulf, near which Eridu was located, was the largest body of water known to the blackheads, Enki was the "father" of all the waters. The oldest settlements of the Euphrates Valley, we should note, are those nearest the Persian Gulf. This is a vital point in tracing Sumerian origins. The part that water plays in the life of mankind and in the development of human cultures is quite sufficient to account for the hallowed position acquired by Enki in the Sumerian pantheon as the protector of humanity. He is the teacher also who instructs humankind in the various sciences. It is Enki who endowed the Sumerian rulers with direction and intelligence, as it is Enki, too, who presides over the fine arts; instructing men in architecture, in working precious metals and stone, and in all the expressions of man's intellectual activities. Thus Enki may briefly be defined as the god of Supreme Wisdom and Civilization itself.

One of the lands most cherished by Enki was Meluhha—a land of mariners, whose prized exports included timber and wooden furniture, copper, gold dust, lapis lazuli and carnelian. There was clearly a close relationship between Meluhha, which was known as "the Black land," and Sumer itself—the land of the "Blackheads." After initially fashioning the blackheaded people themselves, Enki is said to have immediately journeyed to Meluhha to bless it profusely.[1] In post-Sumerian times Meluhha is mentioned repeatedly as a place of "black men," and from the first millennium B.C.E. emerged the designation "Black Meluhhaites."

Meluhha's precise geographic location has frequently been attached by modern scholars to either the African Ethiopia, or the Indus Valley (Harappan) region of Pakistan and western India. Both regions were lands of Black men, but Harappa, whose civilization was larger in area than ancient Mesopotamia and Egypt combined, was much closer to Sumer than African Ethiopia. Harappa and its Dravidian descendant kingdoms are also known for their extensive long-distance commercial activities and mastery of the seas.

The major center of Enki's cult was the southern Sumerian city of Eridu. Originally settled about 3000 B.C.E., Eridu was traditionally the first Sumerian site of kingship before the great Flood. By the end of the third millennium B.C.E. desiccation had let to its gradual isolation and general decline. Although the city and its famous school sank into gradual oblivion towards the fall of Sumer, Lord Enki, the Sumerian god of wisdom and philosophy, of atonement and consecration, continued to hold his place of almost supreme importance in religion, poetry and tradition. So necessary was his cult to the practice of religion that every Sumerian city possessed and dedicated a temple or chapel to Enki specifically.

The city of Eridu eventually lost its position in the political and social history of Sumer, but without real detriment to the stature of Lord Enki himself.

1.8.2.- Kish: the Sumerian city supreme

According to the great pioneer African-American scholar William Leo Hansberry:

> "It was formerly thought that Kish or Cish and their derivations were of Egyptian or Hebrew origin, but the discovery of their counterparts in an Ethiopian record seem to indicate that the words were indigenous to the country and peoples to which they were generally applied. "[2]

The important archaeological site of Kish lies about twenty miles due east of ancient Babylon (the "Gate of God") in central Iraq.[3] The name Kish is used as a short-hand description for many closely related settlements extending far back into prehistory, and existing up to the period of Mongol invasions about 1250 CE. Serious archaeological and related researches on the Kish of the Sumerian Blackheads began in 1923. These efforts were jointly sponsored by the Field Museum of Chicago and Oxford University, and directed by Stephen H. Langdon, Professor of Assyriology at Oxford. Ernest Mackay, a Flinders Petrie trained archaeologist who later achieved wide acclaim for his Indus Valley researches, was field director at Kish until 1926. From 1927 until 1933, the last year of the expedition, Louis-Charles Watelin, a French engineer who had previously dug at Susa, served as field director. Among the physical anthropologists involved in the digs at Kish were L.H.D. Buxton, Henry Field and T.K. Penniman. The published field reports of the 1923-1933 Kish excavations have long been available and should have all by themselves resolved the "problem of Sumerian origins." The real problem is mostly in the arrogant attitudes of European academicians.

According to the Sumerian king list Kish was the seat of kingship after the Flood. It is not mentioned as a pre-Flood city, and never again held the powerful stature which it had during this very early period in Sumerian history. The emergence of Kish as an influential Mesopotamian city-state began in the early third millennium B.C.E. A monumental building at Kish, dated to 2800 B.C.E., was likely the palace of an earthly ruler, rather than a priestly temple. This palace had hundreds of rooms and was considerably larger than the French palace at Versailles thousands of years later. In spite of her general decline Kish for a long time possessed such prestige that Mesopotamian political leaders continued to claim over lordship of the city.

Perhaps the most remarkable single figure in the history of Kish in the Early Dynastic period is recorded in the King List as the "barmaid" ("woman of wine"). Her name was Ku-Baba, and she is said to have "consolidated the foundation of Kish." According to a later account she seized power over Kish from the city of Akshak. Ku-Baba reigned one-hundred years, and after her passing Kish played an increasingly minor role in Sumerian affairs.

1.8.3.- Uruk: The House of Anu

The modern name for Uruk is Warka. The Old Testament name is Erech, or "Healthy." To the Sumerians this extremely ancient city was known as Eanna, the House of Anu. Uruk was dedicated to both Anu and Inanna, the Sumerian goddess supreme. One of Uruk's very earliest structures was the White Temple of Anu, the construction of which may be placed in the latter part of the fourth millennium B.C.E. According to the Sumerian kinglist, after the Flood Uruk assumed power from Kish, only to then lose it to Ur, although the dynasties of all three cities apparently overlapped.

Uruk was also the city of the heroic semi-legendary king Gilgamesh. The Epic says of Gilgamesh that "In Uruk he built walls, a great rampart and the temple of blessed Eanna for the god of the firmament Anu, and for Inanna, the goddess of love."[4]

As God par excellence Anu occupied an independent position, and well before the time of Gudea, the pious priest-king of Lagash (ca. 2060-2042

B.C.E.), he became supreme. Anu was ultimately superseded in his capacity of most exalted god first by Enlil, the "strong man of Sumer," and secondly by Marduk, the tutelary deity of Babylon.

1.8.4.- Nippur: Sumer's religious capital

Nippur, presently known as Tell Niffer, was located towards Sumer's northern borders. In historic times Nippur became the supreme religious center of Sumer. Nippur was also the chief seat of Enlil, who was initially the executive of Anu, and eventually Anu's actual successor. Enlil, sometimes called "Nippur's young man," was later identified with the powerful Babylonian deity called Bel (Lord). Tummal was the name of the district in Nippur consecrated to Ninlil, the wife of Enlil.

Extensive excavations were conducted at Tell Niffer between 1889 and 1900 by the University of Pennsylvania in four campaigns which resulted in the recovery of thirty thousand tablets and fragments. Much of our current knowledge of Sumer is derived from these documents. Some of the results of these digs were published as early as 1893.

1.2.5.- Adab: Sumerian city of Mother Worship

Adab, about twenty-five miles south of Nippur, was supplied by a broad canal which branched from the river Euphrates eastward and passed through the city itself after having fed the adjoining regions along the way. In the centre of Adab the canal divided to form an island on which stood the prehistoric temple of the mother-goddess Aruru. It was known as Emakh, a name common to all the temples of the goddess of birth. The goddess herself had the name Makh, "the far-famed," at Adab. The cult of Adab was devoted entirely to the worship of the mothers-goddess. The stage-tower or ziggurat of Adab is one of the oldest in Sumer.

1.8.6.- Ur: the Heart of Sumer

For most of her history, Sumer consisted of a number of largely independent city-states. Each such entity contained a comparatively large urban center, around which were the smaller satellite towns and villages. At frequent intervals however the Sumerian city-states coalesced to form powerful unified kingdoms led by provincial leaders endowed with divine status. Such was the case during Ur's Third Dynasty. Ur itself, while not the earliest of the great Sumerian cities, was arguably the most important.[5]

Ur-Nammu (circa 2047—2030 B.C.E.), founded the Third Dynasty of Ur of the Blackheads of Sumer in southern Iraq, following a long period of foreign rule. He was succeeded by his son Shulgi, after an eighteen-year reign. His death on the battle-field against the savage Gutians was commemorated in a long Sumerian poetic composition. His main achievement was state-building, and Ur-Nammu is chiefly remembered today for his legal code, the Code of Ur-Nammu—one of the oldest surviving examples in the world. He was also responsible for ordering the construction of a number of stepped temple-mountains, called ziggurats, including the Great Ziggurat of Ur.

The Third Dynasty itself lasted for nearly a century under the reign of five brilliant rulers who elevated Ur to the status of a great empire. The Third Dynasty rulers of Ur assumed the titles of "King of Sumer and Akkad" and this was not the first time a Sumerian city-state had reached out to embrace the surrounding regions. During the reign of its powerful governor Gudea (2142-2122 B.C.E.), Lagash subjugated Susa and much of Elam. From a series of inscriptions we le am of Gudea' conquests, his lack of acknowledgement of a superior, and of the Susians and Elamites who came to Lagash, "to aid him in reconstructing the temple of his god."[6]

Gudea's god was Anu, a name found seemingly whenever the ancient blacks themselves are found. In spite of the scarcity of stone, classical Sumer was an age of colossal construction projects, and each of the major urban centers erected tremendous multiple leveled brick structures called ziggurats. It has been suggested that this ziggurat was the basis of the story of the Tower of Babel.

Amar-Sin (circa 1981-1973 B.C.E.) was the third ruler of the Third Dynasty of the Sumerian Blackheads at Ur in ancient Iraq. He succeeded his father Shulgi. Year-names are known for all nine years of his reign. They record campaigns conducted against several surrounding regions. Amar-Sin's reign is notable for his attempt at regenerating the ancient sites of Sumer. He apparently worked on the unfinished ziggurat (temple mountain) at Eridu. Unfortunately, the city of Eridu was abandoned during his reign as salinity problems made agricultural pursuits in the region unprofitable.

Ur's Third Dynasty Empire, grown expansive and wealthy, unfortunately was built on a very fragile base. First of all, the coalition that constituted the core of the empire was a loosely arranged affair, and there does not appear to have been any genuine efforts towards long term, concrete regional centralization. Secondly, through decades of soil abuse, the agricultural productivity of much of Sumer had become severely limited creating an increasing dependence on foodstuffs grown in the northern provinces of Sumer and Akkad. Thirdly, the continuing spread of Indo-European and Semitic peoples after the mid-third millennium B.C.E. had begun to isolate Sumer and seriously challenge not only her dominance of Lower Mesopotamia but her existence itself. The powerful rulers of the Third Dynasty had initially been able to hold these nomadic and half savage tribes at a distance, but by the end of the third millennium B.C.E. the dam was ready to burst. The northern food producing regions first attracted the attention and then the violent assaults of the interlopers, who through the early domestication of the horse, afflicted the Sumerians with wave after wave of lightning swift attacks, creating both panic and famine in the populous southern city-states. The Sumerians called these roving tribes:

> "The MAR.TU who knows no grain... The MAR.TU who knows no house or town, the boors of the mountains... The MAR.TU who does not bend (to cultivate the land), who eats raw meat, who has no house during his lifetime, who is not buried after his death."[7]

Is this how the now mighty Semites and Indo-Europeans entered history? If so, as seems apparent, it is quite ironic. Any of these factors might have caused the decline of Sumer. Combined, they spelled their doom. The seemingly stable empire rapidly fell apart and Sumer's former vassals turned on her with a vengeance.[8]

Shu-sin was king of the Blackheads of Sumer and ruler of the Kingdom of Akkad. He was the next to last king of the Third Dynasty of Ur. He succeeded his brother Amar-Sin and reigned from about 1972 to 1964 B.C.E. Following an open revolt of his Amorite subjects, he directed the construction of a fortified wall between the Euphrates and the Tigris rivers, intending it to hold off any further attacks. Shu-sin was succeeded by his son Ibbi-Sin, whose reign closed out this historic dynasty of the ancient Blacks of southern Iraq. Night would soon fall on the Blackheads of Sumer.

Ur's collapse at the end of the Third Dynasty is a major turning point in Sumerian history. Ur was probably the most powerful Sumerian city of its era. After the fall of Ur the Sumerians as a nation would rule no more. The Semites, who were really fundamental in the destruction of Ur, became the new masters of the land. What of the Sumerians themselves? The ancient records state that the teeming Blackheaded people were put to the mace and slaughtered.[9]

1.8.7.- The Semitic Ascendancy and the Demise of the Blackheads

The ascension to power of Sargon of Akkad (ca. 2350 B.C.E.) began the first clear phase of Semitic dominance in Mesopotamia. Sargon was West Asia's first empire builder and established a Semitic dynasty which endured about 150 years. He is first identified in the service of Ur-Zababa, the king of Kish. Rising to power swiftly, he outgeneraled and successively defeated the forces of Uruk, Ur, Mari and Lagash. Encountering little opposition from the other city-states, Sargon's armies rather easily subjugated all of Sumer, and shortly thereafter the whole of Mesopotamia. In the *Chronicles Concerning Sargon*, King of Agade, the bold victor boasts that "The blackheaded peoples I ruled."[10] To symbolize his conquests Sargon rinsed his sword in the Persian Gulf, and took the still prestigious title of "King of Kish."

In governing the Sumerian cities of the empire, Sargon appointed only Akkadians to the higher administrative posts, and utilized all-Akkadian garrisons to maintain authority. Later Assyrian rulers of power possessed knowledge of Sargon and his exploits, and were impressed enough to take his name as their own.

The Akkadians, who culturally largely imitated their Sumerian teachers, were ultimately altogether expelled by the onrushing hordes of Guti, nomadic mountain tribes from the Zagros. The Gutian invasion brought down the Sargonic dynasty of Akkad about 2200 B.C.E., and ushered in an era of extreme anarchy. Their only real historical significance is the ruination of the Sargonic line. Of the Guti, Sumerologist C.J. Gadd pointed out that:

"They were doubtless mere destroyers and harpies of the wealth of the country… Nothing was recalled concerning this period, ever afterwards held in humiliating memory by the Babylonians [Sumerians], except its end, a glorious deliverance hailed no less fervently and followed by no less vigorous a reaction, than the expulsion of the Hyksos from Egypt."[11]

The Dynasty of Isin constitutes the last official dynasty in the Sumerian King List. Isin was governed for a short time by a certain Zambia (1836-1834 B.C.E.), after which time Ishbi-Erra established an Isin dynasty which lasted over two-hundred years.

In official inscriptions from Isin the Sumerian language is used exclusively. It must also be emphasized that practically all the great pieces of Sumerian literature found in the famous 'library' of Nippur were composed or carefully copied during the Isin period of dominance at the request of Semitic monarchs craving for Sumerian culture.

And what became of the Blackheads themselves? At the beginning to the Destruction of Black Civilization the marvelous African-American scholar Chancellor Williams recounts a Sumer legend:

"'What became of the Black People of Sumer?' the traveler asked the old man, 'for ancient records show that the people of Sumer were Black. What happened to them?' 'Ah,' the old man sighed. 'They lost their history, so they died.'"[12]

And because of the near physical eradication of the Sumerians and the material evidence of their civilization, combined with the much more tangible evidence of the grandeur of Nile Valley civilization, Diop was able to note with confidence that:

"Millions are spent on excavating clay mounds in Mesopotamia, in the hope of finding evidence to pinpoint with certainty and finality the birthplace of civilization in Western Asia. Although those who undertake this have very slim hope of ever become a permanent habit."[13]

By 1700 B.C.E. the Sumerian Blackheads, who for a thousand years had dominated the Mesopotamian center stage and laid the foundation for every near eastern civilization that was to come after it, had, in essence, vanished from history. Over the Blackheaded people the winds swept.

Notes

1. "Enki, the king of the Abzu, [decrees] (its) fate: 'Black land, may your trees be large trees…'" Samuel N. Kramer, *The Sumerians* (Chicago: University of Chicago Press, 1963), 178.

2. William Leo Hansberry, *Africa and Africans As Seen By Classical Writers*, ed. Joseph E. Harris.(Washington, D.C.: Howard University Press, 1981), 9.

3. "In 1894 an Amorite chief named Sumuabum chose for his capital a site a few miles west of Kish. Sumerian, KA.DINGIR.RA, Akkadian, Babilim, which both mean 'Gate of God.' The Greeks called it Babylon." George Roux, *Ancient Iraq* (New York: Penguin, 1966), 169.

4. *Epic of Gilgamesh*, ed. B. Radice (New York: Penguin, 1972).

5. British archaeologist Leonard Woolley, who from 1907 to 1949 directed major excavations in Egypt, Nubia, Syria, and Iraq, was almost personally responsible for focusing modern world attention on ancient Ur. In 1907, before his work at Ur, Woolley excavated in Nubia in partnership with Randall MacIver. From 1922 to 1934 Woolley directed extensive excavations at Ur on behalf of the joint expedition of the British Museum and the University of Pennsylvania. The best-known artifacts from these excavations are those removed from the so-called "royal cemetery" of Ur's first dynastic period (ca. 2600-2500 B.C.E.). Among the several written works to his credit are *Ur of the Chaldees* in 1929 and *Excavations at Ur* in 1954. These works were particularly designed to appeal to popular consumption, and helped establish the narrow-minded, Oxford University trained Woolley as one of the world's most famous archaeologists.

6. George Cameron, *History of Early Iran* (Chicago: University of Chicago Press, 1936; rpt. 1976), 55.

7. E. Chiera, *Sumerian Epics and Myths*, Chicago, 1934, nos. 58 & 112.

8. "The death blow came at the hands of the Elamites from the eastern hills, who overran Sumer and carried off the last king of the Third Dynasty, the temples plundered of their treasures. At the same time, Amorite tribes led by the ruler of Mari occupied the land of Akkad. This disaster marks the end of Sumerian political leadership in Mesopotamia. The territories of the Third Dynasty broke apart into city-states, such as Isin and Larsa; and the empires to follow in Mesopotamia, down to the Persian, were run by Semites." William H. McNeill, *The Origins of Civilization* (Oxford University Press: London, 1968), 67-68.

9. "Over the black-headed people the winds swept. The people groan… Covered Ur like a garment, enveloped it like linen… The raging storm has attacked unceasingly. The people groan… In its boulevards where the feasts were celebrated they were viciously attacked. In all its streets where they were wont to promenade, dead bodies were lying about; In its places where the festivities of the land took place the people were ruthlessly laid low. Mothers and fathers who did not leave (their) houses were overcome by fire. The young lying on their mother's bosoms like fish were carried off by the waters. The nursing mother-pried open were their breasts. The black-headed people wherever they

laid their heads… were carried off." "Lamentation Over the Destruction of Ur," S.N. Kramer, ed. *Assyriological Studies, No. 12*, Oriental Institute (Chicago: University of Chicago Press, 1940).

10. McNeill, 54.

11. C.J. Gadd, *The Dynasty of Agade and the Gutian Invasion* (Cambridge: Cambridge University Press, 1963), 44.

12. Chancellor Williams, *Destruction of Black Civilization* (Chicago: Third World Press, 1976), 17.

13. 123.

1.9.- The African Presence in Early Arabia

"The suggestion of a `Black Arabia' might seem counter intuitive—the Arab with which most are familiar is the very fair-skinned, hawk-faced Semite. It is the case however that the latter shares the peninsula today with a much different type of Arab."[1]

The Arabian Peninsula, first inhabited more than eight thousand years ago, was early populated by Africans. Once dominant over the entire peninsula, the African presence in early Arabia is most clearly trace able through the Sabeans. The Sabeans were the first people of Arabia to step firmly within the realm of civilization. The southwestern corner of the peninsula was their early home. This area, which was known to the Romans as Arabia Felix, is today called Yemen. In antiquity this region gave rise to a high degree of civilization because of the fertility of the soil, the growth of frankincense and myrrh, and the close proximity to the sea and consequently its importance in the trade routes. The Sabeans have even been called "the Phoenicians of the southern seas."

We hear of the Sabeans in the tenth century B.C.E. through the fabled exploits of its semi-legendary queen. This woman had all the qualities of an exceptional monarch and appears to have ruled over a wealthy domain embracing parts of both Africa and Arabia. She is known as Bilqis in the Koran, Makeda in the Kebra Negast, and the Queen of Sheba in the Bible. The three of these documents provide a relatively clear picture of a highly developed state distinguished by the pronounced overall status of women.

Bilqis/Makeda was not an isolated phenomenon. Several times, in fact, do we hear of prominent women in Arabian history; the documents they are mentioned in providing no commentary on husbands, consorts, or male relatives. Either their deeds or inheritance, perhaps both, enabled them to stand out quite singularly. The Sabeans apparently possessed a dedicated matrifocal culture and society.

Around the beginning of the first millennium B.C.E., the period in which Bilqis/Makeda is thought to have lived, we find the emergence of a number of large urban centers characterized by elaborate irrigation systems. With the domestication of the camel, the people of southern Arabia could effectively exploit the region's greatest natural resources—frankincense and myrrh—which from the earliest historical periods were much prized and sought after. The purest and most abundant sources of frankincense and myrrh were in southern Arabia and Somalia (incorporating at least a part of the land of Punt), just across the Red Sea from Africa.

We hear of the Sabeans during the reign of the powerful Assyrian king Sargon II (721-705 B.C.E.). In a series of inscriptions detailing Assyrian military successes, there is specific mention of:

> "Pir'u, the king of Musru, Sarnsi, the queen of Arabia, It'arnra, the Sabean,— the(se) are the kings of the seashore and from the desert—I received as their presents gold in the form of dust, precious stones, ivory, ebony-seeds, all kind of aromatic substances, horses (and) carnels."[2]

Frankincense and myrrh were very important in the ancient world, and not just in religious ritual. In the Nile Valley, for example, frankincense, while extensively utilized for its perfume-like fragrance, was equally valued for its medicinal properties. It was used both in the stoppage of bleeding and as an antidote to poisons. Myrrh was employed for cosmetic purposes and formed an essential element in the mummification process in Kmt.

In addition to the export of frankincense and myrrh, Southern Arabia, due to its geographic location, was in a position to supplement the vast wealth accrued from the incense trade as an exchange point and haven of safety for the numerous ships involved in the trade in luxury items from east to west. This centuries-old and highly lucrative trade involved vast quantities of products, from silk to produce and spices, ebony and ivory, precious metals and fine jewels. The kingdoms of Southern Arabia, of which Saba was the first and most important, understandably waxed rich in their roles as intermediary between regions. She carefully guarded all knowledge of her commercial enterprises and created the impression that she was the actual source of the great wealth which passed through her hands, and of course other than frankincense and myrrh she was not. One can easily understand why the region was known as Arabia Felix or Happy Arabia.

It was during the seventh century B.C.E. that the Sabean rulers became known as mukarribs (priest-kings). The earliest known Sabean construction projects, including the mighty Marib Dam (South Arabia's most enduring technical achievement) were initiated during this period. Two mukarribs, Sumuhu'alay Yanaf and Yithi'amara Bayyim, cut deep water courses through the solid rock at the south end of the site.

The Marib Dam, which served its builders and their descendants for more than a thousand years, was traditionally believed to have been conceived by Lokman, the marvelous sage and multi-genius of pre-Islamic South Arabia.[3] In effect, the Dam was an earthen ridge stretching slightly more than 1700 feet across a prominent wadi. Both sides sloped sharply upward, with the Dam's upstream side fortified by small pebbles established in mortar. The Marib Dam was rebuilt several times by piling more earth and stone onto the existing structure. The last recorded height of the Marib Dam was slightly more than forty-five feet.

Although the Marib Dam has now practically disappeared, the huge sluice gates built into the rocky walls of the wadi are very well preserved. They continue to stand as silent but effective witnesses to the creative genius of the Southern Arabian people. When the periodic but powerful rains did arrive, the mechanism divided the onrushing waters into two channels, which ultimately sustained the area's inhabitants. Such was the force generated by the turbulent waters, however, that the Marib Dam was periodically washed out. Reconstruction was a formidable task. In one such operation 20,000 workmen were employed, some of them coming from hundreds of miles away.

At some point during this period, perhaps even earlier, there is evidence of Southern Arabian settlement in Africa. The remains of actual Southern Arabian settlements have been found principally at Yeha, Matara, and Haoulti. The resulting co-mingling of Ethiopian and Sabean cultures led to the development of the powerful African kingdom of Axum. The earliest Ethiopian alphabet may be a Southern Arabian type. The Axumite script itself is apparently a derivative of Sabean. Even the name Abyssinia is thought to have been taken from the Habashan, a powerful Southern Arabian family that eventually settled in Africa. From this period Ethiopia became known in Arabic scripts as Habashat, and its citizens Habshi. This early Ethiopian-Sabean era, beginning during the early fifth century B.C.E., lasted a century.

As the scepter of Southern Arabian supremacy passed from Saba's grasp, and also Ma'in (an early rival of Saba and apparently governed by a grand council), Qataban (another regional state) emerged as the area's foremost power. Timna, one of the more archaeologically explored sites in Southern Arabia, was Oataban's capital and its major urban center. Oataban reached its zenith around 60 B.C.E., and right afterwards went into a period of rapid eclipse. The power in Southern Arabia then shifted back towards Saba, in the west, albeit in a lesser form, and Hadramaut in the east, which occupied and destroyed Timna. The kingdom of Ausan, a lesser known state, also became distinct at this time. Ausan had such extensive commercial ties with Africa, that in the Periplus of the Erythraean Sea (ca. 75) the entire East African seaboard is known as the "Ausanitic Coast."

Following the rise of Axum, Africans assumed a highly aggressive role in Ethiopian-Southern Arabian relations. Between 183 and 213, for example the Ethiopian king Gadara, followed by his son, appear to have been the dominant figures in South Arabia. Less than a century later, the Ethiopian king Azbah sent military contingents to South Arabia and apparently settled Ethiopian troops there as well.

Saba was again occupied by Ethiopia from 335 to 370. The effects of this occupation were perhaps more long lasting than those preceding it, in that this one firmly implanted Christianity on South Arabian soil, with the Sabean rulers themselves adopting the faith. Christianity had already made considerable inroads in Arabia, as is evidenced by the attendance in 325 of six Arabian bishops at the historic Council of Nicea. Christianity was to play a critical part in the remaining years of pre-Islamic Arabia. Initially, for example, the church suppressed the age-old burning of incense in religious rituals by deeming that it was a pagan tradition, and consequently an impediment to Christianity itself. When combined with the establishment of direct sea routes linking Asia with the west, Southern Arabian fortunes sharply diminished.

After a brief resurgence of Sabean power under the leadership of Malikkarib Yuhad'in, Southern Arabia, which in addition to its Christian population had attracted large numbers of Jews, witnessed an increasingly antagonistic relationship between the two religions and their adherents. The result was a violent period of Christian persecutions and church burnings. This particularly virulent epoch of Christian martyrdom provoked an immediate response in Ethiopia, then headed by King Ella Asbeha—known as a formidable advocate of "Christian enlightenment." It is said, in fact, that a total of seven different saints lived under Ella Asbeha's generous patronage.

In 524, a powerful coalition composed of the Eastern Roman Empire, Christian refugees from South Arabia, and the Kingdom of Axum, was organized for the specific purpose of invading Southern Arabia and unseating its ruling class. Byzantium supplied the ships, Southern Arabian refugees the advance guard, and the Axumites the bulk of the fighting forces. The coalition soon achieved its goals, and in the Book of Himyarites and the Martyrdom of Arethius, we read of a decisive battle along the Southern Arabian coast where the Southern Arabian king literally lost his head. Ethiopia once again possessed South Arabia's strongholds.

After seven months Ella Asbeha returned to Africa, leaving behind him a joint government of the Southern Arabian nobility and the Ethiopian military. This arrangement lasted until 532 when Abreha, a junior Ethiopian military officer, seized the Southern Arabian throne. The three-thousand man Ethiopian army sent to suppress the revolt quickly defected to Abreha. A second expeditionary force Abreha rapidly and soundly smashed. Abreha's stunning success apparently was facilitated by the deep class contradictions within Ethiopian society, including the military, creating a base from which a former junior officer could rise to become one of the great personalities in Arabian history.

It was during this long series of wars involving Ethiopia, and later Persia, and the Islamic jihads themselves, that many of the major monuments in South Arabia were either damaged or destroyed. Such was the case with the fortress of Ghumdan, a truly superb construction, described most vividly in the tenth century by Al-Hamdani. Standing twenty stories high, the upper levels were composed of polished marble. The roof was made of stone so transparent that a crow could be seen flying overhead from underneath the building. On top of the fortress stood four bronze lions which roared when the winds blew.

Although officially acknowledging Ethiopia's overall supremacy, Abreha worked unendingly to strengthen South Arabia's autonomy, extending her influence into the northern and central portions of the peninsula. Domestically, Abreha is known to have inaugurated major repairs on the Marib Dam. After his death in 558, Abreha's exploits were recorded and embellished in Arabic, Byzantine and Ethiopian literature, and no history of pre-Islamic Arabia is complete without him.

In addition to Abreha, one of the most illustrious single figures in pre-Islamic Arabia was Antar (ca. 525-615). Graham W. Irwin notes that:

> "There has always been a considerable population in Arabia of African origin. Perhaps the most famous of these people was Antara. He had an Arab father and an Ethiopian mother and became in time the national hero of the Arabs. That's not too strong a statement. There was nobody to equal the valor and strength of Antara. He's rather like King Arthur in the English tradition but, in fact, more important, because he was a more historical figure."[4]

Before the advent of Islam, Southern Arabia already possessed, as we have emphasized, large and influential Christian and Jewish communities. She also possessed the sacred Kaaba sanctuary, with its black stone, at Makkah. Makkah was considered a holy place and the destination of pilgrims long before Muhammad. At the same time Allat, the Arabian goddess supreme, was worshipped at Ta'if, in Makkah's immediate proximity. Allat may have been regarded as the ultimate reality in female form. She was worshipped in the form of an immense uncut block of granite, as firm as the earth she represented. The most solemn oaths were sworn to Allat beginning with the words, "By the salt, by the fire, and by Allat who is the greatest of all." Another significant Arabian deity, Dhu-al-Shara, was represented by a quadrangular block of black stone.

It was in this rich religious tradition that the prophet Muhammad, who was to unite the whole of Arabia, was born. The seeds of Islam were already ripe and Africa was instrumental in its growth. According to tradition, the first Muslim killed in battle was Mihdja—a Black man. Another Black man, Bilal, was such a pivotal figure in the development of Islam that he has been referred to as "a third of the faith." Bilal was Islam's first muezzin. Today Bilal has a large tomb and mosque in Damascus, Syria. Many of the earliest Muslim converts were Africans, and a number of the Muslim faithful sought refuge in Ethiopia because of Arabian hostility to Muhammad's teachings:

> "Five years after the proclamation of Islam (615), a number of Muslims sought refuge in neighboring Ethiopia in order to escape the persecutions of the Kurayshites in Mecca Their sojourn in Ethiopia greatly impressed these early Muslim migrants and influenced the future development of their new faith. Muslim biographical sources (tabakat) enumerate not a few Ethiopian converts to Islam who migrated to Medina and ranked amongst the Prophet's companions. They were referred to as the 'Ethiopian monks' (ruhban al-habasha)."[5]

It was this relationship which caused Muhammad to declare that, "Who brings an Ethiopian man or an Ethiopian woman into his house, brings the blessing of God there."[6]

Another eminent Black man, Ata ibn Abi Rabah (ca. 700), became a mufti at Makkah. He was born in Southern Arabia of Nubian parents. Eventually he moved to Makkah and became a famous teacher and jurisconsult there. In his later years his reputation spread far and wide. According to some accounts, including the brilliant black writer and historian Uthman Amr ibn-Bahr al-Jahiz, the prophet Muhammad himself was partly of African lineage. According to al-Jahiz, the guardian of the sacred Kaaba—Abd al-Muttalib, "fathered ten Lords, Black as the night and magnificent." One of these men was Abdallah, the father of Muhammad.[7]

Notes

1. Wesley Muhammad, *Black Arabia and the African Origins of Islam* (Atlanta: A-Team, 2009), 1.

2. James B. Pritchard, *Ancient Near East* (London: Oxford University Press, 1958), 196-97.

3. "Lokman is the most celebrated sage of the East. So great is his fame there that there is still a saying, 'To teach wisdom to Lokman,' which is the equivalent of 'Carrying coals to Newcastle.' In Islam his fame equals that of Solomon in the Christian-Jewish world. Mohammed quoted him as an authority and named the thirty first chapter of the Koran after him.

Much that is said about him is legendary. The Arabs say that he lived about 1100 BC, was a coal-black Ethiopian with woolly hair, and was the son of Baura, who was a son or a grandson of a sister of Job. Lokman is often confused with Aesop, who was also a Negro, and who, it appears, adapted some of Lokman's fables to his own use." J.A. Rogers, World's Great Men of Color, vol. 1 (New York: Collier, 1972), 67.

4. Graham W. Irwin, "African Bondage in Asian Lands," *African Presence in Early Asia*, eds. Runoko Rashidi and Ivan Van Sertima (New Brunswick: Transaction Press, 1988), 146. "The name of 'Antarah ibn-Shaddad al' Absi (ca. 525-615), evidently a Christian, has lived through the ages as the paragon of Bedouin heroism and chivalry. Knight, poet, warrior and lover, Antarah exemplified in his life those traits greatly esteemed by the sons of the desert. His deeds of valor as well as his love episodes with his lady, 'Ablah, whose name he immortalized in his famous Mu'allaqah, have become a part of the literary heritage of the Arabic-speaking world." Philip K. Hitti, *History of the Arabs, 6th ed.* (London: Macmillan, 1956), 96.

"His fame as a literary character transcends that of the modem authors of black blood, such as Pushkin in Russia, and the elder Dumas in France. After his death the fame of Antar's deeds spread across the Arabian Peninsula and throughout the Mohammedan world. ln time these deeds, like Homeric legends, were recorded in a literary form and therein is found that Antar,… has become the Achilles of the Arabian Iliad, a work known to this day after being a source of wonder and admiration for hundreds of years to millions of Mohammedans as the 'Romance of Antar.' The book, therefore, ranks among the great national classics like the 'Shah-nameh' of Persia, and the 'Nibelungen-Lied' of Germany. Antar was the father of knighthood. He was the champion of the weak and oppressed, the protector of women, the impassioned lover-poet, the irresistible and magnanimous knight. 'Antar' in its present form probably preceded the romances of chivalry so common in the twelfth century in Italy and France." A.O. Stafford, "Antar, *The Arabian Negro Warrior, Poet and Hero*," *Journal of Negro History 1, No. 2* (1916), 155.

5. Y. Talib, "The African Diapora in Asia," in *UNESCO General History of Africa. Vol. 3, Africa from the Seventh to the Eleventh* Century, ed. M. El Fasi (Berkeley: University of California Press, 1988), 710-11.

6. E. Cerulli "Ethiopia's Relations with the Muslim World," in *UNESCO General History of Africa. Vol. 3, Africa from the Seventh to the Eleventh Century*, ed. M. El Fasi (Berkeley: University of California Press, 1988), 576.

7. 'Uthman' Amr ibn-Bahr al-Jahiz, *The Book of the Glory of the Black Race*, trans. Vincent J. Cornell (Los Angeles: Preston, 1981), 50.

1.10.- The African Image in Early Afghanistan

by Runoko Rashidi and E. Brunson

Around the fourth century, the ancient central Asian bastion of Toprak Kala in Khwarizm, embracing portions of modem Uzbekistan, Kazakhstan and Afghanistan, contained towered battlements which encompassed an area 1,900 feet by 1,400 feet. The palace itself, which was assembled about an enclosure situated on an elevated platform, ascended to a height of three stories and was overlooked by three tremendous towers. The palace possessed three enormous halls. The decoration of the designated "Hall of Kings" was a consolidation and melding of stucco sculptures and paintings with effigies of the aristocracy of Chorasmia and their families.

Benjamin Rowland notes that the "Hall of Victories" was lined with statues of princes attended by the molded figure of Nikes, and the "Hall of Warriors" was brilliantly decorated with reliefs of men-at-arms painted black with Africoid features. The wavy hair of the figures is perhaps an indication that Dravidian soldiers were affiliated in an important way with the ruling lords of Chorasmia.[1]

John M. Rosenfield contends that another sort of indication of the presence of Dravidian physical types in the portrait assemblies in the Toprak Kala palace are "guards with small stature, dark skins, thick lips, and straight hair. This suggests the presence of armed contingents from South India... Skeletal remains have substantiated the fact that Indians were in the area."[2]

Notes

1. Benjamin Rowland, *The Art of Central Asia* (New York: Crown, 1974), 54.
2. John M. Rosenfield, *The Dynastic Arts of the Kushans* (Berkeley: University of California Press, 1967), 168.

1.11.- The African Presence
in Ancient Pakistan and India

Since the first modern humans (Homo sapiens sapiens) were of African birth, the African presence globally can be demonstrated through the history of the Black populations that have inhabited the world within the span of recent humanity. Not only are African people the aboriginal people of the planet but there is abundant evidence to show that Black people created and sustained many of the world's earliest and most enduring civilizations. Such was the case in India.

As has been noted, the early African presence in Asia extended, and still exists in limited degrees, from the furthest western points to the continent's southern and eastern reaches.

The existence of an isolated Dravidian or South Indian language, namely Brahui, in Baluchistan, is one of the strongest datums in support of ongoing Black migrations into the Asian interior in long distant times. In conjunction with this, extensive studies suggest that Elamite is cognate with the Dravidian family of languages.[1]

Exceptionally valuable writings reflecting linkages between Africa and early India have existed for more than two thousand years. Apollonius of Tyana, who is said to have visited India near the end of the first century C.E., was convinced that "The Ethiopians are colonists sent from India, who follow their forefathers in matters of wisdom."[2] The literary work of the early Christian writer Eusebius preserves the tradition that, "In the reign of Amenophis III [the mighty Dynasty XVIII Ancient Egyptian king] a body of Ethiopians migrated from the country about the Indus, and settled in the valley of the Nile."[3] And still another document from ancient times, the Itinerarium Alexandri, says that "India, taken as a whole, beginning from the north and embracing what of it is subject to Persia, is a continuation of Egypt and the Ethiopians."[4] The commentary of Diodorus Siculus (circa 45 B.C.E.) reflects the same theme:

> "From Ethiopia he (Osiris) passed through Arabia, bordering upon the Red Sea as far as to India, and the remotest inhabited coasts; he built likewise many cities

in India, one of which he called Nysa, willing to have remembrance of that (Nysa) in Egypt where he was brought up."[5]

And then there is the story of the Ethiopian king Ganges, conveyed by Samuel Purchas and cited by J.A. Rogers. The citation reads:

"But of all (the kings of Ethiopia) Ganges was most famous, who with his Ethiopian army passed into Asia and conquered all as far as the River Gangesto which he left that name, being before called Chliaros."[6]

1.11.1.- The Harappan Civilization

In Greater India (Pakistan, India, Sri Lanka, Bangladesh), more than a thousand years before the foundations of Greece and Rome, proud and industrious Black men and women known as Dravidians erected a powerful civilization. The pronounced cultural developments of the Indus Valley complex, with its vast extensions into Central Asia and Peninsular India, where its legacy remains distinct, owe their origins to them.

Based primarily on trade, the Indus Valley civilization was at its height from about 2200 B.C.E. to 1700 B.C.E. This particular phase is called Harappan, the name being derived from Harappa, in the Punjab, one of the earliest known Indus Valley sites. Harappa actually attracted attention as long ago as 1856. No excavations were undertaken however until the 1920s, by which time Harappa had been savagely pillaged for building materials for a British engineered railway line. The severe damage inflicted upon the site through this callous indifference to one of the great cities of ancient times is incalculable.

In 1922, in Pakistan's Sind province (about 350 miles northeast of Harappa), her sister city—Mohenjo-daro (Mound of the Dead)—was identified. Mohenjo-daro was very similar to Harrapa and in this case excavations began the same year. Mohenjo-daro and Harappa were apparently the chief administrative centers of the Indus complex, and since their discoveries several additional sites including Chanhu-daro, Kalibangan, Quetta, and Lothal, have been excavated.

The Indus cities possessed multiple level houses enhanced by sophisticated wells, drainage systems and bathrooms with flushing toilets. A recognized scholar on the Indus Valley civilization, Dr. Walter Fairservis Jr., states that the "Harappans cultivated cotton and perhaps rice, domesticated the chicken and may have invented the game of chess and one of the two great early sources of non-muscle power: the windmill."[7]

The decline and fall of the Indus Valley civilization has been linked to several factors, the most serious of which were the increasingly frequent incursions of the white tribes known in history as Aryans—violent Indo-European tribes initially from central Eurasia, and later Iran. Indeed, the name Iran means the "land of the Aryan."

1.11.2.- The Aryans in India

The White tribes that invaded ancient Pakistan and India and disrupted Black civilization there are known as Aryans. The Aryans were not necessarily superior warriors to the Blacks but they were aggressive, developed sophisticated military technologies and glorified military virtues. After hundreds of years of intense martial conflict between the Dravidians and Aryans, the Aryans succeeded in subjugating most of northern India. By about 800 B.C.E. these nomadic Aryan tribes had conquered Pakistan and all of northern India, naming their newly won territories after themselves, Aryavarta, or the Aryan Land.

Throughout the vanquished territories a rigid, caste-segmented social order was established with the masses of conquered Blacks (the Sudras) essentially reduced to slaves to the Whites and imposed upon for service in any capacity required by their Aryan conquerors. This vicious new world order was cold-bloodily racist, with the Whites on top, the "mixed races" in the middle, and the overwhelming majority of Black people on the very bottom, and imposed upon for service in any capacity required to the higher castes. In fact, the Sanskrit term varna, denoting one's societal status and used interchangeably with caste, literally means color or complexion and reflects a prevalent racial stratification and hierarchy.

Caste in India is the foundation of the religion known as Hinduism. Caste law in India, based originally on race and ethnicity, regulated all aspects of life, including marriage, diet, education, place of residence and occupation. This is not to deny that there were certain elements of the ancient Black aristocracy that managed to gain prominence in the dominant White social structure. The masses of conquered Blacks, however, were regarded by the Whites as Untruth itself. The Whites claimed to have emerged from the mouth of God; the Blacks, on the other hand, were said to have emerged from the feet of God. This was the ugly reality for the Black masses in conquered India.

The highest caste was the Brahmin (the Aryan elite) and identified with the color white; followed by the Kshatriyas (the military and administrative sector) identified with the color red; the Vaisyas (merchants and farmers) and identified with the color yellow; and, of course, the Sudras themselves, identified with the color black. Beneath even the Sudras were the outcastes or untouchables, composed of the unfortunate offspring of Brahmin-Sudra unions and long established Black populations in India which had retreated into the hinterlands to escape the Aryan advances, but ultimately coming under the Aryan sphere of influence.

For the maintenance of the new order a detailed religious and legal code was implemented which regulated even the most minute aspects of daily life. In respect to the Sudras and outcastes the code was quite simply draconian, with few if any ambiguities about it. Because of the critical nature of this subject—the study of early race and cultural relations in South Asia—several illustrative passages from The Law of Manu (Manu being a mythical Indian sage and lawgiver and supposedly a descendant of Brahman) are offered for critical examination:

– "Twice-bom (Brahmins, Kshatriyas, Vaisyas) who, in their fony, wed wives of the low (Sudra) caste, soon degrade their families and their children to the state of Sudras.

– He who weds a Sudra woman becomes an outcast, according to Saunaka on the birth of a son, and according to Bhrigu he who has (male) offspring from a (Sudra female, alone).

– A Brahmana who takes a Sudra wife to his bed, will (after death) sink into hell…[8]

– Let him not allow a dead Brahmana to be carried out by a Sudra, while men of the same caste are at hand; for that burnt-offering which is defiled by a Sudra's touch is detrimental to (the deceased's passage to) heaven.[9]

– A Brahmana… may, at the king's pleasure, interpret the law to him but never a Sudra.[10]

– A Kshatriya, having defamed a Brahmana, shall be fined one hundred (panas); a Vaisya one hundred and fifty or two hundred; a Sudra shall suffer corporal punishment. A Brahmana shall be fined fifty (panas) for defaming a Kshatriya; in (the case of) a Vaisya the fine shall be twenty-five (panas); in (the case of) Sudra twelve.[11] A once-born man (a Sudra), who insults a twice-born man with gross invective, shall have his tongue cut out; for he is of low origin. If he mentions the names and castes of the (twice-born) with contumely, an iron nail, ten fingers long, shall be thrust red-hot into his mouth.[12]

– If he arrogantly teaches Brahmanas their duty, the king shall cause hot oil to be poured into his mouth and into his ears. A low-caste man who tries to place himself on the same seat with a man of high caste, shall be branded on his hip and be banished, or (the king) shall cause his buttock to be gashed.

– If out of arrogance he spits (on a superior), the king shall cause both his lips to be cut off; if he urinates (on him), the penis; if he breaks wind (against him), the anus."[13]

For the Sudras and outcastes, as we have noted and followed with the evidence, the Law of Manu was brutal and vicious, and designed to keep them in their lowly caste position from generation to generation unto eternity. However, there was a way upward, for the Sudras at any rate, and Manu himself articulates the method: "[A Sudra who is] pure, the servant of his betters, gentle in speech, and free from pride, and always seeks a refuge with Brahmanas, attains [in his next life] a higher caste."[14]

As the very name implies, the life of the Indian outcaste was full of misery and impoverishment. Food and drink, if seen by them, were not to be taken. Generally they lived in settlements on the outskirts of villages and towns. In certain periods in Indian history outcastes, or untouchables, were not allowed to enter the adjoining Hindu community at night, in other periods, in daylight. Indeed, the outcaste's very shadow was thought polluting. Outcastes were required to attach a broom to their backs to erase any evidence of their presence. A cup was tied around their necks to capture any spittle that might escape their lips. The untouchable possessions consisted of dogs and donkeys. Their meals were consumed from broken dishes. Their clothing was taken from corpses. The principal functions of the outcastes included street sweeping, the removal of dead animals and human corpses, and the clean-up of cremation grounds; all of which was regarded as impure, even by the Sudras.

1.11.3.- The Nanda and Mauryan dynasties

The Nanda Dynasty of fourth century B.C.E. India was of Sudra origin and is downplayed in Indian histories. The apparent lack of popularity surrounding the Nanda family may be the result of the Sudra founder's determined seizure and consolidation of power, as revealed in early Indian literature:

> "A son of Mahanandin by a Sudra woman will be born a king, Mahapadma (Nanda), who will exterminate all ksatriyas. Thereafter kings will be of Sudra origin. Mahapadma will be sole monarch, bringing all under his sole sway. He will be 88 years on the earth. He will uproot all ksatriyas, being urged on by prospective fortune. He will have 8 sons, of whom Sukalpa will be the first; and they will be kings in succession to Mahapadma for 12 years."
>
> "The non-Aryan protest did not spend itself up only in religion and social matters. Mahapadma Nanda rose as their champion to overthrow the rule of the Kshatriya families in Magadha. He was admittedly of Sudra or non-Aryan origin, and he so terribly punished the Aryan ruling classes that he has been described in the Puranas as 'the exterminator of the Kshatriya race like a second Parasurama."[15]

While we are limited in our knowledge of Mahapadma, by most accounts he was certainly a highly remarkable man, and is credited with halting Alexander's eastern advance with an army of 80',000 horses, 200,000 foot soldiers, 8,000 war chariots, and 6,000 elephants trained for battle.

The center of his powerful, but short-lived dynasty, was Magadha, in what is now the East Indian state of Bihar land dominated by Black people. Ktesias, for example—the first European to write a comprehensive general account of India—known to posterity as the Indika of Ktesias, mentions large concentrations of Blacks in the regions of the eastern Himalayas and the upper Ganges, where most accounts place the birthplace of Gautama Siddartha.[16] Until late in its history the region was notably absent of Aryan settlers, who regarded the region's populace with contempt.

It could be pointed out here, to establish the region's stature, that Gautama Siddartha himself not only travelled to Bihar frequently, but also received enlightenment here, as well as the friendship of its early rulers. Mahavira, a conternporary of Gautama and identified as the Jain's founding figure, was born in Bihar in 599 B.C.E. The Nandas were quite favorably disposed towards the Buddhists and Jains, and were widely known for their patronage of scholarship.

The Nandas were succeeded by the Mauryan Dynasty, which was also of Sudra origin. The dynasty's founder was Chandragupta Maurya, whose opportunity for power came as a result of the withdrawal of Alexander's expeditionary forces around 320 B.C.E. Stepping into the resulting vacuum in the Punjab and western India, Chandragupta assembled a huge army with which he marched east to confront the Nanda forces, which were ultimately vanquished.

During a twenty-four year reign Chandragupta considerably swelled the already large empire seized from the Nandas. Ultimately, from the Magadha kingdom's capital city Pataliputra, the Mauryas would rule what was then the largest empire in the world. Under Mauryan control Pataliputra became a magnificent and highly prosperous city. According to Fa-hien, "the royal palace and the halls in the midst of the city, the walls and the gates and the inlaid sculpture work seemed to be the work of super-human spirits."[17]

Chandragupta was succeeded by his son Bindusara about 300 B.C.E. Bindusara's reign was one of economic expansion, with ever growing plots of land coming under cultivation.

Bindusara was succeeded by his son, Ashoka, the most singularly distinct personality of the Mauryan Dynasty and one of the great kings in India's long history. Ashoka was coronated around 268 B.C.E. after the ouster of several rival princes. Buddhist accounts say that while he began his reign in the militaristic traditions of Chandragupta and Bindusara, in 261 B.C.E. Ashoka underwent a profound transformation. The great human suffering brought on from his successful suppression of a major revolt in Kalinga, in what is now Orissa, caused Ashoka to renounce violence and adopt Buddhism as his personal religion.

Through Ashoka's new vision, a series of social reforms were instituted which were exceedingly humane and even radical for the time. Through Ashoka's own words we read: "There is no better work than promoting the welfare of the whole world. Whatever may be my great deeds, I have done them in order to discharge my debt to all beings."[18]

By Buddhist accounts we learn that in his later years Ashoka became so involved in the Buddhist council of monks that the affairs of state were neglected and the king was overthrown in a palace coup. Ashoka's lasting impact upon the world, however, has been extensive. Buddhist diplomats journeyed far and wide, including Egypt, Libya, Greece, Rome, Southeast Asia and probably China. To Sri Lanka Ashoka sent his own son with a branch of the Bodhi tree, under which Gautama had received enlightenment, as a peace gesture.

The Mauryan dynasty went into a period of rapid decline following Ashoka's reign. Combined, however, the Nanda and Mauryan dynasties represent the spectacularly abrupt seizure of power by the lowly Sudra caste, and their subsequent unbroken rule for more than 150 years. Following the destruction of the Indus Valley civilization, the Nanda and Mauryan dynasties were the next major examples of Black power in South Asia.

1.11.4.- The Dravidians

The Atricoid Dravidians were the founders of the great Indus Valley complex. They were the hated Dasas and Dasyus of the Rig Veda and the perpetual adversaries of the invading Aryan nomadic tribes. These were the very same peoples, Dasas and Dasyus, that later became the Sudras—the conquered Black masses reduced in Aryavarta to the status of slaves. As has been pointed out, the Harappan phase of the Indus Valley complex was already in decline when the Aryan incursions began to grow from a small trickle to a mighty torrent.

The Aryans were undeniably responsible for the destruction of the Indus Valley complex, and most of the identified Indus sites cease to be inhabited after this time. Those Blacks who had continued to people the Indus sites during the decline but prior to, the massive Aryan influx, either lost their lives during the holocaust or fled the region entirely with their remarkable cities ablaze behind them. The evidence is difficult to challenge on this point and the Aryans were cognizant of the ruins around them. The following Aryan passage illustrates our point most succinctly:

> "The people to whom these ruined sites, lacking posts, formerly belonged, these many settlements widely distributed, they, O' Vaisvanara, having been expelled by thee, have migrated to another land."[19]
>
> "Through fear of you (Agni) the dark people went away, not giving battle, leaving behind their possessions, when O Vaisvanara, burning brightly for Puru, and destroying the cities, you did shine."[20]

The lands the Blacks migrated to were both within and without India. This is certainly consistent with Dravidian traditions which recall flourishing cities that were lost or destroyed in ancient times. One might also see the links in the early seafaring posture of the Indus Valley people and the later Dravidian kingdoms of South India which were the great Indian maritime powers of their era.

To be clear then, when we speak of the Dravidians as a people we are speaking of the living descendants of the Harappan people of the ancient Indus Valley who were pushed into South India as the result of the Aryan invasions. The term Dravidian, however, encompasses both an ethnic group and a linguistic group. The ethnic group is characterized by straight to wavy hair textures, combined with physical features that tend to be Africoid.

Dravidian, in addition to its ethnic component, is also an important family of languages spoken by more than a hundred million people, primarily in South India. These languages include Tamil (the largest element), Kannada, Malayalam (from which the name of the Asian country Malaya is derived), Telegu and Tulu. The term Dravidian itself is apparently an Aryan corruption of Tamil.

1.11.5.- The Dravidian Female element

In the Indus Valley the mother goddess figure was conspicuous and this is most consistent with the early Black civilizations of both Africa and Asia. South India is no exception here and it has been noted that the Dravidian village deities are nearly all female, with the few exceptions in the Tamil country. In the Telugu districts, on the other hand, male deities are almost unrecognized in the Dravidian pantheon, the few who are being relegated to the position of subordinate attendants upon the female divinities who hold the supreme power.

James Hornell pointed out that:

> "This dominance of the female sex among the village divinities of the Dravidians who represented the main racial element present in India when the Aryan influx took place is characteristic and is the converse of what we know was the case in Brahmanism and, to a lesser degree in modem Hinduism. In the latter the supreme deities who divide between them the devotional adherence of the great mass of orthodox Hindus are both male—Shiva and Vishnu. It is true that their various energies or active principles, their saktis, are deified in the persons of their

wives, but this seeming exception is to be explained by the modifying influence exerted upon the orthodox Brahman faith by long and intimate contact with the aboriginal culture of the land—a culture which held mother goddesses as the most important divinities in its pantheon."[21]

1.11.6.- Dravidian Kingdoms

From at least the third century C.E. three major Dravidian kingdoms existed in South India—the kingdoms of Pandya, Chera and Chola. Pandya was the southernmost Dravidian kingdom. The major city of Pandya was Madurai, the location of the famous chapel of the Tamil Sangam (Academy). The Sangam, of which there were three, was initiated by a body of forty-eight exceptionally learned scholars who established standards over all literary productions. The Pandyan rulers received these intellectuals with lavish honors.

It is also important to note that in the kingdom of the Pandyas women seem to have enjoyed a high status. This is the exact opposite of the regions of India where the Whites ruled. In these lands of Aryan domination it is said that a woman was never independent. "When she is a child she belongs to her father. As an adult when she marries she belongs to her husband. If she outlives her husband she belongs to her sons." An early queen of the Pandyas, on theother hand, is credited with controlling an army of five hundred war elephants, four thousand cavalry and 13,000 infantry.

To the northwest of Pandya was the kingdom of Chera (present-day Kerala). Northwest of Pandya lay the kingdom of Chola, said to be the place where Saint Thomas the Apostle was buried. The Venetian traveler Marco Polo, who visited India in 1288 and again 1293, referred to Chola as "the best province and the most refined in all India."[22] Polo further exclaimed that:

> "The darkest man is here the most highly esteemed and considered better than the others who are not so dark. Let me add that in very truth these people portray and depict their gods and their idols black and their devils white as snow. For they say that God and all the saints are black and the devils are all white. That is why they portray them as I have described."[23]

The Dravidians were an unusually advanced seafaring people, with the Cholas, in particular, distinguishing themselves amongst the dominant maritime powers of their era. Through its ports, the great kings of Chola traded with Ethiopia and Somalia, Iran and Arabia, Cambodia and China, Sumatra and Sri Lanka, exporting spices and camphor, ebony and ivory, quality textiles and precious jewels.

The kingdoms of the Dravidians produced great poets and writers. Cuntarar, also known as Sundaramurti, was, during the eighth century, the most prominent of the highly esteemed Nayanars poets of Tamil Nadu, India. The Periya Puranam, which collects the legends of the Nayanars, starts and ends with him. The hymns of the seventh volume of the Tirumurai, the twelve-volume compendium of the poetry of Tamil Shaiva Siddhanta, were composed by him. Cuntarar is unique among the Nayanars in that both of his parents are also recognized as Nayanars. The ruler of the local kingdom (Thirumunaipadi-Nadu) adopted him. Tamil legend states that Cuntarar became tired of life and was taken up to heaven by a white elephant.

Kulashekhara Varma (800-820 C.E.), was a Tamil king who founded the second Chera Empire of South India. As king, Kulashekhara Varman united the present-day state of Kerala into a homogenous political entity that became a powerful force in South India for three centuries from 800 to 1102 C.E. He ruled from the capital city of Mahodayapuram (present Kodungallur). He is also one of the famous Hindu saints of the Vaishnavite movement of South India who composed one of the most celebrated devotional works of the Tamil Bhakti cult. It is believed that he renounced the crown to become a holy man and ascetic.

To the northeast of Pandya lay the Kingdom of Chola, said to house the resting place of Saint Thomas the Apostle. Aditya I was a monarch of the South Indian Kingdom of Chola, and led Chola to victory against the rival kingdoms of Pandya and Pallava. Around 885 C.E., in a mighty battle, the armies of Pandya and Nripatunga Pallava were routed by Aparajita Pallava and Aditya I of Chola. The epic Tamil novel Ponniyin Selvan describes this as a battle that changed the course of South India history. Aditya I also built a number of temples for Shiva along the banks of the Kaveri River. Aditya I had a long and victorious reign during which he laid the foundations for the future greatness of the Chola Empire.

The Dravidian kingdoms of South India were well known in the West, having sent several embassies to Rome in particular, in spite of the great distance involved. During the height of their commercial relations South India was said to extract 100 million sesterces annually from the Roman economy

Notes

1. David W. McAlpin, *"Toward Proto-Elamo-Dravidian,"* *Language, vol. 50, no. 1,* 89-101; see also David W. McAlpin, *"Elamite and Dravidian: Further Evidence of Relationship,"* *Current Anthropology, vol. 16, no. 1,* 105-115. The most fruitful efforts in the decipherment of the Indus Valley script have come as the result of utilizing modem Dravidian scripts as the foundation. Linguistic proof: In a combinatory analysis (AZ to 4) the linguistic type of the language of the Indus inscriptions appears to be agglutinative: of the languages known from the Indian subcontinent only the Dravidian languages belong to this type. The declension paradigm discovered fits to the declension of Dravidian. The alteration of a zero suffix and the genitive suffix which is attested in the Indus inscriptions is a characteristic of Dravidian. The decipherment displays an earlier stage of development of Dravidian, which corresponds to expectations (etymologies of suffixes). The word order is the same in Dravidian and the Indus inscriptions. The homophony laws are in accordance with the morpheme structure of Dravidian. *Journal of Tamil Studies,* Special Number on The Decipherment of The Mohenjo-daro Script, vol. 2, no. 1, May 1970.

2. Flavius Philostratus, *The Life of Apollonius of Tyana, book VI.*

3. Eusebius, quoted by George Rawlinson in *Ancient Monarchies, vol. 1* (New York: Dodd, Mead & Co., 1881), 49.

4. *The Itinerarium Alexandri,* 110.

5. Diodorus Siculus. Bk 1: 11, 12.

6. Samuel Purchas, *His Pilgrimage, book 7,* "Africa," page 551. Cited by J.A. Rogers, *100 Amazing Facts about the Negro with Complete Proof* (St. Petersburg: Helga M. Rogers, 1995), 29.

7. Walter A. Fairservis, "The Script of the Indus Valley Civilization," *African Presence in Early Asia,* eds. Ivan Van Sertima and Runoko Rashidi (New Brunswick: Transaction Press, 1985), 64-79.

8. *The Law of Manu,* trans. G. Buhler (Delhi: Motilal Barnarsidas, 1979), 78, 15, 16, 17.

9. 104.

10. 20.

11. 267, 268, 270.

12. 271, 272.

13. 303, 281, 282, 283.

14. 335

15. Nripendra Kumar Dutt, *The Aryanisation of India* (Calcutta: Firma K.L. Mukhopadhyay, 1970), 83-84. "A son of Mahanandin by a Sudra woman will be born a king,

Mahapadma (Nanda), who will exterminate all ksatriyas. Thereafter kings will be of Sudra origin. Mahapadma will be sole monarch, bringing all under his sole sway. He will be 88 years on the earth. He will uproot all ksatriyas, being urged on by prospective fortune. He will have 8 sons, of whom Sukalpa will be the first; and they will be kings in succession to Mahapadma for 12 years."

16. *Ancient India as Described by Ktesias the Knidian*, trans. and ed. J. McCrindle (London: Trubner, 1882), 84-85.

17. B.N. Puri, *Cities of Ancient India* (Meerut: Meenakski Prakashan, 1966), 64.

18. Romila Thapar, *Asoka and the Decline of the Mauryas* (Oxford University Press, 1973), 276.

19. *Hymns of the Rig Veda*, quoted by T. Burrow, "The Aryan Invasion of India," *The Encyclopedia of Ancient Civilizations*, ed. Arthur Cotterell (New York: Mayflower Books, 1980), 184.

20. *Hymns of the Rig Veda*, quoted by T. Burrow, 184.

21. James Hornell, "The Ancient Village Gods of South India," *Antiquity, vol. 18, no. 69* (1944), 82-83.

22. *The Travels of Marco Polo*, trans. R. Latham (Harmondsworth, Penguin, 1982), 277.

23. Polo, 276.

1.12.- Dalits: The Black Untouchables of India

The greatest victims of Hinduism have been those outside the caste system—the outcastes—better known as untouchables. Indeed, probably the most substantial percentage of all the Black people of Asia can be identified among India's two-hundred million Untouchables. These people are the long-suffering descendants of Aryan-Sudra unions and native Black populations who retreated into the hinterlands of India in their efforts to escape the advancing Aryan sphere of influence to which they ultimately succumbed. India's Untouchables number more than the combined populations of England, France, Belgium and Spain.

The existence of Untouchability has been justified within the context of Hindu religious thought as the ultimate and logical extensions of Karma and rebirth. Hindus believe that persons are born Untouchables because of the accumulation of sins in previous lives. Hindu texts describe these people as foul and loathsome, and any physical contact with them was regarded as polluting.

The basis status of India's Untouchables has changed little since ancient times, and it has recently been observed that caste Hindus do not allow Untouchables to wear shoes, ride bicycles, use umbrellas or hold their heads up while walking in the street.

Untouchables in urban India are crowded together in squalid slums, while in rural India, where the vast majority of Untouchables live, they are exploited as landless agricultural laborers and ruled by terror and intimidation. Even when charges are formally filed, justice for Untouchables is rarely dispensed.

Frequently the Untouchables are called Outcastes. Indian nationalist leader and devout Hindu Mohandas K. Gandhi called them Harijans, meaning children of god. The official name given them in India's constitution (1951) is Scheduled Castes. Dalit, meaning crushed and broken, is a name that has come into prominence only within the last four decades. Dalit reflects a radically different response to oppression.

The Dalit are demonstrating a rapidly expanding awareness of their African ancestry and their relationship to the struggle of Black people throughout the world. They seem particularly enamored of African-Americans. The Black Panther

Party, in particular, is revered. In April 1972, for example, the Dalit Panther Party was formed in Bombay, India. This organization takes its pride and inspiration directly from the Black Panther Party of the United States. This is a highly important development due to the fact that the Untouchables have historically been so systematically terrorized that many of them, even today, live in a perpetual state of extreme fear of their upper caste oppressors. This is especially evident in the villages. The formation of the Dalit Panthers and the corresponding philosophy that accompanies it signals a fundamental change in the annals of resistance, and Dalit Panther organizations have subsequently spread to other parts of India. In August 1972, the Dalit Panthers announced that the 25th anniversary of Indian independence would be celebrated as a day of mourning. In 1981, in Bangalore, India Dravidian journalist V.T. Rajshekar published the first issue of Dalit Voice—the major English journal of the Black Untouchables. In a 1988 publication entitled the African Presence in Early Asia, Rajshekar stated that:

> "The African-Americans also must know that their liberation struggle cannot be complete as long as their own blood-brothers and sisters living in far off Asia are suffering. It is true that African-Americans are also suffering, but our people here today are where African-Americans were two hundred years ago. African-American leaders can give our struggle tremendous support by bringing forth knowledge of the existence of such a huge chunk of Asian Blacks to the notice of both the American Black masses and the Black masses who dwell within the African continent itself."[1]

Notes

1. V.T. Rajshekar, *"The Black Untouchables of India,"* in *African Presence in Early Asia*, edited by Runoko Rashidi and Ivan Van Sertima (New Brunswick: Transaction Press, 1988), 242.

1.13.- The African Presence in Early Japan

By Runoko Rashidi, James E. Brunson
and Thabiti Asukile**"For a Samurai to be brave, he must have a bit of Black blood."**[1]

—Japanese Proverb

Although the island nation of Japan, occupying the extreme eastern extensions of Asia, is assumed by many to have been historically composed of an essentially homogeneous population and culture, the accumulated evidence (much of which has been quietly ignored) places the matter in a vastly different light, and though far more study needs to be done on the subject, it seems indisputable that Black people in Japan played an important role from the most remote phases of antiquity through at least the eighth century.

Reverend James Marmaduke Boddy, graduate of Lincoln and Princeton Universities, is the first known African-American writer to address the issue of the African presence in early Japan and China. In October 1905 the Colored American Magazine published Boddy's essay entitled *"The Ethnology of the Japanese Race."*

In *"The Ethnology of the Japanese Race"*, Boddy attempted to document what he considered a prominent and indelible African strain running through early Japanese history, and that the Japanese people are, at least in part, "Asian Negroes." Referencing the work of pioneer ethnologist and anthropologist James Cowles Prichard, M.D. (1786-1848), Rev. Boddy wrote that:

> "They are also described as having `peculiar features, `Crisp hair' and `dark complexion.' Besides their Negro features, which are very observable, the early Japanese historians themselves have described for us the `Black Barbarians of the South,' who, in an age which antedates authentic history, came from the south in ships and settled in Japan."[2]

Boddy concluded that:

"These immigrants mingled and amalgamated one with another and with the natives, and in time became a homogeneous race, whose predominating physical characteristics bespeak the unmistakable presence of a large Negro element."[3]

Meaningful indications of an African presence in ancient Japan have been unearthed from the most remote ages of the Japanese past. To begin with, and as a significant example, a February 15, 1986 report carried by the Associated Press, chronicled that:

"The oldest Stone Age hut in Japan has been unearthed near Osaka... Archeologists date the hut to about 22,000 years ago and say it resembles the dugouts of African bushmen, according to Wazuo Hirose of Osaka Prefectural Board of Education's cultural division."

'Other homes, almost as old, have been found before, but this discovery is significant because the shape is cleaner, better preserved' and is similar to the Africans' dugouts.[4]

1.13.1.- The physical anthropology of ancient Japan

As early as 1911 Professor Neil Gordon Munro, described as "one of the foremost students of Japanese life and culture," wrote that:

"The Japanese people are a mixture of several distinct stocks. Negrito, Mongolian... That the Japanese have inherited an infusion of Mongolian characters goes without saying, but breadth of face intraorbital width, flat nose, prognathism, and bracheephaly might be traced to the Negrito stock as dolichocephaly in Europe appears to have been derived from that of the Negro."[5]

In 1923 anthropologist Roland B. Dixon wrote that "this earliest population of Japan were in the main a blend of Proto-Australoid and Proto-Negroid types, and thus similar in the ancient underlying stratum of the population, southward along the whole coast and throughout Indo-China, and beyond to India itself."[6] Dixon pointed out that, "In Japan, the ancient Negrito element may still be discerned by characteristics which are at the same time exterior and osteologic."[7]

In his last major text, *Civilization or Barbarism: An Authentic Anthropology* (published posthumously in English in 1991), the brilliant Dr. Cheikh Anta Diop (1923-1986) pointed out that:

> "In the first edition of the Nations negres et culture (1954), I posited the hypothesis that the Yellow race must be the result of an interbreeding of Black and White in a cold climate, perhaps around the end of the Upper Paleolithic period. This idea is widely shared today by Japanese scholars and researchers. One Japanese scientist, Nobuo Takano, M.D., chief of dermatology at the Hammatsu Red Cross Hospital, has just developed this idea in a work in Japanese that appeared in 1977, of which he was kind enough to give me a copy in 1979, when, passing through Dakar, he visited my laboratory with a group of Japanese scientists.
>
> Takano maintains, in substance, that the first human being was Black; then Blacks gave birth to Whites, and the interbreeding of these two gave rise to the Yellow race; these three stages are in fact the title of his book in Japanese, as he explained it to me."[8]

As to linguistics, in 1987 former Senegalese president Leopold Sedar Senghor noted that, "The peoples who populate the island of Japan today are descendants from Blacks… Let us not forget that the first population of Japan was Black… and gave to Japan their first language."[9]

1.13.2.- Sakanouye no Tamuramaro: Sei-I Tai-Shogun of early Japan

Of the Black people of early Japan, the most picturesque single figure was Sakanouye no Tamuramaro, a warrior symbolized in Japanese history as "a paragon of military virtues," and a man who has captured the attention of some of the most distinguished scholars of twentieth century America (see appendix). Perhaps the first such scholar to make note of Tamuramaro was Alexander Francis Chamberlain (1865-1914). An anthropologist, Alexander Francis Chamberlain was born in Kenninghall, Norfolk, England, and was brought to America as a child. His family first settled in New York State near Rochester, but soon moved to Peterborough, Canada. In 1868 Chamberlain graduated from the University of Toronto with honors in languages and ethnology. In 1892 he received a Ph.D. from Clark University in Worcester, Massachusetts—the first such degree given for work in anthropology at an American university. Dr. Chamberlain was an assistant professor of Anthropology at Clark, and the department editor for the American Anthropologist and the American Journal of Archaeology. In April 1911 the *Journal of Race Development* published an essay by Chamberlain entitled "*The Contribution of the Negro to Human Civilization.*" While discussing the African presence in early Asia, Chamberlain stated in an exceptionally frank and matter of fact manner:

> "The contributions of the Negro to human civilization are innumerable and immemorial... And we can cross the whole of Asia and find the Negro again, for, when, in far-off Japan, the ancestors of the modem Japanese were making their way northward against the Ainu, the aborigines of that country, the leader of their armies was Sakanouye Tamuramaro, a famous general and a Negro."[10]

1.13.3.- The Sakanouye Family

In E. Papinot's *Historical and Geographical Dictionary of Japan*, the Sakanouye (also written Sakanoue) are described as an ancient family of warriors descended from Achi no Omi.[11] An account of the family's ancestors' move from Korea to Japan is found in the chronicle of Shoku nihongi in a petition for higher official rank made by Tamuramaro's father, Sakanouye no Karitamaro (728-786). Considered the most illustrious branch of the Aya family of immigrant descent, the Sakanouye maintained a long tradition of expertise in archery and horsemanship, becoming hereditary court generals in Japan beginning in the seventh century. Later members of the Sakanouye family, until the early fourteenth century, distinguished themselves as poets, scholars and legal experts.[12]

In 672 C.E., a civil war referred to as the Jinshin Disturbance ensued between the forces of the brother of Emperor Tenchi, Prince Oama, and the former's son, Prince Otomo. Passed over in the royal succession, Prince Oama angrily went into the eastem provinces of Yamato to enlist the military support of local influential families. Among the families solicited is the first mention of a Sakanouye-Okina (d. 699), great-grandfather of Karitamaro. Okina was a close associate of Prince Oama. Serving as a general to Oama, Okina was instrumental in crushing the forces of Prince Otomo, who ultimately committed suicide. With the uprising suppressed, Prince Oama ac-ceded to the throne as the Emperor Temmu.

It is said that the Emperor Temmu was so impressed by the bravery of the warriors of the east that he even thought of transferring the capital to that district.[13]

After the Jinshin Disturbance, the region to the east of Heiankyo became associated with the Azumabito, or "Men of the East."

This refers to a recognizable type, somewhat uncouth by Kyoto's standards, but courageous and skilled in the use of the bow, spear and sword... Heian Japan's frontier country could be called the 'Wild East', meaning the north as well as east of the Fuji Lakes.[14]

By the eighth century C.E., this group of private warriors dominated the country. According to George Sansom, there was no one to match these warriors, particularly the Imperial troops, who were not nearly of the same mettle:

> "They were known as Azumabito or Men of the East, and their praises were sung in early Japanese literature. The regular government forces in the eastern provinces were not of this mettle. Their commanders were so notably unsuccessful that in 783 the Emperor publicly rebuked them for cowardice and ordered a new campaign to be undertaken under competent leadership."[15]

The spread of Buddhism at this time by some Japanese emperors, put an incredible burden upon the general population. In 757 Tachibana no Nakamaro, under the pretext of assisting these people, staged a coup. Sakanouye no Karitamaro (728-786), father of Tamuramaro, helped suppress their revolt. In 764 Karitamaro assisted the Empress Koken Shotoku in crushing the rebellion of Fujiwara no Nakamaro. During this turbulent period Karitamaro demonstrated great bravery and military leadership, and later on became Chinjufu-Shogun.[16] Sakanouye no Tamuramaro continued this tradition, and followed his ancestors in service to the court.

1.13.4.- Sakanouye no Tamuramaro: paragon of Japanese military virtues

Sakanouye no Tamuramo is regarded as an outstanding military commander of the early Heian royal court. The Heian Period (794-1185 C.E.) derives its name from Heian-kyo, which means "the Capital of Peace and Tranquility," and was the original name for Japan's early capital city—Kyoto. It was during the Heian Period that the term samurai was first used. According to Papinot, the "word comes from the verb samurau, or better saburau, which signifies: to be on one's guard, to guard; it applied especially to the soldiers who were on guard at the Imperial palace."[17]

The samurai have been called the knights or warrior class of Medieval Japan and the history of the samurai is very much the history of Japan itself. For hundreds of years, to the restoration of the Meiji emperor in 1868, the samurai were the flower of Japan and are still idolized by many Japanese. The samurai received a pension from their feudal lord, and had the privilege of wearing two swords. They intermarried in their own caste and the privilege of samurai was transmitted to all the children, although the heir alone received a pension.

The "paragon of military virtues," Sakanouye no Tamuramaro (758-811) was, in the words of James Murdoch:

> "In a sense the originator of what was subsequently to develop into the renowned samurai class, he provided in his own person a worthy model for the professional warrior on which to fashion himself and his character. In battle, a veritable war-god; in peace the gentlest of manly gentlemen, and the simplest and most unassuming of men."[18]

According to his biographers, Tamuramaro steadily worked his way up through the military ranks, first serving as a lieutenant of the inner palace guards, advancing to minor captain, and then to middle captain. Tamuramaro, whose career began in the Nara Period (710-794 C.E.), was elevated to the rank of major captain and the office of major counselor by Emperor Saga. He was granted this promotion because of his knowledge of both civil and military codes.

As late as the Nara Period, the Ainu, who were possibly distributed throughout the whole of Japan thousands of years ago, held a considerable portion of northeastern Honshu, Japan's main island. By the eighth century the Ainu had become a formidable enemy of the expanding Japanese rulers.

Unsuccessful commanders in 783 were sharply rebuked by the Emperor Kammu for their cowardice and inability to drive out the Ainu, and were summarily dismissed. In 788 the emperor had the government assemble a mighty army and arsenal to confront this powerful enemy. Kammu demanded tribute from the provinces in the form of military armament. Kanto would provide adequate armor, Dazifu in Kyushu the iron helmets, and Tokaido and Tosando thousands of arrows. In that same year Japanese Imperial troops began fighting a series of bloody battles against mounted Ainu soldiers. This series of campaigns resulted in few victories, and in 791 the emperor summoned a "man of the east," appointing him the the title of "Envoy for the Pacification of the East." The deputy of this individual, who would go on to achieve far greater fame than his nominal superior, was Sakanouye no Tamuramaro. As stated by Sansom:

> "At length, in 791 a commander was appointed and given the title of Seito Taishi, or Envoy for the Pacification of the East; his deputy was one Sakanouye Tamura Maro, celebrated in Japanese history as a paragon of military virtues. Tamura Maro preceded his superior officer to the front in 793, and in 795 they both returned to the capital in triumph. But for a decade or more it was necessary to keep up the pressure against the Ainu and to encourage farmers to settle near the effective frontier so as to provide a permanent defence against raids and sallies, which Tamura Maro's successes had not entirely checked. In order to finish the affair he was given a new commission in 800 and sent off again. In a series of campaigns lasting until 803 he finally accomplished his purpose, and was able to push the frontier as far north as Izawa and Shiba, where strongholds were built and garrisoned. So important was his task in the eyes of the Court that the title of Sei-i Tai-Shogun or Barbarian-subduing Generalissimo, which he was the first to hold, was sought after by the highest military officers in the land for the next thousand years."[19]

Throughout his career, Tamuramaro was rewarded for his services with high civil as well as military positions. In 797 he was named "barbariansubduing generalissimo" (Sei-i Tai-Shogun), and in 801-802 he again campaigned in the north, establishing fortresses at Izawa and Shiwa and effectively subjugating the Ainu. In 810 he helped to suppress an attempt to restore the retired emperor Heizei to the throne. In 811, the year of his death, he was appointed great counselor (dainagon) and minister of war (hyobukyo).

Tamuramaro founded a shrine in the district of Izawa in Mutsu dedicated to Hachiman in which he hung up his bow and arrows. As has been said, this Tamuramaro was one of the very few soldiers whom military exploits had sufficed to raise to power and place in the councils of the State, and it was he that furnished the model on which successive generations of aspiring warriors endeavored to form themselves. Before starting on their expeditions, later Shoguns (Generals) invariably went to worship at his tomb and invoke the aid of his spirit.[20]

Sakanouye no Tamuramaro "was buried at the village of Kurisu, near Kyoto, and it is believed that it is his tomb which is known under the name of Shogun-zuka. Tamuramaro is the founder of the famous temple Kiyomizudera. He is the ancestor of the Tamura daimyo of Mutsu."[21] Tamuramaro "was not only the first to bear the title of Sei-i-tai-Shogun, but he was also the first of the warrior statesmen of Japan."[22] In later ages he was revered by military men as a model commander and as the first recipient of the title shogun-the highest rank to which a warrior could aspire.[23]

Notes

1. Cited by Cheikh Anta Diop, *African Origin of Civilization*, ed and trans. Mercer Cook (Westport: Lawrence Hill, 1974), 281.
2. James Marmaduke Boddy, "*The Ethnology of the Japanese Race*." The Colored American Magazine (October 1905), 582.
3. Boddy, 582.
4. "*African-Like Stone Age Hut is Unearthed in Japan*," Associated Press, February 15, 1986.
5. Neil G. Munro, *Prehistoric Japan* (Yokohama, 1911), 676-78.
6. Roland B. Dixon, *The Racial History of Man* (New York: Scribner's, 1923), 288.
7. Dixon, 287-92.
8. Cheikh Anta Diop, *Civilization or Barbarism*, trans. Yaa-Lengi Meema Ngemi, eds. Harold J. Salemson and Marjolijn de Jager (Westport: Lawrence Hill, 1991), 55.
9. "*Senghor Presents' Actual Facts' on Japanese: They're Descendants from Blacks*," The Final Call 6, No. 5 (1987).
10. Alexander Francis Chamberlain, "*The Contribution of the Negro to Human Civilization*," Journal of Race Development (April 1911), 484-85.
11. E. Papinot, *Historical and Geographical Dictionary of Japan, vol. 2* (New York: Frederick Ungar, 1964), 532.
12. William R. Carter, "*Sakanoue Family*," Kodansha Encyclopedia of Japan, vol. 6 (Tokyo: Kodansha, 1983), 379.
13. "*In Japan, East is East, and West is West*," The East Magazine 33 (1988), 7.
14. Richard Storry, The Way of the Samurai (New York: G.P. Putnam's Sons, 1978), 91.
15. George Sansom, *A History of Japan to 1334* (Stanford: Stanford University Press, 1958), 105.

16. Papinot, 532.
17. Papinot, 536.
18. James Murdoch, *A History of Japan, vol. 1* (London: Kegan Paul, Trench, Trubner & Co., 1925), 917.
19. Sansom, 106.
20. Murdoch, 273.
21. Yagi Atsuru, "*Sakanoue no Tamuramaro* (758-811)," *Kodansha Encyclopedia of Japan, vol. 6* (Tokyo: Kodansha, 1983), 379.
22. Murdoch, 221.
23. Papinot, 532-33.

1.14.- Sakanouye no Tamuramaro in the Works of Twentieth Century African Scholars

William Henry Ferris (1873-1941) attended Yale Graduate School, Harvard Divinity School, and Harvard Graduate School. He rose to assistant president general of the Universal Negro Improvement Association and became the literary editor of Marcus Garvey's Negro World newspaper. Ferris was the author of the highly popular The African Abroad: Or, His Evolution in Western Civilization, Tracing His Development Under Caucasian Milieu, published in two volumes in 1913. In volume two of The African Abroad, Ferris referenced Alexander Francis Chamberlain's article and reproduced his comments on Tamuramaro word for word.[1]

Among the greatest scholars in all of American history stands W.E.B. DuBois. A towering figure, a brilliant scholar and a prolific writer, William Edward Burghardt DuBois (1868-1963) was born February 23, 1868 in Great Barrington, Massachusetts. In 1896 DuBois became the first African-American to receive a Ph.D. from Harvard University. After teaching at Wilberforce University in Ohio and the University of Pennsylvania, he went on to establish the first department of sociology in the United States at Atlanta University. In his book, *The Negro* (first published in 1915), which significantly influenced the lives and careers of Drusilla Dunjee Houston and William Leo Hansberry, among others, Dr. DuBois placed Sakanouye Tamuramaro of Japan within a list of some of the most distinguished Black rulers and warriors in antiquity.[2]

Dubois actually visited Japan in 1937. Dr. DuBois also authored The *World and Africa: An Inquiry Into the Part that Africa has Played in World History*, first published in 1946, and in which mention is made of the Black presence in Japanese antiquity. DuBois was invited to Ghana in 1961 in the twilight of his life by President Kwame Nkrumah to head up a secretariat for an Encyclopedia Africana. W.E.B. DuBois died in Accra, Ghana August 27, 1963 as a Ghanaian citizen.

In 1922 Carter Godwin Woodson and Charles Harris Wesley (1891-1987), in a chapter called "Africans in History with Others," in their book *The Negro In Our History*, quoted Chamberlain on Tamuramaro verbatim.[3] Born in New Canton, Virginia, Carter Godwin Woodson (1875-1950) obtained a B.A. degree from the University of Chicago in 1907. In 1908 he attended the Sorbonne for one semester where he became fluent in French, and received a Ph.D. from Harvard University in 1912. Woodson taught briefly and held educational administrative posts in the Philippines, at Howard University and West Virginia State College. Woodson was a member of the Niagara Movement and a regular columnist for Marcus Garvey's weekly *Negro World*. In addition, he was the author of sixteen books about African people (including the *MisEducation of the Negro*), initiator of the annual February observation of Negro History Week, founder of the Association for the Study of Negro Life and History, and founder and editor of the *Journal of Negro History*. As a contributing writer for the *Journal of Negro History*, Dr. Woodson wrote more than a hundred articles and 125 book reviews. Woodson was also the founder of Associated Publishers, and the founder and editor of the *Negro History Bulletin*.

In the November 1940 issue of the *Negro History Bulletin*, Lois Mailou Jones contributed a brief article entitled "Sakanouye Tamura Maro." Lois Mailou Jones, born in Boston, Massachusetts, was an illustrator, artist, designer and water colorist. Jones was on the editorial board of the *Negro History Bulletin* and served as a professor in the College of Fine Arts at Howard University from the 1930s to the 1970s. In her article Jones pointed out that:

> "The probable number of Negroes who reached the shores of Asia may be estimated somewhat by the wide area over which they were found on that continent. Historians tell us that at one time Negroes were found in all of the countries of southern Asia bordering the Indian Ocean and along the east coast as far as Japan. There are many interesting stories told by those who reached that distant land which at that time they called 'Cipango.'
>
> One of the most prominent characters in Japanese history was a Negro warrior called Sakanouye Tamura Maro."[4]

Very similar themes were expressed in 1946 "In the Orient," the first section in *Distinguished Negroes Abroad*, a book by Beatrice J. Fleming and Marion J.

Pryde in which was contained a small chapter dedicated to "The Negro General of Japan-Sakanouye Tamuramaro."[5]

Joel Augustus Rogers (1880-1966) was a scholar unequaled in assembling data about African people. A real giant, Rogers probably did more to popularize African history than any single scholar of the twentieth century. Rogers was born in Negril, Jamaica September 6, 1880. In 1906 he moved to the United States and spent most of his life in Harlem. Rogers was an anthropologist, historian, journalist and a prolific writer. He covered the Marcus Garvey trial, and though never a member of the Universal Negro Improvement Association, wrote for Garvey's Negro World. In 1930 Rogers was elected to membership in the Paris Society of Anthropology.

Also in 1930, in Ethiopia, he attended the coronation of Haile Selassie as a correspondent for the Amsterdam News. Beginning in 1935, Rogers served as war correspondent for the Pittsburgh Courier during the Italian aggression in Ethiopia. He contributed to such publications as the *Crisis, American Mercury and Survey Graphic*. W.E.B. DuBois wrote that, "No man living has revealed so many important facts about the Negro race as has Rogers."[6]

In 1940 Rogers devoted several pages of the first volume of his *Sex and Race to the Black presence in early Japan*. He cites the studies of a number of accomplished scholars and anthropologists, and even goes as far as to raise the question of "Who were the first Japanese Negroes?" In the words of Rogers:

> "There is a very evident Negro strain in a certain element of the Japanese population, particularly those of the south. Imbert says, 'The Negro element in Japan is recognizable by the Negroid aspect of certain inhabitants with dark and often blackish skin, frizzly or curly hair. The Negritos are the oldest race of the Far East. It has been proved that they once lived in Eastern and Southern China as well as in Japan where the Negrito element is recognizable still in the population.'"[7]

Rogers mentioned Tamuramaro briefly in the first volume of *World's Great Men of Color*, also published in 1946. Regrettably, Rogers was forced to confess that "I have come across certain names in China and Japan such as Sakonouye Tamuramaro, the first shogun of Japan but I did not follow them up."[8]

Sakanouye Tamuramaro was a warrior symbolized in early Japanese history as a "paragon of military virtues." Could it be that this was what Cheikh Anta

Diop was alluding to in 1954 in his first major book, *Nations negres et culture*, when he directed our attention to the tantalizing and yet profound Japanese proverb: "**For a Samurai to be brave he must have a bit of Black blood.**"[9]

Gabriel K. Osei was born in Ghana during the late 1930s. He studied law at the University College and founded the African Publication Society. In 1968 in his book entitled Europe's Gift to Africa, Osei, like Ferris, Woodson and Wesley before him, cited Chamberlain's remarks on Tamuramaro.[10]

Adwoa Asantewaa B. Munroe referenced Tamuramaro in the 1981 publication *What We Should Know about African Religion, History and Culture* and cites Gabriel K. Osei's *African Contributions to Civilization* as the source. Of Tamuramaro, Munroe wrote that "He was an Mrican warrior. He was prominent during the rule of the Japanese Emperor Kwammu, who reigned from 782-806 A.D."[11]

In 1989 Mark Hyman, a doctoral candidate at Temple University, authored a booklet entitled *Black Shogun of Japan*. Hyman concluded his remarks on Tamuramaro by stating that

> "The fact remains that Sakanouye Tammamura Maro was an African. He was Japanese. He was a great fighting general. He was a Japanese Shogun."[12]

However the most comprehensive assessment to date of the Black presence in early Japan and the life of Sakanouye no Tamuramaro is art historian James E. Brunson's *The World of Sakanouye No Tamuramaro: Black Shogun of Early Japan* published in 1991. Brunson had previously published a series of detailed articles, monographs and books on the African presence in early Asia. In *The World of Sakanouye No Tamuramaro* Brunson accurately noted that "In order to fully understand the world of Sakanouye Tamuramaro we must focus on all aspects of the African presence in the Far East."[13]

Notes

1. William Henry Ferris, *The African Abroad, vol. 2* (New Haven: Tuttle, Morehouse & Taylor Press, 1913), 541-42.

2. W.E.B. DuBois, *The Negro* (1915; rpt. London: Oxford University Press, 1970), 84.

3. Carter G. Woodson and Charles H. Wesley, The Negro in Our History, 12th ed. (Washington, D.C.: Associated Publishers, 1972), 45. Historian, educator and admi-

nistrator, Charles Harris Wesley was born in Louisville, Kentucky in 1891. Wesley attended Columbia University and Guilde International in Paris; received a B.A. from Fisk in 1911, an M.A. from Yale in 1913 and a Ph.D. from Harvard in 1925. In 1930-31 he was the recipient of a Guggenheim Fellowship. ln 1913 Wesley joined the faculty of Howard University, eventually becoming a professor, department chairman and dean. Wesley served as editor of the Negro History Bulletin and in 1965 became the Director of the Association for the Study of Negro Life and History.

4. Lois M. Jones, "Sakanouye Tamura Maro," Negro History Bulletin 4, No. 2 (1940), 31.

5. Beatrice J. Fleming and Marion J. Pryde, *Distinguished Negroes Abroad* (Washington, D.C.: Associated Publishers, 1946), 3-9.

6. W.E.B. DuBois, *The World and Africa: An lnquiry lnto the Part thatAfrica Has Played in World History* (1946; rpt. New York: International Publishers, 1965), xi.

7. J.A. Rogers, *Sex and Race, vol. 1* (New York: Rogers, 1940), 68-70.

8. Rogers, *World's Great Men of Color, vol. 1* (1946; rpt. New York: Macmillan, 1972), 20.

9 Cheikh Anta Diop, *The African Origin of Civilization*, trans. Mercer Cook (Westport: Lawrence Hill, 1974), 281. Another recording of the proverb, documented by Maget and cited by Eugene Pittard, professor of Anthropology at the University of Geneva, in 1926 reads: "Half the blood in one's veins must be black to make a good Samurai." Eugene Pittard, *Race and History* (New York: Alfred A. Knopf, 1926), 408.

10. Gabriel K. Osei, *Europe's Gift to Africa* (London: African Publication Society, 1968), 23.

11. Adwoa Asantewaa B. Munroe, *What We Should Know About African Religion, History and Culture* (London: African Publication Society, 1981), 50.

12. Mark Hyman, *Black Shogun of Japan (Philadelphia: Mark Hyman Associates, 1989)*, 5.

13. James E. Brunson, *The World of Sakanouye No Tamuramaro* (DeKalb: Kara, 1991), 4.

1.15.- The Black Presence In Early China

What of the African presence in early China? Have there been Black people in China? If so, what became of them? What happened to the Black people of early China? Are they still there? These are profound questions. Indeed, the African presence in China is perhaps the most challenging area of research within the broad realm of the African presence in Asia. Challenging though it may be, however, it is not an area that can be dismissed. Chancellor Williams, for example, in his classic *Destruction of Black Civilization*, noted that:

> "Ancient China and the Far East, for example, must be a special area of African research. How do we explain such a large population of Blacks in Southern China, powerful enough to form a kingdom of their own?"[1]

While in September 1998, a scientific study posted in the Los Angeles Times concluded that:

> "Most of the population of modern China, one fifth of all the people living today, owes its genetic origins to Africa."[2]

From the realm of the physical anthropology of early China, according to the pre-eiminent scholar in the field, Kwan-chih Chang:

> "Skeletal remains from the Hoabinhian and Bacsoinan strata, similar to those found in southwest China, bear Oceanic Negroids features."[3]

Chinese scholar Chi Li wrote that:

> "Modern writers on Szechuan and Kansu have found traces of both the Negroid and Negrito in China."[4]

The first Black people in China then—the people who are probably the first of any people in China—were apparently Black people akin to the Batwa of Central Africa and the people of the Andaman Islands today—whom we call the Diminutive Africoids. They survived well into the historical periods. The presence of Diminutive Africoids (whom Chinese historians called Black Dwarfs) in early southern China during the period of the Three Kingdoms (ca. 250 C.E.) is recorded in the book of the Official of the Liang Dynasty (502-556 C.E.).[5]

Another of these Diminutive Africoid groups, this one in Taiwan and thought to be the original inhabitants of that island, were the focus of a 2004 report. According to an article in the Taipei Times entitled "In honor of the Little Black People":

> "The Saisiyat tribe of Hsinchu and Miaoli will perform a solemn rite this weekend to commemorate a race of people that they exterminated.
>
> "Drinking, singing and dancing are expected to take place deep in the mountains of Miaoli and Hsinchu when the 'Ritual of the Little Black People' is performed by the Saisiyat tribe once again this weekend.
>
> "For the past 100 years or so, the Saisiyat tribe has performed the songs and rites of the festival to bring good harvests, ward off bad luck and keep alive the spirit of a race of people who are said to have preceded all others in Taiwan.
>
> "In fact, the short, black men the festival celebrates are one of the most ancient types of modern humans on this planet and their kin still survive in Asia today. They are said to be diminutive Africoids and are variously called Pygmies, Negritos and Aeta. They are found in the Philippines, northern Malaysia, Thailand, Sumatra in Indonesia and other places.
>
> "Chinese historians called them 'black dwarfs' in the Three Kingdoms period (AD 220 to AD 280) and they were still to be found in China during the Qing dynasty (1644 to 1911). In Taiwan they were called the "Little Black People" and, apart from being diminutive, they were also said to be broad-nosed and dark-skinned with curly hair.
>
> "After the Little Black People—and well before waves of Han migrations after 1600—came the Aboriginal tribes, who are part of the Austronesian race. They are thought to have come from the Malay Archipelago 6,000 years ago at the earliest and around 1,000 years ago at the latest, though theories on Aborigine migration to Taiwan are still hotly debated. Gradually the Little Black People became scarcer, until a point about 100 years ago, when there was just a small group living near the Saisiyat tribe.
>
> "The story goes that the Little Black People taught the Saisiyat to farm by providing seeds and they used to party together. But one day, the Little Black People sexually harassed some Aboriginal women. So, the Saisiyat took revenge and killed them off by cutting a bridge over which they were all crossing. Just two Little Black People survived. Before departing eastward, they taught the Saisiyat about their culture and passed down some of their songs, saying if they did not remember their people they would be cursed and their crops would fail."
>
> "The Saisiyat kept their promise and have held the Ritual of the Little Black People every year."[6]

These Diminutive Africoids inhabit the Andaman Islands, a remote archipelago east of India, and are direct descendants of the first modern humans to have inhabited Asia, geneticists conclude in new studies. Their physical features, short stature, dark skin, peppercorn hair, and large buttocks are characteristic of so-called African Pygmies. Only four of the numerous groups that once inhabited the Andamans survive, with a total population of about five hundred people. These include the Jarawa, who still live in the forest, and the Onge, who have been settled there by the Indian government.

Similar groups of Black people have been identified in Japan, Vietnam, Cambodia and Indonesia, and it seems almost certain that at one time a belt of Black populations of this type covered much of Asia, including early China and especially southern China.

So there is little doubt that in the early ages of China a Black presence was prevalent. Now what of African presence in the great civilizations of China? Ivan Van Sertima always preached that "It is one thing to say that you were first and yet another to say what you did." So what did Africans do in ancient China? What was their status? What poisitons do we find them in?

Regarding the African presence in early China civilization, three dynasties in particular stand out—the Shang, the Tang and the Yuan.

The Shang Dynasty (1766-1027 B.C.E.), China's first dynasty, dating from the eighteenth to the eleventh century B.C.E., apparently had a Black background, so much so that the conquering Zhou described them as having "black and oily skin."[7] Bronze vessels, such as Le Tigresse are thus an extremely important component to our case and helps buttress our position.

Le Tigresse is by far the most spectacular of such vessels. It is a Yu vessel. In addition to Le Tigresse, in the Cernushi Museum in Paris, there is a similar and near identical artifact in the Sumitomo Collection in Kyoto, Japan.

Le Tigresse is from the late Shang Dynasty period, about 1250 B.C.E. It is from Hunan Province and measures about two feet high. The vessel was intended to hold fermented beverages and is unquestionably the most famous and splendid object in the Cernuschi Museum. The vessel depicts a feline, a tigress with an open mouth, holding a small human in a close embrace with its front paws. For years I had thought of the small human figure as a child. But on closer inspection it appears that it may well be an adult. Is it a Diminutive

Africoid? Whether adult or child, the features are clearly Africoid and may well be a depiction of one of the Diminutive Africoid types associated with early China, protected in the powerful embrace of a tigress.

The entire effect is accentuated by the dark green, almost black, brilliance of the vessel, and the calm demeanor shown in the the person's face suggests an ease and confidence in its surroundings. Le Tigresse was acquired by the Chernushi in 1920.

From the Tang Dynasty (618-907 C.E.) come statues of Africoid-looking dancers. I have photographed two such statues in both the Victoria and Albert Museum in London and the Smithsonian Museum in Washington, DC. They have spiral hair and seem to twirl around with one arm in the air topped by clenched fist. Were these the Black Dwarfs that we have read about in Chinese literature and Chinese tradition? Did they survive into the era of the Tang Dynasty?

In the Yuan Dynasty (1271-1368) founded by Kubilai Khan the Black presence is visible in a number of notable paintings. The first of these paintings is by the Yuan court artist Liu Guandao in 1280, now in the National Palace Museum in Taipei, Taiwan, is of a Mongol hunting scene. Specifically, the painting depicts two powerful looking Black men on horsebook with Kubilai Khan during a hunt. Kubilai Khan was arguably the most powerful man in the world at the time and the easy posture that these men are depicted in gives one reason to think that that they are more than the Khan's body guard, more than mere soldiers but quite possibly nobles or high officials of the Yuan court.

The second painting is a handscroll depicting "tribute bearers" towards the end of the Yuan Dynasty, about 1350 C.E. It is housed in the Asian Art Museum, Avery Brundage Collection, San Francisco. The painting depicts four Black men, one of which is of great prominence.[8]

What is most striking about the Shang Dynasty Yu vessels, the Tang Dynasty statues, and the Yuan Dynasty paintings—all clearly Africoid—is that race and ethnicity of the people depicted are never mentioned, and if one does not see these objects for themselves you would never guess, from reviewing the relevant literature, they were were Black.

Speaking of which, the famous Chinese sage, Lao-Tze (ca. 600 B.C.E.), by tradition, was "black in complexion." Lao-Tze was described as "marvelous and beautiful as jasper." Magnificent and ornate temples were erected for him, inside of which he was worshipped like a god.

Such is our brief sketch of the Black presence in early China. What I have found most interesting in my researches, including the work that I am doing on China today, is the failure, I am sure deliberate, to mention the race or ethnicity of clearly Africoid objects of art. Indeed, it seems to be even more extreme in the case of the African presence in Asia than the cover up of the African origins of ancient Egypt. This cover up—we must call it that—of the African presence in classical civilizations is truly a global phenomenon.

Notes

1. Chancellor Williams, The Destruction of Black Civilization (Chicago: Third World Press, 1976), 44

2. The Los Angeles Times, September 29, 1998.

3. Kwan-chih Chang, The Archaeology of Ancient China (New Haven: Yale University Press, 1963), 129.

4. Li Chi, The Formation of the Chinese People: An Anthropological Inquiry (1928; rpt. New York: Russell and Russell, 1967), 259.

5. Li Chi, 245.

6. Jules Quartly, The Taipei Times, November 27, 2004.

7. Cited by J.A. Rogers, Sex and Race, vol. 1 (St. Petersburg: Helga M. Rogers, 1968), 67.

8. Linda Komaroff, Gifts of the Sultan (New Haven: Los Angeles County Museum of Art, Yale University Press, 2011), 116-117.

1.16.- The Black Presence in Classical Southeast Asian Civilization: Cambodia and Vietnam

In early Southeast Asia the great kingdoms of Angkor in Cambodia and Champa in Vietnam were strongholds of Black power. The most prominent and enduring kingdom of early Southeast Asia was Angkor (802-1431). The builders of Angkor were an Africoid people known as Khmers, a name that loudly recalls Kmt (ancient Egypt). It is also interesting to note that the genealogies of Angkor, like Kmt, were matrilineal in character. In remote antiquity the Khmers established themselves throughout a vast area that encompassed portions of the modem countries of Myanmar, Thailand, Cambodia, Malaysia, Vietnam and Laos.

Much of our knowledge of early Southeast Asia is derived from Chinese and Indian sources. Chinese historical documents speak of the Funanese (the builders of the earliest kingdom in Southeast Asia) as "ugly and black. Their hair is curly."[1] The Khmer men, essentially the same as the Funanese, were described by the Chinese as "small and black."[2] In 1923 Harvard University anthropologist Roland Burrage Dixon noted that the ancient Khmers were physically "marked by distinctly short stature, dark skin, curly or even frizzly hair, broad noses and thick negroid lips."[3]

1.16.1.- The Kingdom of Chenla

By the middle of the sixth century, extensive agricultural reversals combined with the loss of cardinal trade routes had led to a drastic deterioration in Funan's stature and prestige. The focal point of regional domination was then transferred northwards to Chenla, where stone was in great abundance, and utilized as a major building material for the first time in the history of Southeast Asia. The Kingdom of Chenla, initially a vassal state of Funan, was the second significant Khmer kingdom and was divided into two parts—Upper Chenla and Lower Chenla. The southem state (Lower Chenla), bordering on the sea, was covered with lakes and waterways, and was called Water Chenla. The northem state

(Upper Chenla), which consisted of mountains and valleys, extended northward to the present Chinese province of Yunnan, and was called Land Chenla. The Chinese called Upper Chenla Wen Tan and Polieu. In 722 Upper Chenla joined in a war against the Chinese governor of Chiao-chou (Tonkin). Te leader of the revolt defeated the Chinese forces, conquered Chiao-chou and proclaimed himself Hei-ti, "Black Emperor."[4] The chronicle of the Khmer Kingdom of Chenla is much the same as that of Funan. After many decades of prosperity, late during the eighth century trade with India was disrupted, resulting in a severe administrative break down and Chenla's descent into oblivion.

1.16.2.- The Kingdom of Angkor

Early in the ninth century Jayavarman II (802-850) unified the Khmer kingdom and identified himself with the powerful Hindu deity Shiva. The Khmers of Angkor were sophisticated agriculturalists, advanced engineers, aggressive merchants and intrepid warriors. They developed a splendid irrigation system (with some canals extending forty miles in length), and created grandiose hydraulic works. The hydraulic system of Angkor was used for transportation and for rice cultivation to support a surrounding population estimated at one million people. During the reign of King Indravarman I (877-889), for example, the vast artificial lake known as the Indratataka was completed. It was also during the reign of Indravarrnan that inscriptions began to refer to the kingdom of the Khmer as Kambuja, or Kambujadesa—the origin of the modern name of Kampuchea (the country formerly called Cambodia). The Chinese continued to call the whole country Chenla, and the Khmers engaged in extensive international trade with both India and China. For the harsh purposes of war the Khmer engineers designed machines to launch fearsome arrows and hurl sharp spears at their enemies, and rode boldly into battle atop ornately outfitted elephants.

In the Khmer language, Angkor means the city or the capital. In 889 King Yasovarman I (889-900) constructed his capital on the current site of Angkor, and over the centuries Khmer monarchs augmented the city with their own distinct contributions. Notably, it was during the reigns of Rajendravarrnan

II (944-968) and Jayavarrnan V (969-1001) that the East Mebon, Pre Rup, Banteay Srei, Phimeanakas and Ta Keo temples were constructed.

Angkor eventually covered an expanse of seventy-seven square miles and was designed to be completely self-sufficient. The Khmers were magnificent builders in stone and for more than six-hundred years successive Angkor dynasties commissioned the construction of meticulously detailed temples, such as Banteay Samre, marvelous artificial lakes like the Indratataka, and incomparable temple-mountains, including Angkor Wat—the crown jewel of Angkor and estimated to contain as much stone as the Dynasty IV pyramid of King Khafre in Old Kingdom Kmt.

1.16.3.- Angkor Wat

Called "the largest stone monument in the world," Angkor Wat, the most famous of the Khmer stone structures, took thirty-seven years to build.[5] During this period millions of tons of sandstone used in its construction were transported to the site by river raft from a quarry at Mount Kulen, located twenty five miles to the northeast. Angkor Wat rises in three successive flights to five central towers that represent the peaks of Mount Meru—the cosmic or world mountain that lies at the center of the universe in Hindu mythology and considered the celestial residence of the Hindu pantheon. The towers of Angkor Wat (the tallest of which rises about two hundred feet above the surrounding flatlands) are Cambodia's national symbol. The temple's outer walls represent the mountains at the edge of the world, while the moat surrounding the temple represents the oceans beyond.

Angkor Wat dates from the twelfth century reign of Suryavarman II (1113-1150) when the Khmer dominion over Southeast Asia was at its zenith, with an empire "stretching from the South China Sea to modern Thailand, as far north as the uplands of Laos and as far south as the Malay Peninsula. Until the time of Jayavarman VII, Suryavarman II was the most powerful king in the country's history and the first Angkorean king since Jayavarman II to send missions to China. Warlike, aggressive and ambitious, Suryavarman II built Angkor Wat as a funerary temple for himself and dedicated it to the Hindu god Vishnu, whom the king represented on Earth and with whom he integrated on his death."[6]

Angkor Wat is decorated throughout with intricate bas-reliefs depicting stories from the epic Hindu poems, the Mahabharata and the Ramayana (narrating the myths of Krishna, Vishnu and Rama), with marching armies and more than 1,700 vivid and sensual depictions of the celestial female dancers of the Khmers known as apsaras. French architect and archaeologist Henri Parmentier gave his opinion of the apsaras of Angkor Wat in 1923 when he said that, "To me they are Grace personified, the highest expression of femininity ever conceived by the human mind."[7] To the members of the Khmer court, a walk to the center of Angkor Wat was a metaphorical trip of the spirit to the center of the universe.

1.16.4.- The Kingdom of Champa

Angkor was not the only significant kingdom of its time in Southeast Asia. Another major Southeast Asian power and sometimes rival of Angkor was the Kingdom of Champa. Champa was the great kingdom of the Blacks on the coast of Southeast Asia. Indeed, the facial characteristics on the statues of the Cham are as Africoid as any anywhere, including full lips and broad noses.

While Champa, like Angkor, was a substantially indianized kingdom, the Cham are believed to have settled along the coastal plains of mid-southern Vietnam (Annam) more than two millennia ago, The economy of Champa was based on agriculture and maritime trade. They exported rice and forest products, including sandlewood, and essentially dominated the area from about the fourth through the thirteenth centuries.

According to one account, the Kingdom of Champa was born of a victory by the Blacks "over the Chinese province of Je-Nan in + 137; later, it frequently demonstrated its unruliness and spirit of conquest, including against China, of which it had become theoretically a tributary."[8]

Chinese dynastic records from as early as 192 C.E. reference a kingdom of Lin-yi, which meant the "land of Black men."[9] The kingdom of Lin-yi was known as Champa in Sanskrit documents. Its inhabitants possessed "'black skin, eyes deep in the orbit, nose turned up, hair frizzy' at a period when they were not yet subject to foreign domination and preserved the purity of this type."[10] These records expressly state that:

> "For the complexion of men, they consider black the most beautiful. In all the kingdoms of the southern region, it is the same."[11]

Chinese scribes added that the Cham adorned themselves:

> "In a single piece of cotton or silk wrapped about the body... They are very clean; they wash themselves several times each day, wear perfume, and rub their bodies with a lotion compounded with camphor and musk."[12]

H. Otley Beyer believed that between 900 and 1200 C.E. a group of seafarers made their exodus from Southern Annam and found their way to the Philippines. They were called the "Orang Dampuans or Men of Champa." "The Orang Dampuans," wrote Beyer, "were the first civilized foreigners to establish a settlement in Sulu, according to the most reliable of pre-Mohammedan histories."[13] During this same period Cham ships, known to the Chinese by the appellation kun-lun bo (the "vessels of Black men"), were navigating the currents of the Indian Ocean ranging from Southeast Asia to Madagascar.[14]

Among the major centers of Champa were those based near Dong Duong, Tra Kieu and Pandulanga (Phan-Rang). The great southern capital was Vijaya (Binh Dinh), and the early northern capital and religious center was Mi Son.

From its inception in the fifth century, Mi Son was a cardinal center of Brahminic worship. More than seventy temples were constructed at Mi Son from the seventh through the twelfth centuries. The masterpiece of Cham architecture at Mi Son was an enormous, seventy-foot-high stone tower that was destroyed by United States army commandos in August 1969.

1.16.5.- Early Kings of Champa

Fan Hsiung, or Pham Hung, was the king of Champa in the 270s CE. In 270, T'ao Huang, the Chinese governor of Giao Chi, reported that Fan Hsiung was repeatedly assaulting his land with the aid of Funan. Both Champa in Vietnam and Funan in Cambodia were early kingdoms of the Blacks in Southeast Asia. It is said for the men in these lands that "Black was considered the best complexion." In Funan itself, the men were described as "small and Black." This was a time when Blacks were clearly dominant in Southeast Asia. And they would remain so for hundreds of years to come.

Fan Tat, or Pham Dat, was the king of Champa from 284 to 336. In 284, he sent the first Cham envoy to the Eastern Chin Emperor. Fan Tat died in 336 and was succeeded by his commander-in-chief, Fan Wen. At this early date in Southeast Asian history, the Blacks of the region were dominant. Their presence and influence is found in Vietnam, Cambodia, Thailand, and Myanmar. But it is during this very time of the early kings of Champa that their presence is beginning to be challenged by the population pressures of the Asians in China to the north. It is a pivotal time in Black history.

Fan Wen was the king of Champa from 336 to 349. He was the commander-in-chief of the army and, after Fan Tat's death in 336, seized the throne. In 340, he sent an embassy to China to request the province of Giao Chi. His request was denied. Fan Wen recaptured Jen Nan in 347. He died two years later on another campaign. This period is considered the dawn, the morning time, of civilization in Southeast Asia. It is an era dominated by the Blacks, the study of which is still in its infancy. Indeed, Champa was not to reach its apogee until the ninth and tenth centuries CE.

Fan Fat, or Pham Phat, was the king of Champa from 349 to 380. In 353, he was defeated by the Chinese governor of Jiaozhi. The governor also recaptured Jen Nan, which was previously captured by Fan Fo's predecessor, Fan Wen. The Kingdom of Champa lay along the coasts of present-day central and southern Vietnam. It was the kingdom of the Blacks in early Vietnam. It was a civilization heavily influenced culturally by both India and China. It was a contemporary and rival of the much more famous kingdom of Angkor in neighboring Cambodia. It lasted for more than a thousand years.

Fan Hu Ta was the king of Champa, the kingdom of the Blacks in Central Vietnam, from 380 to 413. In 380, Fan Hu Ta took the throne under the royal name Bhadravarman I. In the same year, he moved the capital to Indrapura in Quang Nam Province. He built temples and palaces at the important centers of My Son and Tra Kieu. In 399, he succeeded in capturing the Vietnamese provinces of Nhat Nam and Cuu Chan, and continued on his temple-building campaign as well, building Cham towers along the coast. From 405 to 413, he continuously battled the Chinese governor Do Tue.

1.16.6.- Pressures from the north

By the beginning of the tenth century the Cham were being aggressively pressured and gradually absorbed by Sinicized Vietnamese. By the end of the tenth century, Sinicized Vietnamese had annexed the northern provinces of Champa. In 1225 the Vietnamese once again followed a course of aggression, and in 1283 the Mongols under Kublai Khan desolated the entire coast. All told, however, more than a hundred temples and a multitude of exquisite statuary have survived to remind us of the former splendor of the traders, artisans and royalty of the realm of the Cham.

During the eleventh and twelfth centuries Champa, whose ethnic character was being rapidly transformed by the influx of Sinicized Vietnamese, was engaged in intense martial conflicts with Angkor. In 1177 a Cham fleet sailed up the Mekong River and sacked Angkor—an event chronicled in a bas-relief at the Bayon. In defense of Angkor, an exiled Khmer prince who would come to be known as Jayavarman VII, gathered formidable armies, shattered the Cham forces and drove them from Angkor.

Che Bong Nga ruled Champa from 1360 to 1390 C.E. Che Bong Nga was the last powerful king of Champa and apparently managed to reunite the Cham lands under his rule. Indeed, Che Bong Nga threatened to retake all of the lost Cham territories seized by their enemies, the Viets. In 1383, the Cham even laid siege to the Vietnamese capital of Thang Long—now Hanoi.

1.16.7.- King Jayavarman VII: Angkor's most prolific builder

The reign of Jayavarman VII (1181-1220) marks the height and the beginning of the decline of the kingdom of Angkor. Jayavarman VII (the prefix of whose name, Jaya, in Sanskrit, means "victory") was so successful in his military campaigns with Champa, in fact, that during the last seventeen years of his reign Champa was virtually a Khmer province. Jayavarman VII lived more than nine decades, ruling with strength and wisdom. Almost "all of the earlier kings of Angkor had been Hindus, but Jayavarman VII was a devout Buddhist monarch whose second wife, Indradevi (described as "intelligent by nature, scholarly, very pure, devoted to her husband"), became chief lecturer at a Buddhist foundation.[15]

In 1181, Jayavarman VII was proclaimed king in the battled-scarred and essentially devastated Khmer capital, and many of the monuments of Angkor reflect his Herculean reconstruction efforts and seemingly ceaseless building projects. Jayavarman VII built more than any other Khmer king. Indeed, it is calculated that he built more than all the others put together. In fact, as magnificent as it is, Angkor Wat is only one of 215 sites in the immediate region. Other famous sites include the Bayon, the sculptured stone mountain at the center of the six-square-mile walled city of Angkor Thom, about a mile northeast of Angkor Wat, and the capital of the Khmer empire from the late tenth through the early thirteenth century. "To protect Angkor Thom, Jayavarman constructed a moated stone wall around the city, with five monumental bridges."[16]

1.16.8.- The Bayon

The Bayon, an Angkor temple second in size only to Angkor Wat, is an intricate, eight hundred-year-old shrine celebrated for the gigantic stone faces of its builder, Jayavarman VII. In 1297 a Chinese diplomat named Chou Takuan described the Bayon as shining with gold, and exclaimed that:

> "On the eastern side is a golden bridge, guarded by two lions of gold, one on each side, with eight golden Buddhas spaced along the stone chambers. North of the Golden Tower, at a distance of about two hundred yards, rises the Tower of Bronze (Baphuon), higher even than the Golden Tower: a truly astonishing spectacle, with more than ten chambers at its base. A quarter of a mile further north is the residence of the King. Rising above his private apartments is another tower of gold. These are the monuments which have caused merchants from overseas to speak so often of 'Cambodia the rich and noble.'"[17]

An inscription on the Bayon temple pertaining to Jayavarman states that, "He suffered from the sicknesses of his subjects more than from his own: for it is the public grief which makes the grief of kings and not their personal grief."[18]

1.16.9.- The Ta Prohm and Preah Khan Temples

The Ta Prohm and Preah Khan temples, monuments almost as large as Angkor Wat, were also erected by the prolific Jayavarman VII and were designed by him as mausoleums for his mother and his father (Dharanindravarman II), respectively. The inscription of Ta Prohm reveals that there were 102 hospitals in the Khmer empire when Jayavarman VII reigned. The medical personnel in each hospital consisted of two doctors, two pharmacists, fourteen guardians, eight male nurses, six female nurses, six orderlies, two cooks, two clerks and sixty general assistants.

The Preah Khan temple, a veritable labyrinth of pavilions, halls and chapels, immerses about a square mile of ponderously wooded land just north of the enclosed city of Angkor Thom. According to the dedicatory stele dating to 1191, the site sheltered 515 pietistic portraits, which were embellished with immense quantities of silk veils and golden jewelry set with diamonds, emeralds and pearls.

1.16.10.- The Decline and Fall of Angkor and Champa

After the death of Jayavarman VII Angkor began to decline, and no great monuments were constructed after his reign. Jayavarman VII was succeeded by Indravarman II (1219-1243). His successor, Jayavarman VIII (1243-1295), reestablished Brahminic dominance at the Khmer court, and by the beginning of the fifteenth century the entire kingdom was on the verge of total collapse. During the fifteenth century the Khmers endeavored to repulse a steady series of Thai invasions and preserve the last vestiges of classical Khmer civilization.

Although the early people of the country now known as Thailand clearly reflect a pronounced Africoid phenotype (based on numerous depictions of Buddhas and Bodhisattvas), the people referred to here as Thai (sometimes called Siamese) were originally a tribal people without writing or an organized state. The Thai invaders of Angkor were Sinicized or Mongoloid types generally believed to be ethnically related to modern Chinese. In any case, they, or at least a large group or groups of them, lived in the southern and southeastern portions of the country now known as China. Similar peoples, Sinicized Vietnamese, brought about the final destruction of the kingdom of Champa in 1471.

> "Champa's decline gathered pace. It suffered incessant raids at the hands of the Dai Viet, and also internecine strife, wih five monarchs in succession ascending the throne in a mere thirty years. The final blow came in 1471. In retaliation for an attack by the Cham king, the Vietnamese king Le Thanh Tong mounted a carefullly prepared two-pronged attack by land and sea, putting the Cham army to flight. He captured Vijaya and razed it to the ground, beheading more than forty thousand people, and deporting more than thirty thousand others. He then embarked on the systematic destruction of everything connected with Hinduised Cham culture, thus wiping it out completely."[19]

Just like the pressures of the Dai Viet on Champa, the Thai invasion of Angkor was a life or death struggle for the Khmers. Able bodied Khmer men and the last remnant of the Khmer intelligentsia were abducted as captives and carried away, and the intricate irrigation system of Angkor, which required constant innovation and vigilance, ceased to work effectively. Archaeological excavations have shown that the Thais blocked the canals at Angkor, so that Kingdom of Angkor's complex and elaborate irrigation system was virtually ruptured. In 1431, after a seven month siege, the Thais occupied and ravaged Angkor and pilfered many of its statues. By the end of 1432 came the physical abandonment of Angkor by the Khmer court and the removal of the capital, first to the province of Srei Santhor and later to Phnom Penh and Oudong.

Angkor was eventually retaken from the Thais and even experienced a brief renaissance in the late sixteenth century, but soon afterwards slipped into obscurity. However even as late as 1860, a young French scholar and scientist, Henri Mouhot, recorded in his diary that "It is grander than anything left to us by Greece or Rome."[20] Visiting the site for the first time, Mouhot wrote that:

> "In the province still bearing the name of Ongcor [Angkor], there are... ruins of such grandeur, remains of structures which must have been raised at such an immense cost of labor, that at first view one is filled with profound admiration and cannot but ask what has become of this power-ful race, so civilized, so enlightened, the authors of these gigantic works."[21]

And thus were eclipsed the bright shining lights of the Black presence in Southeast Asian civilizations—the kingdom of Angkor and the kingdom of Champa. The ultimate fate of the Black kingdoms of Southeast Asia can be effectively linked to the rising influx of Mongoloid racial types from the north. Indeed, the fifteenth century Dai Viet destruction of Champa recalls the Roman destruction and eradication of ancient Carthage.

Notes

1. Quoted in Lawrence Palmer Briggs, *The Ancient Khmer Empire* (Philadelphia: American Philosophical Society, 1951), 16.
2. Quoted in Briggs, 50.
3. Roland B. Dixon, *The Racial History of Man* (New York: Scribner's, 1923), 226.
4. Quoted in Briggs, 59.
5. Russell Ciochon and Jamie James, "*The Battle of Angkor Wat*," *New Scientist*, October 14, 1989, 52.
6. Ciochon and James, 52.
7. Hemi Parmentier, quoted in Michael Freeman and Roger Warner, *Angkor: The Hidden Glories*, ed. David Larkin (Boston: Houghton Mifflin, 1990), 182.
8. B. Domenichini-Ramiaramanana, "*Madagascar*," *in UNESCO General History of Africa, Vol. 3. Africa from the Seventh to the Eleventh Century*, ed. M. El-Fasi (Berkeley: University of California Press. 1988), 696.
9. Xu Yun-qiao, quoted in Domenichini-Ramiaramanana, 697.
10. Quoted in Georges Maspero, *The Kingdom of Champa* (New Haven: Yale University Press, 1949), 8.
11. Nan Ts'i Chou, quoted in Maspero, 8.
12. Quoted in Russell Ciochon and Jamie James, "*Land of the Cham*," *Archaeology* (May/June 1992), 52.
13. Quoted in Pedro A. Gagelonia, *The Filipinos of Yesteryears* (Manila: Star Book Store, 1967), 82.
14. Domenichini-Ramiaramanana, 697.
15. Christopher Pym, *The Ancient Civilization of Angkor* (New York: Mentor-New American Library, 1968), 145.
16. Russell Ciochon and Jamie James, "The Glory that was Angkor," Archaeology 47, No. 2 (1994), 43.
17. Chou Ta-Kuan, *The Customs of Cambodia*, trans. Paul Pelliot and J. Gilman d'Arcy Paul (Bangkok: *The Siam Society*, 1987), 1.

18. Quoted in Christopher Pym, 153.
19. Emmanuel Guillon, *Cham Art* (Bangkok: River Books, 2001), 19.
20. Henri Mouhot, quoted in Freeman and Warner, 9.
21. Henri Mouhot, quoted in Russell Ciochon and Jamie James, "*The Glory that was Angkor*," Archaeology 47, No. 2 (1994), 40.

1.17.- A Brief Note on the Black Presence in the Philippines, from the Diminutive Africoids to David Fagen—African-American Rebel

Although the great majority of the people of the Philippines today are Tagalog, the country is not racially monolithic. In spite of their small numbers today the original inhabitants of the Philippines are the Diminutive Africoids, who still live in scattered communities in the Phillipines and are commonly and pejoratively called *Pygmies, Negritos, Aeta*, and a variety of other names based upon their specific locale. The word Aeta, a widely-used Tagalog term meaning filthy, is especially derogatory.

At least one group of Diminutive Africoids in the Philippines is known as the Agta (the People). I am, however, reluctant to the use the term Agta as a blanket term for the entire population of Diminutive Africoids in the Philippines for fear of lumping groups together with broadly similar phenotypes but not necessarily cultural similarities. Such an approach would only tend to perpepuate an injustice to an already wounded sense of humanity to a once proud people. In regard to phenotype, broadly speaking, these Black people can be described as short in stature, dark-skinned, spiral-haired and broad-nosed. They are an extremely ancient people and are no doubt modern representatives of the world's earliest-known modern humans.

In stark contrast to the Diminutive Africoids, the Tagalog majority seem to have only entered the Philippines during the last several thousand years, and while not enough is known of the early history of the Diminutive Africoids in the Philippines it has been well-documented that they engaged in bitter martial conflicts with the Spanish invaders, whose presence in the islands began in the sixteenth century. It was the Spaniards who named the aboriginal people of the Philippines Negritos, meaning Little Blacks.

The Spanish observed that "The Negritos, which our first conquerors found, were, according to tradition, the first possessors of the islands of this Archipelago."[1] Another account observed that "There are black negroes in this island who pay tribute to no one."[2] Similar documents affirm the widespread presence and distribution of Diminutive Africoids in the Philippines at the time of the Spanish intrusion. For example, one account states that, "If we are to believe later historians, the shores of some of the islands fairly swarmed with Negritos when the Spaniards arrived."[3] The Bisayan island of Negroes derives its name from having been a Black population center.[4] Today, however, the Blacks probably comprise less than one per cent of the total population of the Philippines and are treated as outcastes in their own land.

Historically, the Diminutive Africoids amassed quite a reputation as warriors, and although the accuracy of the report is somewhat questionable, it is said that the Blacks were "such enemies to the Spaniards, that if they happen to kill one, they invite all their kindred, and rejoice for three days, drinking out of the skull, clear'd for that purpose; by which means, they afterwards get wives the easier, as being more courageous."[5]

Dr. Pedro A. Gagelonia, a Filipino scholar, citing the commentaries of the European colonizers of the Philippines regarding the Blacks, wrote that:

> "They were the aborigines of the Philippines, and for a long time had been master of Luzon. At a time not very far distant, when the Spaniards conquered the country, the Aetas levied a kind of blackmail from the Tagalog villages situated on the banks of the lake of Bay (Laguna de Bay). At a fixed period they quitted their forests, entered the village, and forced the inhabitants to give them a certain quantity of rice and maize... After the conquest of the Philippines by the Spaniards, the latter took upon themselves the defense of the Tagalogs, and the Aetas, terrified by their firearms, remained in the forests, and did not reappear among the Indians."[6]

These are the Diminutive Africoids—the first people of the Phillipines. Once a proud people, today, they are generally despised by their Tagalog countrymen. They were, however, at one time, for thousands of years, the masters of the land.

Collectively, the story of the first people of the Philippines—the Diminutive Africoids—is truly fascinating. Individually, the story of David Fagen, an African-American soldier in the US Army stationed in the Phillipines during the Philippine Insurection (1899-1901) who defected to the Filipino freedom fighters, is remarkable, and especially in its symbolism.

In November 1899, when in his early twenties, US Arny Corporal David Fagen defected from the Twenty-fourth Infantry Regiment and went over to the revolutionary insurrectionist forces led by Emilio Aguinaldo. Working with the insurrectionist army, Fagen quickly distinguished himself as a guerilla fighter against his former comrades and fought so effectively that he was referred to as "General Fagen" by his Filipino companions. Indeed, as his exploits became widely known he was actually referred to as "General Fagen" in the New York Times newspaper. Officially, he was quickly promoted by the guerillas from first lieutenant to captain. From August 1900 to January 1901 he was involved in at least eight clashes with US forces.[7]

As pressure was brought to bear on the insurrectionist forces and the major rebel leaders were dead or captured, Fagen's position became more and more tenuous. Indeed, the US Army became obsessed with his capture and put a substantial bounty on his head.

Fagen's end is not clear. One account has him assassinated and decapitated. Another has him living long and peacefully in the mountains of the Philippines within a supportive and embracing Diminutive Africoid community. The latter account is very pleasing to me.

Notes

1. Cited in Pedro A. Gagelonia, *The Filipinos of Yesteryears* (Manila: Star Book Store, 1967), 82.
2. Francisco Combes, *Historia de las Islas de Mindanao, Joly y sus Adjacentes* (Madrid, 1667), Cited by Gagelonia, 103.
3. William Allan Reed, *The Negritos of Zambales* (Manila, 1940).
4. A.L. Kroeber, *Peoples of the Philippines, 2d edition* (New York: American Museum of Natural History, 1943), 39.
5. Gagelonia, 111.
6. Gagelonia, 113-15.
7. For an excellent account of Fagen's life see Michael G. Robinson and Frank N. Schubert, "David Fagen: An Afro-Ameriocan Rebel in the Philippines, 1899-1901," *Pacific Historical Review* (February 1975): 68-83.

1.18.- Africans in Asia During the Age of Enslavement

One thing that we have not done here and will not do is begin our survey of the African presence in Asia with enslavement. Indeed, we think that perhaps the greatest crime that we can commit is to teach our children that their history begins with invasion, enslavement and colonization. Our work here is therefore distinguished from the work of other diasporan scholars. Many scholars insist on examining the African Diaspora only from the perspective of enslavement, and use this foundation as the basis for all things.

Enslavement and its aftermath is not the entirety of the African experience in Asia. Yes, obviously, it is important, even essential. But we should not start there. Indeed, what we have endeavored to do here is to look at the enslavement and subjugation of Black people in Asia from the perspective of Black resistance to it and protest of it. We are not looking only at Black people as victims, but as men and women determined to control their lives and destinies.

The story of the African presence in early Asia would be incomplete without an expose of the African role as servant and slave. The subject of African enslavement anywhere is clearly the most sensitive and delicate of historical issues, and all too often it is asserted that the great international movements of Africans occurred only under the guise of slavery. Obviously, as we have seen, this has not been the case. In order to develop a comprehensive understanding of the story of Africans in early Asia, the aspect of servitude must be objectively examined, however painful it might be. What is important to accentuate in this context then is that the period of African bondage in Asian lands is only one part of a much wider story. The period of bondage is in fact dwarfed by the ages of Black glory and splendor in Asia's past, and that even under the guise of slaves and freedmen the Black people in Asia distinguished themselves time and again in a variety of roles and guises and forms.

Probably the most illustrious single figure in pre-Islamic Arabia was Antarah the Lion, called the "father of heroes." Antarah (ca. 525-615), evidently a Christian, had an Arabian father and an Ethiopian mother, and became in time

Arabia's national hero. There was no individual equal to the valor and strength of Antarah. He has been compared to King Arthur in the English tradition but was considerably more important because he was a more historical figure.[1]

It would seem that the notions of chivalry that generally associated with King Arthur and Richard the Lionheart may actually have their roots in Antarah. He was a great warrior, a champion of the weak and the oppressed, and romantic lover of women. Indeed, his love poems became famous, and, 'Ablah, whose name he immortalized in his famous Mu'allaqah, have become a part of the literary heritage of the Arabic-speaking world.[2]

In addition to Antarah, the son of an Arab father and an enslaved African woman named Zabiba, there was Amr ibn al-As—the conqueror of Palestine and Egypt and one of the architects of the Arab empire.[3] Another of the most notable of these Africans was Ubaidallah iban Abi Bakr, who in 698 led an Arab invasion of what is now Afghanistan.[4] Indeed the father of caliph Omar himself had an Ethiopian mother.[5] Another example is Dhu'l-Nun al-Misri, born in Upper Egypt around 796 C.E. Dhu'l-Nun was known as the head of the Sufis and is regarded as a founder of the Sufi doctrine of Islamic mysticism. He is said to have been the initial enunciator of the Sufi concepts of ecstatic states and the mystic ways towards a true knowledge of god.[6] And, of course, there is the man who became one of the great pillars of Islam—the African Bilal ibn Rabah.

The pious Bilal, of Ethiopian birth, was such a pivotal figure in the development of Islam that he has been referred to as "a third of the faith." He was a close companion of the Prophet Muhammad and the first muezzin, the caller of the Muslim faithful to prayer. Some have referred to him as a lawyer. The Prophet Muhammad is said to have told him, "As I journeyed in paradise and was mounting the stairs of God I heard your footsteps before me."[7] Today, Bilal has both a tomb and a mosque in Damascus, Syria.

Ibrahim ibn al-Mahdi (779—839) was an Abbasid prince, singer, composer, and poet. He was the son of the third Abbasid caliph Al-Mahdi. His mother is characterized as an "Afro-Iranian" princess named Shikla or Shakla. Historian Ibn Khallikan reported that Ibrahim was consequently "of dark complexion."[8]

Ibrahim was proclaimed caliph on July 20, 817 by the people of Baghdad, who gave him the royal name of al-Mubarak. He resigned in 819, and spent the rest of his life as a poet and a musician. He is remembered as one of the most gifted musicians of his day, with a phenomenal vocal range.

The issue of African servitude in Asia is intimately connected with the early spread of Islam in the continent's western and southern regions when, with the success of the Arab conquests, large numbers of the conquered "non-believers" of all races fell into Muslim hands and were dispersed throughout the lands they dominated. While slavery was not at all confined exclusively to the Blacks, increasing numbers of enslaved Africans in Muslim lands became so disproportionate that in time the Arabic word abd, meaning slave, became applicable to the Blacks only. And the communities descendants of these enslaved are scattered throughout South Asia.

It is estimated that perhaps as many as eleven million Africans were taken from Africa and transported to Turkey, Syria, Jordan, the Arabian Peninsula, the Persian Gulf, Iraq, Iran, Pakistan and India. Of all the territories of Western Asia it was perhaps in Mesopotamia, or Iraq, that the African presence, albeit in the capacity of slave and slave descendant, manifests itself most prominently.

It should also be pointed out that the enslaved Black people in Asia were not all from Africa. During the fourteenth and fifteen centuries, for example, the Muslim Indonesian sultanate of Tidore was a heavy slave raider of the coasts of New Guinea, transporting their black captives to the slave markets of China, Turkey and Iraq. It was apparently during this period that the Malay term Papuan (literally "kinky-haired") became synonymous with slave.

1.18.1.- Al-Jahiz and the book of the glory of the Blacks over the Whites

Well after the fall of Sumer African people continued to play an imporant role in the region. One of the great men and intellectuals of early Iraq was Al-Jahiz. According to Al-Jahiz, in his Book of the *Glory of the Blacks Over the Whites*:

> "The Ethiopians, the Berbers, the Copts, the Nubians, the Zaghawa, the Moors, the people of Sind, the Hindus, the Qamar, the Dabila, the Chinese, and those beyond them... the islands in the seas... are full of Blacks... up to Hindustan and China."[9]

Abu 'Uthman' Amr Ibn Bahr al-Kinani al-Fuqaimi al-Basri, an outstanding African scholar, the author of two-hundred works and known to posterity as Al-Jahiz (ca. 776-869), has been described by Bernard Lewis as "one of the greatest prose writers in classical Arabic literature."[10] Mounah A. Khouri stated that Al-Jahiz:

> "Brought Arabic prose to the heights of concision and clarity. Al-Jahiz, the grandson of a black slave, grew up in humble circumstances but still managed to gain a wide education in his native Basrah. His wit and learning made him one of Bagdad's leading intellectuals."[11]

Philip K. Hitti wrote that al-Jahiz "was one of the most productive and frequently quoted scholars in Arabic literature. His originality, wit, satire, and learning, made him widely known."[12]

Al-Jahiz was born in Basra, in Southern Iraq, studied philology, philosophy, and science there, and became an outstanding scholar, a prolific writer and a chronicler of the deeds of African people. During the lifetime of Al-Jahiz, Basra was a major trading city on the Shatt al Arab waterway, which empties into the Persian Gulf. So, in addition to the ancient Sumerians, there has been an African presence in Southern Iraq as early as the seventh century when Abu Bakra, an Ethiopian warrior who had been freed by the prophet Muhammad, settled in the Basra. His descendants became elite elements of Basran society.

Al-Jahiz lived during an era marked by a visible increase in overt racial hostility directed by Arabs against Africans in the Islamic world. One of the most extreme reactions to this racial bias was the massive slave insurrection in 868 (around the time of Al-Jahiz's death), known in Arab histories as the Revolt of the Blacks.

Al-Jahiz was the author of the Book of the *Glory of the Blacks Over the Whites*—a special essay in which the global history of African people and the subject of Blackness itself was discussed. During the 1980s, through the efforts of Mr. William Preston, the work was finally translated and published in English. It was long overdue.

The Book of the *Glory of the Blacks Over the Whites* is a remarkable document. It includes penetrating commentaries on great African heroes such as Antarah the Lion—a dashing knight and poet who is considered by some to be the father of the codes of "European" chivalry, Lokman—the celebrated sage of the East, and the African ancestry of the prophet Muhammad himself. According to Al-Jahiz, Abd al-Muttalib (the guardian of the sacred Kaaba in Mecca) "fathered ten Lords, Black as the night and magnificent."[13] One of these men was Abdallah, the father of the prophet Muhammad.

Al-Jahiz returned to Basra after spending more than a half-century in Baghdad, and died in 869 C.E. His exact cause of death is unknown, but a popular tradition states that he died as the result of an accident. The story goes that there was a massive earthquake and he died when his huge library toppled over on him. He died at the age of ninety-three.

1.18.2.- The revolt of the Blacks

The subject of African bondage anywhere is one of the most sensitive historical issues to be discussed, and all to often it is asserted that most, if not all, of the great international movements of African people in history occurred only the guise of slavery and servitude. Obviously, as we have seen, this has not at all been the case. The period of bondage is in fact dwarfed by the ages of magnificent African civilizations, glory and splendor, not just in Africa itself but throughout the whole of the global African community including early Iraq.

It was in early Iraq where the largest African slave rebellions occurred. Here, well over a millennium ago, were gathered tens of thousands of East African slave laborers called Zanj. These Africans, from Kenya, Tanzania, Ethiopia, Malawi and Zanzibar (an island off the coast of mainland Tanzania that gave the Zanj their name) and other parts of East Africa, worked in the humid salt marshes of Southern Iraq in conditions of extreme misery. Laboring in terrible, humid conditions, the Zanj laborers removed layers of topsoil and stripped away tons of earth to plant labor-intensive crops like sugarcane on the less saline soil below. Poorly fed with tiny rations of flour, semolina and dates, they were regularly in contention with the Iraqi system of enslavement.

Conscious of their large numbers and oppressive working conditions the Zanj rebelled on at least three occasions between the seventh and ninth centuries. The largest of these rebellions lasted for fifteen years, from 868 to 883, during which time the Africans inflicted defeat after defeat upon the Arab armies sent to suppress their revolt. This rebellion is known historically in Arab and Persian histories as the Revolt of the Zanj or the Revolt of the Blacks. In the year 871, the Zanj sacked Basra, Iraq.

It is significant to point out that the Zanj forces were rapidly augmented by large-scale defections of Black soldiers under the employ of the Abbassid Caliphate at Baghdad. The rebels themselves, hardened by many years of brutal treatment, repaid their former masters in kind, and are said to have been responsible for great massacres in the areas that came under their sway.

At its height the Zanj revolt spread as far as Iran and advanced to within seventy miles of Baghdad itself. The Zanj even built their own capital, called Moktara (the Elect City), which covered a large area and flourished for several years. They even minted their own currency and actually dominated Southern Iraq. The Zanj rebellion was ultimately only suppressed with the intervention of large Arab armies and the lucrative offer of amnesty and rewards to any rebels who might choose to surrender.

African people have always defied subjugation, and the Revolt of the Blacks is in and of itself a glorious page in African history and Black resistance movements. Through the Revolt of the Blacks, a now relatively little known episode in a part of the world that until very recently some of us regarded as foreign and strange, we see African people doing what they have always done—asserting their basic and essential dignity and standing up for and demanding their inalienable human rights.

1.18.3.- Malik Ambar and the Siddis of India

Although their numbers were dwarfed by those Africans victimized as of result of the trans-Atlantic slave trade, India also received its share of enslaved Africans and we find them scattered over such states as Bengal, Gujarat, Maharasthra, Karnataka, and Andra Pradesh. They are referred to as Siddis, or Sidis, or Habshis. Some of them, as soldiers and administrators, achieved great prominence. In several cases they were the actual powers behind the throne. Their names include: Chingiz Khan, Abhangar Khan, Habash Khan, Saif al-Din Firuz, Malik Andil, Ikhlas Khan and Malik Ambar.

Malik Andil was an enslaved Ethiopian who attained power in India in the fifteenth century. He became commander-in-chief of the armies of Bengal. Malik Andil, taken directly or indirectly from the Horn of Africa, obviously brilliant and gifted with the art of intrigue, cherished the almost inconceivable dream for an enslaved person of becoming sultan and was eventually elected sultan by the people of Bengal with the official title of Feroze Shah. His Ethiopian cohorts supported him to the extent that none of the white Turkish or Afghan chiefs could effectively challenge him. Malik Andil reigned for thirteen years and died in 1494.

Ikhlas Khan was the early seventeenth century de facto master of Bijapur and the subject of more surviving portraits than any of the African leaders in this period of Indian history.

Clearly, however, the most famous of these Africans to achieve distinction during this time period in India, and a contemporary of Ikhlas Khan of Bijapur, was the celebrated Malik Ambar. Like a handful of other Africans in this era in Indian history, Malik Ambar (1548-1626), through hard work and pure raw genius, elevated himself to a position of great authority.

Malik Ambar, whose original name was Shambu or Chapu, was born around 1550 in Harar, Ethiopia. After his arrival in India Ambar, an exceptional man, over time was able to raise a formidable army and achieve great power in the western Indian realm of Ahmadnagar. Ambar was a brilliant diplomat and administrator. He encouraged manufactures and built canals and mosques. He gave pensions to poets and scholars, established a postal service, and ultimately became one of the most famous men in India.

Malik Ambar was chief minister of Ahmadnagar and the defacto power behind the throne. He married his daughter to the sultan of Ahmadnagar, dominated and later ordered the death of his son-in-law.

A contemporary of Malik Ambar wrote that "his charities are beyond description."[14] Another contemporary recorded that, "In warfare, in command, in sound judgement, and in administration, he had no rival or equal."[15] He was the nemesis of the mighty Mughal empeor Jahangir and was never conquered by him. After a full and extraordinary life crowded with achievement Malik Ambar died a mature man in his late seventies. He was buried in an imposing reddish basalt tomb at Khuldabad outside of Aurangabad.

In a collective form, however, and in respect to long term influence, the Africans, some soldiers 1 and some sailors, known as Siddis stand out. Certainly, Siddi kingdoms were established in Western India in Janjira and Jaffrabad as early as 1100 C.E. After their conversion to Islam, the African freedmen of India, originally called Habshi from the Arabic, called themselves Sayyad (descendants of Muhammad) and were consequently called Siddis. Indeed, the island Janjira was formerly called Habshan, meaning Habshan's or African's land. During the sixteenth and seventeenth centuries entire armies of thousands and thousands of these Africans operated in India.

According to R.R.S. Chauhan:

> "Through the foreign powers—the British, Dutch, French and the Portuguese—have left Indian shores forever, the Siddis who are the descendants of Africans brought originally as slaves, are very much here to stay permanently with their unusual cultural heritage. They are found today in quite a large number in different regions of Gujarat, Maharashtra, Karnataka, Andra Pradesh, etc. And although a few of them have assimilated themselves in the Indian society, most of them continue to maintain their indigenous customs, traditions, identity and the way of life despite settling in India for several centures. Their colour, curly hair and thick lips at once reveal the presence of African blood and they generate curiosity in others to know more about their past and history."[16]

The term Siddi signifies lord or prince. It is further said that Siddi is an expression of respectful address commonly used in North Africa, like Sahib in India. Specifically, it is said to be an honorific title given to the descendants of African natives in the west of India, some of whom were distinguished military officers and administrators of the Muslim princes of the Deccan.

The Siddis were a tightly knit group, highly aggressive, and even ferocious in battle. Some of them became sailors. They were employed largely as security forces for Muslim fleets in the Indian Ocean, a position they maintained for centuries.

The Siddi commanders were titled Admirals of the Mughal Empire, and received an annual salary of 300,000 rupees. According to Ibn Battuta (1304-1377), the noted Berber writer who journeyed through both Africa and Asia, the Siddis "are the guarantors of safety on the Indian Ocean; let there be but one of them on a ship and it will be avoided by the Indian pirates and idolaters."[17]

Two Siddi kingdoms, Janjira in Maharashtra, and Sachin, in Gujarat, survived until well into the twentieth century. Indeed, Janjira has been referred to as "The Gibraltar of Siddis."[18]

Notes

1. Graham W. Irwin, "African Bondage in Asian Lands," in *African Presence in Early Asia* (New Brunswick: Transaction Press, 1995), 140.
2. Philip K. Hitti, *History of the Arabs* (London: Macmillan, 1956), 96.
3. Bernard Lewis, "The African Diaspora and the Civilization of Islam," in *The African Diaspora*, Martin L. Kilson and Robert I. Rotberg, eds. (Cambridge, MA: Harvard University Press, 1976), 41.
4. Fitzroy Andre Baptise, John McLeod and Kenneth X Robbins, *African Elites in India* (Mumbai: Mapin, 2006), 13.
5. Lewis, 41.
6. Lewis, 53.
7. J.A. Rogers, *World's Great Men of Color, vol. 1* (New York: Macmillan, 1972), 145.
8. Ibn Khallika, cited by Rogers, *World's Great Men of Color, vol. 1* (New York: Macmillan, 1972), 148.
9. 'Uthman' Amr ibn-Bahr al-Jahiz, *The Book of the Glory of the Black Race* (Los Angeles: Preston, 1981), 55-56.
10. Bernard Lewis, Bernard. *Race and Slavery in the Middle East* (Oxford: Oxford University Press, 1990), 51.
11. Mounah A. Khouri, "Literature," in *The Genius of Arab Civilization* (Cambridge, MA: MIT Press, 1983), 28.
12. Hitti, 382.
13. Al-Jahiz, 50.
14. Richard A. Eaton, "Malik Ambar and Elite Slavery in the Deccan, 1400-1650," in *African Elites in India*, edited by Kenneth X Robbins and John McLeod (Mumbai: Mapin, 2006), 55.
15. Eaton, 60.
16. R.R.S Chauhan, *Africans in India (New Delhi: Asian Publication Services, 1995)*, 1.
17. Ibn Battuta, *The Travels of Ibn Battuta, A.D. 1325-1354, vol. 4* (London: The Hakluyt Society, 1994), 800.
18. Chauhan, 4.

1.19.- Out of Africa to Asia to America: the Gladwin Thesis of "Men out of Asia"

"What we are going to try to do is build up a new theory to explain how the native American civilizations originated... and a first long step in this direction is to show the number, variety and location of the different peoples who were on hand when the seeds of American civilizations first began to sprout."[1]

Harold Sterling Gladwin, 1883-1983, some of whose works and ideas this essay is designed to address, comes to our attention here as a twentieth century archaeologist and historian imbued with an exceptionally keen interest in the early cultures and historical developments of the southwestern sections of the United States, including California, Arizona, New Mexico, Utah, Colorado, and Texas. As for his personal history, we know that Gladwin was born in New York City and that in 1901 he attended Wellington College in Berkshire, England.

From 1908 to 1922 he was employed with the New York Stock Exchange. It was not until 1924 that Gladwin, who was then an energetic forty years of age, became, in the course of a leisurely drive through the American Southwest, suddenly and incurably addicted to the archaeological fever that possessed him for the rest of his life.

Though considered an « amateur » by some academicians because of his disdain for "formal university training," Gladwin's record in actual field research, or what might be called "dirt archaeology," was considerable.[2] In addition to his position as curator at the Santa Barbara Museum, Gladwin was the cofounder and, from 1927 to 1950, Director of the Gila Pueblo Archaeological Foundation, under whose auspices the first significant traces of North America's culture were uncovered. In addition to his extensive excavations, Gladwin either authored or co-authored twenty-four impressively detailed archaeological site reports and several major books, the last one of which, *Men Out of the Past*, was completed as recently as 1975.

We are drawn to him in our current studies primarily because of his authorship of a controversial 1947 publication entitled *Men Out of Asia*. This was the same year, by the way, that W.E.B. DuBois' *World and Africa*, and the still valuable and exciting second volume of Joel A. Rogers' *Worlds Great Men of Color* were first published. Gladwin's text is of particular importance to African-centric analyses of American history because it is one of the few substantial studies backed by specialized field research that claims that the earliest American populations were Black. It is our firm conviction, therefore, that in an age in which a completely new vision of the Black presence in world history is being espoused uncompromisingly, the "Gladwin Thesis" and the bold, compelling and factual manner in which it is presented, should not be ignored, overlooked, or unacknowledged.

In spite of the more than sixty years that have elapsed since *Men Out of Asia's* initial publication, it will probably surprise few to know that the essential message contained within it, or at least the portion of it with which we are concerned, is still unknown to all but a comparatively small number of serious students, and remains unacceptable to Western academicians as a whole. When we add to this the fact that the text is now out of print and has not been available for some time, the necessity for a critical review and reassessment of the "Gladwin Thesis" from an African-centric perspective becomes all the more apparent.

1.19.1- Diminutive africoids: first people on american soil?

It appears extremely likely that small numbers of Diminutive Africoids (whose presence is suggested most strongly by the exceptionally short statures of the Yahgan and Alikuluf peoples who occupy the southernmost tip of South America on Tierra del Fuego) appeared in the New World as its first human occupants.[3]

Initially, and for the purpose of clarification, we should state that when speaking of the Diminutive Africoids, we are referring to the important but much romanticized subgroup of Black people (or Africoids) that are phenotypically characterized by (a) unusually short stature (b) skin-complexions that range from yellowish to dark brown (c) tightly curled hair and (d) in frequent cases, steatopygia. The Diminutive Africoids may be more familiar or better known to us by such terms (some of them pejorative) as: *Pygmies, Negritos,*

Negrillos, Grimaldis, Aeta, Sekai, Orang Asti, Semang, Twa, Black Dwarfs, Khoi Khoi, Hottentots, San, Bushmen,! Kung, Seed People, Little Black Men, and Little Red Men. From their initial places of origin in Mother Africa, these Blacks have scattered around the earth, and are now usually found only in isolated or heavily forested terrains. In spite of Gladwin's doubts, they were in all likelihood the first people to stand physically on American soil.

The Diminutive Africoids are of particular importance to us because they are morphologically related to the world's first Homo sapiens sapiens, and are typically found to be at the population bases of the inhabited zones of the world. In addition to a number of works by relatively early advocates of this view (Armand De Quatrefages serves as an example) we can now stand on the solid foundation of recent scientific studies. The strongest of these is the work of a team of eleven scholars, most of them based at Oxford University. After completing a meticulous analysis of nuclear DNA polymorphisms, this expert scientific body provided the following summary of its labors:

> "The earliest fossils of anatomically modern man (Homo sapiens sapiens) have been found in Africa at Omo in Ethiopia, Border Cave in South Africa and at Klasies River Mouth in South Africa. The data from the last site suggests that H. sapiens sapiens was present in South Africa more than 100,000 yr. ago, and an adult mandible from Border Cave has been dated to about 90,000 yr. BP. Hence, it has been argued that the evolution of modern man took place in Africa. Our data are consistent with such a scheme, in which a founder population migrated from Africa and subsequently gave rise to all non-African populations."[4]

Less than one year after the publication of this revolutionary data assessment, Oxford's Jim Wainscoat, apparently the leader and most actively involved of the scientists engaged in these studies, provided more specific evidence of their validity. In a report just published, Wainscoat elaborates on what is now being labeled "the Out of Africa hypothesis." According to him, "It seems likely that modern man emerged in Africa and... that subsequently a founder population left Africa and spread throughout Europe, Asia and the Americas."[5]

The studies of a team of scientists at the University of California at Berkeley corroborate the Oxford findings. The Berkeley study is based upon the calculation of the slow changes that have occurred in human DNA over the millennia which *"indicate that everyone alive today may be a descendant of a single female ancestor who lived in Africa 140,000 to 280,000 years ago."*[6]

That these early ancestors were "phenotypically Black," in addition to being native African is clear. As the brilliant, late Senegalese scholar Cheikh Anta Diop noted, "The man born in Africa was necessarily dark-skinned due to the considerable force of ultraviolet radiation in the equatorial belt."[7] Fundamental alterations of this "Africoid phenotype" (occurring after distant migrations from their original African base, with resulting adaptations to new environments) could have come about only gradually after extended passages of time.

Traces of the presence of Diminutive Africoids have been identified in the most remote periods of prehistoric Asia. Similar groups of Black people have been identified in Japan.[8] In Malaysia these Small Blacks have been denoted as Orang Asli (Original Man). Pejoratively they are known as Semang, with the connotation of savage. They live in the rainforests of northern Malaysia and are probably the aboriginals of the land. It is tragic that the contributions of these small Black people to monumental high-cultures characterized by urbanization, metallurgy, agricultural science and scripts remain essentially unexamined.

DNA studies published in The New York Times December 11, 2002 focusing on the inhabitants of the Andaman Islands (a remote archipelago east of India) state that they are the direct descendants of the first modern humans to have inhabited Asia: "Their physical features—short stature, dark skin, peppercorn hair and large buttocks—are characteristic of African Pygmies. They look like they belong in Africa, but here they are sitting in this island chain in the middle of the Indian Ocean and are part of what is described as a relict Paleolithic population, descended from the first modern humans to leave Africa."[9]

Dr. Underhill, an expert on the genetic history of the Y chromosome, said the Paleolithic population of Asia might well have looked as African as the Onge and Jarawa do now, and that people with the appearance of present-day Asians might have emerged only later.

The presence of diminutive Africoids (whom Chinese historians called "Black Dwarfs") in early southern China during the period of the Three Kingdoms (ca. 250 C.E.) is recorded in the book of the Official of the Liang Dynasty (502-556 C.E.).[10] In Taiwan there are recollections of a group of people now said to be extinct called "Little Black Man"[11]:

"They were described as short, dark-skinned people with short curly hair... These people, presumably Negritos, disappeared about 100 years ago. Their existence was mentioned in many Chinese documents of the Ching Dynasty concerning Taiwan."[12]

It was the Spaniards who named the native people of the Philippines "Negritos" (Little Blacks). The Spanish observed that "The Negritos, which our first conquerors found were, according to tradition, the first possessors of the islands of this Archipelago."[13] Another account observed that "There are black negroes in this island who pay tribute to no one."[14] Similar documents affirm the widespread presence and distribution of the Agta in the Philippines at the time of the Spanish intrusion.

In the light of such data, it is not difficult to speculate about the probabilities of small groups of Diminutive Africoids entering the Americas in the course of their ancient wanderings.

It is generally agreed that the earliest movements of peoples into the Americas took place across the short span that is now called the Bering Strait. In other words, the first Americans wandered out of Siberia, crossed the narrow but frozen water barrier, and entered Alaska. It is entirely possible that a few of these early folk came to the New World in boats; certainly some of the later migrants from Asia to the Americas did. This very first group of migrants, however, probably entered North America without even getting their feet wet.

The first Americans are believed to have come to their new domains dry shod because of the fact during multiple phases of the geological period known as Wisconsin Glaciation (the last North American phase of the Pleistocene Age) enormous sheets of ice covered most of the northern lati-tudes of the world, including both Eurasia and North America almost totally.

For some reason however (probably because of the low amounts of rainfall), key zones of Siberia's eastern coastal periphery and the extreme western coast of Alaska remained practically ice-free.

The huge amounts of water that the massive northern glaciers drew from the ocean basins of the world caused the earth's sea levels to hover somewhere between two-hundred and five-hundred feet lower than today, exposing a broad, basically flat sub-continent. At certain intervals then, each of varying lengths of time (from about 70,000 to approximately 8,000 years before present), there was no Bering Strait. In its place was a Bering Isthmus: an approximately 3000 foot wide land bridge (sometimes referred to as Beringia) that connected eastern Siberia with western Alaska. Although controversy remains in this area, geophysicists overwhelmingly state that the existence of a land bridge connecting Asia and America is verifiable for at least three different periods of the Wisconsin Glaciation; the first of which remained above water until about 37,000 years ago.

Once having gained the assorted cultural equipment, including clothing, tools and shelter, necessary to withstand exceedingly cold climatic conditions, the existence of Beringia made it possible for early bands of men to literally walk (perhaps following the herds of mastodon, wooly mammoths, and giant bison that had gone before them) in a westerly direction over Beringia's tundra-like surface. Almost certainly without any real consciousness of the significance that modern humankind would attach to their accomplishments, these people ultimately marched directly from Asia right into North America. Eventually, after a space of time that probably consumed many generations and several millennia, they filtered all the way down to South America. These would have been the first people then, almost certainly Diminutive Africoids, to move onto American soil and wander the immense lands of the New World.

Despite the obvious implications of geophysical studies of this nature, the case for human existence in the Americas prior to 30,000 before present was basically sneered at in Gladwin's day and is still met by dogged opposition in our own. The intense debate over the earliest appearance of modern man in the Americas has now crystallized around the newly reported, but firmly documented, carbon-14 dates from the site of Boquierao do Sitio da Pedra Furada in the state of Piaui in Northeastern Brazil. This site had yielded evidence of a series of lithic industries. It is a large, richly painted rock shelter located on the steep bank of a 100 meter high sandstone cliff, and was first reported by the joint French-Brazilian Archaeological Mission in 1973. It has yielded carbon-14 dates from charcoal deposits at the lowest level of an impressively structured hearth. From these miniscule fragments can now be traced periodic human occupations up to 32,160 + or—100 years before present. As far as we know this is the oldest clearly verifiable date for man's presence in the Americas.[15]

Because human skeletal remains have yet to be excavated from the Boqueirao Pedra Furada site, the identities of the shelter's first residents remains something of a mystery. Stray groups of Diminutive Africoids however (the former lords of the earth), must at least be regarded as the most serious candidates, if for no other reason than the vast antiquity of the era itself.

1.19.2.- The first great wave: the australoid migrations

Although in a very remote prehistoric period small numbers of Diminutive Africoids, may have preceded them, what we are dealing with in the context of this essay as the Gladwin Thesis are the first four separate and distinct migratory waves of peoples to enter the New World. Gladwin classifies these four groups, which he calls Australoids, Asiatic Negroids, Algonquins, and Eskimos (Inuit), as actual migrants because they came to the Americas in relatively large numbers.

He further links these paleo-Americans (his men out of Asia) by virtue of their common use of the Bering Isthmus (Beringia) or, depending upon the geological period involved, the Bering Strait as their route of penetration into the Americas.

Finally, Gladwin established firmly the migration of these diverse peoples through his ability to identify their respective Old World cultural prototypes and technologies, and to trace and identify them in their subsequent New World settings.

Gladwin was therefore convinced, based upon the physical evidence then available, that it had been the resulting large-scale intermingling of these various peoples that had constituted the basic ethnic composition of the Americas at the time of the European intrusions that began in the fifteenth and sixteenth centuries.

> "It is extremely important to grasp the significance of these four migrations, who the people were, where they came from, when they came, the things they brought with them and the regions they occupied."[16]
>
> "Contrary to the common belief, the earliest Americans were not Mongoloid but actually were members of the so-called Australoid family, which in the old, old days, roamed over most of the earth."[17]

The four migrations that form the basis of the Gladwin Thesis were all sporadic, probably unplanned, and occurred over long spans of time. The first migration to enter North America, Gladwin says, began about 25,000 before present and lasted for several millennia. Because of the regional climatic variations between Alaska and eastern Siberia during this period, the migration's approximate beginning date of 25,000 B.C.E. seems perfectly valid. The date coincides with the gradual reappearance of Beringia; about 26,000 before present to around 21,000 before present or beyond, when it was once again submerged under water. But even if we were to rule out Beringia's actual existence altogether we would still have to recognize the fact that the frigid strait separating Asia from North America could hardly have been a barrier formidable enough to prevent intercontinental movement.

Because of their close physical and cultural relationships to the people who more than 60,000 years ago colonized Australia and the many Islands off the shores of Eastern Asia, these migrants are called Australoids (derived from "austral" or "southern"). Gladwin was not asserting, of course, that these Black pioneers to the Americas actually came from Australia, but only that they issued from the same physical type as those early folk who had moved into Asia and Australia in prehistoric times.

For a physical description of these migrants, one need go no further than their descendants—the 300,000 Blacks of modern Australia known generally as "Australian Aborigines." Similar Australoid descendant groups can be found today among the six million Mundas of East-Central India, and the easily identifiable Vedda populations of Sri Lanka.

This application of "Blackness" or Africanity to the Australoid segment of humankind has been nothing less than disturbing to Eurocentric "scholars" (Gladwin was not among them). These obstinate individuals, in their apparently relentless attempts to maintain superficial divisions amongst the various members of the Black race, refuse to believe their eyes and continue to stubbornly insist (no matter how ridiculous it appears) upon the "scientific" placement of the Australoids within the Caucasoid racial family. To see the illogicality of this, one need only consider the basic question of whether there can exist groups of human beings that could be called "black-skinned white people." To us, this kind of reasoning simply does not make sense. Cheikh Anta Diop expressed it this way:

> "A racial classification is given to a group of individuals who share a certain number of anthropological traits, which is necessary so that they not be confused with others. There are two aspects which must be distinguished, the phenotypical and the genotypical. I have frequently elaborated on these two aspects.
>
> If we speak only of the genotype, I can find a black who, at the level of his chromosomes, is closer to a Swede than Peter Botha is. But what counts in reality is the phenotype. It is the physical appearance which counts. This black, even if on the level of his cells he is closer to Swede than Peter Botha, when he is in South Africa he will live in Soweto. Throughout history, it has always been the phenotype which has been at issue; we mustn't lose sight of this fact. The phenotype is a reality, physical appearance is a reality. And this appearance corresponds to something which makes us say that Europe is peopled by white people, Africa is peopled by black people, and Asia is peopled by yellow people. It is the se relationships which have played a role in history."[18]

It may help to understand the magnitude of the Australoid migrations to the New World by the fact that they filled in not only the southern section of North America, but also Central and South America. The Australoid migrations occurred during the prolonged period of high rainfall known as the Provo Pluvial, which was really just a continuation of the Wisconsin Glaciation in that the rain belts which had formerly fed the massive ice sheet covering most of Canada moved into the arid regions of the North American Southwest. These southern coastal movements of the Australoids were facilitated therefore by the enormous sheets of iced then covering all but the far western extremities of North America. Again now, it should be clearly stated that all of these movements were slow and gradual processes, continuing over a span of many centuries, with numerous pauses and stops along the way.

The majority of the Australoids continued to move in a southern coastal direction but once beneath the glaciers, near the region that is now California, a few Australoid groups began an eastern trek.[19] Gladwin was able to point out numerous crania found at early sites in Southern California, Southwestern Colorado, Southern Arizona, the Texas Gulf coast, Punin and Paltacalo in Ecuador, and Lagoa Santa in Eastern Brazil, all of which demonstrated "characteristics which link these various instances together and point to their wide distribution and common ancestry with other Australoid people s, as do also certain vestigial traces in some modern people, such as the Pericu of Lower California, the Seri on nearby Tiburon Island, and various tribes in Central and South America… People of Australoid type were once widely distributed, and survivals of some of their features, customs and culture are still to be found in isolated localities."[20]

Possibly the most well-documented single piece of evidence for the early presence of Australoids in the prehistoric Americas during the period of Gladwin's writing was the Punin Skull a female crania found in 1923, embedded in a stratum of volcanic ash near the small village of Punin in the Andean region of Ecuador. In addition to the skull itself, the stratum yielded the remains of a number of long extinct mammals; including an Andean horse-an animal known to have been extinct for more than 10,000 years, The Punin Skull's recovery by the American Museum of Natural History of New York created a sensation. It was, first of all hailed as the earliest evidence of humans in the Americas, and, secondly, it was clearly of an Australoid type. On these two issues "the leading experts" agreed. According to British anatomist Arthur Keith:

> "When the expedition returned to New York from Ecuador, the skull was transferred to the Anthropological side of the Museum, where it was examined and described by Drs. Louis R. Sullivan and Milo Hellman. Both anthropologists were struck by its resemblance to the skulls of the native women of Australia. I agree with them; the points of resemblance are too numerous to permit us to suppose that the skull could be of a sort produced by an American Indian parentage. We cannot suppose that an Australian native woman had been spirited across the Pacific in some migratory movement and that afterwards her skull was buried in a fossilliferous bed in the high plateau of Ecuador… The discovery at Punin does compel us to look in the possibility of a Pleistocene invasion of America by an Australoid people."[21]

Harvard anthropologist Earnest Hooton echoed Keith, although in somewhat less detail:

"The Punin skull, found in 1923 in a fossiliferous bed in the Andean highlands of Ecuador… is a skull that any competent craniologist would identify as Australian in type. It is easier to find Australoid-looking dolichocephals in the more ancient burials in the New World than anything in the way of a skull that resembles a Mongoloid."[22]

1.19.3.- Gladwin's sources

To buttress his views on the physical composition of his men out of Asia Gladwin heavily relied upon the works of three writers (two of whom, Keith and Hooton, we have just quoted) above all others. Their combined influences and interactions with him provided for Gladwin both a measure of credibility and a theoretical framework from which he could develop and grow.

The first of these writers was Sir Arthur Keith; a haughty and arrogant man who was once called the "dean of English anatomists." Keith was the former Keeper of the Hunteriana Collection at the Royal College of Surgeons and the past President of the Royal Anthropological Institute. Interestingly enough, much of Keith's academic reputation was gained as the result of his extensive studies of the famous (or infamous) fossil skull from Piltdown, England.

Quite a blow it must have been for him when in his last years he learned that the prized Piltdown skull, after further studies by other scientists, was actually only a clever hoax. In 1953, through the utilization of flourine testing, the Piltdown Man's jaw was discovered to be in reality that of an orangutan and the whole fossil was declared completely fraudulent. The Keith text most utilized by Gladwin was New Discoveries Relating to the Antiquity of Man, published in 1931, well before the ultimate bursting of his Piltdown Man bubble. Keith lived well into his eighties.

Earnest Albert Hooton, who also contributed the foreword to Men Out of Asia, was a constant base of reference for Gladwin. A prominent anthropologist, and the author of several major books, including Up From the Ape, Hooton served as Curator of Somatology of Harvard University's Peabody Museum. Hooton was trained in anthropology at Oxford University, and was at one point a professor and apparently sympathetic advisor to the great William Leo Hansberry.

Roland Burrage Dixon, 1885-1934, who had a tremendous impact upon Gladwin's thought, was easily one of the most erudite scholars and scientists of his era. Dixon was an Assistant Professor of Anthropology at Harvard University from 1906 to 1915. In 1904 he was appointed Librarian of the Peabody Museum, in 1908 Secretary of its Faculty, and in 1912 Curator of Ethnology. At the time of his death Dixon held all three offices.

Like Gladwin, Dixon was a specialist in the ancient and modern ethnologies of the North American Southwest. The author of numerous scholarly works, Dixon is probably best known for his Racial History of Man, published in 1923. In this comprehensive volume Dixon, through systematic and highly detailed studies of crania, was able to offer what was probably the first really scientific analysis of the racial composition of the American Indians. The book was so brutally received by fellow anthropologists, however, that Dixon was to refer to it in his later years as "my crime."

Nevertheless, the fundamental conclusions presented in Racial History of Man have basically been substantiated rather than disproven by the related archaeological and anthropological researches that have been conducted more recently. Dixon is also known to have spent considerable energy in attacking the diffusionist theories of Elliot Grafton Smith and William J. Perry.

1.19.4.- The second migration: the clovis-folsom point black

"Proto-Negroid or pseudo-Australoid. Terms such as these will be found only in technical papers on physical anthropology, but never in orthodox reconstructions of native American history. We have included them here because we think they cannot fairly be ignored, and, once you accept them as facts to be reckoned with, they turn out to be essential to an understanding of the problem."[23]

The second migration in the Gladwin Thesis began about 15,000 years ago. These migrants Gladwin calls "Asiatic Negroids." He postulates that approximately fifteen millennia ago waves of these Blacks, having entered Asia from Africa, were actively engaged in a broad, wide-ranging population movement.

After firmly establishing themselves in Southern and Eastern Asia, one of their family branches dispersed towards the numerous island chains of the vast Pacific Ocean, while another, after having first penetrated its way northward up the coasts of Asia, began to gradually enter North America. Their arrival in North America differed from the earlier arrival of the Australoids in that it coincided with the eastward recession of the mighty Keewatin ice sheet (which had formerly covered the mass of western Canada), creating for them a sort of corridor along the eastern foothills of the Rocky Mountains. Eventually their movements brought them onto the immense plains where roamed North America's vast bison herds.

These are the Blacks who, decades after their arrival in North America, founded the historically pivotal Clovis and Folsom fluted-point tool industries. Out of respect therefore to their unique and invaluable contribution to the techno/cultural evolution of prehistoric America, we shall henceforth disregard Gladwin's archaic "Asiatic Negroid" designation and refer to them as the "Clovis-Folsom Point Blacks." In physical appearance they closely resembled their Melanesian descendants-the proud, ancient, seafaring Black Islanders of the South Pacific.

Clovis and Folsom were the respective locations (both of them in New Mexico, U.S.A.) that provided the first evidences of the earliest projectile points associated with the Big Game Hunting Traditions of North America. Clovis points have been reliably dated to between 11,000 and 11,500 years before present. Folsom points, which are usually smaller, more refined and sophisticated than their Clovis antecedents, were actually identified before the 'Clovis points, and have been dated to about 10,000 B.C.E. Both Clovis and Folsom spearheads were several inches long and were characterized by smoothly fluted or grooved channels extending lengthwise along both faces. Their precision and firepower were revolutionary and awesome; and their rapidly widespread usage, with the increasingly greater food supplies that resulted, laid the basis for steadily larger American populations. Gladwin associated the delicacy and accuracy of the Folsom points (and the later Yuma points also) with "the better known Solutrean industry of prehistoric western Europe."[24]

It is of further interest that the first known modern discovery and revelation of the existence of these tool industries was made by an African-American; a tantalizingly and frustratingly obscure, self-taught naturalist and archaeologist named George McJunkin. The son of enslaved Africans, McJunkin, whose name may be searched for unsuccessfully in most history books, made the find in 1908 while riding out to check fence posts at a flooded creek. In 1925, three years after McJunkin's death, a dig at the Folsom site revealed a 10,000 year old spear point piercing the ribs of an extinct species of bison. It was McJunkin though, the obscure African-American, who had first documented Folsom points, which were then regarded (this was before the discovery of Ecuador's

Punin Skull) as "the first unequivocal evidence of late Ice Age humans ever unearthed in the Americas."[25]

The Clovis-Folsom Point Blacks seem to have come to North America in relatively small numbers. Later migrations of essentially the same physical type populated most of the rest of North America south of Canada. Their movements into the New World were then slowed, and later halted altogether, by the Australoid populations that were already well established in the North American Southwest. The later period Basket Makers of Arizona (the prehistoric culture bearers who eventually evolved into North America's Pueblo peoples) were probably the result of a fusion of Clovis-Folsom Point Blacks with the numerically larger Australoids.

Roland Dixon was such a strong advocate of this position that he is worth quoting on the subject:

> "In the present area [the Southwest], the Proto-Negroid type is of relatively slight importance. In the islands off the California coast it is lacking amongst the males although present as a small minority among females; it is not found in the Pericue, and occurs only as a trace in the Ute and Piute. The Basket Maker crania, however, show a contrast to the more modern population, in that the Proto-Negroid type is present in large amounts in both sexes. This would appear to indicate that this type was at an early date quite prominent in this portion of the continent; and this belief is corroborated by the crania from the ancient burial caves of Coahuila in northern Mexico, which exhibits this type as clearly dominant! It is interesting in this connection to find that culturally these people of Coahuila were in many respects closely allied to the Basket Makers."[26]

1.19.5.- The third migration: the coming of the Algonquin

> "In dealing with the populating of the New World we are attempting to trace some of the great movements of human history, of which there is no written record and which can only be pieced together by deduction and speculation based on the disconnected and fragmentary evidence of archaeology."[27]

The third migration of the Gladwin Thesis is stated to have begun about 1000 B.C.E. It was believed to have been made up of the people who, since their arrival in North America, have come to be best known as the Algonquin irrespective of what they were called before they reached Alaska. The Algonquin, whose American presence (with the aid of carbon-14 dating methods unavailable to Gladwin) have now been pushed back closer to 2,000 B.C.E., are specifically important to us because they are the first American arrivals who are not known to have been of a Black or Africoid phenotype. For some reason the Algonquin-speakers are the only group of migrants in the Gladwin Thesis for whom the author (much to our misfortune) provides no physical description.

What Gladwin really emphasized about the Algonquin was their pottery. He says that:

> "Once the Algonquin had settled down and made themselves at home they resumed the manufacture of cord-marked pottery, the knowledge of which they brought with them from Asia."[28]

Gladwin positively identified the Algonquin as the first American pottery makers. Their cord-marked pottery, which he defined as "a peculiar kind of prehistoric pottery which shows the imprint of twisted cords or of cord-wrapped paddles used in patting the surfaces," is now known as Jomon pottery ware; the use of which was widely employed in eastern Asia from about 11,000 to 300 B.C.E.

In stark contrast to the Clovis-Folsom Point Blacks, the Algonquin evidently came to North America in fairly big numbers, or so it would appear from the great quantities of pottery shards and other debris that they prominently discarded in the course of their travels. These "traveler's testimonies" have been recovered from village sites in the North American woodlands east of the Mississippi, and the northern states from the Pacific to the Atlantic coasts. These extensive areas of distribution coincide, by the way, with the domains of the known Algonquin-speaking tribes of the European phase of North American history. These tribes include: in Eastern Canada, the Micmac; in Maine, the Penobscot; in New England, the Mohican of Leatherstocking fame; in Pennsylvania, the Delaware; along the Ohio River, the Shawnee; in Illinois, the Kickapoo; near Lake Michigan, the Sauk, Fox and Menominee; and in northeastern Colorado and along the Rocky Mountains, the Blackfoot and the Cree.

1.19.6.- The forth migration: the arrival of the Inuit

The Algonquin were followed, Gladwin believed, around 500 B.C.E. by the last of "four separate migrations, each of which was distinct from all the others in regard to both the physical appearance of the people and the culture which they brought with them."[29]

The fourth migration, which had probably been in full motion well before the estimated date of 500 B.C.: E., was that of the Inuit (Eskimo); a people that Gladwin claims showed absolutely no relationship whatsoever either in physique or culture to any of the peoples of the three earlier migratory waves. The Eskimo entered the New World in large numbers. They came in a steady stream, and they kept on coming for a long time.

It was exceedingly clear to Gladwin that "The arrival of the Eskimo along the Arctic Coasts marked a fundamental transition in the anthropological history of North America. It was the last of a series of long-headed migrations, and the broad faces and slant eyes of the Eskimo marked the initial stage of a long period of Mongoloid domination in lands where Mongoloid people had therefore been unknown."[30]

Mongoloid peoples, in fact, were soon coming to the Americas in such massive numbers, crossing the Bering Strait in boats rather than the Beringia land bridge, that they eventually almost totally absorbed the New World's earlier arrivals. The resulting fusion of peoples came to be the "American Indians." The earlier arrived Blacks (Gladwin's men out of Asia and the very first Americans) tended to fade away with increasing rapidity into the shadowy realms of fairy tales, myths and legends.[31]

Notes

1. Harold S. Gladwin, *Men Out of Asia* (New York: McGraw-Hill, 1947).
2. "Harold Gladwin is not a professional archaeological in the sense of studying the subject at some university or research institute, and then making a meager living by teaching, digging, putting pots in museum exhibition cases. He is an amateur academically in that his record is not besmirched by Ph.D. degree... However, he had done as much dirt archaeology (which means real digging) in contrast to armchair archaeology (which means reading and speculating) as nearly any professional in the American field. He knows fully and utilizes skillfully the elaborate and precise techniques of the science. His excavations are models of method, his reports voluminous, orderly

and overwhelmingly documented. He is not a pot hunter, not a romancer; he is an expert practitioner." E. Hooton, Foreword to Men Out of Asia, x.3. It was in 1833 that the famous British naturalist Charles Darwin, 1808-1882, the author of *Origin of Species* [1859] and *Descent of Man* [1871], found 3,000 Yahgan Indians living naked but healthy at the bleak, cold and windy tip of South America. Darwin reported that "these miserable and abject creatures" slept on the barren ground; that mothers nursed their infants while sleet fell on their naked bodies. Responding to Darwin's writings, "sympathetic Englishmen" sent clothes and blankets. Along with these new items came diseases to which the Yahgan had been previously unexposed. Dreadful and decimating epidemics among the Yahgan was the result.

3. Very few Yahgans now survive. It was reported in 1955 that "a shriveled old woman known only as Julia is believed to be the last pure-blooded Yahgan... The surveying ship Beagle picked up Jemmy Button, a Yahgan, and took him to England for education and a day at the court of King William IV. Jemmy returned two years later. Darwin, who put him ashore, regarded him as a friend and a superior sort of aborigine. Throwing off alien culture, Jemmy 26 years later led a massacre of missionaries." Newman Bumstead, "Atlantic Odyssey: Iceland to Antarctica." National Geographic (December 1955), 765.

4. J.S. Wainscoat, et al. "*Evolutionary Relationships of Human Populations from an Analysis of Nuclear DNA Polymorphisms,*" *Nature, February 6*, 1986, 493.

5. Wainscoat, "*Out of the Garden of Eden." Nature, January 1*, 1987, 13.

6. "DNA Researchers Trace All Humans to Single Woman in Ancient Africa." *New York Times*, March 30, 1986.

7. Cheikh Anta Diop, "Africa: Cradle of Humanity." *Nile Valley Civilizations*, Ivan Van Sertima, ed. (New Brunswick: Transaction Press, 1984), 27.

8. "African-Like Stone Age Hut is Unearthed in Japan." *Associated Press*, February 15, 1986.

9. Nicholas Wade, "An Ancient Link to Africa Lives on in Bay of Bengal," *New York Times*, December 11, 2002.

10. Li Chi, *The Formation of the Chinese People (1928; rpt. New York*: Russell & Russell, 1967), 245.

11. Chen Kang Chai, *Taiwan Aborigines* (Cambridge: Harvard University Press, 1967), 33.

12. Ibid.

13. Pedro Gagelonia, *The Filipinos of Yesteryears* (Manila: Star Book Store, 1967), 82.

14. Gagelonia, 103.

15. N. Guidon, and E Delibrias. "Carbon-14 Dates Point to Man in the Americas 32,000 Years Ago," *Nature*, June 19, 1986, 769-71.

16. Harold S. Gladwin, *A History of the Ancient Southwest* (Portland, Maine: Bond Wheelwright Co., 1957), 16.

17. Cheikh Anta Diop, "Interview With Cheikh Anta Diop," *Great African Thinkers, Vol. 1*: Cheikh Anta Diop, ed., Ivan Van Sertima (New Brunswick: Transaction Press, 1986), 235-36.

18. California may have been mentioned for the first time in *The Adventures of Esplandian*, a novel published in Toledo, Spain around 1516. It was noted as an island paradise wealthy in gold, silver and precious stones. A noteworthy section of the novel reads, "There is an island called California, very near to the terrestrial paradise, which was peopled by black women…" Cortez is thought to have been inspired by the legendary riches of California.

19. Gladwin, *Men Out of Asia*, 66-67; 88-89.

20. Arthur Keith, *New Discoveries Relating to the Antiquity of Man* (London: Williams & Norgate, 1931), 312.

21. Earnest A. Hooton, *Up From the Ape* (New York: Macmillian, 1931), 650.

22. Gladwin, 185.

23. Gladwin, 97.

24. Susan Katz. "Mystery: When Did Ice Age Man Discover The Americas?" *Newsweek*, November 10, 1986, 72.

25. Roland B. Dixon, *The Racial History of Man* (New York: Scribner's, 1923), 109-10.

26. Gladwin, 151.

28. Gladwin, 147.

29. Gladwin, 150.

30. Gladwin, 157.

31. "A man and his wife and their only daughter lived in a remote place. Their daughter was outside, working when she saw a big black speck moving along the ground, coming towards her. When it got closer, she realized it was a man with a sledge. The man and the sledge were all black. He came towards the house, stopped, and said to the girl, 'I have come to take you with me.' He was black all over, even his face. The girl replied, 'Very well. I'll go and tell my parents.' She entered the igloo and the man followed her. He stood outside the door and was told by the father, 'I won't have my daughter going away with a black man like you.' The stranger became angry and made a step forward with his right foot. The whole house shook. Then the father said to his daughter, 'My daughter, you'll have to go away with this man. This will go badly with us if you don't. She got ready and left the house, with the stranger behind her. Before leaving, he put his left foot down hard on the floor and the house shook again. He went out, put the girl on the sledge and shoved the sledge because it had no huskies. After a while they saw a house-the man's house. They stopped and entered. Everything inside was black, and his parents also were completely black." Edwin S. Hall, Jr., *The Eskimo Story Teller* (Knoxville,: n.p., 1975), 289-90.

"For the Greenlander, the color black symbolizes strength and wisdom-traditionally he was not allowed to wear black boots until he had become a skilled hunter and reached a respectable age-but black is also associated with spirits and occult forces. Jean Malaurie, Preface to *An African in Greenland*, by Tete-Michel Kpomassie (New York: Harcourt Brace Jovanovich, 1983), x.

In the Southwest Indian story of the Emergence, a story that is as important in the region as the Book of Genesis is to Christians, the First World is called the Black World. John Bierhorst, *The Mythology of North America* (New York: Quill, 1986).

11. Seated statue of Gudea. The Metropolitan Museum of Art, NYC.
Photo by Runoko Rashidi

12. Images of the Black from Early Iran. Louvre. Photo by Runoko Rashidi

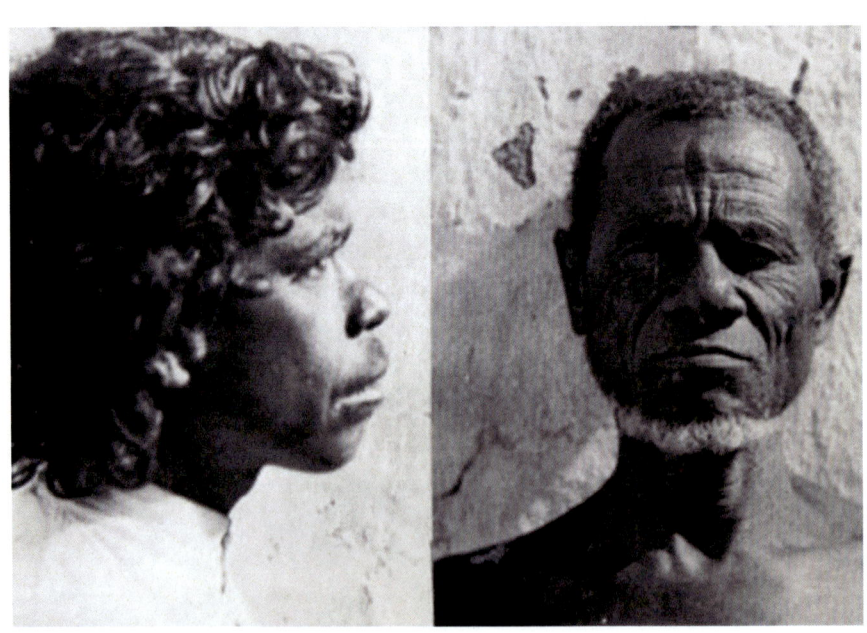

13. Aboriginal Southern Arabians

14. A Black warrior in early Afghanistan, circa 100 C.E.
Photo courtesy of James E. Brunson

15. A Black woman from the ancient Indus Valley. National Museum,
New Delhi

16. Painting of Krishna. The Metropolitan Museum of Art, NYC.
Photo by Runoko Rashidi

17. Kubera, Indian god of wealth. Date unknown.
LACMA Photo by Runoko Rashidi

18. Statue of the Buddha in Bodhgaya, India. Photo by Runoko Rashidi

**19. Painting of Malik Ambar. The Victoria and Albert Museum, London.
Photo by Runoko Rashidi**

20. Painting of a Siddi notable

21. A Tribal man in Tamil Nadu, India

Part Two

AFRICAN STAR OVER ASIA:
TRAVEL NOTES AND LETTERS

2.1.- Journeys to India
in Search of the African Presence

My journeys to Asia began in 1987. In October of that year I inaugurated the First All-India Dalit Writers' Conference held in Hyderabad, Andra
Pradesh. It was historic. In addition, it was my first encounter with the Dalits
(Untouchables or Outcastes). I met the great crusading journalist V.T. Rajshekar
on this trip. On this trip I was taken into the slums and redlight district of
Mumbai (it was still Bombay at the time), I inaugurated the Dalit writer's
conference in Hyderabad and gave a successful keynote address, gave a presentation in Bangalore, Karnataka, and visited an archaeological site and gave a
speech to a Dalit audience in the state of Tamil Nadu. Of all the trips that I have
been on, this was probably the singularly most important travel experience of
life. I felt that I completely left the world that I knew.

The October 1987 trip to India in many ways defined me as a scholar and
historian. Through this trip and its aftermath I helped introduce—for many
people—an entirely new dimension into the African-centered world—the
Dalits: the Black Untouchables of India.

The word dalit is a word peculiar to India and means crushed, broken and
oppressed. It is a synonym for the people officially known as Scheduled Castes
and often called Outcastes or Untouchables. The Dalits are the most oppressed
minority, the most socially ostracized people, in the world. In sheer weight of
numbers, there are more Dalits in India than the entire population of Western
Europe.

I returned to India to be with the Dalits eleven years later. The 1998 trip to
India was perhaps the most adventurous I have ever had. These two India trips
were sandwiched around my first trip to East Asia—to Japan in 1994. On this
1998 trip to India, I went alone and spent nineteen days there, beginning in
New Delhi and then to the state of Bihar where, based in Patna, I toured the
most downtrodden slum communities I have seen, visited with Tribals for the
first time, visited Dalits in villages for the first time, saw the remains of the
ancient Buddhist university at Nalanda, visited the city and stayed overnight

at a guesthouse in Bodhgaya (where the Buddha is supposed to have received enlightenment), took a second class train from Bihar to Maharastra to see the ancient Buddhist paintings in the Ajanta Caves where I got stranded there and hired a car to the city of Nagpur—in the very center of India. Here I gave a speech on African-Dalit unity, interacted with more Tribals, and met for the first time representatives of the Kerala Dalit Panthers.

From the city of Nagpur in Maharastra State, I flew to the Southwest Indian state of Kerala where I was hosted by the Kerala Dalit Panthers. Yes, they took their name and inspiration from the Black Panthers in the United States. Not only was I surrounded by Black people in Kerala, but with the tropical climate I felt like I was actually somewhere in the Caribbean. The Panthers were incredible hosts and escorted me throughout much of Kerala, where I was taken to villages and shrines. In Trivandrum, Kerala with the Panthers I marched through the city streets and gave what I thought was a rousing speech at a late night rally and forum.

From the city of Cochin in northern Kerala I ventured into the rainforests where I met more of the Tribals. When I say Tribals I am referring to the aboriginal occupants of the land—the Adivasis, the people of the forest. Like the ones that I met in Bihar, the Kerala Tribals were extremely small people but perhaps not as dark-skinned. And some of the Kerala Tribals had platinum blond hair. I had never seen anybody like them even in the anthropological texts that I had been examining, and this experience, dramatically and forcefully, reconfirmed for me the importance of international travel and first hand, primary research.

These forest dwellers told me that strangers rarely visited them and if they did they chased them away with their machetes! I assured them that I had come in peace! And what phenomenal care takers they turned out to be! They walked me through the dense foliage of what seemed like half of a mountainside. They took me into their homes and fed me. I drank tea and honey with them and politely asked them all of the questions that I could muster. The highlight and crowning memory of this visit though, came when I was politely confronted by one of the community elders. This lady had been following me all day up and down the mountainside. She was small and serene and projected great dignity. What I remember her telling me through the translators was roughly this:

"I know that you are not from here and must be from somewhere far, far away. But I feel that you are a part of me and I will never forget you."

Of all of the trips that I have taken it is very hard to surpass the emotions that I experienced that day.

Yes, these were true adventures—almost the stuff that legends are made of. I felt young and invincible. And I never wrote in detail about either of these trips. I can only surmise now, twenty-four years after the first trip and thirteen years after the second, that I was simply overwhelmed by the experiences and the emotions that were unleashed.

I have tried to compensate, at least in part, for this absence of writing by including the transcript of the speech that I gave in Trivandrum in April 1998 on the occasion of the anniversary of the birth of Dr. B.R. Ambedkar. As a prelude we include an early letter from the Dalit Panthers of India.

2.2.- We Are One African People: Runoko Rashidi in Trivandrum, India, April 14, 1998 on the Occasion of the Birthday of Dr. B.R. Ambedkar

Statement of solidarity with the Kerala Dalit Panthers and the Black people of India

Dedicated to brother Kwame Ture

Jai Bhim!

I bring you greetings from the Black people of America. I have now been in India for the last two weeks. I have visited Bihar in the North. I have just returned from Nagpur in Central India. And now I am at home with by Black brothers and sisters in Kerala. For the first time since I have been in India I feel that I have finally come to be with my family. I proudly salute the Kerala Dalit Panthers. I have been told that it is my job to inspire you, but instead I am the one who has been inspired by you.

Thousands of years ago the first men and the first women on this planet came out of Africa and they were Black people. Not only were the first people Black, but the people to develop the earliest civilizations in the world were also Black people. It is very important that we talk about the achievements of the past so that we can begin to give our people a sense of pride and dignity.

In India Black people built the earliest civilization. In Africa Black people built the earliest civilization. And then the White man came. In India you call them Aryans. In Africa we call them Europeans. The Aryans came and the Europeans came and they enslaved our people all over the world.

Slaves did not come from Africa. Africans were captured in Africa and enslaved and taken all over the world. In Africa Black men and women and children were hunted like animals. The people were branded with hot irons and all of our women were raped. Shackles and chains were placed on our hands and our feet, and we were taken across the ocean to America. But every step of the way African people—my people, my ancestors, Black people—fought the White man. Even when they burned us alive, even when they castrated us, even when they hung us from trees, our people fought. And that is what I wish to talk to you about tonight—the resistance of Black people to oppression.

I am here tonight to help establish a bond between the Black people of America and the Dalits, the Black Untouchables of India, that will never be broken. Our greatest leader was a Black man named Marcus Garvey. Marcus Garvey to us is what Dr. Ambedkar has been to you. He is our greatest leader. Marcus Garvey organized six million African people. He organized a Black army and he taught Black people in America to be proud of themselves. But the most celebrated of all the Black organizations of America has been the Black Panther Party.

In 1966, in America an organization called the Black Panther Party was formed and it was formed to defend the rights of Black people by any means necessary. Some of the members of the Black Panther Party were sent to prison. Some of the members of the Black Panther Party were murdered. But their deeds and their accomplishments will never die. The Black Panther Party was formed over thirty years ago, but time has not diminished the glory of their deeds.

The Black Panther Party is important to us because it showed that Black men and Black women can stand up and fight for the rights of Black people. The Black Panther Party of America struck fear into the hearts of White people in America—into the hearts of the White oppressors of Black people in America. You must strike that same fear in the heart of the Brahminical forces of India.

Although Black people in America are downtrodden, we are standing up and we will never be defeated. We realize today, perhaps for the first time, both in India and in America, that nobody can save us but us. The Communist Party will not save us. The Brahmins and the Aryans will not save us. Mohandas Gandhi and the Hindus will not save us. The only ones who will save us is us.

Today in America Black people are standing up. Three years ago in the United States more than one million Black men took to the streets of the nation's capitol. One year ago two million Black women took to the streets of America to protest against oppression. This year there is a call for for three million Black youth to take to the streets of New York City in America and stand up for the interests of Black people.

I never imagined when I came to India that I would be marching in a demonstration with my brothers and sisters with their fists in the air saying "Black is beautiful! Black is strong!" When I go back to America, the fact that I have been with you will inspire our people to greater efforts, once I tell them that there is a Black consciousness movement on the rise in India.

I am here to tell you, as I stand here drenched with perspiration, that I love you and that we are one people. I am here to tell you that the Black Untouchables of India, the Dalits, and the Black people of America form one human family. Don't stop! Don't turn back. Be proud of yourselves and realize what a united people can accomplish.

We pledge our undying loyalty and our undying support to the Kerala Dalit Panthers. We will never forget you. We will never forsake you.

Jai Bhim!

2.3.- Looking at India Through African Eyes

April 1999

On April 13, 1999 I returned from a successful tour of India entitled "Looking at India through African Eyes." It was a sixteen day educational tour designed to explore the historical, cultural, social and anthropological components of ancient and modern India from our own perspective—an African perspective. It was my first tour and my third trip to India overall. The tour was of historic significance, being the first such trip I planned and actually carried out. On the tour, accompanied by numerous local people and sixteen African-American brothers and sisters (all experienced travelers), we visited many of the significant temples, tombs, castles, palaces, museums and assorted great monuments in India, including the Taj Majal (reputedly built out of grief for an Ethiopian woman) and described as "poetry in marble," Amber Fort and the Palace of the Winds, the National Museum in New Delhi, the massive Konarak temple in Orissa, the Buddhist temple caves at Ajanta and the magnificent colossal rock cut temples at Ellora. In Patna, in Bihar, we stood on the banks of the Ganges River. We visited the major cities of Delhi, Agra, Jaipur, Patna, Calcutta, Bhubaneswar, Chennai, Trivandrum, Mumbai, Aurangabad and the abandoned city of Fatehpur Sikri.

Overall the people of India were kind and considerate towards us. The Black people of India themselves (the original inhabitants of the land) were wonderful to us and embraced us as family. Among the Black folk we interacted with were the Dom, Santals, Mundas, Dravidians, Dalits and Adivasis (Tribals). We visited them in their homes, offices and villages, rural communities and urban slums, university and academic settings. During our travels we encountered a mosaic of Christians, Hindus, Muslims, Buddhists, Parsis, Sikhs and Animists. Some of them engaged in the religious practices of our ancient African foreparents. Sometimes the sense of oneness and community seemed almost mystical and magical. Everywhere we went we reestablished bonds of brotherhood, sister-hood and familyhood. The individuals in our group were treated like visiting dignitaries, as ambassadors, and I was treated like a prince. At times it was overwhelming.

We were guests of honor at numerous receptions, cultural programs and educational forums, many of whom were sponsored or initiated by the publication *Dalit Voice: The Voice of the Persecuted Nationalities Denied Human Rights*, founded and edited by V.T. Rajshekar. And the Ancestors seemed to be with us. At a major reception in New Delhi the keynote speaker, Union Health Minister Dalit Ezhilmalai, focused on the life of Malcolm X. At a program in Bhubaneswar the moderator, Dr. Radhakant Nayak, who reminded us of John Henrik Clarke, closed the afternoon with a stirring recital of Claude McKay's glorious poem of resistance "If We Must Die!" In Trivandrum I was presented with three ceremonial Ankhs made of coconut shell and adorned with red, black and green beads. At an airport reception we were greeted with shouts of "Free Mumia Abu-Jamal!"

We were hosted by Black youth groups who told of their life stories and village origins, their hopes, their dreams and aspirations. We were entertained by scores of singers and drummers and dancers. We met with Black women's groups who performed skits portraying family life and a vibrant new spirit of resistance to domestic violence and centuries-old oppression. We visited some of the most downtrodden communities on earth, witnessed the miseries of the Black Untouchables of India and were guests on university campuses. In a program in Chennai we were hosted by Bishop Ezra Sargunam of the Evangelical Church of India where I was the guest speaker with Dr. K. Ponmudy, a major Dravidian scholar, in a program designed to address the Black and Dravidian movements.

In Orissa I saw and photographed the blackest human beings I've ever seen. In fact, it was my impression that the blackest people were here the most highly esteemed and considered better than the others who were not so dark! In one city, at an elaborate and heartfelt public ceremony, we presented school supplies to the entire student body of an aspiring educational institution followed by cash contributions for the continuation of the work. We saw ourselves not merely as tourists but at visiting family members come to try to make things better.

"Looking at India through African Eyes" was a resounding success and an incredible high. I came away from India convinced that African people around the world are on the rise and that there is a revolution going on in the hearts, souls and minds of Black people everywhere. It was a great triumph and for me personally clearly only the first in a series of tours to India and other sojourns with African people around the world. Africans Unite!

2.4.- Reflections: In and Around Mumbai

November 27, 2008

I went to bed last night and woke up this morning with India in the news. Specifically, the part of India in the news is the city of Mumbai. According to the latest news report more than a hundred people, in a series of attacks, have been killed in the city of Mumbai. I've been to Mumbai a couple of times and all of the recent news brings back a lot of memories.

Mumbai, a city of about twenty million people, is in the center of India along the coast of the Arabian Sea. Until recently most people called it Bombay. Bombay is the Anglicized version of Mumbai. Mumbai is regarded as the commercial center of India.

In October 1987, on the first of three momentous trips to India, Mumbai was my port of entry and departure. Indeed, that first trip to India helped sharply define my view of the Global African Community.

I recall Mumbai as a huge city with enormous crowds of people sleeping on the streets. Along with sister Njeri Khan and journalist V.T. Rajshekar I stayed at the Sea Green Hotel (the same hotel that the assassins of Mohandas Gandhi stayed at when they were stalking him) and visited the slum areas that housed the headquarters, at the time, of the Dalit Panthers—organized by some of India's Black Untouchables—the Dalits.

Off the coast of Mumbai there is a lot of history relevant to us. There is Elephanta Island, whose main temple is characterized by distinctly Africoid imagery. Also off the coast of Mumbai is Janjira Island, dominated for centuries by the African soldiers known as Siddis.

Some distance due east of Mumbai near the village of Ajanta are the Ajanta Caves. In 1998 during my second trip to India I traveled by train and them by bus all the way from Patna, Bihar to visit these caves. It was a journey and a visit that I will never forget. I even found myself stranded there for a brief while.

There are thirty Ajanta Caves, some of them beautifully adorned with marvelous frescoes depicting the life of Gautama Buddha. The paintings have been dated to as far back as 200 B.C.E.

I believe that these images represent sosme of the finest examples of Buddhist art in the world. The black complexions of the figures and the Africoid hair styles that adorn them speak for themselves, and further reflect the need of including the Black presence in India as an important part of African-centered research. One pioneer African-American scholar, George Washington Williams, referenced this in the early 1880s. Even before that, Godfrey Higgins, an English antiquarian, made similar comments in his colossal work known as the Anacalypsis, published in 1836.

2.5.- The Black Presence in Thailand

March 1999

I came to Thailand fully aware that it is a country with an extremely ancient but little known Black population. Here I am referring to the forest dwelling people called Sekai, sometimes identified by the pejorative term—Negritos. These Black folks live in southern Thailand in the region straddling the border with northern Malaysia. I also realized early on that because of their location (a considerable distance from Bangkok), lack of advance preparation and limited time, the chances of my visiting them were not good.

Not getting to see the ancient Black people of Thailand was pretty much anticipated, and I didn't feel defeated. Perhaps in the future I will get to see them. After all, I plan to return to Thailand again and again. In addition to the Sekai, however, the Black presence in Thailand is apparent in the numerous images of the Buddha. I came to the conclusion a long time ago that only a very ignorant person or a bigot could look at these beautiful sculptures and not see Black people. The highlight, therefore, of my first trip to Thailand was the National Museum, where are housed some of the finest and most African looking Buddhist images in the world, particularly those going back to the cultural phase known as the Mon or Dvaravati cultural period when an independent kingdom flourished in southern Thailand from the sixth to the eleventh century. The Mon people practiced Theravada Buddhism, and it seems that the present Thais adopted Buddhism from them. Indeed, more than ninety-five percent of the Thais today are Theravada Buddhists.

In regard to the physical appearance of many Southeast Asian images of the Buddha, as far back as 1883 African-American scholar George Washington Williams pointed out that:

> "In the temples of Siam [Thailand] we find the idols fashioned like unto Negroes… Traces of this black race are still to be found along the Himalaya range from the Indus to Indo-China, and the Malay Peninsula, and in mixed form through the southern states to Ceylon."

Even before Williams, in regard to the Buddha, Godfrey Higgins, in 1833, argued that "In the most ancient temples scattered throughout Asia, where his worship is yet continued, he is found black as jet, with the flat face, thick lips and curly hair of the Negro."

2.5.1.- Return to Thailand

My second trip to Thailand in 1999 occurred in late November. The trip was highlighted by a slide-presentation entitled African Contributions to the World, a side trip to the city of Ayutthaya. On this occasion the presentation was a rather lively one. I was much more relaxed than I had been at the March presentation to the African-American employees at the US Embassy, and the discussion lasted well into the early morning hours. It is encouraging to know that, all over the world, small groups of African people are discussing our history in a new light and with a new emphasis.

2.5.2.- Ayutthaya

In addition to my slide presentation, on my November 1999 trip to Thailand I visited the ancient city of Ayutthaya, an island city on the Chao Phraya River which was the royal Thai capital from 1350 to 1767. It is the most important historical park within easy striking distance—about forty-eight miles north of Bangkok. Prior to 1350, it was a Khmer outpost. Although sacked, looted and razed by invaders from Myanmar in the eighteenth century, the surviving ruins of Ayutthaya stand as profound witnesses to what was once a magnificent city.

Compared to the frenetic pace of Bangkok Ayutthaya was a quiet and soothing getaway. I have to say, though, that Black tourists are a rare sight in Ayutthaya. In fact, I didn't see a single one. Indeed, the Black community is extremely minute all over Thailand. This was obvious wherever I went. Fortunately, however, my travels were productive and rewarding, and Thailand is now firmly established in my travel plans to Asia.

2.6.- The Mighty Monuments of Angkor

December 11, 1999

> **"For the complexion of men, they consider black the most beautiful. In all the kingdoms of the southern region, it is the same."**
>
> —Early Chinese Chronicler

On December 7, 1999 I returned to the US from a two-week educational tour to Thailand and Cambodia. It was my second trip to Thailand of the year and my first trip ever to Cambodia. Indeed, until quite recently I never really thought that I would have a chance to go to Cambodia, and so my trip there was something of a dream come true. Quite naturally the trip was a search for African people. I am particularly interested in African migrations. We know now, for example, that the first humanity emerged from Africa and that streams of African people have continued to flow across the world from ancient to modern times. It is therefore very important for us to address the questions of exactly where did those Africans go, what did they do when they got there and what has subsequently happened to them. I consider such an approach Pan-African in its nature, African-centered in character and an earnest attempt to reunite a family of people separated far too long.

The most prominent and enduring kingdom of early Southeast Asia was Angkor (ca. 800-1431), located primarily in Cambodia. The builders of Angkor were an Africoid people known as Khmers—a name that loudly recalls ancient Kmt (pharaonic Egypt).

My first full day in Cambodia began with a morning tour of the regal Angkor Wat temple. The temple of Angkor Wat, the most famous of Khmer stone structures, is truly magnificent to gaze upon and took a grand total of thirty-seven years to build. Words do not do it justice.

I love Angkor Wat! But the Bayon is not only my favorite Angkor temple— I believe that it is my favorite temple in the world. From a distance it seems a mere mass of stone. But as one approaches the temple in its park-like setting, you are immediately struck by the hundreds of huge African looking faces that dominate the building. The Bayon, a temple second in size only to Angkor Wat, is an intricate, eight hundred-year-old shrine celebrated for the gigantic stone faces of its builder, Jayavarman VII. In 1297, a Chinese merchant named Chou Ta-kuan described the Bayon as shining with gold and exclaimed that "On the eastern side is a golden bridge, on each side of which are two golden lions, while eight golden Buddhas are placed at the base of the stone chambers." An inscription on the Bayon temple pertaining to Jayavarman states that, "He suffered from the sicknesses of his subjects more than from his own: for it is the public grief which makes the grief of kings and not their personal grief."

I came away from my November 1999 trip to Southeast Asia with the belief that the temples and monuments of Cambodia are about as impressive, with the clear exceptions of Egypt and possibly India, as any that currently exist. Enshrouded as they are by massive jungle growth, the monuments of Angkor are simply splendid to look upon and reflect the sustained creative genius of Black people.

2.7.- The Cham of Vietnam

April 11, 2005

I am now in Hoi An, Vietnam, in the center of the country. Hoi An is a charming port city. I have already been in the north and now the center of Vietnam and I leave for the south today. It has been an excellent trip and I find Vietnam to be a wonderful country. Some of the major highlights so far, besides the general beauty of the country and the people, have been two museums and a visit to the ancient city of My Son. The two museums are the History Museum in Hanoi, in the north, and the Cham Museum in Danang in the center.

The Cham, a clearly Africoid people, were responsible for classical civilization in Vietnam and a major section of the second floor of the History Museum in Hanoi is devoted to them. It was my first visit to Hanoi and I visited the museum on consecutive days. It is simply a delight to see both new pieces and pieces that I had previously only seen in books. The Cham Museum in Danang is incredible and I think that it ranks in the same category with the great museums in Egypt and Europe. My Son was the religious center for the Cham and I was able to visit it for the second time. My tour group found it dazzling.

So today we go to Ho Chi Minh City (formerly Saigon) where we will visit what used to be the National Museum. There is no telling what we will find there.

2.7.1.- Ho Chi Minh City

April 15, 2005

I am now in Ho Chi Minh City in Vietnam. You may know the city as Saigon. Compared to the other cities that I have visited here this one is huge. It seems like a cross between Paris and Manhattan. I arrived this morning with my tour group. The big thing so far is a visit to the History Museum. Those of you who know me understand that I am something of a museum fanatic and I never miss a chance to visit a new one in the quest to find and document the global history of African people.

So far, the primary focus of my visit to Vietnam has been the ethnic minorities (that is the politically correct word for Indigenous people here) and the Cham. It has not been an easy search in either case. The Viets (the Mongoloid people of the region) are as much in denial (perhaps even more) as white folks about the role of Black people in world history. And the Cham were as Black (Africoid) as any group of people that I have ever encountered. I'm telling you that when you see their art you tend to think that you are looking at people from the Congo!

As for the ethnic minorities, there are Africoid people among them too. But it is a devil of a time documenting them. And the Viets themselves consistently tell you that there are no Black people in the country. You can show them the photos in my African Presence in Early Asia book and the photos in the museums and they look you right in the eye and say things like "they are just dark. They are not really Black." Or they might say, "it is simply a bad photo." Or they might say, "The photograph just looks dark." Or they might say, "yes, they used to be Black but are not now." Or they might say that, "yes, they are Black but they are not Black like other Black people!" These guides seem to be nice people but they stepped on my last nerve today with their racial nonsense. Isn't it amazing that that same phenomenon exists here when it comes to the presence of purely Africoid people as exists all over the world.

It is clear to me sisters and brothers that both white supremacy and yellow supremacy are linked and tied hand and hand. And it is so frustrating and illustrates the work that must be done to construct the history of our people in Southeast Asia. Well, perhaps that is simply the mission that the Ancestors have given us.

So it is an emotional day for me. I have found artifacts that I never knew existed. And I have found further evidence for the spread of African people to the far corners of the earth. God almighty and African Ancestors be praised.

2.8.- On The Great Wall of China

March 10, 2004

How many of us have wanted to visit China? I certainly did, and when the opportunity availed itself in March 2001 there I went. I was already in Hawaii anyway and I was excited about going farther. Not only was China the center of a great and ancient civilization, it was a land with a deep history of African contributions, and me being a man with a keen interest in the global African presence, especially in Asia, I felt that I simply had to go.

And so it was that, buoyed by the fact that the trip had been handled by an African travel agency (I love to recycle Black dollars), I arrived, all alone, in Beijing on March 4, 2001. Sure enough, sisters and brothers, it was not long after landing in China that I found myself on the "Great Wall." It was another dream that came true—I was actually standing on the Great Wall of China! But beyond the excitement of being there, how was it really? Actually, I was not that impressed. I suppose that I had been spoiled by Egypt and I've come to the conclusion that after you've visited Egypt a few times everything else pales in comparison.

Indeed, since my first trip to Egypt in 1992, I have visited India's Taj Mahal, Fatehpur Sikri and Pink City, mighty Angkor in Cambodia, Great Zimbabwe in Southern Africa, Bagan in Myanmar, the rock churches in Lalibela, Ethiopia, Cusco and Machu Picchu in Peru, and a whole lot more. And these are impressive areas indeed but nothing really matches up to the pyramids, tombs and temples of Egypt. But at least I could say that I was there—that I stood on the Great Wall! Good for me.

Following the Great Wall I journeyed to the Ming Tombs, which I found interesting but not really awe inspiring. But it was during my visit to the Ming Tombs that something happened that in many ways set the tone for the entire trip. People started to follow me! Both men and women, but especially young women, started following me! Finally, I just stopped in my tracks and asked my tour guide what was going on. He told me that my followers were in admiration of me and thought that I must be some kind of celebrity! Well, with that explanation handed to me I quickly calmed down and went about the important business of sight seeing. But the people continued to follow me and it soon got to the point where folks were shaking my hand and asking to take photographs with me. Well, worse things have happened to me and I pretty much took it in all in stride. But a lot more was to follow on my Chinese odyssey and not all of it was as pleasant.

And so I got through my first day in China. I had had a long trip, checked into a fabulous hotel, climbed China's Great Wall, visited the Ming Tombs and been mistaken for a celebrity. All in a day's work in the life of Runoko Rashidi, fast on his way to becoming "a legend in his own mind." Next day, fresh and relaxed I went to the Forbidden City. I remember a lot of things about that second day. First, that it was cold and windy. Second, I found not a scrap of litter on the streets. Third, that language was going to be a big barrier. Fourth, I never saw any women in tight and revealing clothes. And, perhaps more than important than all of the rest, I had not seen any Black people yet—neither depiction nor actual person! There were none in the Forbidden City, just as there had been none on the Great Wall or in the Ming Tombs. So much for antiquity. And then it suddenly dawned on me that I hadn't seen any in the hotel or in the restaurants or in the streets or anywhere. What was going on here? Trust me when I say that a brother was starting to feel a little lonely.

Next day I visited the Temple of Heaven and the Lama Temple. I was impressed with both places. And this was followed the next day with a trip to the Reed Moat Bridge, the Summer Palace and Tiananmen Square. I went to different restaurants every day and the food was great. So far, pretty good. But still, no Black folks! What could have happened to them I wondered? Wasn't this the place where Chancellor Williams said that we were once powerful enough to build a kingdom of our own? And didn't my brothers James E. Brunson and Wayne B. Chandler document the existence of Black people here? Hadn't Clyde Ahmed Winters done some pioneering work on the subject? And hadn't Rev. James Marmaduke Boddy written about the African presence in ancient China way back in 1905? And what about that 1998 DNA study that concluded that most of the people of modern China had African genetic origins? What was going on here? I was starting to feel confused.

Next day I took an excursion about seventy miles out of Beijing to visit the East Qing Tombs. I thought that if I couldn't find Black people in Beijing itself that I might have better luck elsewhere. The tombs were splendid and it was well worth the journey, although I still had not found what I was looking for. On the other hand, the people that I met that day were said to be peasants of Manchu stock and they weren't friendly at all. Indeed, for the first time on the trip I met folks who actually seemed cold and even a little hostile. I didn't like it. When I asked my tour guides what the local people were saying about me they just shrugged and requested that I not worry about it. I liked it even less.

Well, I guess that you could say that by this time I had seen about enough of Beijing and the surrounding areas and it was more than time to go. And so away I went to city of Xi'an. You know the city—the one with the terra cotta soldiers. I didn't see the soldiers that day but I did make a long anticipated visit to the Shaanxi Provincial Museum of History—said to be China's best museum. What a disappointment! Not a sister or brother—ancient or modern—in the place. Damn!

And then I went to the Tang Dynasty Museum. The Tang Dynasty represents one of the great high points in Chinese history. But there was nothing that I could say was distinctly Africoid in the Tang Museum! They even brought the Museum Director himself out to meet me. I was told that it was his official day off but when he heard that I was coming he showed up anyhow. He told me that he was honored to meet me and that I was the first Black man to ever visit the place. But when I asked him about African people in the history of China I drew a complete blank. He claimed that he knew nothing about such a possibility. At least he was consistent.

Of my three guides, all of whom professed great stores of knowledge regarding early China, I could jar nothing loose from them regarding an ancient African presence. At the same time, however, they all knew about the anti-African riots that took place in China in the mid-1980s. I was beginning to wonder if all of this, I mean the whole experience, was a kind of dream or something.

The following day was my best in China! I went to the Banpo Neolithic Village and drove past the tomb of Emperor Qin Shi Huang, and finally got to the museum of terra cotta soldiers and horses. They were magnificent and represent another high point in Chinese history, and I was impressed by the fact that both the tomb and soldiers and horses all belonged to the same man who began construction of the Great Wall, and I thought that closest comparison that I could make was to the great pyramid builders of Old Kingdom Egypt.

For lunch that day in Xi'an I went to another great restaurant followed by a visit to an actual Chinese tea house. This time all of the waitresses paused in their attention to the needs of the other diners to give me a peep and even the chef came out of the kitchen to take a look. And, oh yes, by this time I had seen a couple of African-American tourists and what appeared to be an African diplomat and one of them actually talked to me! Wow!

The next two days I saw the Xi'an city walls, a Han tomb complex, a drum tower and another museum. And I noticed a few other things too. It seemed that the Chinese, in general, smoked like chimneys, that they were highly disciplined, that there were lots of unemployed laborers, that there was a great deal of industrial pollution and the skies always seemed hazy, that there were many things to buy with aggressive vendors at every site, and that the people as a whole seemed very proud to be Chinese.

Well sisters and brothers, my trip to China was coming to an end and I suppose that it was just as well. I was glad that I had gone but I had found no documentation of the African presence and had spent quite a lot of money in my search. I suppose that I should have been better prepared but based on all the work that had gone into my African Presence in Early Asia anthology I really thought that it would have been a simple process with the African imprint everywhere. It turned out to be far from the case. Even the artifacts that I saw dating from the Shang Dynasty period did not seem Africoid. At least they didn't to me.

And so, rather downcast, I returned to Beijing for one more night before an early morning flight back to the United States. After settling down in Beijing's Mandarin Hotel, where I got a beautiful suite, I went out in search of what I hoped would be a really special meal before I departed the People's Republic of China. But it did not turn out that way. As a matter of fact, I never did get to eat that evening. The first two restaurants that I went to were in the hotel itself. In the first one I waited about thirty minutes for service and never having received any I simply got up and walked out. In the second hotel restaurant

I felt distinctly unwelcome. I don't believe in spending money where I don't feel comfortable and so I soon left that place too. And then I walked around the block thinking that I would have more success outside of the hotel. But the result was just more of the same. At one restaurant that I stopped at I was quickly ushered in with a smile and what appeared to be words of welcome. But then all of a sudden all of the waitresses started to giggle and laugh and I soon got the heck out of there too.

Sisters and brothers, I was livid! I not only let the front desk at the Mandarin Hotel have it at what I considered my overall rude treatment at the hands of the Chinese but I had plenty of venom left for my tour guides the next morning too. All they could do was tell me how sorry they were and rather lamely explain that the local people were just not used to seeing Black folks. And so I blasted them some more.

So I guess that you could say that my trip to China was a kind of bitter sweet affair. I was glad that I had gone because there is nothing like seeing it for yourself. And many of the monuments that I saw there were indeed impressive. But I left China thinking that I would never go there again, and I could not help wondering again and again about what happened to all of the Black people in China.

22. A Tribal man in Tamil Nadu, India

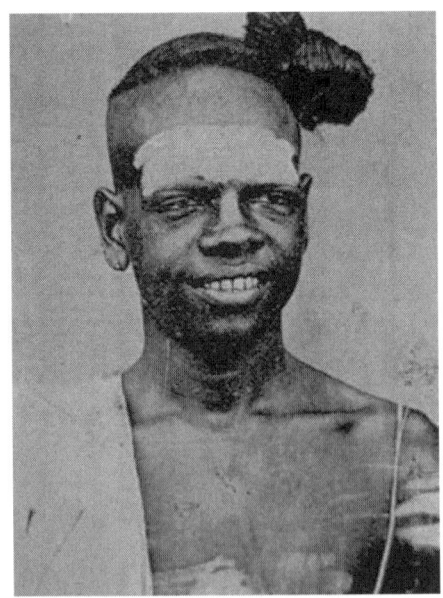

23. A Black Brahman in South India

24. A Tribal woman in India

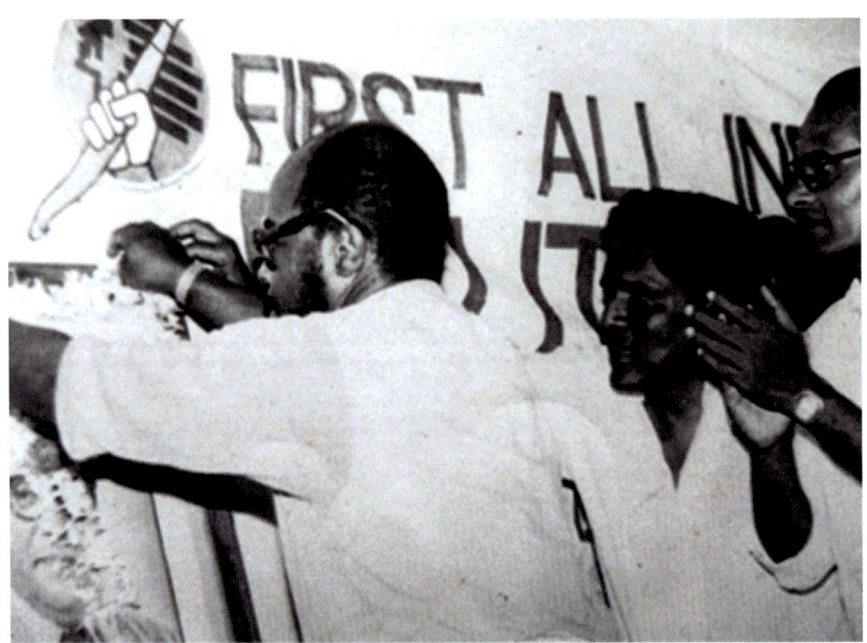

25. Runoko Rashidi in Hyderabad, India in 1987

26. Runoko Rashidi in Trivandrm, India in 1998

27. Fudo Myo. The Metropolitan Museum of Art, NYC.
Photo by Runoko Rashidi

28. Fudo Myo. The Archaeology and Anthropology Museum,
University of Pennsylvania, Philadelphia

29. La Tigresse. The Chernushi Musee, Paris. Photo by Runoko Rashidi

30. A Black Buddha from early Central China

31. A Black Man in Tang Dynasty China. In the Smithsonian Collections, Washington, DC. Photo by Runoko Rashidi

32. A Black Man in Tang Dynasty China. In the Victoria and Albert Museum, London. Photo by Runoko Rashidi

33. A Black dignitary in Yuan Dynasty China. The Asian Art Museum, San Francisco. Photo by Runoko Rashidi

34. A Khmer king or divinity. Victoria and Albert Museum, London. Photo by Runoko Rashidi

35. An Apsara from Angkor Wat, Cambodia. Photo by Hamara Holt

36. A Boddhisatva in the innermost sanctuary of Angkor Wat.
Photo by Runoko Rashidi

37. A face from Angkor. Photo by Hamara Holt

38. A statue from Bantei Srei, Cambodia. Photo by Runoko Rashidi

39. A face from the entrance to Angkor Thom, Cambodia.
Photo by Hamara Holt

40. An Africoid face from the Bayon. Photo by Hamara Holt

41. Africoid faces from the Bayon. Photo by Hamara Holt

42. Statue of Shiva. Rietberg Museum, Zurich. Photo by Runoko Rashidi

43. Statue of Shiva. Rietberg Museum, Zurich. Photo by Runoko Rashidi

44. Head of Vishnu. Cham Museum, Vietnam. Photo by Hamara Holt

45. Colossal head of Buddha. Musee Guimet. Photo by Runoko Rashidi

46. Statue of Shiva. Cleveland Museum of Art.

2.9.- The African Experience In Turkey:
A Family Gathering

November 8, 2004

Now and then in the course of travel something approaching magic happens. Today in Turkey one of those moments occurred. You surely should have noticed by now that when I travel I am always in search of the African presence and this trip is no exception. I am now in the Aegean seaside city of Kusadasi. I was driven here this morning through the Black Mountains from the city of Izmir. Well, after a diligent search, some prayer, an excellent travel agent and an outstanding guide I am finally connecting with a long established African presence in Turkey.

It was not easy but far off the beaten path I was guided to a house inhabited by a mother, daughter and grandchild of Sudanese ancestry. It was raining (which I considered a good sign), and the guide, himself guided by a small Turkish boy that we picked up in a village, stopped at a house and knocked on the door. Two African women peeked out of the window to see who it was and seemed utterly shocked but very pleasantly surprised to see my face. It was like they could not believe what they were seeing! They then beckoned me inside. I removed my shoes and with a big smile I entered their house. The older sister, I guess about fifty-five, and her daughter, about twenty-five, seemed a little nervous but they never wavered in their courtesy. With that the older woman indicated to my driver, guide and translator that she would return shortly and left us for a few moments and the young sister entertained us with small talk still obviously flabbergasted by my presence. When I asked her if she had ever met an African-American before, she reacted like I had just asked her if she had ever been to the moon. The answer was an emphatic no!

Within a few moments the older woman returned and within another few minutes we were joined by three other women. They were all African and they all seemed overjoyed to see me and indicated that I was their brother. I have rarely felt such joy and contentment. My search had been rewarded! They served me Turkish tea and we spent the morning together and all of the time they never stopped beaming at me.

In summary, this is what they told me. After I introduced myself as an African historian looking for documentation of the African presence in Asia these sisters informed me that their families had been in the community for generations and as far back as they recall. They told me that originally they had come from Sudan and that all of their husbands were dead. They told me that they had never met an African from America before and that I looked just like them, and that I was their brother. They told me that they were discriminated against by the white Turks and that they were very poor and desolate and that they felt very much abandoned. It was all very emotional.

They told me that they were all Muslims and that each of them had three children and that the children went to the small local school. They told me that they generated money from agricultural labor but only for about three months a year and that life for them was very hard. They told me that the Turks treated them differently because of their color and called them Zanj (Black). They told me that Sudanese government representatives had come to visit them about two years earlier but had never followed up on their promises to stay in touch. They implored me not to forget about them. They told me that African people were sprinkled here and there throughout the region. I was overwhelmed.

I then asked them if I could take pictures and they were really happy at the chance. So I photographed them individually and then collectively. And then I had my picture taken with them and then took some of them and my guide. And then I gave them one of my cards but the sister that I gave it to told me that she could not read and so I gave it to her daughter. The daughter was married to a white Turk, by the way, who had been imprisoned for a reason that I did not press her on.

And then I asked, knowing that they were very poor but maintained their dignity, if I could offer them a bit of money and they said yes. And so I gave each of the elders about twenty million Turkish lira, and the youngest one ten million Turkish lira. It is not as much as it might sound but it was a substantial gift nevertheless. And then I gave the eldest sister fifty US dollars and told her that is was for all of them to share. And then they cried and I got kind of emotional too and I felt even better that I asked them to accept the money and they did not ask for it themselves. It was my idea, for I do believe that people should always be able to maintain their human dignity. And then they blessed my trip and I excused myself, telling them as I departed that the morning that we spent together was by itself worth the entire trip to Turkey. And they really liked that.

And they asked me never to forget them and they told me that they would never forget me. And with that I left. Yes, every now and then on one of my trips there are magic moments such as these. I guess that you could even say that we made a bit of history.

I think that I better end this little travel note now as the emotion is starting to overwhelm me once again. I trust that you understand.

2.9.1.- Mary's house

November 10, 2004

I am now back in London and missing Turkey. I left Istanbul for Amsterdam and London late this afternoon feeling a little sad about going. So many incredible things happened during the nine days that I was there. I could give multiple lectures on the subject! For example, I met some other African people including a Black Egyptian family whose relatives had been in the region for at least two-hundred years and at least three other brothers as well, although I did not get to talk to them for very long. I also visited the city of Ephesus where St. Paul preached and where St. John was buried. I actually saw John's grave. There is also a temple of Isis there, and the African deity Bes was very prominent. And I visited an ancient library there. But there was one other experience, among so many, that really stands out and you can make of it what you will.

On Sunday morning I went to an ancient house reputed to be the dwelling where the Virgin Mary is said to have lived after the crucifixion of Jesus. That is what the locals believe, both Christian and Muslim, and pilgrims come from all over the world to pray for miracles. Now, although I was raised a Christian I really had no interest in seeing the place, but my driver and guide took me there anyway! And then I decided not to bother to take my camera as I was saving film and then at the last minute I took it anyway.

Outside of the house is a brown statue of Mary. She did not look African, but at least the statue was brown. So we go in the place and there is a young Christian nun sitting at the entrance. Inside the house were a number of images of Mary, most of which I was not impressed by. But then I laid my eyes on a black image of Mary and the infant Jesus. There is supposed to be no talking inside the house but I quietly asked my guide about the statue's age. In spite of my protests he immediately went to ask the nun about it and I reluctantly followed just to see if she would say anything. She mentioned again, very quietly, that there was to be no conversation in the house but if we were really interested we could step outside very briefly for a word or two.

When we got outside she said that she thought that the statue was from either Egypt or Ethiopia and that she believed that it was about five hundred years old. She also said that she believed that the black color represented something profound. Well I thought that that was a pretty good response and was prepared to let the matter rest. But then she continued to talk about the statue's symbolism. Well she said that she had no time but she just kept right on talking and other people were starting to gather. And so I told her that I had already seen a few Black Madonnas in my time and gave her the details. She seemed very impressed and asked for more information. More people started to gather.

I told her that I had seen Black Madonnas in Russia and Spain and and Costa Rica and France. And then she said that although she believed that the Madonna statue in Mary's house had originally come from Egypt or Ethiopia that it had been brought to Mary's house directly from Le Puy in France. I could not believe it! I had been trying to see this statue for twenty years and here it was right in front of me! And so I began to give a small lecture on the history of Le Puy and the Black Madonna complete with references! I told her that Joan of Arc used to pray before it. And she said, "really?" And I said "yes!" And she said, "really?" And I said "yes!" By this time a large crowd had started to gather— Greeks, Turks, Italians, Spanish, French, Japanese. And so I went on. I told her that one of the Crusades was launched from Le Puy. And she said "really?" and I said "yes!" This young nun was so flushed with excitement that she ran inside and brought the Madonna statue out of the house and into the sunlight in front of everybody and I just continued to lecture! Thirty minutes had passed and the crowd continued to grow! I got even bolder and asked her if I could photograph the statue even though I knew that it was strictly forbidden and without hesitation she said "yes!" And so I took about eight pictures of it including one of her holding it. She even let me touch it! I thought that I was dreaming!

And then she told me to wait a minute and that she had some information inside for me. This woman ran off and left me with the statue! Can you believe it? I could have put it in my bag and walked off with this precious icon! Anyway, a few minutes later she came back with a lot of literature about her order and implored me to share it with the African community! Just to humor her I agreed. This nun, this young white woman, then took my right hand and held it tightly for about five minutes and did not seem to want to let it go! I had to finally almost snatch it away! I think that we both had an experience that we will never forget.

And that is how I began my last day in Turkey. That is a true story sisters and brothers. Believe it or not.

2.10.- A Black Man in Jordan

March 22, 2005

After a lot of flying I arrived in Amman last night. Amman is the capital of Jordan and it is the first visit to a "purely" Arab country, as I consider Egypt more African than Arab. Getting my visa was no problem and in a short time there I was in the lobby of my hotel with the head of the tour company, a Palestinian with Jordanian citizenship. Indeed, about half the population of Jordan is Palestinian—including Black Palestinians.

Today I did a tour of the city, including the big and beautiful King Abdullah Mosque (there were two churches right across the street from it) and the Citadel, of course, the archaeological museum. The museum was not impressive but like all of the museums that I have visited of late there were a number of artifacts from Egypt. The Citadel also contained an ancient Roman temple built during the reign of Emperor Hadrian.

From Amman I journeyed to Jerash—an early Roman city. Jerash is even larger than Ephesus in Turkey. It seems that I am becoming something of an expert on the Romans and I rather liked the place. It too had a museum and there were a bunch of young and not so young and energetic Jordanian children out on a field trip. It was a pleasure to see them and the site was so large that it was easy to find a bit of solitude within. And then came the highlight of the day—a journey to the Dead Sea and my first meetings with Black folks in Jordan, the most important of which, by far, was brother Raja Juma.

Raja Juma was the Assistant Food and Beverage Manager at the Movenpick Resort and Spa Dead Sea. The hotel itself is wonderful and as I am sure to bring a group of us to Jordan and Turkey I will see the place again. Brother Raja, let me see if I can quickly tell his story, is about thirty five years old. Raja was a very handsome brother, extremely confident and proud, who looks like he could be straight from the Congo. He spoke very good English and told me that either his father or grandfather, I forget which, was born in South Africa and moved to Palestine. It must have been his grandfather. The father then moved to Jordan.

To hear Raja tell it there are about seven thousand Black people in Jordan with various origins. Some come from the Sudan and others, like Raja himself, are from other parts of Africa. Some have been in Jordan for a very long time, just how long he could not specify. He told that me that a lot of the Palestinians in Israel, Palestine, and Jordan are Black, especially in Haifa and Jericho. He told me about all of the dignitaries that he had met including Bill Clinton, President Bush, Colin Powell (he said that Colin Powell was a "really cool brother"), Jacques Chirac and many more. He worked personally for King Hussein and the current King Abdullah and liked them both very much. He even showed me photos that he had taken with them. He is the "boss" of 270 people and introduced me to several of them, three of them African, including a couple of family members.

Brother Raja told me that Black people were not discriminated against in Jordan and during his travels throughout the Middle East, including Saudi Arabia and the Gulf States, that the situation was very similar. He told me that in Jordan Blacks occupied high positions, particularly in the the military. During all of this I had a stunned and rather incredulous look on my face but he just laughed and continued. He said that the only time that he had faced racial discrimination was during his three trips to the United States! He also told me that a lot of African-American military personel came to Jordan from Iraq on vacation. He told me that the reason that he spoke such good English was through watching TV and talking to people. He told me that he identified himself first as a Black man, then a Jordanian, then an Arab, and then a Muslim. And then he paid for my entire, expensive, I must say, lunch and beverages. It was quite an afternoon and I think that we definitely bonded. I think of brother Raja as a friend now and we are definitely going to stay connected. Those are some of today's highlights. Tomorrow I leave Amman and head south to the ancient city of Petra with numerous stops along the way. What a life!

2.10.1.- A note from southern Jordan

March 23, 2005

I am in Petra, Wadi Musa, Jordan. Yesterday I went to the ancient city of Petra. It is almost beyond words. Perhaps if I were to call it marvelous, or wonderful, or remarkable, or overwhelming I might be able to come close. But I have never seen anything like it or been anywhere like it.

The city of Petra is a couple thousand years old. It was originally built by people called Nabateans. I am not sure who they were. Then the Romans came along and built some more. It is I think that biggest ancient city that I have ever seen. Just getting to the entrance point from the ticket office is about an hour's walk. Then you walk through this gorge for about an hour before you get to the first building. This first building is called the Treasury but it is really an ancient tomb. I had never seen anything quite like it. The stone is a kind of rust color with a lot of other shades blended in. And then the city itself expands for many kilometers. I don't remember the last time I walked so much.

Inside Petra you meet the people called Bedouin. Very interesting folks, the Bedouin. Some of them are very dark. They reminded me of the Gypsies that I see when I travel to Europe. I shared a glass of tea with a few of them and they told me that many of the Bedouin are Black. I hope to meet some when I return with a tour group.

One of the big highlights of my visit to Petra was an ancient building known as the Monastery. It is an ancient tomb that was eventually converted into a church. Once again, I have never seen anything like it. But first I had to get there. It is up by a mountain and there are about nine hundred steps to reach it. I was walking up the mountain and then I saw this young Black Bedouin teenager who offered to take me up there on a donkey for five dinar (the local currency is known as the Jordanian dinar). So since I figured that this would be a good way to chat with this young brother I agreed and even though I thought several times that both me and the donkey were going to fall off the side of a cliff I am glad that I did it. I am not sure if I would have made it otherwise. I am talking steep mountainside here! But it was worth it. And getting down was no joke either!

Following the Monastery I visited the local museum and found a depiction of the Ancient Egyptian god Bes and what was described as "the face of a Black man." And I bought a book on the history of Petra. And then there was the walk back to my hotel! This time I was glad to find a donkey to ride and was looking for a horse or a camel or a carriage but I was fresh out of dinars. All things considered, it was quite a day. I ate some Bedouin food in the city of Wadi Musa and slept good last night.

So now I am ready to fly away. I have seen a number of Black people, talked to a few, ate some interesting food, made some contacts and seen Petra. Indeed, I am feeling humbled and subdued right now and thinking about my upcoming adventures in Vietnam and Cambodia.

2.10.2.- Reflecting on Jordan

March 25, 2005

Throughout my trip to Jordan, with one exception, I did not see more than one Black person at a time. By that I mean that the only time that I saw Black folks were as individuals. I never saw a group except when I was in the Movenpick Hotel at the Dead Sea with brother Raja Juma. There he introduced me to two more brothers and we took photos together. But beyond that I only saw one here and there. I thought this rather odd also. And most of the ones that I saw were very dark! I met one brother working in a restaurant at a place called Kerak and he told me that a lot of the Black people in Jordan were "Sudani." And I would see one here standing on the street, and another one there working on a construction site, and a sister here walking down the street with a shopping bag, and a brother there walking down the street talking on a cell phone. And I saw this really fine sister working in a booth at the airport early this morning but she seemed too interested in talking to these white boys to notice me. I never got the sense that there was a Black community in Jordan and none of the sisters and brothers that I saw looked "oppressed." Does that make sense to you? They just seemed like ordinary folks going about their business. And absolutely everybody that I talked to, Black or white, Christian or Muslim, Bedouin or city dweller, assured me that there no difference between them. It was tempting to believe them but I guess I have been in America too long, and I am cynical about such things.

The stars in the desert were beautiful last night. The moon was full and bright and I had no problems. Jordan was a good experience and I am glad that I went. I want to see more of the region, including Syria, Lebanon, Yemen and even Israel and Palestine when the time is right. African people are a global people. We are scattered far and wide and have made fantastic contributions to the world. And there is no where on earth that I do not want to go in order to find and further document the Global African Presence.

2.11.- The African Presence in Syrian Antiquity

October 31, 2005

I spent the past weekend in Istanbul, Turkey and arrived early this morning in Damascus, Syria. It is my first visit here and this makes country number fifty-nine that I have visited.

I like Syria. I must confess that I was more than a little nervous about coming here but I want to see the world and so here I am. The people seem friendly and you certainly don't get the impression that it is the kind of police state projected on CNN and the US news media.

My day this morning started, naturally enough, in the National Museum of Syria where I saw a number of important artifacts relating to the African presence, including a number of pieces from Kmt and other artifacts that reflect a strong Nile Valley influence. There was also an exquisite vase depicting an African nobleman dated to about eighteen hundred years ago during the time of Roman dominance in this part of the world.

I also visited the Ummayad Mosque, considered the fourth most important mosque in the world. I was really impressed. Next to the mosque near the medina is the house of one of modern Syria's early heads of state. In the house are three excellent paintings of Antar—a dashing knight and poet, and the Black man regarded by Arabs as the father of modern chivalry. I took some good photos here.

The highlight of my day was a visit to the tomb of Bilal. I actually saw it! This was not on my itinerary but I found a way to squeeze it in anyhow. Bilal, you know, was an African from Ethiopia regarded as the closest companion of the Prophet Muhammad and so important in history that he is considered "a third of the Islamic faith." I read many years ago that he had a tomb in Damascus and today I actually saw it. It is covered in a green shroud. I photographed the tomb and the magnificent mosque right next to it that carries his name.

I saw many Africans along the streets of Damascus. In fact, I was surprised at so many Black folks! When I asked about them I was simply told in a matter of fact manner that "they are just Syrians."

African family, I am now in the city of Palmyra. I had to cross the Syrian Desert to get here as Palmyra is about one hundred and fifty miles from Damascus and about the same distance from the Iraqi border. It is an ancient city and full of history. Indeed, the dominant personality from ancient Palmyra is a woman named Zenobia that J.A. Rogers devoted a chapter to in his World's Great Men of Color.

So that is about it for now. By the way, someone asked me recently "Brother Runoko, don't you ever get scared going to all these places, especially by yourself?" My answer is, "Of course I do!" I get plenty nervous and, yes, sometimes I am afraid and I definitely get lonely and wish that I had some other Africans to talk to and share the experience with.

Tomorrow I visit the ruins of Palmyra and the following day I get back on the road to Damascus with some nice stops along the way. My travel agents are trying to arrange for me to meet with some members South African community here. By the way, did you see the letter from South African President Thabo Mbeki last week referencing my work on the Moors? He gave me a really nice recognition. I am extremely proud of that and I hope to meet him during my Southern Africa lecture tour next May! My only regret so far is that my trip to Syria is not long enough. So far I have found an incredible friendliness among the local people. Absolutely nobody has given me a hard time and I think that I am safer here than most places in the good old USA. I like it here.

2.12.- Looking Back at Lebanon

July 27, 2006

You know that I was just in Lebanon in January 2006. I was told that it was a very safe place to travel, and I went there all alone in search of the African presence ancient and modern. And I found a lot of it too.

It was a very satisfying trip. I flew in from Paris via Italy and spent five days in Lebanon. I toured Beirut, traveled to the Bekaa Valley, had tea in the home of a noted local archaeologist, and visited all of the major ruins at Baalbek, Byblos, Tyre, and Sidon.

The people were extremely friendly and welcoming. During my visit to Lebanon I talked to African people and Christians and Muslims and even Druze. I even went to south Beirut where so much of the recent devastation has taken place. What a shame. What a tragedy.

I am glad that I went to Lebanon when I did because, as a country, Lebanon will never be the same. It was a safe country to visit then but it is certainly not safe anymore.

2.13.- Letters from Indonesia

March 6, 2007

Runoko Rashidi is fine and well in the middle of Central Java, Indonesia. Specifically I am in a very nice hotel in the city of Yogyakarta (a city of about 500,000 people) called the heart and soul of the big island of Java.

Most of the people here are Muslims. Indeed, Indonesia has the largest concentration of Muslims in the world—a population of more than two hundred million people. But so far I have not felt uncomfortable even though I have only seen one clearly phenotypically Black person. This was a fairly light complexioned young Black woman in the airport in Denpasar, Bali. I spoke to her but got little response. I think that she may have been from New Guinea.

Indonesia invaded West Papua New Guinea more than three decades ago and reports tell us that many atrocities have taken place.

But the real reason that I am here in Indonesia is within an hour's drive. And believe me when I say that it was a real effort to get here.

And now I am where I am supposed to be and I just hope that it will be worth it. I should know in a relatively short time as just a couple of hours from now I will be on my way by car to the temple complex of Borobudur—the largest such structure in all of Southeast Asia, and I don't know anyone who has visited the place. So I suppose that I am something of a pioneer. I have a car, a driver, a guide, a camera and plenty of film, and now it is just a matter of going.

2.13.1.- Borobudur

March 7, 2007

This morning I went to the magnificent Buddhist temple at Borobudur. Borobudur is about an hour's drive northwest of Yogyakarta and is one of major reasons that I came to Indonesia in the first place. Borobudur is a large temple built around a small hill and ranks with the greatest temples in Southeast Asia, including those at Angkor in Cambodia and Bagan in Myanmar.

I've already been to Angkor three times and Bagan twice, and so I have been very fortunate. As a matter of fact, I think that Southeast Asia has the greatest monuments in the world outside of Egypt. It is true that I have not been to the Sudan, Libya, Yemen, Iraq and Iran yet but I have laid eyes on a lot of monuments in a lot of places, including Egypt, Ethiopia, Zimbabwe, Tunisia, Morocco, Peru, Mexico, Central America, India, China, Japan, Jordan, Syria, Lebanon, Turkey and all over southern Europe, but Southeast Asia is hard to top. As I said, so far only the monuments, temples and tombs of ancient Egypt have impressed me more. And Egypt, you know, is in a category all by itself.

Borobudur was built by the rulers of the Buddhist Sailendra dynasty in Central Java about twelve hundred years ago. It is made up of volcanic stone, and from a distance it has the appearance of a large pyramid. It took about a hundred years to build and it was in use for only a hundred years afterward.

The monument is said to have been conceived as a Buddhist version of the cosmos in stone. The lower levels of the temple have intricately carved reliefs, while the upper levels represent nirvana. Almost five hundred statues of the Buddha stare down at you from the temple and at the very top is a large ornamental stupa. The edifice stood abandoned for almost a thousand years until the English and Dutch began the colossal task of restoration beginning in the nineteenth century.

This is the low tourist season here in Indonesia and therefore there were not a lot of people at Borobudur this morning. And I am happy to say that by taking my time I managed to climb all the way to the top of the temple. This part of the temple is called the Sphere of Formlessness.

Although I did a lot of huffing and puffing it was actually not a bad climb. The heat and humidity is what made it seem tough. And the view from the top was magnificent. The entire area is surrounded by lush green hills and volcanoes, or what some of the local people call fire mountains.

I also went to two related temples. The first of these is known as the Mendut temple and has a ten foot high statue of the Buddha inside. The second temple is called Candi Pawon. This is a small temple with a pyramidal roof.

Tomorrow I visit the Hindu temple complex at Prambanan village. I should then be able to say mission accomplished in Indonesia! In the next note, god willing, I will tell you about Prambanan and some other things I hope you'll find interesting.

2.13.2.- The Prambanan

March 8, 2007

This morning I visited the Prambanan temple complex just northeast of the city of Yogyakarta. It is essentially Hindu in character and it is indeed impressive.

All of the more than two hundred temples in the Prambanan area were built between the eighth and tenth centuries when the southern part of Java was ruled by the Buddhist Sailendra dynasty and the northern part ruled by the Hindu Sanjaya dynasty.

The biggest of the Prambanan temples is called Candi Shiva. Candi is the Javanese word for temple and this particularly grand temple is dedicated to the great Hindu deity Shiva. Candi Shiva is most imposing and stands close to fifty meters high. Like the Borobudur temple, Candi Shiva is composed of dark volcanic stone and covered with intricate reliefs telling the story of the Hindu epic called the Ramayana.

The Prambanan temples are spread out over an area of several miles. This morning I was only able to see a few, including the larger ones. I would have seen more but I accidentally ripped my pants climbing inside the big temple. I wasn't supposed to be inside at all, as there is a high wire fence surrounding the place installed to keep people out. But I could not resist the temptation to go inside and so I bribed a couple of the local guards and there I went.

The Borobudur and Prambanan temples were nice but the imagery, the statues and reliefs, unlike Vietnam and Cambodia and even early Thailand and Myanmar, did not quite reflect what I consider a phenotypically Africoid character. The statues and the reliefs just did not look overtly African to me. And that was the grand disappointment. Indeed, only one of the statues, dubbed "the slender virgin", that I saw inside a highly darkened Prambanan temple, looked like a Black woman. Hopefully, I will have something more substantial to share with you then. But, for now, Indonesia is behind me. I am glad that I went. But Runoko Rashidi, the pioneer traveler and historian, would have loved to have seen more Africoid looking things on his Indonesian journey.

2.14.- Reflections about Myanmar (Burma)

May 28, 2008

I was blessed to visit Myanmar (Burma) twice, first in late August/early September 2001 on my own and again, I think in either November 2002 or 2003, as a group tour leader, and I was nervous all of the time. Myanmar is a generally poor, fairly isolated, country with a military government that places a lid on political expression and social activism.

Myanmar is a relatively large country by Southeast Asian standards and was known under British rule as Burma. I thought that the place was absolutely fascinating but few Africans go there. Indeed, it was one of those places where just by walking down a street you tend to stop traffic. The big draw in Myanmar for me was her temples. In a place in north central Myanmar called Bagan there are the remains of close to five thousand temples in an area of about twenty-five square miles. It is truly a temple field and I don't think that there is anything else quite like it in the world—not even in the Nile Valley in Africa. I don't know who the builders were but these are Buddhist temples erected over a period or about two-hundred-fifty years from around 1050 to 1300 C.E.. The temples are spread out over grassy fields on or near the banks of the Irrawaddy River. And no two temples are the same.

The Irrawaddy in Myanmar is similar to the Nile in Egypt and the Niger in West Africa. It is the region's lifeline. One evening I got a boat and journeyed on the river and watched the life of the country unfold about me—farmers using the river to irrigate their fields, fishermen casting their nets, children swimming and frolicking, women bathing and washing their clothes and their cooking utensils, and everybody watching me watch them. Everybody seemed friendly and most people smiled and waved at me. Life, for me at that moment at least, rarely seemed so tranquil.

The area was so agrarian that once you got away from the river it was easy to get a bicycle or a horse and buggy and move leisurely from temple to temple. Indeed, I worked hard to secure a room in the Bagan Hotel, constructed along the banks of the river, with an ancient temple on the hotel grounds and the hotel itself built in the likeness of an early Bagan temple. I was in paradise!

Unfortunately, I only saw one African from the West (I think that she was an African woman from France) all of the time that I was there, and so I really had no one to talk to. There was virtually no TV or radio and all that I could do besides visit temples was read and dream about all of the other places that I was going to visit. Of course, this was before September 11, 2001 and so on my list of places to see were such destinations as Yemen, Pakistan, Iran and Sri Lanka. It was all a dream I guess as I returned to the US exactly two days before the bombing of the Pentagon and the World Trade Center—when the world was turned upside down—and now I wonder if I will ever get to see these fabulous lands. But who knows? After all, I did get to visit Indonesia last year and so the dream hasn't completely died.

One of the things that stood out about Myanmar was the chalky type substance that most women and many men spread about their faces. I was told that it was designed to keep them from getting dark and that light skin was much desired. And this may have been as much about class as race and ethnicity. I was told that if you are a woman and you are dark that means that you are probably a peasant. And that if you are light that it meant that you do not work laboring in the fields.

Outside Bagan I spent most of the time in what was then the capital city of Myanmar—Yangon. Even here the city is dominated by a temple—the massive and splendid Shwedagon Paya. And of course I visited the big archaeological and ethnographic museums in Bagan and Yangon. In Bagan a group of young men made fun of my African features. But this was nothing compared to the museum visit in Yangon. There I bumped into a group of young school children and one of them, in particular, was absolutely terrified of me. I've never had a experience like that and the look in one little girl's eyes could not have reflected more fear than if she had seen the devil itself! She was simply horrified by my presence! It is something that I will never forget. These experiences, and those like them, have only happened to me in Asia and nowhere else.

As to the African presence in Southeast Asia itself, including Myanmar, this should be a special area of research. Some would deny the very existence of Africans there. But during my 2002 group tour to Myanmar our tour guide informed me that twenty miles south of Yangon resided a community of African pearl divers. I wonder if they are still there? Or did time and circumstance, particularly the massive cyclone, destroy or displace this African community? And how did they get there in the first place?

I miss Southeast Asia, including Myanmar. It is an archaeological treasure house. Maybe next year I will go back and pay the region another visit. And maybe I will do it right this time by returning to the old sites in Thailand, Vietnam, Cambodia, and Myanmar, and new places like Laos, Malaysia and even the Philippines. That is where my mind is leading me—perhaps a last grand trip to Southeast Asia in search of the African presence. Other local guides in Southeast Asia have informed me of "unmixed" Black people in east-central Cambodia. And there are clearly Black people in southern Thailand and northern Malaysia. And there is the fairly-well documented existence of indigenous Black people in the Philippines and the Montagnard communities in Central Vietnam.

Those are some of my reflections for today.

47. Black captives of Assyrians at Lachish, Judea. Circa 700 BCE.
Photo by Runoko Rashidi

48. A Black captive of Assyrians at Lachish, Judea. Circa 700 BCE.
Photo by Runoko Rashidi

49. Assyrian depiction of a Nubian hunter. Metropolitan Museum of Art, NYC. Photo by Runoko Rashidi

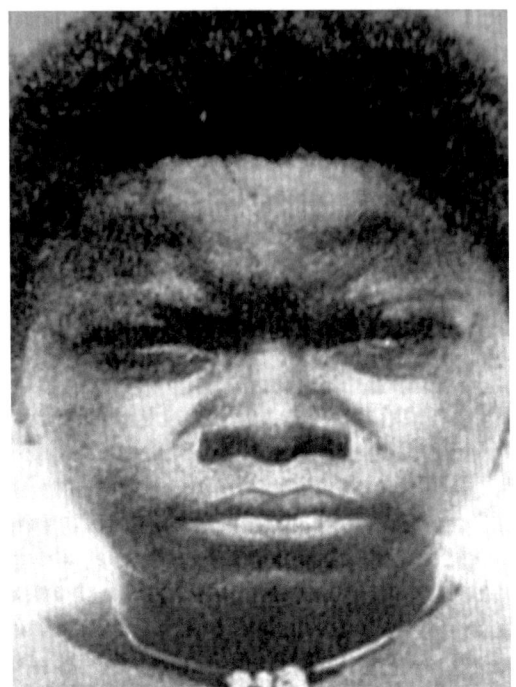

50. A Black woman in the Philippines

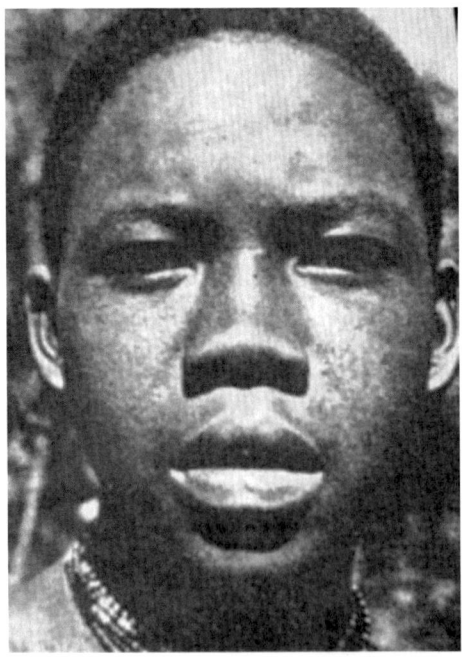

51. A Black youth in the Philippines

52. A Black woman and child in the Philippines

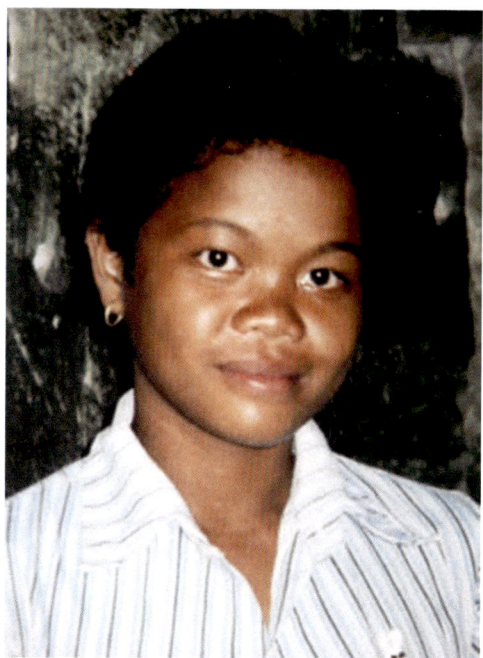

53. A young Khmer woman in Siem Reap, Cambodia.
Photo by Hamara Holt

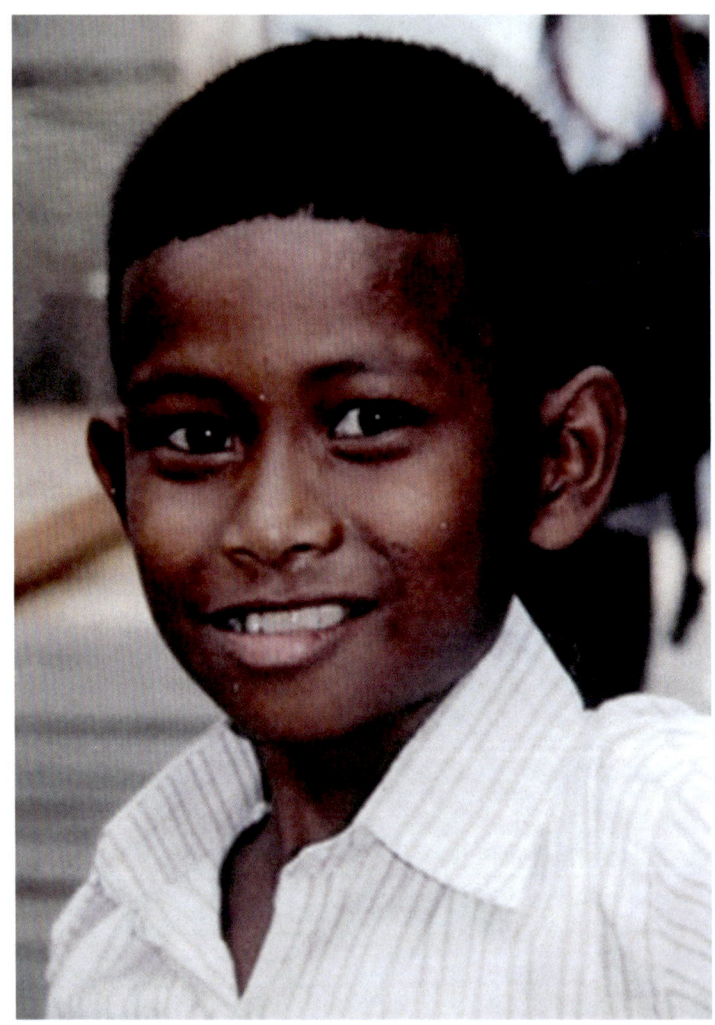

54. A Khmer boy in Siem Reap, Cambodia. Photo by Hamara Holt

55. An Africoid mask from Western Canada. Louvre.
Photo by Runoko Rashidi

56. Head of a Black man in Hellenistic Turkey. Brooklyn Museum of Art.
Photo by Runoko Rashidi

57. A painting of Antarah in the Medina in Damascus, Syria.
Photo by Runoko Rashidi

58. Runoko Rashidi being welcomed in New Delhi, India in 1999

59. Runoko Rashidi with a Tribal woman in North Kerala, India in 1998

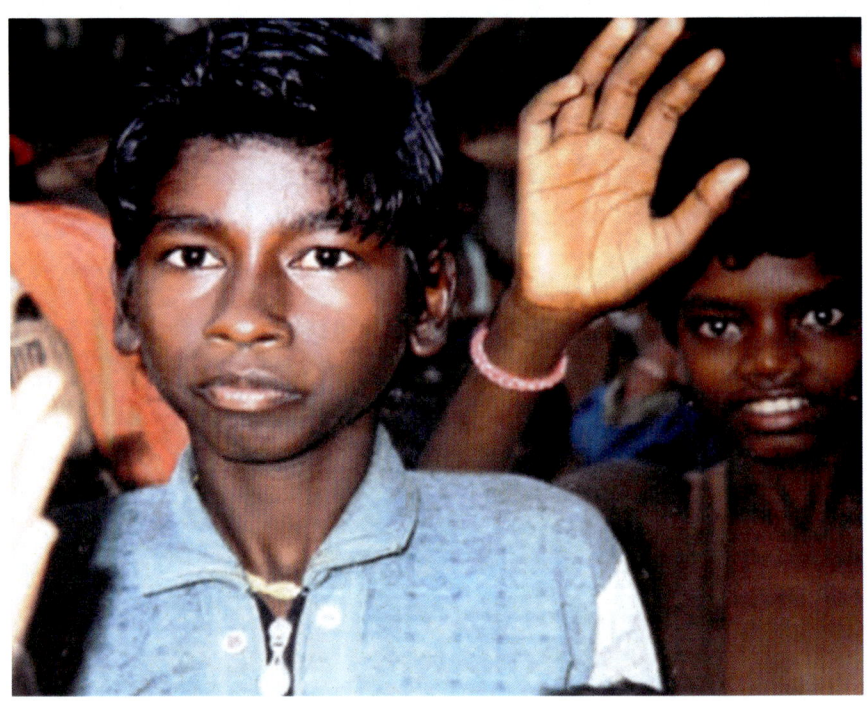

60. Munda children in Orissa. Photo by Runoko Rashidi

Part Three

AFRICAN STAR OVER ASIA:
MUSEUM COLLECTIONS

3.1.- Images of the African in the West Asian Collections in Paris, London and Brussels

Of all of the museums in the Western world, the one that seems to have the most impressive collection of art reflecting the African presence in early Iraq and Iran is the Louvre, the national museum of France. Indeed, there is an entire room filled with statues of Gudea, the ensi or governor of the ancient Sumerian city-state of Lagash during the late third millennium B.C.E.

Of the most outstanding of the Blackheads of Sumer Diop singles out Gudea. He probably did not come from the city, but had married Ninalla, daughter of the ruler Urbaba (2164-2144 B.C.E.) of Lagash, thus gaining entrance to the royal house of Lagash. Gudea was a formidable ruler and after him both Lagash specifically and Sumer in general began a significant decline. He was succeeded by his son Ur-Ningirsu.

Interestingly enough, Gudea, in spite of the general scarcity of stone in Mesopotamia, had numerous, almost life-size statues of himself carved from hard black diorite, as though he could have actually anticipated the historical dilemma his African descendants would find themselves in, and they us left his personal calling cards in the medium of stone that would shout to the world his African roots.

At least twenty-six statues of Gudea have been found thus far and many of the best of them are in the Louvre, with the Metropolitan Museum of Art also in possession of one of the best of them.

The impressive art reflecting the African presence in early Iran in the Louvre is not to be missed. Just nearby the Gudea room in the Louvre is a collection of magnificent colored reliefs of Black members of the Immortals—the imperial bodyguard of the Persian shahs (during the fifth century B.C.E.), identified by the nineteenth century French archaeologist Marcel A. Dieulafoy. Dieulafoy stated that:

> "On removing a tomb placed across a raw-brick wall which was part of the forti-fications of the Elamite gate, the workers uncovered a funeral urn. The urn was encased in a masonry covering composed of enameled bricks. These came from a panel depicting a personage superbly dressed in a green robe with yellow, blue,

and white embroidery. He wore a tiger skin and carried a cane or a golden spear. Most surprising of all, the personage whose lower jaw, beard, neck, and hand I found was black. His lips were thin, the beard thick; the embroidery, of archaic style, seemed to be the work of Babylonian artisans.

In other Sassanid walls built of earlier materials, were found glazed bricks revealing two feet shod in gold, a very well-shaped hand, a wrist covered with bracelets; the fingers held one of those long canes that became the emblem of the sovereign power under the Achaemenides. There is a piece of the robe bore the coat-of-arms of Susa, partly hidden under a tiger skin. Finally, a flowered fringe on a brown background. His head and feet were black. It was even evident that the whole decoration had been designed to blend with the dark complexion of the face. Only powerful personages had the right to carry long canes and wear bracelets. Only the governor of fortified post could have his image embroidered on his tunic. Yet, the owner of the cane, the master of the citadel was black. It is therefore highly probably that Elam was ruled by a black dynasty and, judging by the features of the face already described, an Ethiopian dynasty…"[1]

The Greek historian Herodotus (circa 450 B.C.E.) wrote of their presence and substantiates the observations of Dieulafoy:

"The Ethiopians, in their leopard skins and lion skins, carried long bows made of palm-wood—as much as six feet long—which were used to shoot small cane arrows tipped not with iron but with stone worked to a fine point…"[2]

And further:

"The eastern Ethiopians—for there were two sorts of Ethiopians in the army—served with the Indians. These were just like the southern Ethiopians, except for their language and their hair: their hair is straight, while that of the Ethiopians in Libya is the crispest and curliest in the world."[3]

Images of African soldiers, specifically Ethiopians, in the Persian armies of the fifth century B.C.E. are also prominently depicted on several alabastra displayed in museums in Boston, Berlin, Brussels and London. Two of the best preserved of these, in Brussels and London, are shown here.

Notes

1. Cited by Cheikh Anta Diop, *The African Origin of Civilization* (Westport: Lawrence Hill 1974), 104.
2. Herodotus, *The Histories* (Middlesex: Penguin, 1972), 467.
3. Herodotus, 468.

3.2.- The Black Presence in Early Vietnam: Cham Artifacts

Images of deities, whether Buddhist or Hindu, in Cambodia and Vietnam and Thailand provide unmistakable testimony to the form that god was worshipped in these ancient lands. The Cham civilization was the great early classical civilization in what is now Central and Southern Vietnam. Emerging during the second century, it endured and flourished for more than a thousand years before finally meeting its destruction at the hands of the Viets in 1471. Fortunately, at least some of the material vestiges of Cham civilization have survived and the Africoid features of these statues do not cease to astound us.

The foremost collection of Cham artifacts in the world are, not surprisingly, in Vietnam itself, especially those in the Cham Museum in Danang, followed by the Vietnam History Museum in Hanoi and the Museum of Vietnamese History in Ho Chi Minh City. Outside of Vietnam the major Cham collections are in the Musee Guimet in Paris, followed by the Rietberg Museum in Zurich, with important pieces in the Metropolitan Museum of Art in New York City and the Cleveland Museum of Art. I have viewed and photographed all of these collections, including multiple visits to the Musee Guimet and two visits to the Cham Museum in Danang. Apparently there is also a Cham collection, or at least a history of a Cham collection, in the Musee Guimet in Lyon, France which, at the time of this writing, I have not been able to view. The Cham artifacts depicted here are among the finest in the world.

3.3.- The Black Image in Buddhist Art from Thailand

Early Thailand produced some of the most brilliant and beautiful images of the Black in Southeast Asia. And nowhere is this more evident than in the Dvaravati phase in Thai history. Dvaravati refers both to a culture and a conglomerate of ancient city-states in the lower plain of the Chao Phraya River. The style of art known as Dvaravati is distinct from subsequent Thai and Cambodian (Khmer) art forms. Indeed, the art from the Dvaravati period in Thailand rivals that of neighboring Cambodia and Vietnam in regard to the portrayal of Africoid features. But it does not end there, as even in the some of the later periods of Thai history we continue to find Buddhist images with the features of Black men.

By the tenth century, Dvaravati began to come under the influence of the Khmer Empire. During the twelfth century it was incorporated into the Khmer Empire in the golden age in the reign of the great Khmer king Suryavarman II, builder of the splendid Angkor Wat.

In addition to Angkor in Cambodia, Dvaravati was significantly impacted by Indian culture and was instrumental in introducing Buddhism and Buddhist art to Souheast Asia.

Exquisite examples of the Black image in the Buddhist art of Thailand are found in abundance in the temples and museums in Asia, and fine arts museums in Europe and the United States. The images depicted here are among the very best.

Part Four

AFRICAN STAR OVER ASIA:
CONTRIBUTIONS
TO THE AFRICAN PRESENCE
IN ASIA

4.1.- Seeing Asia Through Joel Augustus Rogers (1880-1966)

By Thabiti Asukile

"There are Negro peoples with naturally straight or frizzly hair: others with kinky hair, that is more or less abundant as some of the West Africans; and still others with sparse, tiny beads of hair, the so-called peppercorn. Malay Negritos who are alike in color and features have, some of them, straight hair, others, woolly hair."[1]

"There is a tendency to deny that the ancient Buddhas were Negroes despite the fact that they are portrayed with Negroid hair and features. We are told that the curls on the heads of the Buddhas were originally snails that settled on the scalp to protect it from the burning sun. But is not the ethnological explanation less miraculous? Negro peoples lived and still live in India."[2]

When I was very young, one of the first things that stuck out to me the first time I read J.A. Rogers' *Sex and Race: Negro-Caucasian Mixing in All Ages and All Lands, Volume I, The Old World* (1940) were the pictures of the different types of Buddhas in the appendix. Before reading this work I had never thought about any type of representation of Buddha being associated with Black people. The westernized education that I received in K-12 in Los Angeles, California never prepared me to think of people of African descent outside of European controlled Trans-Atlantic enslavement of Africans to the Americas during the sixteenth through the nineteenth centuries, and the enslavement of people of African descent in the formation of the United States. Reading about Black people in Asia during antiquity and in the modern era in Rogers' *Sex And Race: Negro-Caucasian Mixing In All Ages And All Lands, Volume I, The Old World and Worlds Great Men of Color: 3000 B.C. to 1946 A.D., Volumes I* forced me to re-conceptualize my westernized education in K-12 before I went to college. Before matriculating into college, I never dreamed that much later on in my life that I would become a J.A. Rogers scholar or even have the possibility of meeting and having a lengthy conversation his much younger widow twice in St. Petersburg, Florida in 2006 and 2007. (He married her, Helga

Rogers-Andrews, in the mid 1950s). As a very young man, I was just very fascinated with Rogers' resesearch which led me to other scholars, and I found out to my surprise later that Rogers never received any type of university or institutional funding for the type of domestic and international research he conducted in his lifetime.

Rogers during his lifetime traveled extensively throughout United States, Europe, and Northern Africa and conducted probably more archival African research overseas than any person of African descent into uncovering valuable historical facts and popularizing Africana history from antiquity to the modern era (covering Africa, Europe, the Americas, and certain parts of Asia). Rogers very informative African diasporic scholarship that highlighted certain important aspects of Black people in Asia was ignored and not appreciated by many white American scholars in the American academy (including Black academicians) because of the absence of a Ph.D. behind his name and the nature of the scholarship he chose to write about concerning race-mixing and Black diasporic biographies which was not in vogue between the 1930s and 1950s.

In this latest edition of the African Presence in Asia it is hoped that this essay will encourage other people no matter what their ethnic background is to read the works of Rogers for the following reasons. First, it is amazing how many Americans especially African American youth have never heard of Rogers, although he dedicated his life's work that young people may understand the totality of African history that includes the African diaspora of Asia. Rogers without any research assistants or any institutional financial support spent over forty years visiting famous museums, libraries, art museums, portrait galleries, antiquarian bookstores, and churches. Second, the tenacity Rogers gave to conduct archival research was impeccable and on a par with any academic twentieth historians who had research assistants and institutional funding to help them with their own scholarship. Rogers' archival and photo-anthropolgy research and historical writing vindicated and disproved the claim projected on people of African descent by Europeans and white Americans in all walks of life that people of African descent in Africa, and throughout the African diaspora (that includes all of Asia) never made any civilizational contribution from antiquity down through the modern era. It is also important to stress here that Rogers' historical writings was not limited to his self-published books. There is an abundance of historical references about people of African descent history in the *Pittsburgh Courier* from the 1920s until 1966, and *The New York Amsterdam News* during the 1920s and 1930s.[3]

4.1.1.- The Black presence in Asia contextualized in *Sex and Race*

For anyone who has not read Rogers' *Sex and Race* trilogy it is highly suggested as an important preliminary read in learning about Africa and the African diaspora. Although space does not permit this author to go into great detail about the importance of this work, two important points must be clarified from the start. First, it is one of the first major African and African diaspora works during the twentieth century that is still worth reading because of broad range of historical information presented throughout the trilogy. Rogers' scholarship is based on his own primary research and latest scholarship of his era. In reading *Sex and Race*, one can learn fascinating historical information from antiquity through the modern era. Furthermore, Rogers' scholarship that some scholars snubbed during his lifetime and is now in vogue today opened its readers into a world that was during his lifetime and can still be argued today still not taught in the American and British public schools and in most colleges and universities. This became a scholarly contribution in itself considering the shameful reality during first part of the twentieth century in the United States where many African-Americans were never taught about people of African descent historically living outside of Africa in Europe, Central and South America, and Asia.

Second, the western education that people of African descent have received in the United States cannot be underestimate the way African American have evolved as people in this country. This is important because along with institutionalized Jim Crow racism during the 1930s and 1940s, the education taught to many Americans about African Americans influenced hate crimes and segregation, and contributed towards the stagnation of the intellectual growth of all Americans in understating the great intellectual contribution of people of African in this country and throughout the world. Since the late seventeenth century, there were people of African descent born in the United States who lived and died that could not fathom or honestly believe outside American slavery, that in Africa, sub-Saharan Africans, or people of Black African descent were histori-cially intertwined with Europeans and Asians in influencing all aspects of world history and different cultures. *Sex and Race* introduces us to the fact that people of African descent were engaged in scientific discoveries, old and new world arts, and the formation of old and new world religions which is very important in relationship to people of African descent participation in the rise of Islam in Asia and Africa. Third, it must be stressed Rogers' scholarship in *Sex and Race* had an immediate impact on the historical scholarship of many African Americans including the great scholar-activist W.E.B. DuBois (1868-1963).

In the Introduction of DuBois' *The World And Africa: An Inquiry Into The Part Which Africa Has Played In World History* (1947), he openly acknowledged that he had learned a great deal from Rogers, and that no man alive had revealed so many facts about people of African descent. Rogers' influence on DuBois, by coincidence, was evident in DuBois' own chapter entitled "Asia in Africa." DuBois cites *Sex and Race* in describing the Black presence in India, China, and the heroic Moorish Muslim general Tarik-bin-Ziad who in 711 A.D. conquered Spain when led an army of Muslims to defeat the King Roderick of the Visigoths.[4]

DuBois cited Ziad from a letter sent to Rogers from Mme. Halideh Edib former Minister of Education in Turkey and according to Rogers a leading authoress. In this letter Edib explained to Rogers the civilizing role that people of African descent contributed to the history of Turkey. Edib mentioned to Rogers that the Ottoman Turks did not have a race question and did not view people of African descent as inferior. According to Edib, many men of African descent evolved out of slavery to become great rulers:

> "For good or for evil, men of African descent have played very great parts in Turkish history. Further, quite a number of them were patrons of art and lite-rature, they themselves being very well educated. It would be possible, though it would mean a great deal of time, to make a list of them and of their activities from the Turkish Annals. In my own time I have seen a considerable number of coloured officers in the Turkish Army of all grades. They have commanded white soldiers, and have been known as good and brave men."[5]

The Edib letter that was sent in 1933 suggests that Rogers may have initially written a letter to Edib to find out about people of African ancestry in Turkey because it does appear Edib is responding to him. What is not known at this time is if Edib followed up and sent Rogers a list of these great men mentioned in the letter. The letter also speaks to what we are taught here in the American public school systems which is virtually bankrupt concerning learning about people of African descent outside this country, especially in Asia. The question that must be asked is how many young African Americans actually think about or are interested in people of African descent in Asia, and if one would be interested, would Turkey be the first place one would think of? Although Rogers never traveled throughout Asia it apparent he was very interested in making contact with people of Asian descent that could help him re-write the missing parts of world history. Another question that must be raised is based on their westernized education how many African American thought Rogers was imprudent to write about an African presence in Asia through history and biography. In thinking about what happened in Rogers' lifetime and where we are today. One can reflect and think about the following of what Rogers said about a certain African American male concerning his scholarship:

> "I have several times been attacked in print and on the platform. In 1919 {sic} 1929 when I was writing sketches of great Negroes as General Dumas, Antar, Kafur, Bilal, an Aframerican who was studying in Germany wrote to the leading Negro newspaper in America saying that I was talking all fable. His German professors had never told him of these things, ergo, they couldn't possibly be true. The professional Nordic and his henchmen in the universities and elsewhere, are adept at raking into their fold every great man regardless of race, and claiming that he was Caucasian, the object being to prove that Negroes are incapable of outstanding accomplishment and thus only fit for labor battalions and the rougher and the badly paid jobs."[6]Rogers' statement raises another question: do we still have that problem today in the United States? It is the opinion this writer we still do. In *Sex and Race Volume I*, Rogers briefly through other scholars, ancient eye-witness testimony, and biblical reference highlighted the Black presence in Syria, Palestine, Arabia, Persia, and India. In reference to India, Rogers pointed out that "In Southern India are to be found Negroes of a type almost as pure as those of Africa." In citing the latest scholars of his era who he believed were honest about the Black presence in India Rogers said. "As Professor Hooton says, 'A large share of responsibility for the great civilization of India

must be assigned to Negroes since there is unquestionably a very strong Negro strain in the Indian population."[7]

Sex and Race is a reference point to the Black presence in Asia. It was not Rogers' specialty per se, but he gathered enough pioneering information for future scholars to use if they were interested in the Black Presence in Asia. By the mid-1940s Rogers self-published a two-volume work that he had gathered historical research since he became interested in Africana history. Through the writing of short biographies in Africa and throughout the African diaspora *World's Great Men of Color* would complement the scholarship of *Sex and Race* and once again contextualize the Black presence in Asia within world history.

4.1.2.- The african diaspora of Asia in world's great men of color

In *World's Great Men of Color Volume I* (1946), Rogers had honestly made it clear concerning Asia that he had not done comprehensive research about Black personalities in the Far East:

> "I have come across certain names in China and Japan as Sakonouye Tamura-maro, the first Shogun of Japan, but I did not follow them up. In India, also, I did little on the Negroes among the Mohammedans there, while in Turkey I did no intensive research though the number of great Turkish Negroes, some of whom were virtual rulers of the empire, is considerable."[8]

Looking back one would have to question what would the biographical scholarship of WGMC had been if Rogers actually did archival and field research throughout Asia. It would have been very expensive from him to say the least, not being supported by any university fellowships or institutional endowments that were not available to him because of his race and the type of research he did about people of African descent which was not in vogue during the 1930s through the 1950s.[9]

Although Rogers did not do extensive biographical research in Asia, he did have a small section in WGMC (World's Great Men of Collor) that highlighted nine biographical personalities of African descent from antiquity to the modern era. Out of the nine biographical personalities mentioned seven are more than likely to had immediate or generational African ancestry in their lineage. Antar,

Bilal, Ibrahim Al Mahdi, Al Jahiz, Malik Ambar, Malik Andeel, and Eugene Chen are all wonderful people of African descent to read about in relation to Asia.

Although, Rogers believed all throughout his life that there was no color line in the religion of Islam, while doing research it was most difficult for him to acquire pictures of people of African descent in Islamic lands because of the early wishes of Muhammad discouraging any type of portraits of Muslims. One can understand how this would have been a major problem in writing about the history of people of African descent in Islamic lands especially in Asia.[10]

If Rogers would have been able to obtain any type of iconic representation of important Islamic figures it is more than likely that the section of Asia in WGMC would have definitely been larger. Notwithstanding, the Black Islamic personalities in the section of Asia really stand out in WGMC. For example, Rogers' biographical representation of one of Islam's greatest scholars Al-Jahiz (a.d.776-868) was very important in 1946 because of his importance in the history of Islam. Al-Jahiz became a towering intellectual, and his writings were very influential especially *The Superiority in Glory of the Black Race* over the White which highlighted the humanity of the Black Zenghs many who were brought over as enslaved Africans from Africa. Overall this influential Islamic work by Al-Jahiz countered the white American and European racist notion of the humanity of Black people. In explaining the importance of this work Rogers asserted:

> "It must also be noted that when Jahiz refers to Negroes he is speaking principally of those in Africa and the first generation of Africans living in Arabia, and that when he speaks of "whites" he is also including Arabian-born mulattoes. An Arab, near-white, or mulatto, and even black, was inclined to look down on the incoming blacks from Africa and to consider them inferior much as a Northern Negro is inclined to consider himself superior to a Southern one or a Black city-dweller does someone from the country, that is, the East it has never been so much a question of color as it is of culture, therefore, what Jahiz refers to here is not to be confused with Western color prejudice. The testimony of Jahiz on certain great Negroes among the Arabs is important also because he wrote at the time, or near the time, they lived. What he says about the color of the Ethiopians, (now that the latter are claimed to be white), is very important also. He wrote partly in the eighth and partly in the ninth centuries, which was long before the coming of the

Portuguese and other Europeans to the admixture with whom is due to the lighter color and straighter features of a small percentage of Ethiopians of our time."[11]

Rogers' mention of Al-Jahiz being an eyewitness is important because between the eighteenth and nineteenth century people of Afican descent received so much information about their history filtered through Europeans travellers and savants that were prejudiced in their interpretation of the life of different types of Black peoples no matter where they resided in the world. Rogers' precursor to what he mentioned about people of African descent in *WGMC* can actually be found in the index of *Sex and Race* "Notes and References to the Negro Under Islam". In this section Rogers suggests that the founder of Islam, Muhammad, had African in his ancestery. He cites the African missionary Dan Crawford:

> "Bound to the African by the two great bonds of polygamy and slavery, he (the Arab) is a witness, not at all poisoned by prejudice, albeit he is so long bought the Negro as two-legged animal. Take and try these six nuts our Arab asks us to crack. Was not the Prophet descended from an African woman?"[12]

Rogers also cited Washington Irving who mentioned that Muhammad's biological mother died when he was young and he was reader by an African slave named Barakat. This is one of the reasons why in *WGMC, Volume II*, Rogers in the section "Additional Celebrities" listed Muhammad in the back of the book along with other Muslims listed in the section entitled "Arabia and Eastern Islam."[13]

Whether it's biographical or regular history for anyone who does not know much about the African presence in Asia, reading both *Sex and Race* or *WGMC* will introduce to them to information that they can follow up on themselves. This is Rogers' contribution to the scholarship about Asia. Although, it is not extensive as his work about Black people in Africa, Europe or the Americas, it has very good information that can lead you to other sources.

Notes

1. J.A. Rogers, *Sex and Race, vol. 1* (New York: J.A. Rogers, 1940), 74.
2. Rogers, *Sex and Race*, 268.
3. Concerning Rogers' self-published historical and biographical scholarship consult, *World Greatest Men of African Descent* (1931); *World's Greatest Men and Women of Afri-*

can Descent (1935); *Sex and Race, 3 volumes* (1940, 1942, 1944); *World's Great Men of Color: 3000 B.C. to 1946 A.D., 2 volumes* (1946, 1947); *Nature Knows No Color-Line* (1952); and *Africa's Gift to America* (1958).

4. W.E.B. DuBois, *The World and Africa* (New York: Viking Press, 1947), 177, 180, 183-184.

5. Rogers, *Sex and Race*, vol. 1, 286.6. Rogers, 289.

7. Rogers, 63, 66.

8. *Rogers, World's Great Men of Color, vol. 1* (New York: J.A. Rogers, 1946), 20.

9. *Rogers, World's Great Men of Color, vol. 1* (New York: J.A. Rogers, 1946), xx.

10. Rogers was the first to admit that errors may have crept into his scholarship yet he labored alone with no research assistants to help him. It is interesting that Rogers started out the section about Asia with Zenobia of Palmyra because he does not list her ancestry, and it is virtually impossible without having his research notes to understand why she was included in this section, especially when the overwhelming iconographic representation that has come down to us today and the ancestral lineage cited by most scholars seem to support that she was not of any type of African/Black ancestry. Although not on the same scale as the representation of males, Rogers did include Black women throughout both volumes of *World's Great Men of Color*, and he chose Zenobia to represent the first Black person to learn about in Asia in his own work. According to Rogers, "Next to Cleopatra, Zenobia was the most famous woman of antiquity. Her empire, Palmyra stretched from the Euphrates almost to the Golden Horn and including Egypt and Syria."(67) The same research problem without seeing Rogers research notes or having a conversation with him can be said about the famous Arab Ibn Saud (1880-1953). It is also difficult to gauge why Rogers listed him as a possible person of African/Black ancestry when he did not cite any racial lineage in Saud's ancestry.

11. Rogers, *Worlds Great Men of Color*, 94-95. WGMC is not the first time that Rogers' publications mentioned the African presence in Islam in Asia or Africa. In *Sex and Race*, Rogers has an appendix entitled "Notes and References to the Negro under Islam." In this section Rogers quotes a list of scholars who mentioned Black Muslims in this religion.

12. Rogers, *Sex and Race*, vol. 1, 284.

13. Rogers, *Worlds Great Men of Color, vol. 2* (New York, J. A. Rogers, 1947), 692-93.

4.2.- Dr. Cheikh Anta Diop and the Cultural Roots of the Dalits: India's Black Untouchables

By V.T. Rajshekar[*]

It is not generally appreciated that Blacks live all over the world, comprising the world's largest oppressed group. That Asia has a large Black population is also not well known. Indian Blacks themselves are not aware of this fact. Lately, a strong Black identity has emerged and the slogan, "Black is beautiful" is catching up fast, at least among militant Blacks. Such a feeling is putting pride back into the broken hearts of Black natives, also uniting them with the struggle of their Black comrades in Africa and elsewhere. The Black liberation struggle against white racism, inequality and male domination is an international struggle.

A distinguished Black physicist, historian and linguist, Dr. Cheikh Anta Diop was among the first to establish that Egypt was the world's first civilization and that it was Black. He showed that humanity originated in Africa, and that the first human being, the first person, was Black. The Blacks migrated from Africa to other parts of the world. The Blacks are also the ancestors of Indian Untouchables (Dalits). That is why the Blacks, wherever they are, belong to one single family. Hence, the relevance of Diop's work, for India's Black Indus Valley Civilization is now widely accepted.

Diop's discoveries, therefore, establish that India's Black Untouchables (with their African origin) are the ancestors of all humankind. Hence, they have to be proud of their Black Untouchable origin and their glorious cultural past. The whole world owes its origin to Black people—our people. African history laid the foundation of world history.

Collective historical consciousness is a means of survival. If India's Black Untouchables are today hiding their identity, ashamed to own their origin and admit that they are Untouchables, it is because they are not aware of their

---

*. [Dravidian journalist V.T. Rajshekar is the editor of *Dalit Voice: The Voice of the Persecuted Nationalities Denied Human Rights.* He is the author of many books and is widely traveled internationally.]

glorious past. Diop says that the Blacks can regain their personality, can become proud of their past if they are told "who they are," and "what they are." That means we have to discover our roots, our goddesses, our religion, our ancestors, our history.

Cheikh Anta Diop has proven that the core of our problem is cultural root-lessness. The most important task facing us, therefore, is to reconstruct the links that tie us as communities. Humanity was born and developed in Africa. The first human was Black, and Black is beautiful. The Blacks lost their historical memory because we were fed by false history books. The rule of oppression will soon end with the reconstruction of world history, taking the aid of the tools provided to us by authorities like Diop, Ivan Van Sertima, and Runoko Rashidi—all world famous Black scholars.

4.3.- The Blacks of East Bengal: A Native's Perspective

By Horen Tudu

The Black race in its entirety has been the victim of subjugation and extermination by the Caucasoid race from the dawning of modern humanity. However, it truly remarkable that this unique community has survived and accomplished remarkable feats that have redefined the world in every possible way. As the groundbreaking historian Runoko Rashidi has often used the words "Black" and "African" interchangeably, I will remain loyal to his terminology and define all members of the Black race to be of Austroloid and Negroid descent. This merger of noble humanity is to include all the Aborigines of Australia, New Guinea, The Philippines, and Indonesia. It embraces the proto-Austroloids of Bangladesh and eastern India, the lower castes and tribal Dravidians of India, Sri-Lanka, the Andaman/Nicobar Islands, and ultimately all members of the African continent and its far-reaching diasporas on the western hemisphere of the Earth. One of the most daunting tasks for a truth finder is to form an unbiased perspective in an era where most historical documents are corrupted by Euro-centric bigotry and Indo-Aryan white supremacy. There are few if any documents written truly from a native's perspective. I will attempt to provide an account that exposes a truth, of which many in the world are simply not ready to bring to light and internalize. Moreover, it forces us as human beings to genuinely view the world for what it is. The truth hurts far more than the facade that allows so many in the world to live comfortable lives.

It is the primary focus of this document to answer many serious questions: Who were the inhabitants of East Bengal before the arrival of the Muslims? Where are those people now? How have the Arabs and the Hindus destroyed Bangladesh? Most importantly, how can Pan-African politics help unite and possibly save the country?

4.3.1.- The original inhabitants of Bengal

The word Bangladesh is derived from the term "Vangla", a word given by the Bodo Aborigines of Assam to connote "wide plains." The original inhabitants of modern day Bangladesh were the Proto-Austroloid Kols, otherwise known as Kolarians. The term Kol has ubiquitously been corrupted by the Aryan-Sanskritic speakers to the word "kalu", meaning both "black" and "ugly" in almost all of the sixteenth languages of the Indian Sub-Continent. The Kolarians are a Dravidian sect, whose descendant communities can be found also in West Bengal and elsewhere in the eastern belt of the Indian-Subcontinent. Most geological scholars will contend that most of Bangladesh was fashioned between one and 6.5 million years ago during the tertiary era. Semi-recent excavations in the Deolpota village of western Bengal seem to suggest that a Paleolithic civilization in the region existed about one hundred thousand years ago. A 10,000 to 15,000 year old stone structure in Rangamati is the primary evidence of Paleolithic civilization along with a hand axe found in the mountainous inclines of the Feni district. This Neo-stone age began 3,000 B.C.E. lasting almost 1500 years. Similar tools were found in Sitakunda of the eastern region Chittagong, and near Comilla district. The sparsely forested hills in eastern Bengal strewn with fertile valleys imparted a hospitable location for Neolithic settlements.[1]

Physically, the indigenous people were longheaded, dark skinned, broad-nosed, and short in stature. Sometimes labeled as "Negritos" and "Negroids", their physical features are unchanged today among the lowest castes of Bengal, mainly the peasants, as well as 95% of population of Bangladesh today who derive from these lower castes and tribes.

4.3.2.- The Aryan invasion and destruction of ancient Bangladeshi civilization

Most present day anthropologists and scholars will confirm that the people of the ancient Indus Valley Civilization were of the same racial stock as the present day Bangladeshis and lower castes of India. The Indus Valley Civilization marked a period of wealth and prosperity in Indian history. Noted developments include the development of yoga, the erection of ziggurats and the discovery of zero. All these inventions were later appropriated by the Aryan priests in what must have been the greatest case of scientific theft on record. The golden Harappan age came to an abrupt and brutal end when hordes of barbaric Aryans swept into India in 1500 B.C.E. through the Khyber Pass. Most of these Caucasians were under the flexible leadership of the moon worshipping Aryan named Indra. The 1000 years that followed imparted irreversible destruction and darkness. During this Vedic Dark Age (1500.-500 B.C.E.) no civilization survives, no writing, nor any trace of the existence of even a semi-civilization. There is, even now in the late 21st century, complete ignorance concerning this era of Indian history. It was a seemingly endless orgy of slaughters and massacres of native Bangladeshis by the Caucasoid, barbaric invaders who considered it meritorious to butcher those of a different race, a Black race.[2]

Bharata launched the second Aryan invasion from Afghanistan, and conquered much of the upper Ganges valley. The mayhem and murder continued throughout this period, the end of which no trace of the Indus Valley civilization was left and the Aborigines had been displaced from all of Northwest India. The massacres perpetuated by the Aryans in India during the thousand years of the Vedic Dark Ages are unparalleled in history, exceeding the Holocaust of the Jews by the Nazis (which was inspired by the Vedic Aryans), and the slaughter of the South American native populations by the invading Spaniards and Portuguese. Almost all of the five million inhabitants of the Indus Valley civilization perished, the rest being displaced east into Bangladesh and south into present day Tamil Nadu and Sri Lanka. Thus, Bangladesh is a melting pot of various Black tribes with a separate Mongoloid presence to the east in modern day Myanmar.[3]

The armies of 'Lord' Ram initiated the Aryan invasion into Bengal during 600 B.C.E. Subsequently, the apartheid varna system was strictly imposed. Those Black Aborigines who accepted Aryan enslavement were relegated to the 'Clean Sudra' caste, and those who fought the Aryans were relegated to the "Untouchable" outcastes of Dalits and Adivasis. The worship of the Aryan religion of Vaishnavism was introduced and the aboriginal king of Kol was promptly murdered. In contrast to north India, the number of Dravidian Blacks was much higher and the number of Aryans low. Hence, extermination of the non-Aryan native population was not possible here in Bengal, as it had been done in north India, but a progressive agenda of Aryanization of the Kolerians and their assimilation into the varna system of racial apartheid was undertaken by the Aryans. Today the natives of East-Bengal speak Bengali or Bangla, a Sanskrit based Indo-European tongue hybridized with various indigenous Dravidian elements.[4]

4.3.3.- The Arabs come to Bengal

The conversion of the native Bengalis to Islam began in the eighth century, when the Arabs began invading north India and present day Pakistan. Additionally, other East African Muslims were transplanted into India; most historians agree that 5-12% of the Muslims that entered India were Ethiopian mercenaries. Because Brahmanical tyranny and oppression of native Bengalis had reached a climax, the Muslims were hailed as liberators and saviors. Islam gained much support by the lower caste and "untouchable" Bengalis because it allowed them for the first time in their lives to reach upward mobility in society. Many indigenous and Hindu worshipping sites were destroyed and transformed into mosques. Although many Arabs freely mixed with the native Black population, the majority kept themselves racially distinct, keeping various titles such as ADM (Abu D. Muhammed), Sheikh and Sayed. Many Brahmans remained Hindu as well as a large number of low castes and "untouchables" masquerading under the false identity of Brahmanism. The others that were forcibly converted retained their caste names such as "Chowdhury", "Biswas", and "Das."[5]

4.3.4.- The Legacy of the Arabs and the Hindus

Hitherto, most Sheikhs and Sayeds boast of their light skin complexions and will not marry into a Black Aboriginal family. Even though these descendants of Arabs and Caste Hindus identify themselves as ethnic Bengalis, they have always looked down upon native Bengalis as "Village Kalus"(another term for "nigger") and remain highly bigoted with regard to skin color.

In modern times, Arab Sayed landowners have collaborated with the Brahman landowners to slaughter the tribal Santhals and Kols for financial gain via acquisition of tribal land. Most Muslim Aborigines from the village are in destitute poverty and remain illiterate; they typically work as housemaids and servants of the Arab Bangladeshis especially in places like the Chittagong district. They have no concept of their Aboriginal/tribal ancestry and have made no attempt to join hands with their tribal brothers that are raped and tortured every year by Hindu landowners all throughout Bengal, east and west. Most Islamic scholars in Bangladesh have written out the pre-Islamic past brainwashing the Black Bengalis into believing that they are dark skinned Arabs and are racially distinct from the Austroloid tribals. Today, the residual "untouchables" that did not convert to Islam perform the most inhuman and menial forms of labor as sanctioned by the Bangladeshi government. They are forced to work with human carcasses and clean human feces from the street gutters as their ancestors have done for centuries under Hindu oppression.

The introduction of a Caucasoid racial element into Bangladeshi society has had one of the most

devastating effects on the development of the country. Most upwardly mobile and successful men tend to marry tall, and lighter skin women with long noses. The influx of India's openly racist film industry has done more to shatter whatever moral ethos the Black Bengali women carried before the Aryans and Arabs came to Bengal, Black is not beautiful in Bangladesh although 90-95% of the population is black Austroloid.

Following Bangladesh's independence in 1971, there has been a strong lack of political unity within Bangladesh because most politicians and government leaders are bigoted Caucasoids that only seek to better the financial standing of the Sayed and Sheikh elite rather than work for the better welfare of the people.

4.3.5.- The need of the hour: Pan-Africanism in Bangladesh and all of the black world

During the African-American Holocaust of North-America, the Black descendants of slaves were forced to engage the cruel Anglo-Caucasian oppressor without any assistance whatsoever from the world at large, it was largely a local effort and a astonishing one indeed for many victories were won and many intellectuals were produced to assist fellow Blacks worldwide. In the coming decade the Black race as whole faces new and precarious predicaments such as HIV, crime, illiteracy, and infant mortality. These are only but a few to name, but the local populations

on average cannot possibly solve them without help from their blood brothers and sisters from across the globe. With the Aborigines of Australia, The Philippines, and Andaman Islands nearing extinction along with massive proliferation of AIDS in Africa, Pan-Africanism is the need of the hour! According to the article "Pan-Negroism and the Tamil-Sinhala Conflict in Sri Lanka" written by Hadwa Dom of the *Dalitstan Journal*, the collaboration between Blacks has been proven effective in the struggle for humanity and the right to exist. In this effort, Nelson Mandela provided military manpower in aid of the indigenous Black LTTE (Liberation Tigers of Tamil Eelam) rebels in Sri Lanka leading to several important military successes. Only time can tell whether globally, the Black race will survive into the next millennium.[6] I am confident that it will.

4.3.6.- Pan-Africanism in south Asia

The early stages of human civilization in South Asia marked a glorious era in which African people practiced sustainable development, lived in peaceful, close-knit kinship societies virtually without conflict. As the barbaric Indo-European rose from the depths of his shallow burrows, he knew only those actions that were innate to his cold environment in the Caucasus, namely murder, war, rape, torture, genocide, conflict and destruction, the proceedings having been documented in the celebrated Hindu text, the Rig Veda. However, history has taught us that this is not a unique circumstance of South Asia, wherever the Aryan has encountered African human beings; the end result has been tragedy beyond the comprehension of the human mind.

India has maintained the stability of its social order through race-based fascism. Literally meaning skin color, the "Varna" system of racial apartheid was imposed upon the native Africoid inhabitants with the utmost brutality centuries ago in Northwestern India. Most characteristic of Modern

Hinduism is the sheer hatred and contempt for black African people. As clearly stated in widely read Hindu scriptures such as the Rig-Veda section II.12.4, "Black Skin is Impious and Lowly". Citing section I.130.8, "Indra protected in battle the Aryan worshipper, he subdued the lawless for Manu, and he conquered the black skin." In section IX.73.5 "The black skin, the hated of Indra, were swept out of heaven." Moreover, along with the disdain for blacks Indo-Aryan white supremacy is endorsed, as section I.100.18 states, "The thunderer bestowed on his white friends the fields, bestowed the sun, and bestowed the waters."

The invading Aryans enforced the caste system on the Black population with a merciless and bigoted spiritual philosophy, having whites occupy the top echelons of society, mixed races in the middle and the mass of the conquered Blacks at the bottom, today known as Dalits and Dravidians. The physical differences between the black-skinned Dravidian races of southern and eastern India, Bangladesh, and Sri Lanka and the Caucasoid Aryan races mainly comprising of upper caste Hindus and Sikhs is not the mere design of European colonialist historians, but a fact of human existence in the apartheid state of India. The indigenous people of the Indian Sub-Continent are the descendents of the Dravidian tribes that founded the celebrated Indus Valley civilization. Recent genetic evidence has confirmed what anthropologists have known all along, that the Dravidians, tribals, and lower caste Hindus belong to the greater African Diaspora. As affirmed in the pioneering mitochondria DNA studies published in *Human Biology vol. 68* (1996) p. 1, "The caste populations of Andhra Pradesh cluster more often with Africans than with Asians and Europeans". Additionally, another study performed by the Department of Medical Genetics in Umea University, Sweden discovered that "significant ethnic differences in single polymorphisms were found between all groups except for African Blacks-Dravidian Indians, who differed only in their MspI7-16-bp duplication haplotype distribution".

The early stages of Pan-Africanism in the western hemisphere focused on the principles and rhetoric of the great Jamaican born leader, Marcus Garvey. In recent times, global Negroland movements have sprouted all over the Indian Sub-Continent and are undergoing exponential growth in support. These movements comprise of all constituents of the Asiatic black race (Sudroids), from the Santhal insurgents of Bangladesh, to the tribal Gond militants of Madhya

Pradesh and the Dalit Panthers of Bombay, Chennai, and Kerala. Furthermore, it must be made abundantly clear that these populations are by no means marginal, it totals over 350 million people, exceeding the combined populations of several western European countries.

Apparently, the foundation and direct inspiration for these political and social movements come from the literature of great African-American intellectuals such as Booker T. Washington, W.E.B. DuBois, Frederick Douglass and many others. In search for their true identity and history, the Dalits and Dravidians are making great efforts to expand on their African ancestry, making connections with their black brothers and sisters around the globe. As stated by the great historian and lecturer Runoko Rashidi, "They (Dalits) seem particularly enamored with African-Americans. African-Americans, in general, seem almost idolized by the Dalit, and the Black Panther Party, in particular, is virtually revered." In 1972, taking inspiration from the Black Panther Party, the Dalit Panther party was fashioned with circulating myths of actual Black Panthers being transplanted to India to fight Aryan fascist regimes such as the RSS (Rashtriya Swayamsevak Sangh) and the Ranvir Sena. Particularly in South India, several universities and political establishments have made African-American literature required reading and continue to promote a "black is beautiful" type philosophy that empowers the next generation of Dravidians.

In the spirit of Marcus Garvey and John Henrik Clarke, Pan Africanism has become the need of the hour in South Asia. Based on genetic, cultural, and historical relatedness it was only natural for Dravidians and Africans to tie up struggles. History is in the making, and many prominent Dravidian intellectuals as we speak are exploring the call for an independent black "Dravidistan" nation. That day is heavily anticipated.

Notes

1. "Bangladesh Towards 21st Century". Dhaka, Ministry of Information, Government of the People's Republic of Bangladesh. ASNIC
2. "*The Bible of Aryan Invasions*; 1500 B.C.—1000 AD, Vol. 2" by Prof. Uthaya Naidu
3. "The Bible of Aryan Invasions; 1500 B.C.—1000 AD, Vol. 3" by Prof. Uthaya Naidu
4. Ibid.

5. "BRAHMIN GOLD The Plunder of Paradise Vol. III Exploitation of Individual Nations" by Shankar Nadar

6. "*Pan-Negroism and the Tamil-Sinhala Conflict in Sri Lanka*" *Dalitstan Journal, Volume 1, Issue 3*, December 1999. Written by Hadwa Dom.

4.4.- The Black East

By Paco D. Taylor

As a child growing up on the Far South Side of Chicago, whenever I would envision the physical features of Asian peoples—since those I saw most were in martial arts movies and Ultramen reruns on television—a fairly narrow set of characteristics always came to mind. Perhaps not surprisingly, brown skin and curly black hair were never among them. But one fateful day my father would tell me of an eye-opening experience he'd had as a young man serving in the United States Marines. While stationed in the Philippines between 1961 and 1963, "Pops" learned of Asians whose physical features were significantly different from what most Americans have been conditioned to expect.

There in the Philippines my father would see native Filipinos who, albeit small in stature, looked a lot like him, with dark brown skin, curly black hair and—stranger still—African facial features.

To say the very least, the sight of such people living in the heart of Southeast Asia was completely unexpected.

It was also unsettling.

Perhaps equally as unsettling, my father learned that these puzzling pint-sized people were referred to locally as the "little blacks."

4.4.1.- Facts of life

As the Earth's largest and most populous land mass, Asia is home to sixty percent of the planet's human population. Included in this sum are the continent's lesser known groups called the Negritos—indigenous Asians who look at lot more like the relatives of Gary Coleman than Jackie Chan.

The term Negrito was first applied by Spanish explorers in the sixteenth century, after encounteres with such people during early forays into the region. And through wholly unscientific, the term is still used today to refer to distinct ethnic groups living in parts of Southeast Asia and the Asian Pacific island of Papua New Guinea.

According to James J.Y. Liu, author of the book *The Art of Chinese Poetry*, the term Kunlun is the equivalent of Negrito in the Chinese language, and there are several mentions of Kunlun people in the early literature of China. The most well known of these can be found in the classic adventure romance entitled The Kunlun Slave.

In the language of their Malay-speaking neighbors, they are known as the orang asli, meaning, first people or original people. This term would come into general use in the 1930s, in response to efforts by the Malaysian government to officially recognize them as the region's earliest inhabitants.

Prior to the adoption of a more respectful designation, such people were commonly called by the pejorative term semang (debt slave), a word bonded to times when, like other blacks, Negritos too were abducted from their home-lands and sold into slavery, but in Asia.

4.4.2.- Family tree

The defining physical features of Negrito people included dark brown to black skin, curly black hair and diminutive stature. The average height among men is five feet, five inches, and the average height among women is four feet, eight inches.

And through seemingly orphaned from humanity's family tree, Maury Povich won't be needed to pop for a DNA test to figure out "who is the father?" According to geneticists, these peculiar peoples are actually the modern descendants of the first migrant populations to venture into Asia more than 50,000 years ago.

That there is a strong resemblance between Negritos and African groups like the Pygmies of Uganda and Congo is obvious. What is impossible to see, however, is that on the DNA level, these people share closer genetic bonds to other Asians than they do to now distant cousins back in the Motherland.

4.4.3.- Stunted growth

Fossil finds from across the continent suggest that these nomadic hunter-gatherers once lived across Asia from India to southernmost Japan. The southern islands of the Pacific Ocean (Oceania) were also once part of their domain, as were the southern continent of Australia and the neighboring island of Tasmania.

Their stomping grounds today, however, are but mere traces of what they once were.

Challenged by the continuous spread of larger, more organized and more technologically advanced human groups, their once wide open range has been limited only to isolated parts of the Philippines, Southern Thailand, Malaysia, Indonesia, the Andaman Islands (off the coast of India), and Papua New Guinea.

What's more, populations that were documented as recently as the late nineteenth century to have numbered in the tens of thousands now number only in the thousands. But the numbers for some groups have become even smaller.

Today, the tribal population of the Onge people in the Andaman Islands number less than one-hundred. And it is conceivable that in the proverbial blink of an eye this ancient tribe of humankind will simply ceast to exist.

4.4.4.- Collective memory

For most of my adult life, I have been tirelessly collecting old photographs of the so-called "little blacks" of Asia. Is is a captivating hobby.

Yellowed volumes published in the late 1800s and nearly 1900s have been a good resource for many of these finds. Antique postcards made from the plates of globetrotting photographers are another. Snapshots taken by military personnel who, like my father, were stationed in thei region has been yet another.

It has become important to me to collect these images because, as the old expression goes, "a pictures paints a thousands words." And too few actual words have been written about these intriguing humans and the living, breathing bridge they form between the peoples of Africa, Asia and the rest of the planet.

For me, the photos also serve as a personal reminder of jus thow big an impression my father's words on these people made on me now so many years ago. And how, as the stories our parents tell often have the power to do, one small anecdote shared on a summers's day could shape so much of my worldview.

4.5.- In Search of the Original Filipinos

By Hamara Holt

In 2006 I traveled independently from the United States to the Philippines in search of the indigenous Black population there. These mountain dwelling (highlander) people are scattered in relatively small communities throughout the Philippines. Their dark skin, tightly curled hair and African features make them physically distinct from so called lowlander Filipinos that have a much more Mongoloid appearance, albeit with a wide range of complexions from dark to light.

These Indigenous Africoids are in fact the first inhabitants of not only the Philippines, but of all of Southeast Asia. These Blacks—the parent people of Southeast Asia—are known by several names—Aeta, Agta, Ati, Negrito, and others. However, the people have their own names, and never refer to themselves by the aforementioned. Due to the derogatory and sometimes misleading nature of these names, and for the sake of accuracy and respect, I will refer to them by their self-appointed names (in specific terms), and the Indigenous Africoids (in general terms) throughout this account.

My purpose in visiting the Philippines was to find and interact with members of this population, and gain knowledge of their sense of their own history and origins, as well as their current social status within the country.

4.5.1.- First contact

As my guide and I set off to visit a community of Batak people in the mountains of Northern Palawan, my excitement was almost palpable. This was the first day, for which I'd been researching and planning for months. We first stopped to buy gifts for the village chief (cigarettes, coffee, canned sausages). Our driver then took us to the entry point, where we met our two Batak guides who led us into the mountains and to the village. The trek was about two hours.

Upon arriving at the village, I must say that I was stunned. My research had not prepared me for the people that greeted us. My Batak guides were two dark-skinned gentlemen (a bit lighter than chocolate) with broad features and straight hair. They certainly looked as if they had Black ancestry, but they would not in the US commonly be considered phenotypically Black.

While conducting research on the Batak I learned that they are considered to be of so called "negrito stock", but all of the photographs that I saw, save one, were of lighter-skinned people with a much more "mixed" appearance. I was pleasantly surprised to find that most members of the community were "distinctly Black", including the chief. Their complexions are an array of colors from gold to dark brown, and their hair ranges from very tightly curled to straight. They are small in stature and build—I am just over five feet in height and I was the same height or a little taller than most of them, including the men.

My guide introduced me as a history student from the United States that was doing research on the "Agta". Most of the adults seemed to be only mildly interested in me, but a small group formed around me that seemed delighted by our physical similarities. I found it very interesting that they referred to my hair as "original hair", made even more so by the fact that the people that actually said it had straight hair.

I was formally introduced to the chief. He is a short, slender Black man with brown skin, curly hair cut very low and a mustache. His demeanor was quiet and laid back. Traditionally, the chief was always the eldest member of the community. The Batak of this village speak Tagalog (Filipino), and my guide translated for us.

According to the chief, his group consists of about thirty families. They are experts with wood and bamboo. This village's chief export is rattan. They make the rattan from bamboo trees, roll it up into big bundles and take it down the mountain, into town, to be sold. Until very recently, they have always moved around, settling in an area, using its resources, and moving on to the next place. Now, again due to outside influences, they have abandoned their ancient nomadic lifestyle in favor of "conservationism". In fact, upon our arrival at the village, some Korean conservationists were conducting a class on preserving the resources of their area. I asked the chief what his beliefs or opinions were regarding this change in their way of life were, and he simply responded that it was fine with him.

The average lifespan of the group is only sixty-five. Their major cause of death is infection, such as tuberculosis. They have very little access to medical care, most of which is by way of one visiting nurse/midwife from outside of the community that happened to be there at the time to see some patients suffering from leprosy.

There is no clinic or school in this village, but I was not surprised to find that a ramshackle church has been constructed by some visiting missionaries. Apparently about five years ago they trekked up the mountain and into the community dragging their load of Catholicism behind them and dispensing it to whomever would have some. The chief stated he does not believe in Catholicism or Christianity. Like many of us, he believes in God, but not religious groups. I asked if there was any resistance to the missionary presence, why specifically did they allow the missionaries to come in, and if their presence bothered him-as chief. In his quiet manner, he answered that there was not much resistance, he was not chief when they came and has no idea of why the former chief agreed to allow them in, and that as chief, their presence does not bother him, but he does not believe in their teachings. I asked if there was any religion practiced, other than Catholicism, now and before the missionaries came. He stated that no, historically there was and is no other organized religion, and his people just lived their lives. Only about one third of the community has converted.

Historically, this group of Indigenous Africoid people have no real knowledge of their origins before their presence in the Philippines. They believe that they have always been there, in the mountains of Palawan, and that is where their history began. When asked about the racial/ethnic identity of the Batak, the chief responded that they are the original people of Palawan and the Philippines, and they do consider themselves to be a separate group that are racially and ethnically distinct from lowlander Filipinos. At no time were the words black, white, yellow, or other terms used to describe racial categories.

4.5.2.- Civilization or Barbarism

Clearly apparent on this tour and throughout the entire trip was the attitude of superiority shared by the lowlanders towards the Indigenous Africoid groups of the country. They are largely seen as lazy, less intelligent, dirty, wild, primitive, and are heavily discriminated against in every place in Filipino society, from the media to the markets.

The most commonly stated idea is that the Indigenous Africoids are uncivilized. This was probably the most prevalent statement that I heard in reference to them, and is often stated very casually in conversation, as if it's just a matter of fact and no big deal. One instance of this occurred on the way to the village.

My guide, a lowlander of Malay descent, stated (again very casually) that our two Batak guides were more civilized than their brethren because they spoke some English, and wore western style clothing. I quickly corrected him, stating that what he really meant was that they were more assimilated into the outside culture—not more civilized. He offered no response to this rectification. I found myself having to explain the difference between a primitive people (unchanged for many centuries) and an uncivilized people (barbaric), several times during my stay.

4.5.3.- Olongapo

After a short flight back to Manila, I took the bus to Olongapo City. Olongapo is a city in the Southwest of the island of Luzon, about a 4 hour drive from Manila. It is home to the Subic Bay area, which is now home to the Indigenous Africoid community I planned to visit. This community lives on a resettlement site that was established after their displacement by the 1991 eruption of Mt. Pinatubo.

The people of this village, like most of the Indigenous Africoid communities, keep to themselves, and aside from the marketplaces, live separately from the majority population. While in the cities, I only saw a few Black faces, and while I saw many homeless and despondent people, I only saw one Black man, through a restaurant window, peeping into trash cans as he walked along. My guide, Bonifacio told me that there are people and charity groups that claim that there are Indigenous Africoid street children in need of assistance, but this is absolutely not true, and is usually stated for financial gain. Throughout my stay I saw many beggars—mothers with their children, children alone, men with hollow eyes like black holes, void of all hope (many of them clearly indigenous). But in that entire time, I never saw one that was Indigenous Africoid.

As explained earlier, the indigenous people here have their own distinct names and do not refer to themselves as Aeta, Agta, or any other foreign names reserved for them by the non-indigenous population. These names change from region to region, and group to group. The community I was in refers to themselves as the Kulat. This term is a racial distinction reserved for indigenous Blacks with curly hair. The term Unat is used to refer to all Filipinos—indigenous and non-indigenous—with straight hair and a Mongoloid phenotype.

Shortly after our arrival, the chief of the community came by to meet me. He is a short, brown-skinned Black man, very slim, with closely cropped hair. Like the Batak chief, he spoke softly, and seemed to have a very quiet manner. He speaks Tagalog, and a tiny bit of English.

The community is currently made up of sixty-five families, some of whom, including the chief and his family, were here before the resettlement site was founded. Again, like the Batak, I visited, they have changed old customs and now elect their chief. Women in the community are social equals. They work alongside the men, serve on the governing committee, and a woman can be elected as chief.

The historical knowledge of the chief and his community is again very similar to that of the Batak. They know that they are the original people of these islands and consider themselves to be racially/ethnically distinct from other indigenous groups and lowlander Filipinos of Malay descent. Their belief is that they have always been here, and they have no knowledge or sense of any origin outside of the Philippines. Their original name for God is Apu Maliare. However, about eighty percent of the community has converted to Catholicism. The chief and his family are all Catholic.

Any child of a Kulat/Unat union, is automatically considered to be Kulat. This was not a shock to me, being that this practice is very similar to racial distinctions in the United States. What I did find interesting though is that very often, while these children have the deep complexion of their Kulat parent, they also have the straight hair texture of their Unat parent. It was not unusual to see Black parents with afro-textured hair carrying children with their exact complexions, but completely straight hair. Seeing the children of such unions, it became easy to imagine how the Indigenous Africoid populations have been swallowed up and genetically assimilated into the majority population, leaving traces of their physical characteristics (seen throughout the Filipino population). The chief himself, is married to a lighter-skinned indigenous Unat woman.

Towards the end of our chat, the chief invited me to sit in on their community meeting that afternoon. I started to thank him in closing for allowing me to visit his community and sharing his time with me when, to his surprise and my own, I started to cry. He asked in his broken English, why I was crying, so in my broken voice, I tried to answer. I initially said that it was the opportunity to be able to speak with the representative of a people so old, and with such a strong link to their original culture that was so astounding to me, but it was not only that. It was also the culmination of all the time I'd spent researching, all the years of wanting to do something like this and knowing that I had just scratched the surface of what I would like to achieve. I also believe that being a product of the America that I live in, interacting with a people that seem to have no pretense of superiority, bigotry, or greed was a bit overwhelming for me.

4.5.4.- The origin of Things

As a student historian, for me, starting with the original people of any country is tantamount to truly understanding its history. This is true on a micro and macro scale, whether studying the history of an individual group, or of humankind in general. To quote our great ancestor, Malcolm X, "When you deal with the past, you're dealing with history, you're dealing actually with the origin of a thing. When you know the origin, you know the cause. If you don't know the origin, you don't know the cause. And if you don't know the cause, you don't know the reason. You're just cut off. You're left standing in mid-air. So the past deals with the history or the origin of anything—the origin of a person, nation, or incident. And when you know the origin, then your get a better understanding of the causes that produce whatever originated there and it's reason for originating, and its reason for being. It's impossible for you and me to have a balanced mind in this society without going into the past..."

Studying the origins of nations brings us to the question and eventual discovery of how and why they started, and is essential to the realization of Black people as a global population, and the originators not only of civilization, but of humanity itself.

4.6.- The African Presence in Arabia

By Wesley Muhammad

Archaeology, anthropology and ethno-historical studies indicate that the original Arabians were much different from the moderns. As Bertram Thomas, historian and former Prime Minister of Muscat and Oman, reported:

> "The original inhabitants of Arabia… were not the familiar Arabs of our time but a very much darker people. A proto-negroid belt of mankind stretched across the ancient world from Africa to Malaya. This belt… (gave) rise to the Hamitic peoples of Africa, to the Dravidian peoples of India, and to an intermediate dark people inhabiting the Arabian peninsula. In the course of time two big migrations of fair-skinned peoples came from the north… to break through and transform the dark belt of man beyond India (and) to drive a wedge between India and Africa… The more virile invaders overcame the dark-skinned peoples, absorbing most of them, driving others southwards… The cultural condition of the newcomers is unknown. It is unlikely that they were more than wild hordes of adventurous hunters."[1]

While these white invaders will impact the demography of the area, 2 the indigenous Black Arabians for the most part seem to have resisted miscegenation on any significant level, instead retreating to the southern portion of the peninsula. This black-skinned southern Arab is best represented today by the Mahra, Qara, and Shahra tribes of Oman and Hadhramaut.[3] Undoubtedly a modified version of Arabia's original inhabitants, these groups show an affinity to both the so-called 'Hamites' of East Africa (Somalis, Abyssinians) and the South Indian Dravidians, and they possibly represent a 'genetic link' between these two populations.[4] Speaking of the Qara, J. E. Peterson notes: "European observers have made much of their physical resemblance to Somalis or Ethiopians".[5]

Today the dark-skinned South Arabian is short and "extremely round-headed (brachycephalic)"[6] but he was no doubt originally much taller and dolichocephalic (long-headed) like the so-called Hamites of East Africa. In the 13th century C.E. the Muslim traveler Ibn al-Mujāwir described the Mahra as "tall, handsome folk" in his Tārīkh al-mustabsir, 271.1.17 and early pre-Christian skulls found in Hadramawt were markedly dolichocephalic.[7] It has been suggested that the 'definite change' in the racial constitution of the people of Hadramawt resulted from the invasion and inbreeding of brachycephalic whites such as Armenoids or Persians.[8] Henry Field suggested that Arabia's current ethnography is the result of the mixing of two distinct basal stocks: The dolichocephalic (long-headed), dark-skinned Mediterranean/Eur-African and the brachycephalic (round-headed) fair-skinned Armenoid.[9]

Craniofacial measurements in nearly 2,000 recent and prehistoric crania from major geographical areas of the Old World indicated that ancient West Asians and Africans resembled each other.[10] Rock-art from the Rub al-Khali dated to the 4th-2nd millennia B.C.E. depict, according to renowned archeologist and Near Eastern ethnologist Emmanuel Anati, a "Cushite" population of "oval-heads" who were a "beautifully built people of high stature, with elegant body features, slender and long legs and harmonious shapes and movements."[11] According to Cheikh Anta Diop: "In the Riyadh Museum, in Saudi Arabia, one can see the reproductions of cave paintings showing the Negro type that inhabited the Arabian Peninsula in Neolithic times."[12]

4.6.1.- Arabia as North East Africa

These ancient black Arabians no doubt originated as Africans. During the Precambrian (c. 5000 million—590 million BP 13) Arabia was a part of Africa.[14] The environment of central and eastern Arabia during the Miocene (c. 25—12 million BP) and the Pliocene (c. 5.3—1.8 million BP) "has been called 'lush' and compared to that of a tropical Savanah".[15] Geomorphological evidence suggests great rainfall during the Pliocene and the faunal remains imply a tropical or subtropical climate as well. At that time, as Michael Rice suggests in his book, The Archaeology of the Arabian Gulf: "Arabia probably would have looked much like East Africa now".[16]

Plate tectonics caused the Arabian plate to break off from the African shield, creating the Red Sea as recently as the Pliocene. Nevertheless Arabia remains today the geological and ecological continuation of Africa, despite the Red Sea cleavage. In an important study Maurizio Tosi confirms:

"In general, Arabia is the continuation of the African system across the Red Sea, spanning the Saharo-Arabian phytogeogrphical region comprising its northern and central parts and the Sudanese one for its tropical southern and eastern coastlands. Physically the (Arabian) peninsula is a part of Africa, landscaped by the same geological and climate processes as the eastern Sahara and the Ethiopian highlands."[17]

In terms of geomorphology and climatology Arabia is part of what's called the "Saharo-Arabian Region." But the ecological evidence (phytogeographical and zoogeographical) also points to Arabia being "Africa across the Red Sea." As A.H. Keane wrote: "Arabia has, on the whole, an African climate… In the animal kingdom an African character prevails generally."[18] In 1982 Stacey International published its Saudi-endorsed study of the region, noting as well:

"Maps and geography books make Arabia a part of Asia, but plant and animal life clearly bear out the theory that it is really an extension of Africa… Saudi Arabia's wildlife is… an African complex of species… The animals and plants of northern and northeastern Saudi Arabia are generally closely related to or identical with Saharan species…"[19]

Put simply, the Arabian Peninsula is actually just the north-eastern extremity of the African continent:

Geologically, the whole of the Arabian peninsula must be considered as unitary with the African continent… the Red Sea… is best thought of as an inland Lake with a small opening into the Indian Ocean…[20]

Africa thus does not end at the Red Sea, but extends across it into Arabia. This fact is obscured by what Ali Mazrui calls the 'tyranny of the Red Sea.'

"European power and European pre-eminence in map making decided that Africa ended on the western side of the Red Sea and on the west bank of the Suez Canal, in spite of the similarity of the geology of north-eastern Africa and Arabia on either side of the Red Sea, in spite also of the similarity of language and culture, and the artificiality of a continental boundary based on a man-made canal… In spite of the geological unity of Arabia and Africa and the former land link between the two continents at the Suez Isthmus, European geographers classified Arabia as being part of Asia… It is arguable that Europe dis-Africanized the Prophet Muhammad by declaring the Red Sea rather than the Persian (or Arabian) Gulf as Africa's north-eastern boundary."[21]

4.6.2.- **Africans in Arabia**

Arabia is also an ethnological extension of Africa. Dr. Charles S. Finch correctly affirms:

> "It has been customary to separate the Near East from Africa. Ethno-culturally though, in the light of increasing Neolithic evidence, it is perhaps more nearly correct to consider the lands between Khartoum in the south and the Tigris-Euphrates in the north as constituting one broad horizon in the period between 10,000 and 5,000 B.C. This broad horizon was composed substantially of 'Saharo-Nilotic' ethno-cultural elements. Regional differences and variations were certainly evident in this larger cultural complex, but ongoing techno-commercial relations linked the various groups of this horizon. It is certainly true that what is known as the Near East is more properly thought of as Africa's 'Northeast extension,' because geologically and geographically that is in fact what it is."[22]

The first hominids of the Arabian Peninsula were African migrants. Lower Miocene (c. 17-14 million BP) hominid remains similar to those found in East Africa have been found in Arabia.[23] In fact, Arabia was likely the first territory reached as these migrants expanded out of Africa. As Michael D. Petraglia remarks, the Arabian Peninsula was "a key geographic region that, without doubt, played a critical role in Out of Africa dispersals."[24] Recent genetic research has confirmed Arabia's role as the migrating Africans' first 'home away from home' or, in the words of Fernandes et al: "Arabia was indeed the first staging post in the spread of modern humans."[25] Recently (26 January 2012) UPI.com published a Science News article, "Arabia saw first humans out of Africa," announcing that: "European researchers say genetic studies suggest the first humans leaving the Horn of African to the rest of the world first settled in Arabia."[26]

Archaeogenetics indicate that today's modern human population outside of Africa can be traced back to a progenitor African group that migrated out of Africa into Arabia about 70,000 years ago.[27] These African migrants likely entered the peninsula by the south over the Bab el-Mandeb and by the north through the Levantine corridor. As Norman M. Whalen and David E. Peace point out:

"whether migration (out of Africa) proceeded by way of the north or the south, it was necessary to cross Arabia first before continuing further. For that reason, the oldest cities in the world, next to those in Africa, should be found in Arabia, which occupied a pivotal position astride the path of early intercontinental migration in Lower Pleistocene times... Arabia (is) humankind's doorway to the world."[28]

After adapting in Arabia for approximately 5,000 years, these Africans in Arabia went on to populate the rest of the world. P.A. Underhill et al have done genetic research with the non-recombining portion of the Y-chromosome (NRY) polymorphisms suggesting that human diversity today can be traced back to a migration out of Africa ca 50-45 kya (kya=thousand years ago) to the Middle East. From there, after adapting for ca 5-10 ky, these groups expanded North to Europe, East to India and Southeast Asia, and West (back to Africa?).[29]

We are thus not surprised to find the cultural affinities that we do between the peoples on both sides of the Red Sea. Arabian archaeology shows links with African materials.[30] Prof Benard Leeman, linguist and historian of Africa reports: "Archaeological evidence shows that a common culture did exist on the opposite shores of the Red Sea, ca. 1500-1000 B.C.E."[31] That these dark-skinned 'Ethiopic'-type Arabs belong to an African cultural complex was highlighted in The Encyclopedia Britannica [9th Edition; 1: 245-46 s.v. Arabia] which lists ten literary, linguistic, cultural, and ethnological evidences indicating some relation between South Arabians and Africa.

"Regarding the origin of the Arab race... the first certain fact on which to base our investigations is the ancient and undoubted division of the Arab race into two branches, the 'Arab' or pure; and the 'Mostareb' or adscititions... A second fact is, that everything in pro-Islamitic literature and record... concurs in representing the first settlement of the 'pure' Arabs as made on the extreme south-western point of the peninsula, near Aden, and then spreading northward and eastward... A third is the name Himyar, or 'dusky'... a circumstance pointing, like the former, to African origin. A fourth is the Himyaritic language... (The preserved words) are African in character, often in identity. Indeed, the dialect commonly used along the south-eastern coast hardly differs from that used by the (Somali) Africans on the opposite shore... Fifthly, it is remarkable that where the grammar of the Arabic, now spoken by the 'pure' Arabs, differs from that of the north, it approaches to or coincides with the Abyssinian... Sixthly, the pre-Islamic institutions of Yemen and its allied provinces-its monarchies, courts, armies, and serfs-bear a marked resemblance to the historical Afro-Egyptian type, even to modern Abyssinian. Seventhly, the physical conformation of the pure-blooded Arab inhabitants of Yemen, Hadramaut, Oman, and the adjoining districts-the shape and size of head, the slenderness of the lower limbs, the comparative scantiness of hair, and other particulars-point in an African rather than an Asiatic direction. Eighthly, the general habits of the people,-given to sedentary rather than nomade occupations, fond of village life, of society, of dance and music; good cultivators of the soil, tolerable traders, moderate artisans, but averse to pastoral pursuits-have much more in common with those of the inhabitants of the African than with those of the Western Asiatic continent. Lastly, the extreme facility of marriage which exists in all classes of the southern Arabs with the African races; the fecundity of such unions; and the slightness or even absence of any caste feeling between the dusky 'pure' Arab and the still darker native of modern Africa… may be regarded as pointing in the direction of a community of origin."

That Arabians and East Africans derive from a 'community of origin' is indicated by more modern studies as well. As Dana Reynods (Marniche) records in an important article:

"In the days of Mohammed and the Roman colonization of Palestine, North Arabia and Africa, the term Arab was much more than a nationality. It specifically referred to peoples whose appearance, customs and language were the same as the nomadic peoples on the African side of the Red Sea… The evidence of linguistics, archaeology, physical remains and ethnohistory support the observations and descriptions we find in the histories of the Greeks and Romans and in later Iranian documents about nomadic Arabians of the early era. The Arabs were the direct progeny and kinsmen of the dark-brown, gracile and kinky haired 'Ethiopic' peoples that first spread over the desert areas of Nubia and Egypt…

It is clear from the ancient writings on the 'Arabs' that the peoples of the Arabian peninsula and the nonimmigrant, indigenous nomads of the Horn were considered ethnically one and the same and thought to have originated in areas near the cataracts of the Nile."[32]

Regarding the linguistic evidence, the Proto-Semites (i.e. the original group of Semitic speakers) were no doubt a group of Africans that migrated into Asia.[33] According to Nicholas Faraclas in 1995, several lines of evidence converge to suggest that they separated from the Proto-Afroasiatic group in Middle Africa and followed the Blue Nile to the Ethiopian Highlands (where most of the Semitic languages are found to this day), crossing over into Arabia from the

Bab el-Mandeb; other Proto-Semites probably continued north down the Nile eventually entering Syria-Palestine from the Isthmus of Suez. He suggests:

> "the origins of the Ancient Egyptian, Hebrew, Babylon, Assyrian, and Arabic languages (trace) back to a central African homeland… many of the speakers of the languages from which all these languages developed may have participated in a black civilization that was driven out of Central Africa by the expanding Sahara Desert some 7,000 years ago…"[34]

That Arabic in particular originated with African peoples is further supported by the work of University of Michigan Professor Emeritus George Mendenhall, one of the world's leading authorities on the Near East and Near Eastern languages. He notes that "Arabic could not be a gift of the prophet Muhammad, as many Islamic clerics claim, since its origins are in the early Bronze Age," over 3,000 years before Muhammad.[35] Mendenhall has identified the "earliest identifiable Arabic-speaking social group" as the Midianites, an important political entity that came into existence suddenly in the 13th century B.C.E. in northwest Arabia. This highly sophisticated culture spoke a language which is an archaic ancestor of modern Arabic.[36] This is significant because, as David Goldenberg affirms: "Kush is the ancient name of Midian."[37] These Midianites, the earliest identifiable Arabic-speaking social group, are documented as a Kushite tribe.[38]

According to Jan Retsö the priestly author(s) of the Hebrew Bible offer(s) us the earliest attempt at a systematic description of peoples living on the Arabian peninsula around the 7th century B.C.E.,[39] and these peoples in general are there identified as Kushites (Gen 10: 7).[40] Kushites were the dominant ethnic group in Syria-Palestine in late 8th and 7th centuries B.C.E.,[41] though the Africoid presence there went back as far as the Natufian culture of the 10th millennium B.C.E.[42] These were no doubt black or dark-skinned (though not necessarily Negroid) Syro-Palestinians.[43] Being that peoples designated as Arabs first appeared in sources connected with events in Syria in the first centuries of the first millennium B.C.E.,[44] it is not unlikely that the historical Arabs emerged out of these various groups of Arabian Kushites.

This identification of the Arabs as Kushites is recorded as well in Jewish literature on the eve of the rise of Islam. Rabbi Akiba, famous first century Rabbi who is said to have visited Arabia, is presented in a 5th/6th century Jewish text commenting on Numbers 5: 19, a passage dealing with how one knows if a wife has committed adultery. The Jewish (midrashic) text Numbers Rabbah says:

> "The King of the Arabs put this question to R. Akiba: 'I am black (kushi) and my wife is black (kushi), yet she gave birth to a white son. Shall I kill her for having played the harlot while lying with me?'"[45]

As Jan Restö notes, while this Midrash is probably completely legendary, it does give us a hint of Arabian ethnography, or what the views of the 5th/6th century redactors of this text were regarding Arabian ethnography at the time. See also the Jewish text Targum Shir ha-Shirim commenting on *Song of Songs* 1: 5 ("I am black and comely, O Daughters of Jerusalem, [black] as the tents of Qedar"):

> When the people of the House of Israel made the Calf, their faces became black like the sons of Kush who dwell in the tents of Qedar.

The Qedar was a black Arab tribe, the most powerful Arab tribe of Syria and North Arabia who fought the Assyrians in the 7th century B.C.E.[46] Here they are identified as Kushites. They were not active at the time of Rabbi Akiba's 5th/6th century B.C.E. redactors, but apparently their black memory was still alive and was transferred to the contemporary Black Arabs of the time and their Kushitic origins remembered. As Restö points out:

> "The blackness of the Arabian king is due to his dwelling in the land of the Qedar whose inhabitants are black, according to the Song of Songs... Rabbi Aqiba's Arabia is thus identical with that of Qedar, which was the area between Egypt and Palestine."[47]

4.6.3.- The Black Arabs of the islamic period

"In the morning of the world, when the fingers of Love swept aside the curtains of Time, our dusky mother, Ethiopia, held the stage. It was she who wooed civilization and gave birth to nations... Her spirit called to Arabia and out of the mystic desert surged the black soldiers of Islam, who welded the world into a new empire and sang of love and victory in the vales of Andalusia." George Wells Parker, "The African Origin of Grecian Civilization," *Journal of Negro History 2* (1917)

Invasions, migrations, slavery, and miscegenation have severely changed the complexion of the peninsula. However, on the eve of Muhammad's reform movement in Mecca 48 and beyond the Arabs were still black. This is well documented in the Classical Arabic/Islamic sources.[49] Ibn Manzur (d. 1311), author of the most authoritative classical Arabic lexicon, Lisan al-'arab ("Language of the Arabs"), notes the opinion that the phrase aswad al-jilda, 'black-skinned,' idiomatically meant khalis al-'arab, "the pure Arabs," "because the color of most of the Arabs is dark (al-udma)."[50] In other words, blackness of skin among the Arabs indicated purity of Arab ethnicity. Likewise, the famous grammarian from the century prior, Muhammad b. Barri al-'Adawi (d. 1193) noted that an Akhdar or black-skinned Arab was "a pure Arab ('arabi mahd)" with a pure genealogy, "because Arabs describe their color as black (al-aswad)"[51] Finally Al-Jahiz (d. 869), in his Fakhr al-sudan 'ala l-bidan, ("The Boast of the Black over the White") declared: "The Arabs pride themselves in (their) black color (al-'arab tafkhar bi-sawad al-lawn)".[52]

A particularly instructive illustration of the renowned blackness of the Arabs of the Islamic period is the case of the Arab poet Rabi' b. 'Amir of the early Umayyad period, better known as aal-Darimi ("The poor man from the tribe of Darim"; d. 708). Miskan was a distinguished member of noble ancestry from the Banu Darim from Tamim of Iraq.[53] A pure Arab born to a wealthy family, he was known for being "very dark, handsome, courageous, and eloquent".[54] At a certain point in his life Miskin became a very religious ascetic. He gave up his wealth with its finery and his poetry, and all but locked himself in a mosque in Medina.

Though Miskin was a famously black-skinned (al-aswad; al-sumra) pure-blooded Arab, [55] this was no handicap to him in seventh century Hejaz, as least for the most part, as a famous anecdote reveals. We are told that a merchant arrived in Medina once with a load of black veils, which he had a difficult time selling. Disappointed, this merchant was informed that the only one who could help him was the famous poet Miskin, who now was an ascetic who abandoned his poetry. The merchant found Miskin in his mosque and impressed upon him to help. Though the Muslim ascetic initially resisted, Miskin eventually agreed, left the mosque and donned some of his old finery. Miskin recited verses suggesting that a beautiful woman in a black veil distracted him from his prayer. The word spread enthusiastically that the handsome, wealthy poet had returned to his former lifestyle, enamored by a black veiled beauty. Every unmarried woman in the city thus had to have a black veil, and the merchant sold out within days. Mission accomplished, Miskin went back to his religious asceticism.

This anecdote nicely illustrates the general mood at that time vis-à-vis blackness. No stigma was yet attached to it, for the most part. While Miskin was black, he was famous for being a handsome and wealthy poet. It is important to note also that his blackness was a consequence of his noble Arab ancestry. However, I have qualified my statements with "for the most part." This is because another famous anecdote reveals the minority opinion, but even more forcefully makes our point.

It is reported that Miskin proposed to a woman of his tribe who rejected him because of both his blackness and (now) poverty. She instead married a wealthy, fair-skinned man who was not a pure Arab. Clearly the seed of self-hatred was growing among some Arabs of seventh century Hejaz. One day Miskin passed the two on the street and recited some verses to them, boasting of his noble heritage and denigrating her spousal choice for his lack of the same. He said before them:

> "I am Miskin to those who know me.
> My complexion is dark brown (al-sumra),
> the complexion of the Arabs".[56]

Regarding her husband Miskin said: "the wealth of his house (samin al-bayt) is poverty with respect to genealogy (mahjul al-nasab),"[57] i.e. his material wealth cannot equal Miskin's pure Arab genealogy, which her choice lacks.

Moroccan scholar Tariq Berry has insightfully drawn out some significant implications of this anecdote. Firstly, it articulates an important historical truth: pure Arabs are black-skinned Arabs. And secondly, related to this latter point, fair-skinned Arabs were considered of ignoble birth.[58] True Arabs were black Arabs.

A further illustration is that of the Arab linguist and genealogist al-Hasan b. Ahmad (d. 1044-45), better known as al-Aswad al-Ghandajani, "the black-skinned man from Ghandajan." He was also known as al-A'rabi, the Arab, and it is said that he was excessively proud of his Arab heritage, particularly the dark skin (al-sumra) of the Arabs.[59] The latter was so important to al-Hasan, in fact, that he would not only apply tar to his skin and frequently sit in the very hot sun of Ghandajan to blacken his own complexion making it more 'Arab-like,' but would also throw his son in oil and have him sit in the sun so that his complexion would be dark brown like the Arabs. The poor boy died from this.[60] So important was it to al-Hasan for his son to be black like the Arabs.

4.6.4.- Muhammad, the great african general

"Note, too, fact that Mohammed was of these black Arabs. When he appealed to the Arabians he called himself an 'Arab of the Arabs, of the purest blood of your land, of the family of Hashim that founded the House of the Abbasids, and thus are we brought face to face with the fact that the third of the world's greatest religions was founded by a man in whose veins flowed black blood." George Wells Parker, The Children of the Sun (1918)

"Mohamet himself, by all accounts, was a Negro... It was this empire founded by the black Mohamet with the help of brown, yellow and white mongrels that aroused proud Europe from the slumber of the Dark Ages, and laid the foundations of its present culture." J.A. Rogers, *Sex and Race* (1968).

It was a bit of a shock to many when astrophysicist and racial separatist Dr. Michael Hart published in 1978 and 1992 his *The 100: A Ranking of the Most Influential Persons in History*. This list includes the likes of Homer (# 98), Jean Jacques Rousseau (#78), William the Conqueror (#67), Genghis Khan (#29) Jesus Christ (#3) and Isaac Newton (#2). But the real eye-opener was who Dr. Hart determined was the most influential person in all of human history: the Prophet Muhammad of Arabia. Hart argued:

> "My choice of Muhammad to lead the list of the world's most influential persons may surprise some readers and may be questioned by others, but he was the only man in history who was supremely successful on both the religious and secular levels... unified by Muhammad for the first time in history, and inspired by their fervent belief in the one true God... small Arab armies now embarked upon one of the most astonishing series of conquests in human history... Muhammad (unlike Jesus) was a secular as well as a religious leader. In fact, as the driving force behind the Arab conquests, he may well rank as the most influential political leader of all time..."[61]

It did not dawn on Professor Hart that the most influential man in history was a Black Arab or African Arabian. Africa-centered scholars, however, were quite aware of this fact.[62] While this Africa-centered scholarship reached its conclusion without the benefit of the Classical Arabic sources, their intuition is vindicated by a close examination of those sources. The two most authentic descriptors used for Muhammad in the early Islamic literature are abyad and asmar.

Anas b. Malik reported: "While we were sitting with the Prophet in the mosque, a man came riding on a camel. He made his camel kneel down in the mosque, tied its foreleg and then said: 'Who amongst you is Muhammad?' At that time the Prophet was sitting amongst us (his companions) leaning on his arm. We replied, 'This abyad man reclining on his arm.'"[63]

Anas b. Malik reported: "The Messenger of Allah was of medium stature, neither tall nor short, [with] a beautiful, asmar-complexioned body. His hair was neither curly nor completely straight and when he walked he leant forward."[64]

In Classical Arabic abyad was the standard term for 'white' when referring to non-human subjects, i.e. milk, teeth, etc. However, when abyad was used as a descriptor of human complexions it took on its opposite (didd) mean-ing: black.[65] Thus, according to Shams al-Din Abu ʿAbd Allah al-Dhahabi (d. 1348), in his Siyar aʿlam al-nubalaʾ [II: 168]: "When Arabs say, 'so-and-so is abyad,' they mean a golden brown complexion with a black appearance (al-hinti al-lawn bi-hilya sudaʾ)." This description of Muhammad as abyad, "black with a golden hue," is consistent with the description of him as asmar, brown. Dark brown, not tan, is the normal connotation of this term as evidenced by other formations from the same root: samar "darkness, night"; al-garra al-samra "the black continent (Africa)".[66] In the context of human complexions sumra/asmar has been associated with khudra, adam, and aswad, i.e. black.[67] Muhammad was thus a dark brown-skinned Arab with a flawless complexion that shinned. He was a pure Arab, and as such was a descendent of those Africans who had much earlier indigenized in the Arabian Peninsula. The Prophet Muhammad was indeed one of the greatest Africans in history. As leader of a political empire, he was in fact a great African king, and should be counted among great kings of African history.

Notes

1. Bertram Thomas, *The Arabs* (London: Thornton Butterworth LTD., 1937) 355f. More recently Runoko Rashidi documents: "The Arabian Peninsula… was, like much of Asia, first populated by Black people… Some of the surviving Black populations, known as the Veddoids, are major portions of the Mahra population found still in the extremities of Arabia." Runoko Rashidi, "Africans in Early Asian Civilizations: A Historical Overview," in Runoko Rashidi and Ivan Van Sertima (ed.), *African Presence in Early Asia* (New Brunswick: Transaction Publishers, 1999) 28f. See further Wesley Muhammad, *Black Arabia and the African Origin of Islam* (Atlanta: A-Team Publishing, 2009), Chapter I.

2. See e.g. Dr. Jivanji Jamshedji Modi, "The Physical Character of the Arabs: Their Relations with Ancient Persians," *Anthropological Society of Bombay 11* (1919): 724-768.

3. On these tribes see J. E. Peterson, "Oman's diverse society: Southern Oman," *The Middle East Journal 58* (Spring 2004): 254ff; *Encyclopedia of Islam* [Second Edition; hereafter EI2] 6: 81-84 s.v. Mahra by W.W. Müller; Bertram Thomas, "Among Some Unknown Tribes of South Arabia," *Journal of the Royal Anthropological Institute 59* (1929): 97-111; For photos of these black-skinned South Arabians see further D. Van der Meulen, "Into Burning Hadhramaut" *The National Geographic Magazine 62* (1932): 393-421; Richard F. Nyrop (ed.), *The Yemen Country Studies* (Washington D.C.: The American University, 1985): 5-7; Sir Arthur Keith and Dr. Wilton Marion Krogan, "The Racial Characteristic of the Southern Arabs," in Thomas, *Arabia Felix*, 327 facing, 330 facing 333.

4. Vitaly V. Naumkin, *Island of the Phoenix, an Ethnological Study of the People of Socotra* (Ithaca Press Reading, 1993) 67 notes also: "Socotra, and possibly all of Southern Arabia, may after all be the missing intermediate link in the race-genetic 'west-east' gradient for which anthropologists search in order to fill the gap between the African Negroids and the Australo-Veddo-Melanesian types in the equatorial area."

5. "Oman's diverse society," 261.

6. Henry Field, "Racial Types From South Arabia," *The Open Court 50* [1936]: 33-39.

7. G.M. Morant, "A Description of Human Remains Excavated by Miss G. Gaton Thompson at Hureidha" in G. Caton Thompson, *The Tombs and Moon Temple of Hureidha* (Hadhramaut) [Reports of the Research Committee of the Society of Antiquaries of London # 8; Oxford: University Press, 1944] 107-112.

8. See e.g. Jivanji Jamshedji Modi, "The Physical Character of the Arabs: Their Relations with Ancient Persians" *Anthropological Society of Bombay 7* [1919]: 724-68 and Keith and Krogan, "Racial Characteristic," 301-333.

9. See his "Ancient and Modern Inhabitants of Arabia," *The Open Court 46* (1932): 854 [art.=847-869]. See also Bertram Thomas, "Racial Origin of the Arabs," in idem, *The Arabs: The life-story of a People who have left their deep impress on the world* (London: Thorton Butterworth Ltd., 1937) 353-359; C.G. Seligman, "The Physical Characters

of the Arabs," *Journal of the Royal Anthropological Institute of Great Britain and Ireland* *47* (1917): 214-237.

10. See Tsunehiko Hanihara, "Comparison of Craniofacial Features of Major Human Groups," *American Journal of Physical Anthropology 99* (1996): 389-412. On the ancient colonization of Western Asia from Africa see further Ofer Bar-Yosef, "Early colonizations and cultural continuities in the Lower Palaeolithic of western Asia," in Michael D. Petraglia and Ravi Korisettar (edd.), *Early Human Behaviour in Global Context: The Rise and Diversity of the Lower Palaeolithic Record* (London: Routledge, 1998): 221-279. On ancient migration from Ethiopia to the south of Arabia, then north into the Levant see O. Bar-Yosef, "Pleistocene connexions between Africa and Southwest Asia: an archaeological perspective," *The African Archaeological Review 5* (1987): 29-38. For a discussion of the recent genetic data suggesting ancient and more recent gene-flow from Africa to Yemen see Rídl, Edens, and Lerny, "Mitochondrial DNA Structure of Yemeni Population," 69-78.

11. Emmanuel Anati, *Rock-Art in Central Arabia. Vol. 1*: The "Oval-Headed" People of Arabia (Louvain and Leuven, 1968) 180.

12. Cheikh Anta Diop, *Civilization and Barbarism: An Authentic Anthropology* (Brooklyn: Lawrence Hill Books, 1991) 54.

13. BP= Before Present.

14. D.T. Potts, *The Arabian Gulf in Antiquity, Vol. I: From Prehistoric to the Fall of the Achaemenid Empire* (Oxford: Oxford University Press, 1990) 9.

15. Potts, Arabian Gulf in Antiquity 16.

16. Michael Rice, *The Archaeology of the Arabian Gulf* (London and New York: Routledge, 1994) 69

17. Maurizio Tosi "The Emerging Picture of Prehistoric Arabia," *Annual Review of Anthropology 15* (1986): 461-490.

18. *The New International Encyclopedia, 2nd edition* (ed. Frank Moore Colby and Talcott Williams; New York: Dodd, Mead and Company, 1914) s.v. *Arabia* by A.H. Keane.

19. *The Kingdom of Saudi Arabia* (Stacey International, 1982), apud Dr. Khalid Abdullah Tariq al-Mansour, *Seven African Arabian Wonders of the World: The Black Man's Guide to the Middle East* (n.d.: First African Arabian Press, 1991) 116.

20. Paul Bohannan, *African Outline* (Harmondsworth, Middlesex: Penquin Books, 1966) 42.

21. Ali A. Mazrui, *The Africans: A Triple Heritage* (Boston and Toronto: Little, Brown and Company, 1986) 30, 32, 36.

22. Charles S. Finch, "Nile Genesis: Continuity of Culture from the Great Lakes to the Delta," in Ivan Van Sertima (ed.), *Egypt: Child of Africa* (New Brunswick and London: Transaction Publishers, 1994) 44

23. P. Andrews, W.R. Hamilton and P.J. Whybrow, "Dryopithecines from the Miocene of Saudi Arabia," *Nature 274* (1978): 249-51; Pott, *Arabian Gulf in Antiquity*, 11.

24. "The Lower Paleolithic of the Arabian Peninsula: Occupations, Adaptations, and Dispersals," *Journal of World History 17* (June 2003): 173 [art.=144-179].

25. Verónica Fernandes et al, "The Arabia Cradle: Mitochondrial Relicts of the First Steps along the Southern Route out of Africa," *The American Journal of Human Genetics 90* (2012): 1-9.

26. http://*www.upi.com/Science*_News/2012/01/26/Arabia-saw-first-humans-out-of-Africa/UPI-65001327616469/#ixzz1ksJQNUqh

27. Richard Gray, "African tribe populated rest of the world," http://*www.telegraph.co.uk/science/science-news/*5299351/African-tribe-populated-rest-of-the-world.html. Accessed July 25, 2009.

28. Norman M. Whalen and David E. Peace, "Early Mankind in Arabia," *ARAMCO World 43: 4* (1992): 20, 23. Jeffrey I. Rose and Michael D. Petraglia confirm the same in their article "Tracking the Origin and Evolution of Human Populations in Arabia," in Michael D. Petraglia and Jeffrey I. Rose (edd.), *The Evolution of Human Populations in Arabia: Paleoenvironments, Prehistory and Genetics* (London and New York: Springer, 2009) 1. See also Michael D. Petraglia, "The Lower Paleolithic of the Arabian Peninsula: Occupations, Adaptations, and Dispersals," *Journal of World History 17* (June 2003): 173.

29. See P.A. Underhill et al, "The Phylogeography of Y chromosomes binary haplotypes and the origins of modern human populations," *Annals of Human Genetics* 65 (2001): 43-62. See further J.R. Luis et al, "The Levant versus the Horn of Africa: Evidence for Bidirectional Corridors of Human Migrations," *American Journal of Human Genetics* 74 (2004): 532; Bernard Vandermeersch, "The Near Eastern Hominids and the Origins of Modern Humans in Eurasia," in Takeru Akazawa, Kenichi Aoki, and Tasuku Kimura (edd.), *The Evolution and Dispersal of Modern Humans in Asia* (Tokyo: Hokusen-sha, 1992): 29-38.

30. As noted in Jakub Rídl, Christopher M. Edens, and Viktor Lerny, "Mitochondrial DNA Structure of Yemeni Population: Regional Differences and the Implications for Different Migratory Contributions," in Michael D. Petraglia and Jeffrey I. Rose (edd.), *The Evolution of Human Populations in Arabia: Paleoenvironments, Prehistory and Genetics* (London and New York: Springer, 2009) 71. On the cultural links between Bronze Age Yemen and the Horn of Africa see Christopher Edens and T.J. Wilkinson, "Southwest Arabia During the Holocene: Recent Archaeological Developments," *Journal of World History 12* (1998): 55-119.

31. Bernard Leeman, *Queen of Sheba and Biblical Scholarship* (Queensland, Australia: Queensland Academic Press, 2005) 176.

32. Dana Reynolds (Marniche), "The African Heritage & Ethnohistory of the Moors," in Ivan van Sertima, *Golden Age of the Moor* (New Brunswick: Transaction Publishers, 1992) 100, 105-106.

33. Gregorio del Olmo Lete, *Questions of Semitic Linguistics. Root and Lexeme: The History of Research* (Bethesda, Maryland: CDL Press, 2008) 115; Christopher Ehret, *The Civilizations of Africa: A History to 1800* (Charlottesville: University of Virginia Press, 2002)

38, 57; Edward Lipiński, *Semitic Languages: Outline of a Comparative Grammar* (Leuven: Uitgeverij Peeters and Departement Oosterse Studies, 1997) 42-43; A. Murtonen, *Early Semitic* (Leiden: E.J. Brill, 1967), 74; George Aaron Barton, *Semitic and Hamitic Origins: Social and Religious* (Philadelphia: University of Pennsylvania Press, 1934); idem, "The Origins of Civilization in Africa and Mesopotamia, Their Relative Antiquity and Interplay," *Proceedings of the American Philosophical Society 68* (1929) 303-312.

34. Nicholas Faraclas, "They Came Before the Egyptians: Linguistic Evidence for the African Roots of Semitic Languages," in Silvia Federici (ed.), *Enduring Western Civilization: The Construction of the Concept of Western Civilization and Its "Others"* (Westport, Connecticut and London: Praeger, 1995) 175-96

35. Quoted in interview by Jeff Mortimer, "Language of the Desert," Michigan Today, Spring 1997 online version: http://*www.ns.umich.edu*/MT/97/Spr97/mta8s97.html accessed July 30, 2009.

36. George E. Mendenhall, "Arabic in Semitic Linguistic History," *JAOS 126* (2006): 17-26; *The Anchor Bible Dictionary*, ed. David Noel Freedman et al, 6 vols. (New York: Doubleday, 1992) 4: 815 s.v. Midian by George E. Mendenhall; idem, "The Syro-Palestinian Origins of the Pre-Islamic Arabic," in Studies in the *History and Archaeology of Palestine, vol. III* (Aleppo University Press, 1988) 215-223.

37. David M. Goldenberg, *The Curse of Ham: Race and Slavery in Early Judaism, Christianity, and Islam (Jews, Christians, and Muslims from the Ancient to the Modern World)* (Princeton: Princeton University Press, 2005) 28, 54.

38. "the people of Northwest Arabia (Midian) were called Kushites." Goldenberg, *Curse of Ham*, 54.

39. Jan Retsö, *The Arabs in Antiquity: Their History from the Assyrians to the Umayyads* (London and New York: RoutledgeCurzon, 2003) 212. Fred V. Winnett similarly saw the genealogies of Gen. 10: 7 as Arabian genealogies which "contain information of considerable value for the reconstruction of early Arabian history." He assumes these genealogies reflect the political and tribal situation in 6th cent B.C.E. Arabia. Fred V. Winnett, "The Arabian Genealogies in the Book of Genesis," in Harry Thomas Frank and William L. Reed (edd.), *Translating and Understanding the Old Testament. Essays in Honor of Herbert Gordon May* (Nashville and New York: Abingdon Press, 1970) 173.

40. Regarding the genealogies of Gen. 10: 7 Claus Westermann, *Genesis 1-11: A Commentary* (Minneapolis: Augsburg Publishing House, 1984) 511 notes: "It is certain that the majority of the names describes peoples in Arabia," not Africa.

41. On the Kushite presence in the Syro-Palestine region see Roger W. Anderson, Jr. "Zephaniah ben Cushi and the Cush of Benjamin: Traces of Cushite Presence in Syria-Palestine," in Steven W. Holloway and Lowell K. Handy (edd.), *The Picture is Broken: Memorial Essays for Gösta W. Ahlström* (JSOTSupp 190; Sheffield: Sheffield Academic Press, 1995) 45-70. William Foxwell Albright documented a district or tribe called Kush in southern Transjordan in the 19th century B.C.E. and a Kusan-rom, "high Kushan" in Northern Syria in 13th-12th cent B.C.E. Williams Foxwell Albright, Archaeology and the Religion of Israel (Baltimore: The John Hopkins Press, 1956) 205

n. 49. On the Kushite presence in North Arabia see also Goldenberg, *Curse of Ham*, 20: "The existence of a Kushite people in the general area and references to it in the Bible have become well accepted in biblical scholarship."

42. On the Natufians of Palestine see C. Loring Brace et al, "The questionable contribution of the Neolithic and the Bronze Age to European craniofacial form," *Proceedings of the National Academy of Sciences, USA 103* (2006): 242-247; Margherita Mussi, "The Natufian of Palestine: The Beginnings of Agriculture in a Palaeoethnological Perspective," *Origini 10* (1976) 89-107; F.J. Los, "The Prehistoric Ethnology of Palestine," *Mankind Quarterly* 7 (1966): 53-59; Sir Arthur Keith, "The Late Palaeolithic Inhabitants of Palestine," *Proceedings of the First International Congress of Prehistoric and Protohistoric Sciences, London August 1-6* 1932 (London: Oxford University Press, 1934) 46-47; idem, *New Discoveries Relating to the Antiquity of Man* (New York: W.W. Norton & Company, 1931) 210-211.

43 As Roger W. Anderson, Jr. notes: "The Cushites were probably dark-skinned or burnt-faced people, ones whom we would classify today as black." Anderson, "Zephaniah ben Cushi," 68. But Anderson wants to connect these Syrian Kushites with the Nubian rulers of Egypt's 25th Dynasty who had some influence in the area. On the other hand Robert D. Haak has shown that this association is untenable. "'Cush' in Zephaniah," in Holloway and Handy, *Picture is Broken*, 238-251. On Kushites in the area see also Israel Eph'al, *The Ancient Arabs: Nomads on the Borders of the Fertile Crescent 9th-5th Centuries B.C.* (Leiden: E.J. Brill, 1982) 78-79. The ancient Egyptians also depicted Syro-Palestinians as having "dark hair, brown complexions and Semitic features": Frank J. Yurco, "Were the Ancient Egyptians Black or White," *BAR 15* (Sept/Oct 1989): 26. In sum, in Near Eastern, Greco-Roman, Biblical and post-biblical Jewish literatures, Kushites are noted for their black skin. Goldenberg, *Curse of Ham*, 113-114.

44. Retsö, *Arabs in Antiquity*, 119.

45. Num. R. IX.34 (Soncino translation).

46. The verbal root qēdār < q—d—r means "to be dark". As Marvin Pope informs us, "The root qdr itself carries the idea of darkness." *Song of Songs*: A New Translation with Introduction and Commentary (*The Anchor Bible; Garden* City, NY: Doubleday and Company, 1977) 319. See also Tremper Longman III, *Song of Songs* (Grand Rapids, Michigan and Cambridge: William B. Eerdman's Publishing, 2001) 97. Qedar is related to the Arabic root kh-d-r, from which we get akhdar "of blackish hue inclining to green, black-complexioned." See Jaroslav Stetkevych, *Muhammad and the Golden Bough: Reconstructing Arabian Myth* (Bloomington and Indianapolis: Indiana University Press, 1996) 73.

47. Restö, *Arabs in Antiquity*, 530.

48. On which see Muhammad, *Black Arabia*, 164-171.

49. See especially Berry, *Unknown Arabs*.

50. Ibn Manzur, *Lisan al-'arab* (Beirut: Dar al-Sadir—Dar al-Bayrut, 1955-1956) s.v. رضخإ IV: 245f; See also Edward William Lane, *Arabic-English Lexicon* (London: Williams & Norgate 1863) I: 756 s.v. رضخ.

51. Ibn Manzur, *Lisan al-'arab*, s.v. خرض IV: 245.

52. Al-Jahiz, Fakhr al-sudan 'ala l-bidan, in *Risa'il Al-Jahiz*, 4 vols. (Cairo, 1964) I: 207. See also the English translation by T. Khalidi, "The Boast of the Blacks Over the Whites," *Islamic Quarterly 25* (1981): 3-26 (17). See further Ignaz Goldziher, *Muslim Studies (Muhammedanische Studien)* 2 vols. (London, Allen & Unwin, 1967-), 1: 268 who notes that, in contrast to the Persians who are described as red or light-skinned (ahmar) the Arabs call themselves black.

53. On him see Abu al-Faraj al-Isfahani, *Kitab al-aghani* (Beirut: Dar al-Thaqah, 1955) 20: 167-178; EI2 7: 145 s.v. MiskÊn al-DŞrimÊ by Ch. Pellat.

54. EI2 7: 145 s.v. *Miskin al-Darimi* by Ch. Pellat.

55. al-Isfahani, *Kitab al-aghani*, 174.

56. al-Isfahani, *Kitab al-aghani*, 174.

57. al-Isfahani, Kitab al-aghani, 175.

58. Berry, *Unknown Arabs*, 59.

59. 'Ali b. Yusuf al-Qifti, *Inbah al-ruwah 'ala anbah al-nuhah* (Cairo, 1973) 168-169.

60. Al-Qifti, *Inbah al-ruwah*, 169; Yaqut b. 'Abd Allah al-Hamawi, *Kitab irshad al-arib ila ma'rifat al-adib*, ed. D.S. Margoliouth (Leiden: E.J. Brill, 1910) III/i, 22-23.

61. Michael H. Hart, *The 100: A Ranking of the Most Influential Persons in History* (New York: Carol Publishing Group, 1993) Chapter I.

62. George Wells Parker, *The Children of the Sun* (Hamitic League of theWorld, 1918; reprint Black Classic Press, 1981) 22; J.A. Rogers, *Sex and Race Volume I: Negro-Caucasian Mixing in All Ages and All Lands* (New York: Helga M. Rogers, 1968) 95-96; Yosef A.A. ben-Jochannan, *African Origins of the Major 'Western Religions'* (1970; Baltimore: Black Classic Press, 1991) 237: "none of the Gods, prophets, or founders of any of the three religions—Judaism, Christianity, and Islam—… was indigenous to Europe (a Caucasian, or White man.)… Judaism and Islam, both, had indigenous Africans in the leadership roles from the first day of their recorded origin… Islam had Mohamet—whose grandfather was of African origin… Al-Jahiz's description and identification of the Prophet Mohamet placed him, Mohamet, in the family of the Black Race"; Mamadou Chinyelu, "Africans in the Birth and Spread of Islam," in Ivan Van Sertima (ed.), *Golden Age of the Moor* (New Brunswick: Transaction Publishers, 1993) 360: "African blood figures in Mohammed's lineage"; Wayne B. Chandler, "Ebony and Bronze: Race and Ethnicity in Early Arabia and the Islamic World," in Runoko Rashidi and Ivan Van Sertima (edd.) *African Presence in Early Asia* (New Brunswick: Transaction Publishers, 1995) 280: "All the chronicles that survive intact agree that Ishmael and Muhammad were of the Black race… A careful examination of history reveals that the Prophet Muhammad… was of the Black race and was black in complexion."; Cheikh Anta Diop, *The African Origin of Civilization* (Westport: Lawrence Hill & Company, 1967): 25ff: "the entire Arab people, including the Prophet, is mixed with Negro blood. All educated Arabs are conscious of that fact."

63. al-Bukhari, *Sahih, kitab 'alim*, # 63.

64. *Sunan al-Tirmidhi* 6: 69 # 1754.

65. EI2 s.v. Lawn by Morabia "One of the most striking manifestations of the symbolic connotations of colours among the Arabs, is the phenomenon of opposites (al-addad). We have seen, in studying the semantic value of certain adjectives of colour, that they were sometimes capable of embracing two diametrically opposite meanings. This phenomenon is particularly to be noted in the case of white and black... To signify wine, the Arabs used a number of euphemisms of the type 'the fair drink', 'the golden one', etc... Even today, in certain parts of the Orient and the Maghrib, in order to avoid pronouncing the word 'black'... opposites are used. In Morocco, al-abyad sometimes denotes tar or coal."; Jehan Allam, "A Sociolinguistic Study on the Use of Color Terminology in Egyptian Colloquial and Classical Arabic," in Zeinab Ibrahim, Nagwa Kassabgy and Sabiha Aydelott (edd.), *Diversity in Language: Contrastive Studies in English and Arabic Theoretical and Applied Linguistics* (Cairo and New York: The American University on Cairo Press, 2000) 78: «[The Arabic term Abyaḍ ('white')] is derived from the root /b/y/D/ ('to become whitened')... In [Classical Arabic], the sense of [abyaḍ] usually revolves around purity and light... Figurative meanings may vary with different derivatives of the root... in fact, [abyaḍ] is used euphemistically to refer to a black man.»

66. J M. Cowan (ed.), Hans Wehr *Arabic-English Dictionary 4th edition* (Ithica: Spoken Language Services, Inc., 1994) 500 s.v. رمس.

67. Ibn Manzur, *Lisan al-'arab*, s.v. رضخ IV: 245; s.v. رمس IV: 376: "al-udma is al-sumra, and al-§dam among people in al-asmar." See also Ibn Abi al-Hadid, Sharh nahj al-balaghah, V: 56. Lane's note, Lexicon, I: 1425 s.v. رمس: "tawny... like the various hues of wheat" does not accurately capture the chromatic implications of this term. See also Hidayet Hosain's translation of Anas b. M§lik's report as found in Tirmidhi's al-Shama'il (#2): "his complexion was tawny": Hidayet Hosain, "Translation of Ash-Shama'il of Tirmizi," *Islamic Culture 7* (1933): 397. K. Vollers, "*Über Rassenfarben in der arabischen Literatur,*" Centenario della nascita di Michele Amari 1 (1910): 88, is more accurate in his definition of asmar as dunkle Bräune, dark brown.

APPENDIX
LETTER TO RUNOKO RASHIDI

September 26, 1983

Dear Mr. Rashidi,

It is really fascinating to have your letter of September 15, 1983. We are equally anxious to develop relations and mutual cooperation with Blacks in general and American Blacks in particular.

It is undoubtedly true that Dalits (oppressed and suppressed) who were abused to the extent of being called untouchables have a black background. But we are sympathetic towards American Blacks because they have no identity in American society. American Blacks are also second class citizens in practice as we are in ours. This is more harmful than foreign rule. Battle against foreign rule, and you have sympathies and support all over the world, whereas you are totally missing this when you fight against discrimination that you are facing in your daily life. Do you not think the Blacks in various newly independent countries are honourable and enjoy better status in the eyes of whites, including American Whites, than the Blacks in America?

This is how we are always sympathetic towards American Blacks. When American Blacks showed militancy and started talking about Black Power, we were highly impressed and we named a most militant organization of Dalits at present, as Dalit Panther. Undoubtedly, the word Panther is taken from Black Panther. I do not know whether you are aware or not that Dalit literature, is also influenced very much by the pro test literature being written by the Blacks.

So, we have very much in common. And, if we realise, that we have to fight back the situation, which is the worst type of exploitation, we can at least build strong world opinion against this. Similarly exploited class such as Burakumen in Japan, can also join us.

More when I hear from you. Meanwhile please accept my warmest greetings.

Yours in struggle,
Bapurao Pakhiddey,
Dalit Panther of India
New Delhi, India

BIBLIOGRAPHIES

1. Nineteenth and Early Twentieth Century African Diasporan Scholars and the African Presence In Asia Bibliography

Bergman, Peter M., editor. *The Chronological History of the Negro in America.* New York: Harper and Row, 1969.

Blyden, Edward Wilmot. "The Negro in Ancient History." *Methodist Quarterly Review* (January 1869): 71-93.

Boddy, James Marmaduke. "The Ethnology of the Japanese Race." *The Colored American Magazine* (October 1905): 577-85.

Brown, Lois. *Pauline Elizabeth Hopkins: Black Daughter of the Revolution.* Chapel Hill: University of North Carolina Press, 2008.

Brunson, James E. *Africans in Early Asia: An African-Centric Historiography* (1827-1991). DeKalb: Kara, 1991.

Cornish, Samuel E., and John Russwurm. "European Colonies in America." *Freedom's Journal 1, No. 18* (July 18, 1827).

Franklin, John Hope. *George Washington Williams: A Biography.* Chicago: University of Chicago Press, 1985.

Hill, Robert A., editor. *The Marcus Garvey and Universal Negro Improvement Association Papers. Vol. 1*: 1826—August 1919. Berkeley: University of California, 1983.

Hill, Robert A., editor. *The Crusader.* New York: Garland, 1987.

Homer. *The Iliad. Translated* by A.T. Murray. 2 Volumes. London: Heinemann, 1925.

Hopkins, Pauline Elizabeth. "The Dark Races of the Twentieth Century, Pt. 2: The Malay Peninsula, Borneo, Java, Sumatra and the Philippines." *The Voice of the Negro* (March 1905): 186-91.

Hopkins, Pauline Elizabeth. A *Primer of Facts Pertaining to the Early Greatness of the African Race and the Possibility of Restoration by its Descendants*—With Epilogue Compiled and Arranged from the Works of the Best Known Ethnologists and Historians. Cambridge: P.E. Hopkins & Co., 1905.

Houston, Drusilla Dunjee. *Wonderful Ethiopians of the Ancient Cushite Empire, Book I: Nations of the Cushite Empire. Marvelous Facts From Authentic Records.* Oklahoma City: Universal Publishing, 1926. Reprinted with a New Introduction by W. Paul Coates. Afterword by Asa G. Hilliard III. Commentary by James G. Spady. Baltimore: Black Press, 1985.

Jacobs, Sylvia M. *The African Nexus: Black American Perspectives on the European Partitioning of Africa, 1880-1920.* Westport: Greenwood Press, 1981.

Johnson, Edward A. *The Negro Race in America.* Raleigh: Edwards & Broughton, 1891.

Logan, Rayford W., and Michael R. Winston, editors. *Dictionary of American Negro Biography.* New York: W.W. Norton, 1982.

Martin, Tony, compiler and editor. *African Fundamentalism: A Literary and Cultural Anthology of Garvey's Harlem Renaissance.* Dover: The Majority Press, 1991.

Norris, John William. *The Ethiopian's Place in History* (Baltimore, 1916).

Parker, George Wells. *The Children of the Sun. Omaha: The Hamitic League of the World*, 1918. Rpt. Baltimore: Black Classic Press, 1978.

Perry, Rufus Lewis. *The Cushite: or, The Children of Ham*, (The Negro Race) As Seen by the Ancient Historians and Poets. Introduction by Thomas McCants Stewart Brooklyn: *The Literary Union*, 1887.

Perry, Rufus Lewis. *The Cushite: or, The Children of Ham*, (The Negro Race) As Seen by the Ancient Historians and Poets from Noah to the Christian Era. Introduction by Thomas McCants Stewart. Springfield, MA: Willey & Co., 1893.

Schomburg, Arthur A. "The Negro Digs Up His Past." *Survey Graphic* (March 1925): 670-72.

Shockley, Ann Allen. "Pauline Elizabeth Hopkins: A Biographical Excursion in Obscurity." *Phylon 33* (Spring 1972): 22-26.

Shockley, Ann Allen. "Pauline Elizabeth Hopkins, 1859-1930." *In Afro-American Women Writers 1746-1933: An Anthology and Critical Guide.* Boston: G.K. Hall, 1988: 289-95.

Simmons, William J. Men of Mark, *Eminent, Progressive and Rising. 1887*; rpt. Chicago: Johnson, 1970.

Stafford, Alphonso Orenzo. "Antar, The Arabian Negro Warrior, Poet and Hero." *Journal of Negro History. Vol. 1, No. 2* (1916): 151-62.

Stafford, Alphonso Orenzo. "Africa and Asia." *Negro History Bulletin. Vol. 4, No. 2* (1940): 29.

Stafford, Alphonso Orenzo. "Antar." *Negro History Bulletin. Vol. 4, No. 2* (1940): 27.

Stafford, Alphonso Orenzo. "Why Study Asia with Respect to Africa?" *Negro History Bulletin 4, No. 2* (1940): 27.

Williams, George Washington. *History of the Negro Race in America from 1619 to 1880.* Negroes as Slaves, as Soldiers, and as Citizens: Together with a Preliminary Consideration of the Unity of the Human Family, an Historical Sketch of Africa, and an Account of the Negro Governments of Sierra Leone and Liberia, in Two Volumes. New York: G.P. Putnam's 1883.

2. The African Presence in Early Southwestern and Southern Asia Through the Eyes of Nineteenth Century European Scholars: Bibliography

Baldwin, John D. *Pre-Historic Nations* (New York: Harper & Brothers, 1872).

Dieulafoy, Marcel A. *L'Acropole de Susa* (Paris: Hachette, 1892).

Forlong, J.G.R. *Rivers of Life* (London: Bernard Quarith, 1883).

Higgins, Godfrey. *Celtic Druids. 1829;* rpt. (Los Angeles: Philosophical Research Society, 1977).

Higgins, Godfrey. *Anacalypsis.* 1836; rpt. (Mokelume Hills, CA: Health Research, 1972).

Lenormant, François. *Ancient History of the East* (London: Asher & Co., 1869).

Massey, Gerald. *Books of Beginnings, Vol. 2.* 1881; rpt. (University Books, 1974).

Massey, Gerald. *Ancient Egypt* (New York: Samuel Weiser, 1970).

Rawlinson, George. *History of Herodotus. Vol. 1.* London: John Murray, 1858.

Rawlinson, George. *Ancient Monarchies. Vol. 1.*(News York: Dodd, Mead, 1881).

Rawlinson, George. *Origin of Nations* (New York: Scribner's, 1881).

3. A Selected Bibliography of John Glover Jackson (1907-1993)

Compiled by Runoko Rashidi

Jackson, John G. *Ethiopia and the Origin of Civilization: A Critical Review of the Evidence of Archaeology, Anthropology, History and Comparative Religion—According to the Most Reliable Sources and Authorities.* New York: The Blyden Society, 1939; rpt. Baltimore: Black Classic Press, 1985.

Jackson, John G. *Pagan Origins of the Christ Myth.* New York: Truth Seeker Co., 1941.

Jackson, John G. *Introduction to African Civilizations. Introduction and Additional Bibliographical* Notes by John Henrik Clarke. Secaucus: Citadel, 1970.

Jackson, John G. *Man, God, and Civilization.* New Hyde Park: University Books, 1972.

Jackson, John G. *Foreword to Gerald Massey's Lectures.* New York: Samuel Weiser, 1974.

Jackson, John G. *The Mysteries of Egypt.* Chicago: MASS, 1980.

Jackson, John G. *The African Origin of Christianity.* Chicago: L&P, 1981.

Jackson, John G. "Egypt and Christianity." *Egypt Revisited.* Edited by Ivan Van Sertima. New Brunswick: Transaction Press, 1982: 65-80.

Jackson, John. G. *The African Origin of the Myths and Legends of the Garden of Eden.* Chicago: MASS, 1984.

Jackson, John G. *Was Jesus Christ a Negro?* Chicago: MASS, 1984.

Jackson, John G. *Christianity Before Christ.* Austin: American Atheist Press, 1985.

Jackson, John G. *Black Reconstruction in South* Carolina. Austin: American Atheist Press, 1987.

Jackson, John G. *The Golden Ages of Africa.* Austin: American Atheist Press, 1987.

Jackson, John G. Hubert H. Harrison: *The Black Socrates. Austin: American* Atheist Press, 1987.

Jackson, John G. "Krishna and Buddha: Black Gods of Asia." *African Presence in Early Asia. Rev. ed.* Edited by Runoko Rashidi and Ivan Van Sertima. New Brunswick: Transaction Press, 1996: 106-11.

Jackson, John G. *Ages of Gold and Silver and Other Short Sketches of Human History.* Foreword by Madalyn O'Hair. Austin: American Atheist Press, 1990.

Jackson, John G. *Introduction to The Story of the Moors in Spain*, by Stanley Lane-Poole. Baltimore: Black Classic Press, 1990.

Jackson, John G. "The Empire of the Moors." Compiled, with an Appendix, by Runoko Rashidi. *Golden Age of the Moor.* Edited by Ivan Van Sertima. New Brunswick: Transaction Press, 1992: 85-92.

Works by Willis Nathaniel Huggins and John Glover Jackson

Huggins, Willis Nathaniel, and John Glover Jackson. *A Guide to the Study of African History: Directive Lists for Schools and Clubs.* New York: New York Federation of History Clubs, 1934.

Huggins, Willis Nathaniel, and John Glover Jackson. *An Introduction to African Civilizations with Main Currents in Ethiopian History.* New York: Avon House, 1937; rpt. New York: Negro Universities Press, 1969.

Williams, George Washington. *History of the Negro Race in America from 1619 to 1880. Negroes as Slaves, as Soldiers, and as Citizens: Together with a Preliminary Consideration of the Unity of the Human Family*, an Historical *Sketch of Africa, and an Account of the Negro Governments of Sierra Leone and Liberia, in Two Volumes.* New York: G.P. Putnam's 1883.

Williams, Larry Obadele, compiler. *Towards an African Historiography: A Bibliography.* Atlanta: Ipet Isut, 1989.

Woodson, Carter G. "Alphonso Orenzo Stafford," *Journal of Negro History. Vol. 26, No. 1* (1941): 277-78.

4. African Presence In Early Western Asia

Hakim, Musa Abdul."Diop on Cultural Kinship between Arabs and Africans." *The Challenger 24, No. 6* (1988): 15.

Hansberry, William Leo. *Africa and Africans As Seen By Classical Writers*. Edited by Joseph E. Harris. Washington, D.C.: Howard University Press, 1981.

Herodotus. *The Histories*, trans. Aubrey de Selincourt. New York: Penguin Books, 1972.

Houston, Drusilla Dunjee. *The Wonderful Ethiopians of the Ancient Cushite Empire*. 1926; rpt. Introduction by W. Paul Coates. Afterword by Asa G. Hilliard III. Commentary by James Spady. Baltimore: Black Classic Press, 1985.

Keith, Arthur, and M. Krogman."The Racial Character of the Southern Arabs." Chapter in *Arabia Felix*, by Bertram Thomas. London: Jonathan Cape, 1932.

Kramer, Samuel N., editor. "Lamentation Over the Destruction of Ur." *Assyriological Studies, No. 12*, Oriental Institute. Chicago: University of Chicago Press, 1940.

Kramer, Samuel N. *The Sumerians*. Chicago: University of Chicago Press, 1963.

Lenormant, Francois. *Ancient History of the East, Volume. 2*. London: Asher & Co., 1869.

Muhammad, Wesley. *Black Arabia and the African Origin of Islam*. Atlanta: A-Team, 2009.

Perry, Rufus Lewis. *The Cushite: or, The Children of Ham, (The Negro Race) As Seen by the Ancient Historians and Poets*. Introduction by Thomas McCants Stewart. Brooklyn: *Brooklyn* Literary Union, 1887.

Perry, Rufus Lewis. *The Cushite, Or the Descendants of Ham as Found in the Sacred Scriptures and in the Writings of Ancient Historians and Poets from Noah to the Christian Era*. Springfield, MA: Willey & Co., 1893.

Rawlinson, George. *Ancient Monarchies, Volume 1*. New York: Dodd, Mead & Co., 1881.

Rawlinson, George. *Origin of Nations*. New York: Charles Scribners' Sons, 1912.

India, caste, color and race

Aravaanan, K.P. *Dravidians and Africans*. Madras: Tamil Koottam, 1977.

Dutt, N.K. *Origin and Growth of Caste in India*. Calcutta: Mukhopadhyay, 1968.

Dutt, N.K. *The Aryanisation of India*. Calcutta: Mukhopadhyay, 1970.

Jayasuriya, Shihan De Silva and Richard Pankhurst, editors. *The African Diaspora in the Indian Ocean*. Trenton: Africa World Press, 2003.

Laws of Manu. Translated by G. Buhler. Delhi: Motilal Banarsidas, 1979.

Possehl, Gregory L., ed. *Harappan Civilization*. New Delhi: Oxford, 1982

Pritchard, James Cowles. *Researches into the Physical History of Man*. Chicago: University of Chicago Press, 1073.

Puri, B.N. *Cities of Ancient India*. Meerut: Meenaskshi Prakashan, 1966.

Rajshekar, V.T. *Dalit: The Black Untouchables of India*. Atlanta: Clarity Press, 1987.

Rashidi, Runoko and Ivan Van Sertima, eds. *African Presence in Early Asia*. New Brunswick: Transaction Press, 1995.

Travels of Marco Polo. Translated by R. Latham. Middlesex: Penguin, 1982.

Upadhyaya, U.P. *Dravidian and Negro-African*. Karnataka: Samshodhana Prakashana, 1983.

Wobogo, Vulindlela I. *Cold Wind from the North: The Prehistoric European Origin of Racism Explained by Diop's Two Cradle Theory*. Introduction by Legrand Clegg II. Foreword by Nozipo Wobogo. Charleston: Books on Deman, 2011.

The african presence in early China

Boddy, James Marmaduke. "The Ethnology of the Japanese Race." *The Colored American Magazine* (October 1905): 577-85.

Brunson, James E. Black Jade: *The African Presence in the Ancient East and Other Essays*. Introduction by Runoko Rashidi. DeKalb: Kara, 1985.

Brunson, James E. *The Image of the Black in Eastern Art*. Pt. 1, Black Roots in Most Ancient China (1766 B.C.-950 B.C.) DeKalb: Kara, 1989.

Brunson, James E. *Kamite Brotherhood: African Origins in Early Asia*. DeKalb: Kara, 1989.

Brunson, James E. "African Presence in Early China." *African Presence in Early Asia*. Rev. ed. Edited by Runoko Rashidi and Ivan Van Sertima. New Brunswick: Transaction Press, 1995: 120-37.

Brunson, James E. "Unexpected Black Faces in Early Asia: A Photo Essay." *African Presence in Early Asia. Rev. ed.* Edited by Runoko Rashidi and Ivan Van Sertima. New Brunswick: Transaction Press, 1995: 206-33.

Chai, Chen Kang. *Taiwan Aborigines: A Genetic Study of Tribal Variations. Cambridge*: Harvard University Press, 1967.

Chandler, Wayne B. "The Principle of Polarity." *African Presence in Early Asia. Rev. ed.* Edited by Runoko Rashidi and Ivan Van Sertima. New Brunswick: Transaction Press, 1995: 360-77.

Chandler, Wayne B. "Bodhidharma: Founder and First Patriarch of Zen Buddhism." *African Presence in Early Asia*. Edited by Runoko Rashidi and Ivan Van Sertima. New Brunswick: Transaction Press, 1995: 378.

Chang, Kwang-chih. *The Archaeology of Ancient China*. Rev. ed. New Haven: Yale University Press, 1968.

Chang, Kwang-chih. *Art, Myth, and Ritual: The Path to Political Authority in Ancient China*. Cambridge, MA: Harvard University Press, 1983.

Chang, Kwang-chih, editor. *Studies of Shang Archaeology: Selected Papers from the International Conference on Shang Civilization*. New Haven: Yale University Press, 1986.

Chi, Li. *The Formation of the Chinese People: An Anthropological Inquiry. 1928*; rpt. New York: Russell & Russell, 1967.

Duyvendak, J.J.L. *China's Discovery of Africa*. London: Probsthain, 1949.

Filesi, Teobaldo. *China and Africa in the Middle Ages*. Translated by David L. Morison. London: Frank Cass, 1972.

Horton, Mark. "The Swahili Corridor." *Scientific American* (September 1987): 86-93.

Hotz, Robert Lee. "Chinese Roots Lie in Africa, Research Says." *Los Angeles Times*, September 29, 1998.

Rashidi, Runoko and Ivan Van Sertima, eds. *The African Presence in Early Asia*. Rev. ed. New Brunswick: Transaction Press, 1995.

Winters, Clyde-Ahmad. "Trade Between East Africa and Ancient China." *Afrikan Mwalimu 4, No. 3* (1978).

Winters, Clyde-Ahmad. "The Relationship of Afrikans and Chinese in the Past." *Afrikan Mwalimu* (January 1979): 25-31.

Winters, Clyde-Ahmad. "Blacks in Ancient China, Pt. 1: The Founders of Xia and Shang." *Journal of Black Studies* (1984): 8-13.

Sakanouye Tamuramaro and the black presence in japanese antiquity

"African-Like Stone Age Hut is Unearthed in Japan." *Associated Press, February 15,* 1986.

Boddy, James Marmaduke. "The Ethnology of the Japanese Race." *The Colored American Magazine* (October 1905): 577-85.

Brunson, James E. *The World of Sakanouye No Tamuramaro: Black Shogun of Early Japan.* DeKalb: KARA, 1991.

Chamberlain, Alexander Francis. "The Contribution of the Negro to Human Civilization." *Journal of Race Development 2* (April 1911): 458-71.

Diop, Cheikh Anta. *The African Origin of Civilization: Myth or Reality.* Translated from the French and edited by Mercer Cook. Translator's Preface by Mercer Cook. Westport: Lawrence Hill, 1974.

Dixon, Roland B. *The Racial History of Man.* New York: Scribner's, 1923.

Fleming, Beatrice J., and Marion J. Pryde. "The Negro General of Japan-Sakanouye Tamuramaro." Chapter in *Distinguished Negroes Abroad.* Washington, D.C.: Associated Publishers, 1946: 3-9.

Hulse, Frederick S. "Physical Types Among the Japanese." *In Studies in the Anthropology of Oceania and Asia.* Edited by Carleton S. Coon and James M. Andrews IV. Cambridge, MA: Peabody Museum of American Archaeology and Ethnology, Harvard University, 1943: 122-33.

Hyman, Mark. *Black Shogun of Japan and Sophonisba: Wife of Two Warring Kings: Other Events from Ancient Times.* Introduction by Edward Sims, Jr. Philadelphia: Mark Hyman Associates, 1989.

Jones, Lois Mailou. "Sakanouye Tamura Maro." *Negro History Bulletin 4,* No. 2 (November 1940): 31.

Munro, Neil Gordon. *Prehistoric Japan.* Yokohama: Morice, 1908.

Munroe, Adwoa Asantewaa B. What We Should Know About African Religion, History and Culture. London: *African Publication Society*, 1981.

Murdoch, James. *A History of Japan, Volume 1: From the Origins to the Arrival of the Portuguese in 1542 A.D.* London: Kegan Paul, Trench, Trubner & Co., 1925.

Rashidi, Runoko, and Ivan Van Sertima, eds. *African Presence in Early Asia*. New Brunswick: Transaction Press, 1995.

Rogers, Joel Augustus. *Sex and Race. Vol. 1*, The Old World. New York: Rogers, 1940.

"Senghor Presents `Actual Facts' on Japanese: They're Descendants from Blacks." *The Final Call 6, No. 5* (1987).

Suzuki, Hiroe. "September Meeting Report." *JAFA News:* Japan Afro-American Friendship Association Dedicated to Friendship and Mutual Understanding Between Japanese People and the Black Community in Japan (December 1993): 5-6.

Winters, Clyde-Ahmad. "Further Thoughts on Japanese Dravidian Connections." *Dravidian Linguistics Association News 5, No 9* (September 1981): 1-4.

Black kingdoms in southeast Asia bibliography

Briggs, Lawrence Palmer. *The Ancient Khmer Empire*. Philadelphia: American Philosophical Society, 1951.

Cham Sculpture Album. Hanoi: Social Sciences Publishing House,1968.

Chou, Ta-Kuan (Zhou Daguan). *The Customs of Cambodia*. Translated into English from the French Version by Paul Pelliot of *Chou's Chinese Original* by J. Gilman d'Arcy Paul. Bangkok: The Siam Society, 1987.

Ciochon, Russell, and Jamie James. "The Battle of Angkor Wat." *New Scientist 124 (October 14, 1989)*: 52-57.

Ciochon, Russell, and Jamie James. "Land of the Cham." *Archaeology (May/June 1992)*: 52-55.

Ciochon, Russell, and Jamie James. "The Glory that was Angkor." *Archaeology 47, No. 2* (March/April 1994): 38-49.

Cunningham, Michael R., et al. Masterworks of Asian Art. Cleveland: *Cleveland Museum of Art*, 1998.

Dixon, Roland B. *The Racial History of Man.* New York: Scribner's, 1923.

Domenichini-Ramiaramanana, B. "Madagascar." In *UNESCO General History of Africa, Vol. 3. Africa from the Seventh to the Eleventh Century.* Edited by M. El Fasi. Berkeley: University of California Press, 1988: 681-703.

Fontein, Jan. *The Art of Southeast Asia: The Collection of the Museum Rietberg Zurich.* Zurich: Museum Rietberg, 2007.

Freeman, Michael, and Roger Warner. Angkor: *The Hidden Glories.* Edited by David Larkin. Boston: Houghton Mifflin, 1990.

Gagelonia, Pedro A. *The Filipinos of Yesteryears.* Manila: Star Book Store, 1967.

Guillon, Emmanuel. *Cham Art: The Treasures of the Da Nang Museum,* Vietnam. Bangkok: River Books, 2001.

Jacques, Claude. *Angkor.* Preface by Federico Mayor. Cologne: Koneman, 1999.

Majumdar, B.K. "Cambodia and Indian Influence (Circa 200-1432 A.D.)." *IndoAsian Culture* (January 1965): 36-41.

Majumdar, R.C. *Kambuja-Desa, or an Ancient Hindu Colony in Cambodia.* Madras: University of Madras, 1944.

Majumdar, R.C. *India and South East Asia.* Edited by K.S. Ramachandralt and S.P. Gupta. Delhi: B.R. Publishing, 1979.

Maspero, Georges. *The Kingdom of Champa.* Preface by John G. Embree. New Haven: Yale University Press, 1949.

Mazzeo, Donatella, and Chiara Silvi Antonini. *Monuments of Civilization: Ancient Cambodia. Foreword by Han Suyin.* New York: Grosset & Dunlap, 1978.

Parmentier, Henri, Paul Mus and Etienne Aymonier. Translated by Walter E.J. Tips. *Cham Sculpture of the Tourane Museum (Da Nang, Museum), Religious Ceremonies and Superstitions of Champa.* Bangkok: White Lotus Press, 2001.

Pym, Christopher. *The Ancient Civilization of Angkor.* New York: Mentor-New American Library, 1968.

Rawson, Philip. *The Art of Southeast Asia.* New York: Praeger, 1968.

Reuters. "U.N. Seeks to Save Fabled Khmer Temples." *Los Angeles Times, October 1,* 1991.

Van Beek, Steve, and Luca Invernizzi Tettoni. *The Arts of Thailand.* Periplus, 1999.

Vella, Walter F., editor. *The Indianized States of Southeast Asia* by G. Coedes. Translated by Sue Brown Cowing. Honolulu: University of Hawaii Press, 1964.

Diminutive Africoids: first people in the Philippines bibliography

Bennagen, P.L. "The Negrito: A Rallying Call to Save a Filipino Group from Cultural Extinction." In Filipino Heritage: The Making of a *Nation*. Manila: Lahing Pilipino, 1977.

"Black People Are Catching Hell in the Philippines." *Zamani 9, No. 3* (1990): 10.

Branigin, William. "'Angry' Mt. Pinatubo Evicts Aboriginal Tribe." *San Francisco Chronicle*, July 14, 1991.

Drogin, Bob. "Pinatubo's Agonizing Aftermath." *Los Angeles Times, October 9, 1991*: 1.

Gagelonia, Pedro A. "Negritos." Chapter in *The Filipinos of Yesteryears*. Manila: Star Book Store, 1967: 101-33.

Griffin, P. Bion, and Agnes Estioko-Grifin, eds. *The Agta of Northeastern Luzon: Recent Studies*. Cebu City: San Carlos Publications, 1985.

Headland, Thomas N. "Agta Negritos of the Philipines." *Cultural Survival Quarterly 8, No. 3.* (1984): 29-31.

Hutchcroft, Paul. "This is Whose Land? The 'Squatter Problem' at Clark." *Southeast Asia Chronicle* (April 1983): 20-26.

Kingdon, Jonathan. "Eve's Descendants." Chapter in *Self-Made Man: Human Evolution from Eden to Extinction?* New York: John Wiley, 1993: 255-93.

Lebar, F.M. *Ethnic Groups of Insular Southeast Asia, Volume 2: Philipines and Formosa*. New Haven: HRAF, 1975.

Maceda, Marcelino N. *The Culture of the Mamanua (Northern Mindanao) as Compared with that of the Other Negritos of Southeast Asia*. Second Edition. Cebu City: University of San Carlos, 1975.

Noval-Morales, Daisy Y., and James Monan. *A Primer on the Negritos of the Philippines*. Preface by Rudolf Rahmann. Manila: Philippine Business for Social Progress, 1979.

Peterson, Jean Treloggen. *The Ecology of Social Boundaries: Agta Foragers of the Philipines*. Urbana: University of Illinois Press, 1978.

Rashidi, Runoko and Ivan Van Sertima, eds. *The African Presence in Early Asia*. New Brunswick: Transaction Press, 1995.

Reed, William Allen. *The Negritos of Zambales*. 1905; rpt. Manila: Bureau of Public Printing, 1940.

Taylor, Paco D. "Black East." *Kung Fu Grip!* (February 2011): 9-15.

Warren, Charles P. "Minority Student Response to the Anthropology of Asian Black Populations." *Chicago: Department of Anthropology*, University of Illinois at Chicago, 1982.

Men out of Asia (to America)

"African-Like Stone Age Hut is Unearthed in Japan." *Associated Press, February 15* 1986.

Boule, Marcellin and Henri V. Vallois. *Fossil Men*. 1921; rpt. New York: Dryden Press, 1957.

Bowles, Gordon T. *The People of Asia*. New York: Scribner's, 1977.

Cobb, Gayleatha B. "An Interview with Roosevelt Brown: Black Nationalism in the South Pacific." *Black World* (March 1976): 32-43.

Brunson, James, E. Black Jade: *African Presence in the Ancient East*. Chicago: Kara, 1985.

Chang, Kwang-chih. *The Archaeology of Ancient China*. New Haven: Yale University Press, 1968.

Clegg II, Legrand H. "The Beginning of the African Diaspora: Black Men in Ancient and Medi-eval America? Pt. 1." *Current Bibliography on African Affairs, Vol. 2, No. 2, 1969:* 19-32.

Clegg II, Legrand H. "Who Were The First Americans?" *Black Scholar* (September 1975): 33-41.

Clegg II, Legrand H. "The First Americans." *Journal of African Civilizations* (April 1979): 98-107.

Clegg II, Legrand H. "The Mystery of the Arctic Twa: A Letter to the Editor." *African Presence in Early Europe*. Edited by Ivan Van Sertima. New Brunswick: Transaction Press, 1985: 245-50.

Davies, Nigel. *Voyagers to the New World*. New York: Morrow, 1979.

Diop, Cheikh Anta. "Africa: Cradle of Humanity." *Nile Valley Civilizations*. Edited by Ivan Van Sertima. New Brunswick: Transaction Press, 1984, 23-28.

Dixon, Roland B. *The Racial History of Man*. New York: Scribner's, 1923.

"DNA Researchers Trace All Humans to Single Woman in Ancient Africa." *New York Times*, March 30, 1986.

Finch, Charles S. "Race and Evolution in Prehistory." *African Presence in Early Europe*. Edited by Ivan Van Sertima. New Brunswick: Transaction Press, 1985: 288-312.

Gladwin, Harold S. Excavations at Casa Grande. Los Angeles: *Southwest Museum Papers No. 2*, 1928.

Gladwin, Harold S. "Independent Invention Versus Diffusion." *American Antiquity 3*. 1937: 156-160.

Gladwin, Harold S. *Men Out of Asia*. New York: McGraw-Hill, 1947.

Gladwin, Harold S. *A History of the Ancient Southwest*. Portland, Maine: Bond Wheelwright, 1957.

Gladwin, Harold S. *Men Out of the Past*. Santa Barbara, California, 1975.

Guidon, N., and E Delibrias. "Carbon-14 Dates Point to Man in the Americas 32,000 Years Ago." *Nature, June 19*, 1986: 769-71.

Hooton, Earnest A. *Up From the Ape*. New York: Macmilllan, 1931.

Imhotep, David. *The First Americans were Africans: Documented Evidence*. Foreword by Clyde A. Winters. Afterword by Molefi Asante. Bloomington: Authorhouse, 2011

Katz, Susan. "Mystery: When Did Ice Age Man Discover the Americas?" *Newsweek, November 10*, 1986: 72.

Keith, Arthur. *New Discoveries Relating to the Antiquity of Man*. London: Williams & Norgate, 1931.

Kpomassie, Tete-Michel. *An African in Greenland*. Translated from the original French by James Kirkup. Preface by Jean Malaurie. New York: Harcourt Brace Jovanovich, 1983.

Lemonick, Michael D. "Everyone's Genealogical Mother: Biologists Speculate that 'Eve' Lived in Sub-Saharan Africa." *Time*, January 26, 1987: 66.

Quatrefages, Armand De. *The Pygmies*. New York: D. Appleton, 1985.

Rashidi, Runoko, and Ivan Van Sertima, eds. *African Presence in Early Asia*. New Brunswick: Transaction Presss, 1985.

Rouse, Irving. *Migrations in Prehistory*. New Haven: Yale University Press, 1986.

Van Sertima, Ivan, ed. *Great African Thinkers, Vol. 1:* Cheikh Anta Diop. New Brunswick: Transaction Press, 1986.

Wainscoat, J.S., et al. "Evolutionary Relationships of Human Populations from an Analysis of Nuclear DNA Polymorphisms." *Nature, February 6*, 1986: 491-93.

Africans in Asia during the age of enslavement

Abdul-Rauf, Muhammad. *Bilal Ibn Rabah: A Leading Companion of the Prophet Muhammad*. n.p.: American Trust Publications, 1977.

Cerulli, E. "Ethiopia's Relations with the Muslim World." Chapter in *UNESCO General History of Africa. Vol. 3, Africa from the Seventh to the Eleventh Century*. Edited by M. El Fasi. Berkeley: University of California Press, 1988: 575-85.

Drake, J.G. St. Clair. "The Black Experience in the Muslim World." Section in Black Folk Here and There: An Essay in *History and Anthropology, Vol. 2*. Los Angeles: Center for Afro-American Studies, UCLA, 1990: 77-184.

Fleming, Beatrice J., and Marion J. Pryde. "Antar of Arabia." Chapter in *Distinguished Negroes Abroad*. Washington, D.C.: Associated Publishers, 1946: 10-20.

Fleming, Beatrice J., and Marion J. Pryde. "Bilal, Black Muezzin." *Distinguished Negroes Abroad*. Washington, D.C.: Associated Publishers, 1946: 21-30.

Hakim, Musa Abdul. "Diop on Cultural Kinship between Arabs and Africans." *The Challenger 24, No. 6* (1988): 15.

Hawley, John C., editor. *India in Africa, Africa in India: Indian Ocean Cosmopolitanisms*. Bloomington: Indiana University Press, 2008.

Hayes, John R., ed. *The Genius of Arab Civilization: Source of Renaissance*. Second Edition. Foreword by Bayly Winder. Introduction by John Stothoff Badeau. Cambridge: The MIT Press, 1983.

Hitti, Philip K. *History of the Arabs from the Earliest Times to the Present*. New York: St. Martin's Press, 1970.

Hunwick, J.O. "Black Africans in the Islamic World: An Understudied Dimension of the Black Diaspora." *Tarikh 20* (1978): 20-40.

Irwin, Graham W., ed. *Africans Abroad: A Documentary History of the Black Diaspora in Asia, Latin America, and the Caribbean During the Age of Slavery*. New York: Columbia University Press, 1977.

Al-Jahiz, Uthman Amr Ibn Bahr. *The Book of the Glory of the Black Race*. Translated by Vincent J. Cornell. Los Angeles: Preston, 1981.

Keith, Arthur, and M. Krogman. "The Racial Character of the Southern Arabs." Chapter in *Arabia Felix*, by Bertram Thomas. London: Jonathan Cape, 1932.

Komaroff, Linda. *Gifts of the Sultan: The Arts of Giving at the Islamic Courts*. New Haven: Los Angeles County Museum of Art, Yale University Press, 2011.

Lewis, Bernard. "The African Diaspora and the Civilization of Islam." *The African Diaspora: Interpretive Essays*. Edited by Martin L. Kilson and Robert I. Rotberg. Cambridge, MA: Harvard University Press, 1976: 37-56.

Lewis, Bernard. *Race and Slavery in the Middle East: An Historical Enquiry*. Oxford: Oxford University Press, 1990.

Al-Mansour, Khailid Abdullah Tariq. *The Destruction of Western Civilization as Seen through Islam, Christianity and Judaism*. San Francisco: First African Arabian Press, 1982.

Al-Mansour, Khalid Abdullah Tariq. *Seven African Arabian Wonders of the World: The Black Man's Guide to the Middle East*. San Francisco: First African Arabian Press, 1991.

al-Mansour, Khalid Abdullah Tariq. *The Lost Books of Africa Rediscovered: We Charge Genocide*. San Francisco: First African Arabian, 1995.

Mekasha, Getachew. "Ancient Ethiopia. Pt. 3, Islam and Ethiopia." *Ethiopia Review 1, No. 3* (1991): 18-22.

Muhammad, Wesley. *Black Arabia and the African Origin of Islam*. Atlanta: A-Team, 2009.

Pellat, Charles, trans. and ed. *The Life and Works of Jahiz.* Berkeley: University of California Press, 1969.

Popovic, Alexandre. *The Revolt of African Slaves in Iraq in the Third/Ninth Century.* Translated from the French by Leon King. New Introduction by Henry Louis Gates, Jr. Princeton: Markus Wiener, 1999.

Rashidi, Runoko, and Ivan Van Sertima, eds. *African Presence in Early Asia.* New Brunswick: Transaction Press, 1995.

Richmond, Diana. *Antar and Abla.* London: Quartet Books 1978.

Rogers, J.A. "Al-Jahiz, Lord of the Golden Age of Arab Literature." *World's Great Men of Color, Vol. 1.* New York: Macmillan, 1972: 163-71.

Stafford, Alphonso Orenzo. "Antar, the Arabian Negro Warrior, Poet and Hero." *Journal of Negro History 1, No. 2* (1916): 151-62.

Stafford, Alphonso Orenzo. "Africa and Asia." *Negro History Bulletin 4, No. 2* (1940): 28.

Stafford, Alphonso Orenzo. "Antar." *Negro History Bulletin 4, No. 2* (1940): 29.

Stafford, Alphonso Orenzo. "Why Study Asia with Respect to Africa." *Negro History Bulletin 4, No. 2* (1940) 27.

Talib, Y., based on a contribution by F. Samir. "The African Diaspora in Asia." *UNESCO General History of Africa. Vol. 3, Africa from the Seventh to the Eleventh Century.* Berkeley: University of California Press, 1988: 704-33.

The Siddis in India

"African Races to Bring Glory to India." *Dalit Voice 10, No. 18* (August 1-15, 1991): 10.

Banaji, D.R. *Bombay and the Siddis.* Bombay: MacMillan, 1932.

Chandrashekaraiah, B.M. "Siddis: A Negroid People of Karnataka." *Vanyajati 13, No. 1* (1965): 9-14.

Chandrashekaraiah, B.M. "Life Organization of the Siddis." *Journal of the Indian Studies in Social Sciences 1, No. 1* (1967): 55-57.

Chauhan, R.R.S., *Africans In India: From Slavery to Royalty.* New Delhi: Asian Publication Services, 1995.

Harris, Joseph E. *The African Presence in Asia: Consequences of the East African Slave Trade.* Evanston, IL: Northwestern University Press, 1971.

Harris, Joseph E. "Malik Ambar: African Regent-Minister in India." *African Presence in Early Asia*. Edited by Runoko Rashidi and Ivan Van Sertima. New Brunswick: Transaction Press, 1988: 152-58.

Irwin, Graham W., ed. *Africans Abroad: A Documentary History of the Black Diaspora in Asia, Latin America, and tha Caribbean during the Age of Slavery*. New York: Columbia University Press, 1977.

Irwin, Graham W. "African Bondage in Asian Lands." *African Presence in Early Asia*. Edited by Runoko Rashidi and Ivan Van Sertima. New Brunswick: Transaction Press, 1988: 146-51.

Jayasuriya, Shihan De Silva, and Richard Pankhurst, editors. *The African Diaspora in the Indian Ocean*. Trenton: Africa World Press, 2003.

Khalidi, Omar. "African Diaspora in India: The Case of the Habashis of the Dakan." Islamic Culture 53, Nos: 1-2 (1989): 85-107.

Parkhurst, Richard. "The Habashis of India." Appendix to *An Introduction to the Economic History of Ethiopia*. London, 1961: 409-22.

Prasad, Kiran Kamal. Siddis in Karnataka: *A Report Making Out A Case That They be Included in the List of Scheduled Tribes*. Bangalore: Prasad, 1984.

Rao, Vasant D. "The Habshis: India's Unknown Africans." *Africa Report 18, No. 5* (September-October 1973): 35-38.

Rao, Vasant D. "Siddis: African Dynasty in India." *Black World* (August 1975): 78-80.

Rao, Vasant D. "Unknown Afican Dynasty in India." *India News, April 24*, 1978: 6.

Rashidi, Runoko. "Black Bondage in Asia." *African Presence in Early Asia*. Edited by Runoko Rashidi and Ivan Van Sertima. New Brunswick: Transaction Press, 1988: 144-45.

Robbins, Kenneth X, and John McLeod. *African Elites in India: Habshi Amarat*. Mumbai: Mapin, 2006.

Rogers, Joel A. "Malik Ambar." Chapter in *World's Great Men of Color, Vol. 1*. New York: Collier-Macmillan, 1972: 172-76.

Rogers, Joel A. "Malik Andeel." Chapter in *World's Great Men of Color, Vol. 1*. New York: Collier-Macmillan, 1972: 177-78.

Seth, D.R. "The Life and Times of Malik Ambar." *Islamic Culture: The Hyderabad Quarterly Review 31, No. 2* (April 1975): 142-55.

Tamaskar, B.G. "An Estimate of Malik Ambar." *Quarterly Review of Historical Studies* 8 (Calcutta, 1968-69): 247-50.

"Warrior Tribe of African Descent in Gujarat Struggling to Keep Alive." *India Tribune*-Chicago Edition, September 17, 1994: 4.

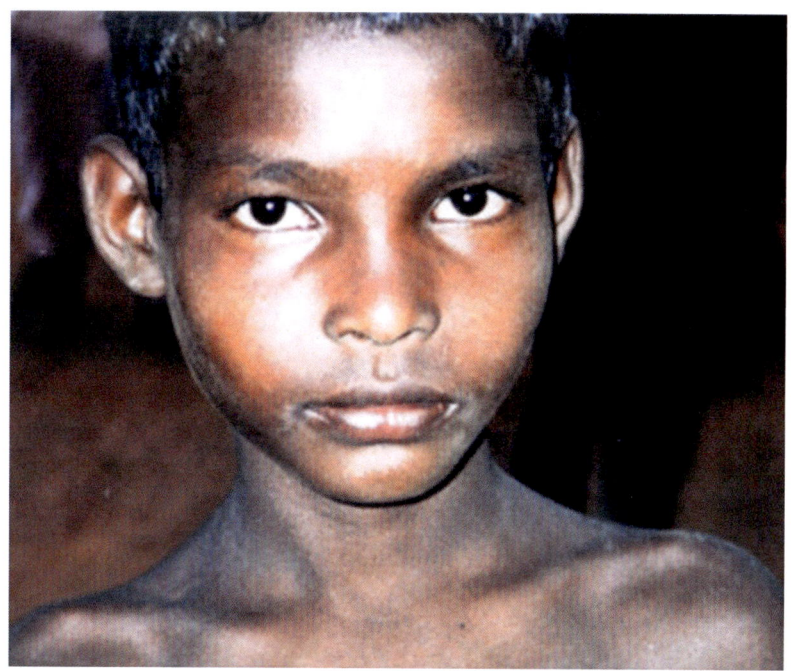

61. A Munda boy in Orissa. Photo by Runoko Rashidi

62. A Munda man and Runoko Rashidi in Orissa in 1999

63. An Oraon man in India

64. A seated statue of Gudea. Louvre. Photo by Runoko Rashidi

65. A Black soldier from ancient Persia. Louvre. Photo by Runoko Rashidi

66. Black soldiers in Susa, Persia. Louvre. Photo by Runoko Rashidi

67. A Black soldier in the Persian army. British Museum.
Photo by Runoko Rashidi

68. A Black soldier in the Persian army. Royal Museum of History and Art,
Brussels. Photo by Runoko Rashidi

69. Statue of Shiva. Metropolitan Museum of Art, NYC.
Photo by Runoko Rashidi

70. Seated statue of Buddha. National Museum, Bangkok

71. Dvaravati Buddha. Metropolitan Museum of Art, NYC.
Photo by Runoko Rashidi

72. Dvaravati Buddha. Asian Art Museum, San Francisco.
Photo by Runoko Rashidi

73. Detail of seated statue of Buddha. Musee Geimet.
Photo by Runoko Rashidi

74. A Black man in early Persia

75. Ethiopian Crusaders at the Battle of Jerusalem. Pantheon, Paris.
Photo by Runoko Rashidi

76. Former Crown Prince of Kuwait

Glossary

Aboriginal: Being the first of its kind present in a region. Aboriginal people are the first inhabitants of a country.

Absolute/Relative Age: An absolute date applies to a specific time in calendar or radiocarbon years, whereas a relative age only indicates whether an item is younger or older than other items.

Adivasis/Tribals: The original inhabitants of India.

Agriculture/Domestication: Practice of cultivating the soil and bringing animals under human control.

Akkadian: An important language of ancient Iraq, significantly influenced by Sumerian.

Alabastron: In antiquity a type of pottery used for holding oil, especially perfume or massage oils, particularly in ancient Greece. Most types of alabastron have a narrow body with a rounded end, a narrow neck and a broad, splayed mouth.

Angkor: The heart of the Khmer Kingdom. A Khmer word, based on the Indian Sanskrit meaning the city or the capital.

Anthropology: The study of humankind.

Archaeology: Study of the material traces of the human past.

Artifact: Any object made by human agency.

Aryan: A member of the Indo-European speaking tribes which invaded Pakistan, India and Iran in ancient times; Nordic.

Asparas: The celestial female dancers depicted in the art of early Southeast Asia.

Assyrians: An ancient people who lived approximately in the area of modern-day Iraq from the mid-third millennium B.C.E. and who ravaged West Asia and invaded the Nile Valley twice in the seventh century B.C.E.

Bas-relief: A carving or sculpture that projects slightly from the background on which it is carved.

B.C.E.: Before the Common Era.

Beringia: Refers to the ancient land mass that formerly connected Siberia with Alaska.

Bodhisattva: A person destined for enlightenment, a future Buddha, who embodies the ideas of compassion by assisting or caring for others. The Bodhisattva idea is a characteristic feature of Mahayana Buddhism.

B.P.: Before the present.

Brachycephalic: Short-headed or broad-headed with a cephalic index of over 80.

Brahmin: The highest ranking Hindu caste.

Caliph: Chief executive officer of the Islamic religion (Successor or Representative of Muhammad).

Carbon-14: A heavy radioactive isotope of carbon of mass number 14 used especially in tracer studies and in dating archaeological and geological materials.

Caste System: A hierarchical system of classification of peoples by which social privileges, duties and prohibitions are rigidly assigned. In India caste is determined by birth, but was originally based on ethnicity.

Cham Civilization: An Indianized state that flourished in Central and South Vietnam from the second to the fifteenth century.

Circa/Ca: Approximately.

City State: An autonomous state consisting of a city and the surrounding territory.

Cranial: Of or relating to the cranium or skull, which forms the enclosure of the brain, excluding the lower jaw.

Craniometric: The comparison and contrast of crania and cranial features based on metric measurements.

Cuneiform: An ancient West Asian system of writing with wedge-shaped characters incised on clay tablets.

Cyclopean Architecture: Architecture characterized by the use of very large close-fitting irregular stones.

Dalits: The only name which India's Black Untouchables have given themselves. Presented designated Scheduled Castes, the Dalits are descended from the original Black founders of the Indus Valley civilization, who were subjugated and kept in conditions of enslavement and apartheid called untouchability, from the time of conquest until the abolition on paper of "untouchability" in 1951.

Diminutive Africoids: The sub-division of African people phenotypically characterized by: unusually short statures, skin-complexions that range from yellowish to dark brown to near black, tightly curled hair, and, in frequent cases (like many other Blacks), steatopygia. The Diminutive Africoids, especially in Asia, are also known by such pejorative terms as Aeta, Negritos, Semang and Pygmies.

DNA: Deoxribonucleic acid; an essential component of all living matter and a basic material in the chromosomes of the cell nucleus. It transmits the hereditary pattern.

Dolichocephalic: Having a skull long in proportion to its breadth; having a skull whose width is less than 80% of its length.

Dravidian: An autonomous family of languages which spread in antiquity from Southern India to Eastern Iraq. It was likely the language of Harappa. The best-known representatives of the family are Tamil and Telegu, which continue to thrive in Southern India, and Elamite, the language of the ancient Elamite high-culture of Iran.

Dvarapala: Divine guardian of a gate.

Dvaravati: Mon kingdom or principality in Central Thailand that began to flourish from the sixth century, which left significant Buddhist works of art.

Dynasty: A line of rulers belonging to the same family; also the period during which a certain family reigns.

Elam: The ancient civilization of Southwestern Iran. The chief city of Elam was Susa.

Empire: A major political unit having a territory of great extent or a number of territories or peoples under a single sovereign authority; also the period during which such a government prevails.

Epicanthic Fold: A skin fold on the eyelid that, when the eye is open, comes down over and runs on a line with the edge of the upper eyelid.

Eponym: A real or mythical person from whose name thename of a nation, community or institution is derived or supposed to have derived.

Erythraean Sea: The term applied by Greek and Roman geographers to the Red Sea.

Fossil: Any hardened remains or traces of plant or animal life of previous geological periods, preserved in rock formations in the earth's crust.

Funan: The Chinese name for the Indianized kingdom in Cambodia that preceded the kingdom of Angkor.

Genotype: The fundamental constitution of an organism in terms of the hereditary factors.

Greater India: Outer India; a broad geographic region encompassing at various periods what is now Bangladesh, India, Pakistan and Sri Lanka (Ceylon) and sometimes portions of Southeast Asia.

Hadith: A hadith is a reliably transmitted report of what the prophet Muhammad said, did, or approved.

Hajj: The annual pilgrimage to Makkah (Mecca).

Harappan Civilization: The high culture of the ancient Indus Valley in what is now Pakistan and related centers in northwest India dating from circa 2700 B.C.E. to 1500 B.C.E.

Harijans: Children of God, a term applied by M.K. Gandhi to the Black Untouchables of India.

Hijra: The migration in the year 622 by the prophet Muhammad and his followers from Makkah to the city of Madinah. The Hijra marks the beginning of the Muslim calendar.

Hominid: A member of the family Hominidae, which includes Homo (mankind) and Australopithecus but excludes the apes.

Homo: The generic hame given to the hominid group containing fossil and modern man.

Homo erectus: A species of humans that preceded modern humans.

Homo habilis: A group of fossil hominids and the earliest population named "Handymen."

Homo sapiens sapiens: Modern human beings.

Hydraulic: Operated, moved, or effected by means of water.

Interglacial: Warmer period between colder glaciations periods.

Interstadial: Short, relative warm interlude within a longer glacial period.

Isthmus: A narrow strip of land connecting two masses of land that would otherwise be separated by water.

Jati: Sanskrit term for caste.

Ka'ba: The sanctuary at Makkah; of very ancient date. It was a small square temple of black stones that had for its corner-stone a meteorite.

Khmer: Referring to the people, language and culture of the civilization of Cambodia and especially Angkor.

Koran: Believed to be the exact words revealed by God through trhe Angel Gabriel to the prophet Muhammad.

Laterite: A red, porous, iron-bearing rock that is easy to quarry but extremely hard when dried.

Linga: Shiva worshipped in the form of a phallic stone.

Linguistics: The study of human speech including the units, nature, structure, and modification of language.

Lithic: Of, or pertaining to stone.

Littoral: Near, or along a coastal region.

Mahabharata: Classical Sanskrit to epic probably compased between 200 B.C.E. and 200 CE. The Bhagavad-Gita, a religious classic of Hinduism, is contained in the Mahabrarata.

Material Culture: The tangible objects produced by a society.

Matrifocal: The strong presence and importance of the mother.

Megalithic: Constructed of large stones.

Mesolithic: The Stone Age period between the Paleolithic and the Neolithic. The prefixes indicate Old, Middle and New Stone Ages.

Mesopotamia: A Greek term denoting the land between the rivers Tigris and Euphrates. In 1921 the British changed the name from Mesopotamia to Iraq, an Arabic word which means "well-rooted country."

Mongoloid: Term commonly used to describe Eastern Asians.

Monolith: A single gigantic stone or similarly huge object, often in the form of an obelisk or column.

Mudra: A hand gesture or posture of the Buddha.

Naga: Mythical serpent, a water spirit.

Natufian: An ancient tool industry and culture in Western Asia named for settlements extending from Turkey to the Egyptian Delta.

Paleo: Ancient, historically early or prehistoric.

Paleolithic: The Old Stone Age. The Paleolithic is the pre-agricultural are beginning with the emergence of humankind and the manufacture of the earliest tools.

Paleontology: A science dealing with the life of past geological periods as known from fossil remains.

Pancharma: M.K. Gandhi's name for suggested fifth lowest caste, which he proposed be created for the purpose of incorporating the Dalit into the caste system, purportedly to correct the ill of defining and maintaining them outside it as Untouchables.

Periplus: The name applied to a class of writings which answered for both a sailing chart and traveler's handbook.

Phenotype: The visible characteristics of an organism that are produced by the interation of the genotype and the environment.

Physical Anthropology: Study of the physical nature of humankind.

Platyrrhine: Denoting a short broad nose.

Pluvial: Prolonged periods of high rainfall marked by a major changes in lake levels, flora and fauna.

Prehistoric: The period before written history.

Prognathous: Jaws projecting beyond the upper face.

Proto: The first in time, original, principal.

Pseudo: False, pretended, spurious or illusory.

Ramayana: Classical Sanskrit epic of India, probably composed in the third century B.C.E. The Ramayana relates the adventures of Rama.

Reflex-bow: The much-feared weapon of the horse nomads of the Eurasian steppes. It was made of wood or other organic material reinforced by bone. At rest, it curved outward and had to be bent back to string. The reflex-bow possessed great range and penetrating force.

Rig Veda: The oldest and probably the most important of the Hindu sacred texts.

Riverine: On, or near, the banks of a river.

Saba: Biblical Sheba, with its capital at Marib in South Arabia.

Samurai: Literally, "those who serve"; the knights of Medieval Japan.

Sanskrit: An ancient Indo-European language regarded by many as "the sacred and classical language of India and Hinduism."

Scheduled Castes: Indian bureaucratic designation for the Dalit, replacing their previous label accorded by Hinduism of "Untouchable."

Scheduled Tribes: Indian bureaucratic designation for tribal peoples. They appear on a schedule of tribal communities enjoying a legal status distinct from other Indians. They number approximately forty million and not long ago were referred to as Aboriginals, a term justified by the well-founded believes that in all probability they had dwelt in their present habitat long before the first Aryan haed set foot on Indian soil.

Semitic: Related to a subfamily of Afro-Asiatic languages including Arabic, Hebrew, Ethiopic, Amharic, Aramaic and others.

Shang: The first historical dynasty of China, from circa 1800 B.C.E. to circa 1060 B.C.E.

Sharia: The Divine Law; the detailed code of conduct comprising the precepts, governing modes and ways of worship and standards of morals and life.

Shogun: Name given to the military governor of Japan prior to the Meiji era.

Siddis: A term applied to Africans and the descendants of enslaved Africans in India.

Steatopygia: A physical trait characterized by an excessive accumulation of fat on the buttocks.

Stela: A stone column or upright slab decorated with carvings or inscriptions.

Steppe: Vast grasslands capable of supporting herds of grazing animals, but generally too cold and arid for the growing of crops.

Stupa: Mortuary or commemorative monument erected over the relics of the Buddha or other Buddhist saints.

Sudras: Originally they lowest of the four castes of Hinduism; now divided into hundreds of subcastes. In Hindu tradition, a Sudra who intentionally reviles twice-born men by criminal abuse, or criminally assaults them with blows, shall be deprived of the limb with which he offends. If he has criminal intercourse with an Aryan woman, his organ shall be cut off, and all his property confiscated. If the woman had a protector, the Sudra shall be executed. If he listens intentionally to a recitation of the Veda, his tongue shall be cut out. If he commits them to memory his body shall be spilt in twain.

Sumer: The oldest known civilization of Western Asia, located in the Tigris-Euphrates river valley and flourishing during the third millennium B.C.E.

Sumerian: The earliest recorded language of the southernmost part of Mesopotamia or Southern Iraq, used during the third millennium B.C.E., and later preserved as the language of religion and ritual.

Suttee: The rite recorded from India of a widow taking her own life in order to accompany her deceased husband.

Tara: Female savior and the Buddhist embodiment of compassion.

Taxonomy: Classification of living things into groups.

Tundra: A level or undulating treeless plain that is characteristic of arctic and subartic regions where the subsoil is frozen.

Varna: Classical division of Hindu society; Sanskrit term denoting color or complexion.

Vedas: The four religious books that instruct Brahmanic ritual, of which the most famous is the Rig Veda.

Wadi: An Arabic word meaning dried-up river-bed.

Wat: In Southeast Asia a Buddhist temple or religious complex.

Ziggurat: Massive rectangular shaped, step-temple structures or stage-towers in early Western Asia, generally composed of mud bricks.

Biographical notes

RUNOKO RASHIDI

Runoko Rashidi is an historian, anthropologist and world traveler. His has authored or edited more than a dozen books, in English and French, on the global African presence, both ancient and modern. He considers as his major mission in life the restoration to African people of much of what has been falsified about them. He has traveled to more than a hundred countries, colonies and overseas territories in search of the African presence, and has lectured in more than fifty-five countries. His most recent English language text is *Black Star: The African Presence in Early Europe* in October 2011, published by Books of Africa Ltd (London, United Kingdom).

JAMES E. BRUNSON

Art Historian Dr. James E. Brunson is a pioneer author and researcher on the African presence in ancient civilizations, especially in Asia. He was a regular contributor to the *Journal of African Civilizations*, founded by Ivan Van Sertima. His written works include *Black Jade* and *Predynastic Egypt*.

THABITI ASUKILE

Dr. Thabiti Asukile received a Ph.D. in American History from the University of California-Berkeley in 2007 with a special concentration in African American Intellectual History and a secondary concentration on the African Diaspora. He has published numerous articles about Joel Augustus Rogers that have appeared in *The Black Scholar, The Journal of African American History, Afro-Americans in New York Life and History*, and the *Western Journal of Black Studies*.

HAMARA HOLT

Hamara Holt, based in New York City, is a writer and veteran traveler with an avid interest in world history and the global African presence. She is an excellent photographer and her photos have graced both of Runoko Rashidi's French language books. She is currently in the early stages of translating the works of major African scholars from English into Spanish.

WESLEY MUHAMMAD

Dr. Wesley Muhammad is an historian of religion and author of several books, including *Black Arabia* and the *African Origin of Islam* (2009). Dr. Muhammad earned a Bachelor of Arts in Religious Studies from Morehouse College (1994) and a Masters and Doctorate in Islamic Studies from the University of Michigan (2003, 2008) and he has taught at several universities, including the University of Toledo, the University of Michigan, and Michigan State University.

V.T. RAJSHEKAR

V.T. Rajshekar is a long-time crusading journalist in India and the founder and Editor of *Dalit Voice: The Voice of the Persecuted Nationalities Denied Human Rights*. Rajshekar is the author of many books, including *Dalit: The Black Untouchables of India*. V.T. Rajshekar is very much a Pan-Africanist in his thinking and writing, and facilitated all three of Runoko Rashidi's historic tours to India.

PACO D. TAYLOR

Paco D. Taylor has written for *Giant Robot* magazine and is author and editor of *Kung Fu Grip!*, *In His Image*, *Distant God Meditation*, and other critically-acclaimed 'zines. Born and raised on the South Side of Chicago, he currently resides in Tucson, Arizona.

HOREN TUDU

Horen Tudu is a Bangladeshi-Santhal born scientist, engineer and physicist raised in the United States. He is a staunch Pan-Africanist and research specialist. His work emphasizes the plight of the Dalit and the tribal historical/political situation in Bangladesh and India.

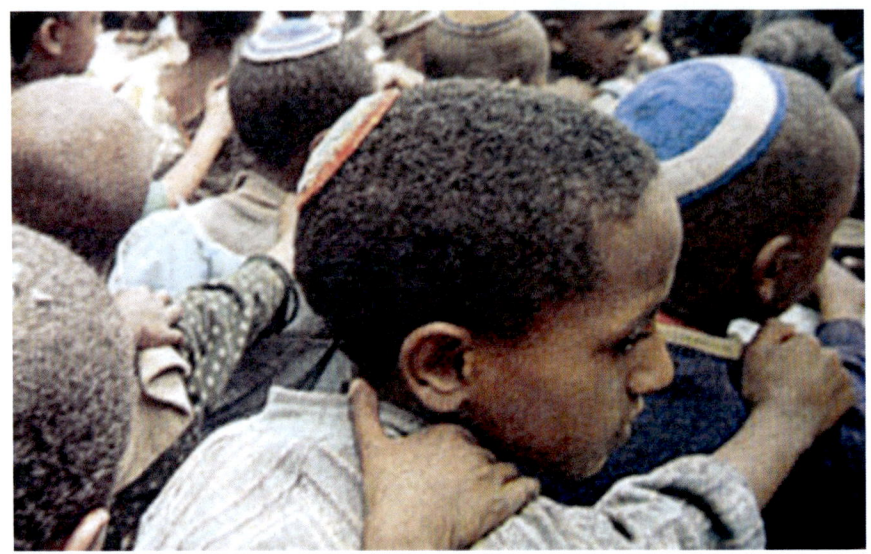

77. Black children in Israel

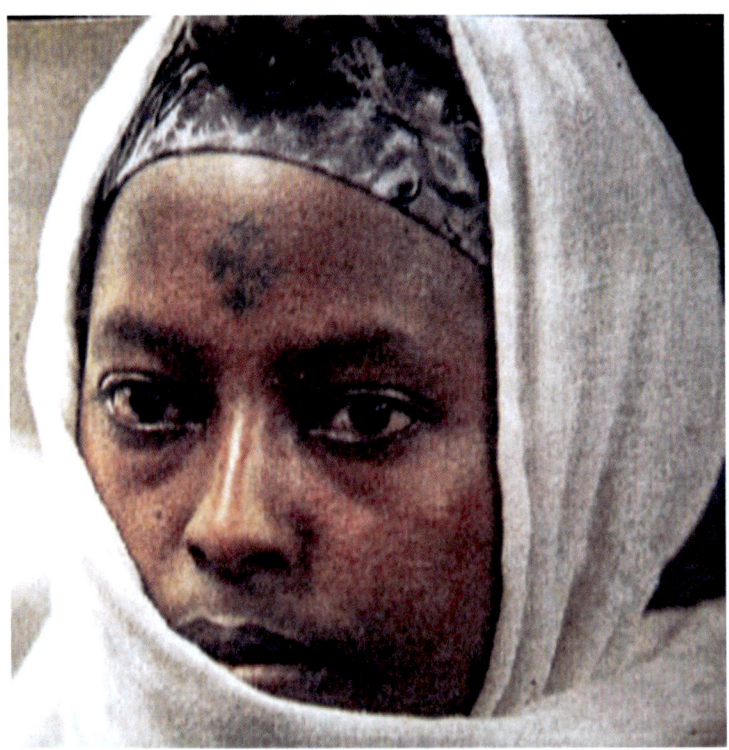

78. A Black woman in Israel

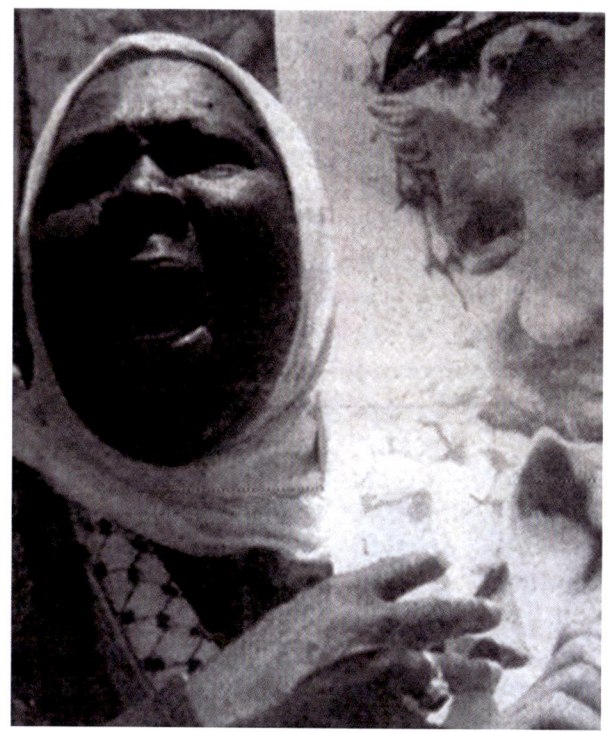

79. An African-Palestinian. Courtesy Final Call Newspaper

80. Runoko Rashidi and African women in Southwest Turkey. November 2004

81. An African woman in Southwest Turkey. Photo by Runoko Rashidi

82. A mannequin of the Chief of the Black Eunuchs in the Tokapi Palace, Istanbul. Photo by Runoko Rashidi

83. Raja Juma and Runoko Rashidi at the Dead Sea in Jordan

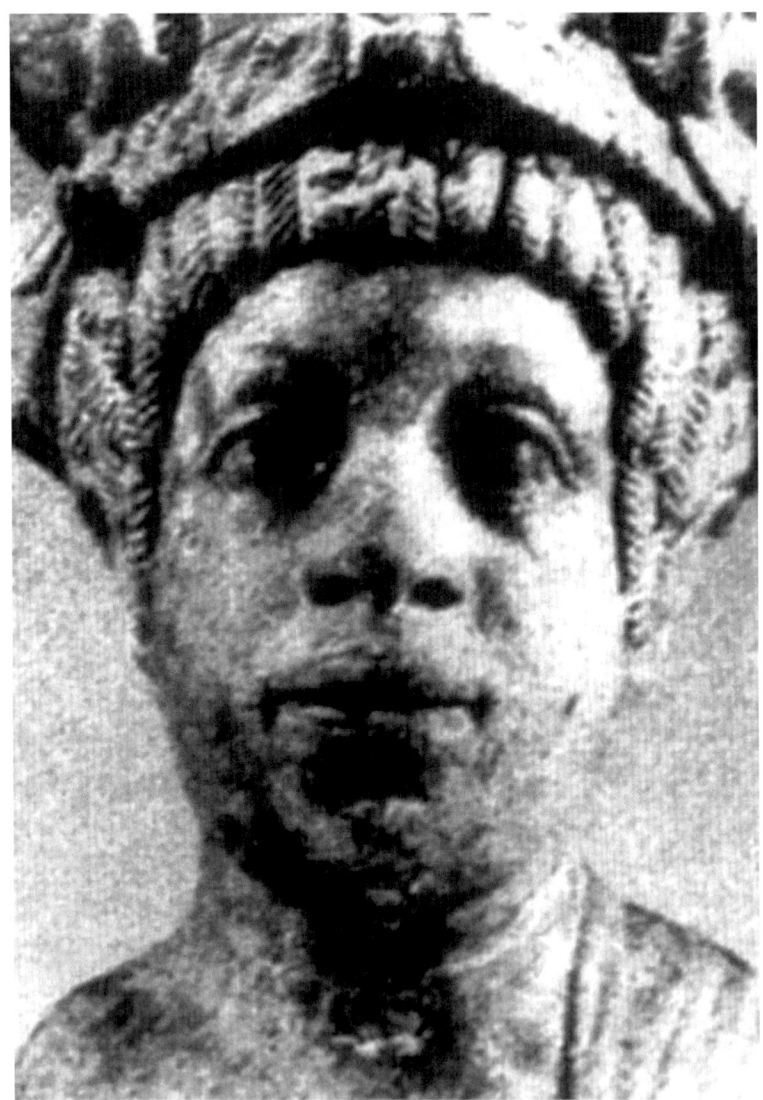

84. A Black man in ancient Syria. National Museum, Damascus

85. The Tomb of Bilal in Damascus. Photo by Runoko Rashidi

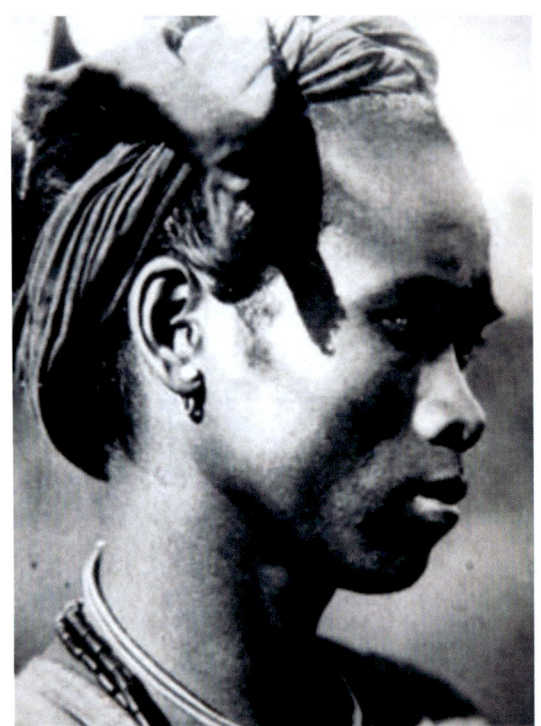

86. A Black man in Vietnam

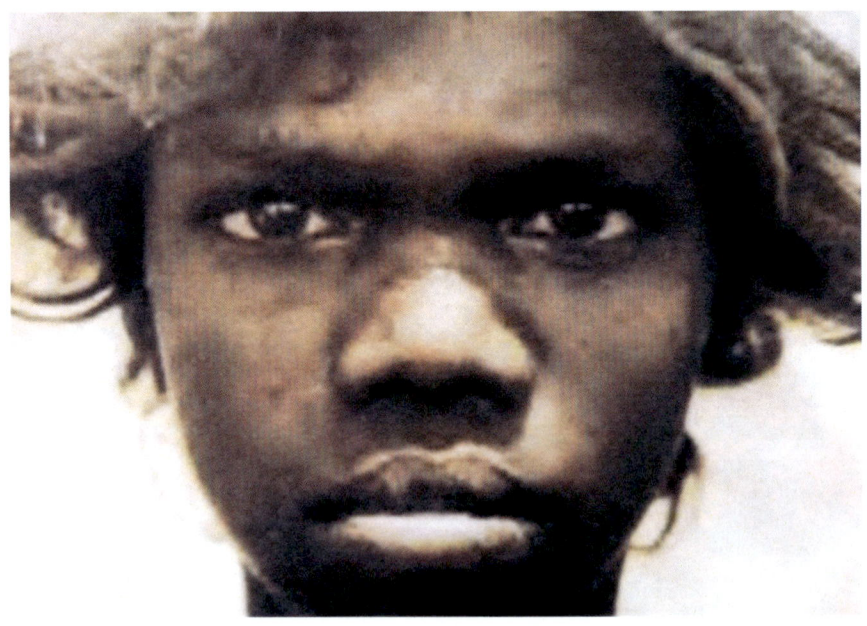

87. A Tribal in Southern India

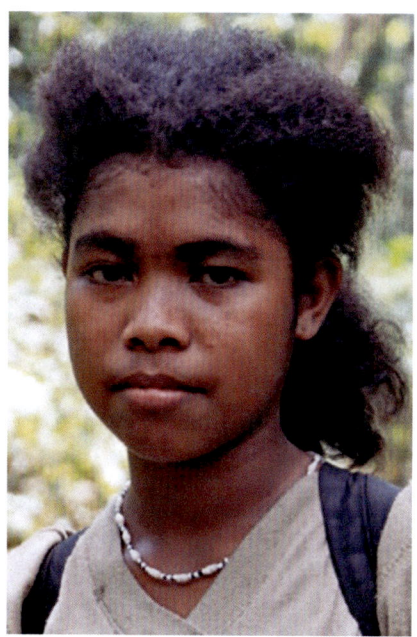

88. A Black girl in the Philippines. Photo by Hamara Holt

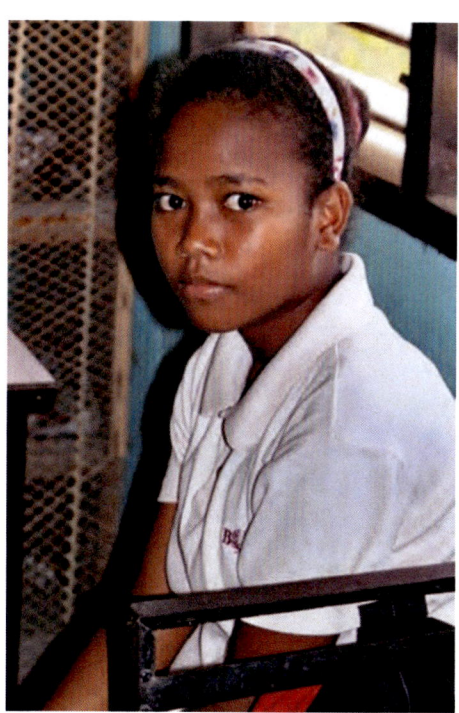

89. A Black girl in the Philippines. Photo by Hamara Holt

90. Black children in the Philippines. Photo by Hamara Holt

91. A Black man in the Philippines. Photo by Hamara Holt

92. A Black man in the Philippines. Photo courtesy of Paco D. Taylor

93. Black women in Northern Malaysia. Photo courtesy of Pace D. Taylor

94. A Black woman and child in Southern Thailand.
Photo courtesy of Paco D. Taylor

95. Joel Augustus Rogers

5. Index

Photo captions